The New Constitutional Order

The New Constitutional Order

Mark Tushnet

PRINCETON UNIVERSITY PRESS

PRINCETON AND OXFORD

Second printing, and first paperback printing, 2004
Paperback ISBN 0-691-12055-2

The Library of Congress has cataloged the cloth edition of this book as follows

Tushnet, Mark V., 1945–
    The new constitutional order / Mark Tushnet.
    p.   cm.
    Includes bibliographical references and index.
    ISBN 0-691-11299-1 (alk. paper)
    1. Constitutional law—United States.   I. Title.

    KF4550 .T87 2003
    342.73—dc21   2002070394

British Library Cataloging-in-Publication Data is available

This book has been composed in Galliard

Printed on acid-free paper. ∞

pup.princeton.edu

Printed in the United States of America

3   5   7   9   10   8   6   4   2

To Louis Michael Seidman and Vicki C. Jackson

Collaborators extraordinaire

CONTENTS

PREFACE

IN LIGHT OF the common perception among legal academics that the analytic approaches associated with the critical legal studies movement are moribund, I think it is worth noting here that the argument in this book is, in my view, continuous with the arguments about constitutional law and theory I have been making since I began writing in the field. The critical legal studies approach had—or has—two components, usefully described by Peter Gabel as a critique of certain claims about objectivity and rationality, particularly but not exclusively in law, *and* as a interpretive approach to history and contemporary society, again particularly but not exclusively focused on the development and place of law in society.

Red, White, and Blue: A Critical Analysis of American Law (1988) had two parts, tracking the two components of critical legal studies. The first part argued that the theories of constitutional interpretation with numerous adherents at the time did not, and could not, satisfy the demands that liberal political theory placed on theories of constitutional interpretation. The second part was a descriptive sociology of some aspects of constitutional doctrine as it stood at the time, linking constitutional doctrine to some aspects of the social organization of what I described as liberal society. *Taking the Constitution away from the Courts* (1999) pursued the strategy of *Red, White, and Blue*'s first part by developing a critique of constitutionalism itself (although of course my views had changed somewhat, becoming, as I see them, more sophisticated in the course of a decade of thinking). This book pursues the second part's strategy, again with modifications. Instead of linking specific constitutional doctrines to large-scale social structures, I link the structure of constitutional doctrine to some aspects of the way in which political institutions actually operate in the present day.

The distinction between the analytic approach and the descriptive sociology approach was part of discussions in critical legal studies almost from the start. Aficionados know it as the issue of "tilt." My position has been throughout that nothing analytic constrained the structure or content of constitutional (or, more broadly, legal) doctrine but that a descriptive sociology would identify some tilt at any particular historical moment. The issue mattered, and perhaps still does, because some thought that the descriptive point suggested a degree of (social) determinism that was inconsistent with the analytic one and, more important, that might have politically debilitating effects. My view was and is that there is no inconsistency or misleading political lesson. The descriptive sociology developed in this book suggests to me the people with political views like my own would do well to develop two kinds of legal arguments. One would support, and push to the limit, the kinds of reformist programs described in the conclusion as compatible with the political structure of the present constitutional order. The other, not inconsistent, would make proposals that are wildly utopian in the present political context, such as the proposal for abolishing judicial review that concluded *Taking the Constitution away from the Courts*.

• • •

I would like to thank Bruce Ackerman, Elizabeth Alexander, Samuel Bagenstos, Michael Dorf, Dan Ernst, William Eskridge, Daniel Farber, Heidi Li Feldman, Robert Ferguson, Bastien François, Frederick Mark Gedicks, Mark Graber, Vicki Jackson, Sanford Levinson, John Manning, Carrie Menkel-Meadow, Gerald Neumann, Richard Parker, Eric Posner, Matthew Porterfield, Jeff Rosen, Louis Michael Seidman, Peter Spiro, Peter Strauss, Cass Sunstein, Rebecca Tushnet, Carlos Manuel Vázquez, and Eugene Volokh for comments on prior versions of parts of this book. Participants in several Faculty Research Workshops at Georgetown University Law Center and Columbia University Law School, the Public Law Lunch Group at Columbia University Law School, the Legal Theory Workshop at Emory University, the Workshop on Comparative Constitutional Law at the University of Virginia Law School, and the University of Chicago Constitutional Theory Workshop also made helpful comments on parts of the work. Neysun Mahboubi, Rachel Lebejko Priester, and Jacqueline Shapiro provided valuable research assistance. Parts of the book have appeared in the following articles: "Foreword: The New Constitutional Order and the Chastening of Constitutional Ambition," 113 *Harvard Law Review* 29 (1999); "Globalization and Federalism in a Post *Printz* World," 36 *Tulsa Law Journal* 11 (2000); "What Is the Supreme Court's New Federalism?" 25 *Oklahoma City University Law Review* 927 (2000); "Mr. Jones and the Supreme Court," 4 *Green Bag*, 2d ser., 173 (2001); "Federalism and International Human Rights in the New Constitutional Order," 47 *Wayne Law Review* 841 (2001); "The Redundant Free Exercise Clause?" 33 *Loyola University Chicago Law Journal* 71 (2001). I have reorganized and elaborated the argument, sometimes quite substantially, from the versions of its elements that have been published elsewhere.

The New Constitutional Order

THE IDEA OF A CONSTITUTIONAL ORDER

PRESIDENT BILL CLINTON announced in his 1996 State of the Union Address that "[t]he age of big government is over."[1] Many Republicans thought that the president was cynically appropriating Republican themes to preserve his presidency after the apparent public repudiation of Clinton's approach to government in the 1994 elections, when Republicans attained a majority in both the House of Representatives and the Senate for the first time since 1954. Many traditional Democrats thought that the president was betraying the Democratic Party's principles as they had been developed in Franklin Roosevelt's New Deal agenda and Lyndon Johnson's Great Society programs.

We ought to take President Clinton's observation quite seriously. His statement demonstrated his understanding that what I call a new constitutional order had been consolidated. By *constitutional order* (or *regime*), I mean a reasonably stable set of institutions through which a nation's fundamental decisions are made over a sustained period, and the principles that guide those decisions.[2] These institutions and principles provide the structure within which ordinary political contention occurs, which is why I call them *constitutional* rather than merely political.[3]

Both institutions and principles constitute a constitutional order. On the institutional level, a constitutional order extends well beyond the Supreme Court and includes the national political parties, Congress, and the presidency. Indeed, as I argue in chapters 1 and 2, the constitutional principles articulated by the Supreme Court cannot be understood except in the context of the institutional arrangements prevailing in the national government's other branches. For me, a constitutional order is more like the small-c British constitution than it is like the document called the United States Constitution. And, just as scholars of constitutionalism have found it productive to think about the British constitution, so I think it productive to think about constitutional orders in the United States that go beyond judicial doctrine and the written Constitution to encompass relatively stable political arrangements and guiding principles.

Franklin D. Roosevelt's State of the Union message in 1944 defined the guiding principles of the constitutional order that prevailed from the 1930s to the 1980s, which I call the New Deal–Great Society constitutional order. Roosevelt called for implementing a "Second Bill of Rights" that included "the right to earn enough to provide adequate food and clothing and recreation" and rights to "adequate medical care," "a decent home," and "a good education," as well as "the right to adequate protection from the economic fears of old age, sickness, accident, and unemployment."[4] Clinton's claim that the age of big government had passed did not mean that the national government had nothing left to do. Rather, the initiatives of the new constitutional order would be small-scale. The aspirations expressed by Roosevelt, and in the New Deal–Great Society constitutional order, have been chastened in the new order.

In the most general terms, the principles that guide the new constitutional order make it one in which the aspiration to achieving justice directly through law has been substantially chastened. Individual responsibility and market processes, not national legislation identifying and seeking to promote justice, have become the means by which that aspiration is to be achieved. Law, including constitutional law, does not disappear, but it plays a less direct role in achieving justice in the new constitutional order than it did in the New Deal–Great Society regime. Statutes and constitutional doctrines establish the conditions within which individuals and corporations seek their own ends, which include, for some, achieving justice. Statutes and constitutional doctrine form the framework within which these efforts take place. The new order's vision of justice, that is, is one in which government provides the structure for individuals to advance their own visions of justice.

Constitutional orders are gradually constructed and transformed: At any moment we can observe a dominant set of institutions and principles, some residues of a prior regime, and some hints of what might be the institutions and principles that may animate a succeeding one.[5] As I argue in chapter 1, the present constitutional order began to take shape with Ronald Reagan's election in 1980, was given greater definition in the 1994 elections, and was consolidated during the final years of the Clinton presidency. The gradual processes of regime construction and transformation make it particularly difficult to describe "a" constitutional order, because one must always be concerned that some feature is a residue of the past or an anticipation of the future rather than a central feature of the existing regime. My descriptions of those central features will be less qualified than perhaps they should be, but recurrently observing that my argument is tentative would be distracting.

Throughout this book I contrast the new constitutional order with the New Deal–Great Society constitutional order. For my purposes it is unnecessary for me to identify other constitutional orders in U.S. constitutional history, but it does seem appropriate at this point to distinguish my approach from two others, to which it is most closely related in constitutional scholarship.[6] Law professor Bruce Ackerman has described constitutional history as a series of constitutional moments followed by extended periods of what he calls normal politics.[7] The periods of Ackerman's normal politics correspond roughly to what I call constitutional orders, and his constitutional moments might be the points at which new constitutional orders come into being.

Building on Ackerman's insights, law professors Jack M. Balkin and Sanford Levinson also describe revolutionary transformations in constitutional orders.[8] They disagree with Ackerman in emphasizing that these transformations can, and ordinarily do, occur gradually. They implicitly criticize Ackerman's metaphor of a *moment*, which suggests—misleadingly, at least with respect to the new constitutional order—that constitutional orders necessarily come into being quickly.[9] For Balkin and Levinson, constitutional revolutions happen through a process of what they call partisan entrenchment, in which one party with a guiding ideology gains control—sometimes suddenly but more usually gradually—of all three branches of the national government. Balkin and Levinson frame their essay with *Bush v. Gore* in the background, for they take that case, which installed George W. Bush in the presidency, as a step in the direction of partisan entrenchment. As they see the case, the Supreme Court's conservative justices took steps to ensure that the next justices to be appointed would consolidate Republican control of the courts and thereby complete the partisan entrenchment that constitutes a constitutional revolution.[10]

I agree with Balkin and Levinson, and thus disagree with Ackerman, that constitutional regimes can come into being over extended periods rather than in convulsive moments. So, for example, some of the Supreme Court's decisions discussed in chapter 2 as exemplary of the demise of the New Deal–Great Society constitutional order pre-date 1980, and some doctrines that flourished in the late 1990s had precursors in the 1970s. The emphasis Balkin and Levinson place on partisan entrenchment, however, means that they cannot consider the possibility, developed in this book, that a constitutional regime can be characterized by persistent divided government, and that divided government produces policies with their own guiding principles. To Balkin and Levinson, *Bush v. Gore* placed us on the verge of a constitutional revolution; I suggest, in contrast, that we have already made the transition to a new constitutional order.

Another difference between my approach and Ackerman's is that Ackerman insists on identifying constitutional moments because he wants to develop a normative constitutional theory that can explain what he calls the intertemporal difficulty with constitutional law,[11] the problem of explaining why decisions taken by people generations ago should restrict the choices people today wish to make. Ackerman solves the intertemporal difficulty by arguing that decisions made in constitutional moments have greater normative weight than those made during periods of normal politics.[12] The reason is that the political sequences producing constitutional moments elicit from the public a greater degree of attention to constitutional fundamentals than the public gives those fundamentals during normal politics, when quotidian concerns understandably and properly distract many from political deliberation and permit narrowly focused interest groups to influence policy development more than occurs during constitutional moments.

Ackerman's normative concerns lead him to develop a number of formal criteria that, in his view, must be satisfied before we can say that a constitutional moment has occurred: Because duties of fidelity to the Constitution arise from constitutional moments, people deserve to have some clarity about the precise occasions from which those duties arise. I am less concerned than Ackerman with the normative problems associated with the intertemporal difficulty.[13] For that reason, I do not think it necessary to demonstrate that the new constitutional order came into being by satisfying some specific formal criteria.[14] There was no particular critical election, for example.[15] Ackerman's way of thinking about our constitutional order has influenced my approach, but I believe that Ackerman's formalism, derived from his normative concerns, obscures our ability to see clearly the present constitutional order.

Ackerman's formal criteria do have an important advantage: They allow us to identify when one constitutional order replaces another. My approach, unfortunately, lacks the crispness of Ackerman's. Without formal criteria to rely on, I cannot avoid making judgments, which others can readily contest, about which institutional arrangements and guiding principles are stable enough to be part of a constitutional order. Chapters 1 and 2 present, as forcefully as I can, the arguments supporting my judgments, while chapter 3 addresses some challenges to those judgments, with the inevitable effect of weakening the force of my arguments. In the end, I think my judgments remain good ones, but I hope at least to have acknowledged the most vulnerable points in my analysis.

Ackerman's concern with the intertemporal difficulty produces another difference between his approach and mine. That difficulty is closely tied up with judicial enforcement of the principles that guide a constitutional order: It is a difficulty only to the extent that we worry about being bound by decisions taken decades ago, and only courts issue directives that are formally binding. My approach to regime principles is less Court-focused than Ackerman's or Balkin and Levinson's. Unlike them, I believe that *constitutional* principles can be, and typically are, reflected in the statutes that characterize successive constitutional regimes. For the New Deal constitutional order, the social security system and Roosevelt's proposed Second Bill of Rights are as important as any Supreme Court decisions. For the Great Society, no Supreme Court decisions match the Civil Rights Act of 1964, the Voting Rights Act of 1965, and Medicare in expressing the regime's guiding principles. Of course a constitutional order's principles guide some judicial decisions as well, but we lose some purchase on how our institutions are organized if we confine our attention to the courts.

Chapter 1 describes the institutional arrangements in Congress and the presidency, with a short glimpse at developments in state government. The most important feature of the modern constitutional order is divided government, which places important constraints on what the national government can do. I examine why divided government has arisen, how it has affected relations between presidents and Congress, and how it has affected the internal organization of Congress. Here I rely heavily on works by political scientists. Unfortunately for my project, often the political scientists differ among themselves over describing and explaining developments in national political institutions. Acknowledging the existence of controversy when it exists, I have chosen to invoke those analysts who seem to me most insightful.

Chapter 2 examines the Supreme Court's most important decisions over the past decades. For reasons I discuss in chapter 1, the Court was something of a "leading indicator" for the new constitutional order, repudiating the New Deal–Great Society constitutional order and developing the new order's constitutional principles somewhat in advance of the development of institutional arrangements that eventually provided the larger context for those principles. But, I argue, the Court at present fits reasonably well into the new order and is unlikely to foment a true constitutional revolution that would push the constitutional order into territory not yet occupied.

Chapters 1 and 2 adopt the rhetorical strategy of asserting that there *is* a new constitutional order. Chapter 3 takes up a number of challenges to a strongly put argument that we are in a new constitutional order. Perhaps we are in a sort of interregnum, a period *after* which we will enter a new constitutional order through Supreme Court appointments of the sort Balkin and Levinson fear or through the creation of unified government produced by presidential leadership. Or, perhaps what I call a new constitutional order is simply a general characteristic of American political development: We have occasional convulsions, Ackerman's constitutional moments, followed by periods of drift during which the constitutional aspirations that animated the American people earlier are inevitably chastened. What I call a *new* constitutional order, that is, may be the *usual* constitutional order. My position on these questions is simple: They may be correct, but we can clarify our thinking about our present situation by considering the possibility that what we have is sufficiently stable, and distinctive, to be called a new constitutional order. In some ways, then, Chapters 1 and 2 should be sprinkled with phrases like, "This shows that we might be in a new constitutional order." For rhetorical purposes, however, I have decided to keep such qualifications to a minimum even though they more accurately reflect my position than the stronger assertions I actually make.

Chapter 4 examines some recent developments in constitutional scholarship, particularly the work of Cass Sunstein, arguing that these works present a constitutional jurisprudence compatible with, and perhaps designed for, the new constitutional order. Chapter 5 moves beyond the established contours of existing doctrine to examine the ways in which the new domestic constitutional order may have to adjust to a new international context or, to use the trendy word, to globalization. The development on which I focus is international interest in promoting universal human rights, and the implications such an interest might have for the domestic law of federalism, because federalism has been an important focal point in the development of the new order's constitutional doctrine. A brief conclusion describes some interesting developments in regulatory theory, which might provide the basis for a modest progressive reformist element in the new constitutional order.

I conclude by mentioning a second difficulty that attends my reliance on political science materials and sheds light on some general problems associated with this book's project. Before the 2000 elections, political scientists confidently presented models that predicted relatively large margins of victory for Vice President Al Gore. The models relied on predictions based on theories according to which voters responded almost exclusively to economic conditions, their assessment of the prior administration's performance, and the like, and not at all to the candidates' personal characteristics or the ways they campaigned. The models were an embarrassing failure; they all predicted correctly that the vice president would receive a majority of the votes cast for the two major parties, but that minimal success was overshadowed by their failure to predict how close the election would be.[16] The reason is that the "science" in political science cannot take human willfulness—campaign decisions, voter reactions to specific personalities and events—and mere chance into account. But, as we all know, willfulness and chance play a large role in the day-to-day workings of politics. At best, then, I can describe large trends that seem likely to prevail but that might be changed at any moment by unpredictable events or human decisions.

My analysis describes the structures within which people make decisions based on their own preferences, beliefs, and values. These structures provide incentives and opportunities, but political actors may resist the incentives or fail to grasp the opportunities.[17] Divided government plays a large role in what follows, but voters may simply decide to reject or reconstitute the new regime, for example by providing large-scale support to a third party or by changing their preferences in ways that produce a unified ideological government.

Law professor Jack Balkin, a scholar whose intellectual formation occurred during the New Deal–Great Society constitutional order, comments indirectly on these issues in reflecting on the Supreme Court's decision in *Bush v. Gore* that "[d]uring the last five years or so, I have been consistently wrong about what the Court was willing to do to promote its conservative agenda. Repeatedly . . . I have thought to myself: 'They can't possibly do *that*. That would be *crazy*.' And each time I have been proven wrong."[18] Balkin's initial impressions were right in one sense: The modern Court's positions are indeed crazy when assessed against the constitutional doctrine of the New Deal–Great Society order. Younger scholars, particularly those in harmony with the Federalist Society, have a better sense of where the Court is and where it may be going. The real question is whether the positions the Court has staked out to this point define the modern constitutional order's limits. They might instead be harbingers of an even more revolutionary transformation. Undoubtedly the Court's decisions are susceptible to aggressive, revolutionary readings that would reshape constitutional law even more dramatically than has as yet occurred. I believe that a revolutionary change in constitutional doctrine is unlikely, because the modern Court's doctrine is compatible with the regime principles that characterize the new constitutional order's other institutions. But I am quite aware of the observation (by either Yogi Berra or Neils Bohr—no one appears to be sure) that prediction is hazardous, particularly about the future. I rely, in contrast, on another observation (by either Damon Runyon or H. L. Mencken—again the source is unclear): "The race is not always to the swift, nor the battle to the strong, but that's the way to bet."

Chapter One

THE POLITICAL INSTITUTIONS OF
THE NEW CONSTITUTIONAL ORDER

CONSTITUTIONAL ORDERS combine novel guiding principles with distinctive institutional arrangements. Simplified greatly, the new constitutional order is characterized by divided government and ideologically distinct and unified parties. Its principles are chastened versions of the aspirations that guided the New Deal–Great Society order. Its first solid institutional gain was the election of Ronald Reagan in 1980.[1] The new constitutional order has been consolidated since the 1994 elections produced a Republican majority in the House of Representatives and the Senate.

The New Deal–Great Society order was characterized by bargaining among pluralist interest groups, many of which obtained footholds in the national government's bureaucracies.[2] Its guiding principle was egalitarian liberalism, though of course there was substantial disagreement within the regime's adherents over the best methods of ensuring equality among all Americans. The moderately conservative principles that guide the new regime are well-known, and so in what follows I focus on the new order's institutional characteristics, setting them against the background of the New Deal–Great Society order that it replaced and that still affects policy outcomes in the new order.[3]

Constitutional regimes bind institutions and behavior together, and we need not give any particular institution analytic priority. But we must begin somewhere, and one promising place is with the relation between voters and the parties as constructed by presidents and politicians seeking congressional office. Historically regime shifts have occurred in the United States through a process of partisan realignments as a result of critical elections, which produced large-scale and seemingly permanent shifts in party affiliation among large numbers of voters.[4] The new constitutional order came about differently.[5] Many observers thought that the 1980 election would be a critical realigning election, with traditional Democrats permanently converting to Reagan Republicanism.[6] It was not.[7] Instead, the 1980 election was part of a longer term process of partisan dealignment and adjustment, in which many voters reduced their attachment to *any* party and other voters shifted from the Democratic to the Republican Party in numbers sufficient to eliminate the large advantage Democrats had during the New Deal–Great Society order but not enough to give Republicans a permanent and guaranteed majority.[8] One result of adjustment, in particular, was an increase in the "philosophical coherence" of the two parties: Liberal Republicans nearly disappeared, and the number of conservative Democrats dropped, though not as much.[9] Dealignment and adjustment are connected, in turn, to the way in which successive presidents constructed their parties. Dealignment and adjustment may not have *produced* the new constitutional order, but it created the conditions under which the new regime flourishes.

I take up the institutions of the new constitutional order in the next sections. First I describe the ways in which presidents contribute to the construction of constitutional orders, emphasizing in particular the relation between the president whose administration initiates regime change and successor presidents from both the same and the opposition party. Then I turn to Congress, describing the sources of congressional polarization in the new constitutional order and the apparent preference voters have for divided government. I argue that the interaction between presidents and Congress in the new regime produces a government of chastened constitutional aspiration. The final sections discuss some concrete implications of the preceding argument: for the scope of national policy, presidential initiatives, impeachment, individual rights, and judicial review generally.

PRESIDENTIAL POWER

Stephen Skowronek identifies a process in which presidents play central roles in initiating regime transformation.[10] In the terms I have been developing, Skowronek argues that each constitutional order has a president who initiates the new order, both by articulating the new order's principles and by beginning the processes of institutional transformation that ultimately produce a constitutional regime that differs from what has gone before.[11] So, for example, Franklin Roosevelt gradually developed modern liberalism's principles and began to create institutions in which interest groups could be embedded, and Lyndon B. Johnson aggressively pursued a more robust egalitarian vision while accepting and attempting to manipulate the competition among interest groups for control over the policy agenda. Ronald Reagan came to office challenging liberalism's principles and sought, with limited success, to dismantle the interest group–dominated institutions of the New Deal–Great Society order.[12]

Although the government was not transformed during Ronald Reagan's tenure, the new regime has since been consolidated, and its current form is more important than the limited achievements of the Reagan administration during 1981–89. Notably, the Contract with America proposed a series of reforms entirely consistent with the Reagan vision. The Contract's terms were not enacted immediately, but by 1999 many of its key features had been enacted in some form, usually with President Clinton's support.[13] This outcome strongly suggests that the new constitutional order has taken root: A president from the opposition party could not resist, and sometimes endorsed, the initiatives associated with the new regime.[14]

Presidents who follow the regime initiators play a variety of roles. Those from the initiator's own party seek to perpetuate his legacy but also strike some new paths on their own to demonstrate that they too are leaders worthy of respect. They often have trouble emerging from the shadow of the president they seek to emulate, as Skowronek shows was George H. W. Bush's difficulty.[15]

More interesting, perhaps, are the presidents from the party that opposed the new regime's creation. These successors practice what Skowronek calls a "politics of preemption" if that regime is firmly in place.[16] They accept the new regime's general outlines but seek to modify particular details. Sometimes they seek to temper what their party regards as the regime's excesses.[17] In this they will be supported by the prior regime's partisans, who see in these modest initiatives some hope for a larger reversion to the former order. This course, however, does little to satisfy whatever ambition the president has to define himself distinctively as the nation's leader.

An alternative path is open: to continue forward with the new regime's initiatives. This is a true politics of preemption. The president appropriates the programs of the party that is formally his opposition. Bill Clinton chose this role.[18] As a so-called New Democrat, he articulated themes not dramatically different from some associated with the Republican Party: "[P]olicy would work through market mechanisms or the states, and it would 'reinvent' government"; "policy would set clear expectations for individual responsibility and impose sanctions on bad behavior"; and "policy would highlight the long-term benefits of 'investing' in people so that they could be productive workers and citizens."[19] Two of the three major initiatives taken during Clinton's first two years in office—deficit reduction and the adoption of the North American Free Trade Agreement—were projects entirely compatible with Republican Party principles.[20]

Presidents who practice the politics of preemption face challenges from two directions. They must somehow impose their vision on their own party, whose activist members are likely to remain embedded in the now-displaced older constitutional order. And they must overcome challenges by their opponents to their sincerity, and outrage at their appropriation of their opponents' themes.[21]

Skowronek identifies other roles presidents may play. Presidents seek to demonstrate that they are leaders. They therefore welcome new challenges, ones that their predecessors did not face or failed to resolve. But every constitutional order gradually decays, and as it does the challenges may prove intractable. Whether they are affiliated with the party that instituted the regime or have practiced a politics of preemption, presidents increasingly find the institutional arrangements that have been built up to implement the regime's principles unsuited to the new challenges they face. But they rarely have alternative institutional resources at hand. Innovators who propose to displace the old order with a new one turn these late-regime presidents into perceived failures.

President Clinton's State of the Union Address signaled that he saw himself as a practitioner of the politics of preemption. His widely noted political strategy of triangulation, in which he distanced himself both from what he characterized as the rigid and excessive conservatism of the Republicans who controlled Congress and from what he characterized as the old-fashioned New Deal–Great Society liberalism of many Democrats in Congress, is precisely what a practitioner of a politics of preemption would do.[22] His frequently quoted statement to his advisers, "I hope you're all aware we're all Eisenhower Republicans. . . . and we are fighting the Reagan Republicans," suggests the content of Clinton's program.[23] Preemption for Clinton consisted of lessening the ambitions of the national government. And, by early 1999, it appeared that he had done a great deal to change the Democratic Party. Not only was the congressional party united in its opposition to Clinton's impeachment, but candidate Al Gore began to define the themes of his campaign, and they were small ones.[24] Indeed, all presidential campaigns in the new constitutional order may involve the presentation of large packages of small programs, suggesting the cynical observation that "politicians . . . [will] substitute lists of many small, nearly empty promises . . . for a few large, empty promises,"[25] which is what politicians clinging to outdated New Deal–Great Society assumptions offer.

The relation between presidents who initiate regime changes and their successors occurs *within* each regime. Skowronek also identifies an important trend as the nation experiences successive regimes: Each regime leaves behind some sedimentary residue, with which its successors must somehow deal. The important legacy of the New Deal–Great Society regime in this regard is the accumulated weight of interest groups in national politics.[26]

Sidney Milkis describes the process by which Franklin Roosevelt built interest groups into the New Deal–Great Society constitutional order.[27] Roosevelt found himself confronting a national party system based in the states, which posed an obstacle to the accomplishment of his program.

The national parties were coalitions of state and local parties, an important function of which was to dispense patronage. State institutions obstructed the implementation of New Deal programs.[28] Roosevelt challenged the state parties directly, but with mixed success at best. His true
accomplishments lay elsewhere, in displacing the patronage-oriented
state parties with a national political organization with a distinctive programmatic agenda.[29]

Roosevelt's contribution to the party system was to create a distinctive
national presidential party, independent of the state parties that continued to play a central role in selecting members of Congress. He did so by
drawing on an important intellectual and organizational strand in the
progressive politics that provided one source of his support: the availability of a cadre of liberal professionals, such as social workers, who accepted
Roosevelt's regime principles.[30] Roosevelt relied on these progressive professionals to staff the bureaucracies of the New Deal regime, displacing
political patronage as the ground for selection. The bureaucracies in turn
operated independently of the state parties, directly connecting constituencies to the national government without the mediation of local political parties.[31] Roosevelt also initiated the now universal practice of developing a presidential campaign organization that operates independently
of the organization of the national political party of which the candidate
is nominally the head.[32]

Together, as they developed over time, these innovations produced
what Milkis calls a "politics centered on government rather than the electorate."[33] As the New Deal–Great Society constitutional order decayed,
so did the efforts by interest groups to mobilize their constituencies. In a
government-centered politics, interest groups devoted their efforts to influencing the bureaucracies, relying on their leaders' judgments that what
they did was consistent with the interests of their nominal constituents.
Political sociologist Theda Skocpol describes the new interest groups as
"advocates without members."[34] Skocpol argues that the new form of
interest group politics "responded to—and in turn helped to fuel—major
changes in U.S. government and electoral politics."[35] The importance of
day-to-day lobbying in Washington, the availability of foundation funding for start-up costs, ongoing fund-raising by mass mailings, and easy
access to the media creates a "top-down" world of interest group politics.
Skocpol emphasizes as well that funding through mass mailings "mag-
nifies polarized voices" because "mailing-list members tend to be at once
fickle and motivated by intense policy preferences. . . . Shouting and
deadlock can easily result."[36]

The new constitutional order continues to be affected by the residue of
the New Deal–Great Society regime. Interest groups remain important,
particularly in structuring the policies implemented by national bureau-

cracies. This "institutional thickening" of the executive branch, as Skow-ronek calls it, enhances the president's formal power, and sometimes his effective power, but it also makes it possible "for other actors to mount more formidable resistance" as they deploy their bureaucratic resources to resist presidential or congressional initiatives.[37] And politics remains centered on government. Further, campaigns for the presidency remain "candidate centered,"[38] and elections for Congress have become increas-ingly so. But the new constitutional order imposes some discipline on those who eventually are elected. An important feature of the new consti-tutional order appears to be the reunification of the presidential and con-gressional parties.[39] The Contract with America accomplished the re-unification of the Republican Party,[40] and the impeachment of President Clinton, coupled with strenuous efforts by Clinton and his allies to shift his party's ideological center of gravity, appear to have done the same for the Democrats. Policymaking has again been taken over by unified na-tional political parties. But these parties no longer have the connections to the electorate that the parties did before the New Deal.

A POLARIZED CONGRESS IN A DIVIDED GOVERNMENT

The new constitutional order has several components. I have already dis-cussed the role that government-centered presidential parties play. This section deals with other components. First, the new order contains a public that does not participate in politics. This contributes to the devel-opment of weak *congressional* parties, whose members run campaigns al-most as independent entrepreneurs. The congressional parties may be weak as parties, but they are ideologically coherent.[41] They are also highly partisan because candidates must obtain nomination by appealing to the most active, and therefore most partisan, of their constituents, in districts that have themselves become more ideologically homogeneous. Finally, the new constitutional order appears to take divided government, with different parties controlling the presidency and at least one house of Con-gress, as a norm.

Over the past one hundred years, voter turnout has declined by 25 percent.[42] Observers disagree about whether the decline results from voter alienation or voter satisfaction,[43] from legal obstacles to voting,[44] or from the transformation of political parties from organizations that mo-bilized mass participation in politics to something else.[45] Its consequences are reasonably clear. Politics has become dominated by relatively small groups of voters, and not by party organizations. The congressional par-ties in the New Deal–Great Society regime were heterogeneous: conser-vative Southern Democrats caucused with liberal Northern Democrats, and the Republican Party contained international-minded "Rockefeller

Republicans" and isolationist conservatives. Heterogeneity resulted from candidate selection by local party organizations rather than by the voters themselves.

Today candidate selection occurs in primaries. People with aspirations to national office essentially offer themselves to the public, with no screening by any party organization. But the electorate to which they appeal is now smaller and dominated by its most partisan segments. The shrinking effective electorate means that candidates and therefore legislators have become increasingly ideological.[46] Once elected, legislators must protect themselves against challenges in primary elections, where the main threat is from highly ideological members of their own party. And even in general elections, ideologically motivated citizens are more likely to vote than those without strong views.[47] The result is that Republican legislators are more conservative than the general population and Democratic ones more liberal.[48] As a result of these factors, members of Congress are increasingly unresponsive to the overall views of their constituents.[49] The increased ideological coherence of the national parties feeds back to the level of voters: Republican voters are more uniformly conservative and Democratic ones more uniformly liberal than in the past.[50]

Nomination of candidates in primary elections reduces the importance of local party organizations. Rather than seek the blessing of party leaders, candidates go directly to voters, to the candidates' own personal checkbooks, and to those who can contribute funds to their campaigns. This nomination process simultaneously increases the ideological distance between the parties, because "primary voters are more ideologically inclined than the general electorate" and because party activists tend to orient themselves to national interest groups and to allies they find in wider geographic areas than congressional districts.[51] The overall effect has been to "empty" "the center of today's congressional party system," leaving almost no overlap between liberal Democrats and conservative Republicans.[52] One measure of partisan division revealed that the most conservative Democrats in Congress were more liberal than the most liberal Republicans.[53]

Congressional districts themselves have become increasingly homogeneous in partisan terms. In 1998, for example, 94 incumbents ran unopposed, and 114 had only nominal opposition, primarily because the districts were solidly in the hands of one party.[54] That in turn resulted in large measure from the Supreme Court's reapportionment decisions, which eliminated a host of traditional reasons for drawing district boundaries. Politicians drawing the lines could focus almost entirely on securing partisan advantage through districting, with their ability to achieve results enhanced by the development of computer programs that could compare alternative districting decisions to evaluate their partisan implications.[55] Partisan advantage sometimes means protecting even moderate incumbents by giving them internally diverse districts, but more often it means creating homogeneous districts that will be safe for the incumbent and, perhaps more important, for a representative from the same party once the incumbent leaves office.

Districting decisions obviously cannot have an impact on the Senate, but voter decisions about where they want to live may. One journalist suggests, for example, that people move to places where they expect to find like-minded neighbors.[56] A more systematic inquiry indicates that people who move from one state to another are more likely to be Republicans than Democrats: Moving is expensive, people with more money move more often than people with less, and people with more money tend to be Republicans.[57] The effect is to make the states they leave more Democratic and the states they enter more Republican.[58] One effect may be to increase the number of Senate delegations with both senators from the same party.[59]

In homogeneous districts, incumbents face challenges largely from the most politically active *within* their parties, and, again, activists tend to be more ideological than the general electorate. Selecting candidates in primary elections lets people select *themselves* as potential candidates, then appeal to the party's politically active members. People who choose to do that are likely to be highly partisan individuals.[60] The result is that partisan homogeneity in Congress has increased substantially over the past several decades.[61] As one member of Congress put it, "It can all be traced back to the 1962 *Baker v. Carr* decision. . . . Because the districts in Congress are more and more one-party dominated, the American Congress is more extreme. What you have in Congress after 30 years of this redistricting is more and more polarization by party."[62] The polarization of candidates, in turn, appears to have induced an increase in the polarization of the public that participates in politics.[63]

The general electorate, observing these partisan differences, appears to have decided that its best response is to create a divided government, "balancing the policies or ideologies of the opposing parties by placing them in control of different institutions."[64] That formulation suggests that divided government results from voters' preferences: Observing ideological polarization in the national parties, enough voters decide to split their votes to ensure more moderate outcomes.[65]

This explanation for divided government is quite controversial among political scientists.[66] A preference-based explanation for divided government sometimes may require an implausibly high degree of coordination among voters. Preferences might explain why voters elected Bill Clinton in 1992 and a Republican Congress in 1994, but coordinating preferences to produce divided government in a presidential election, as in 1996, is quite difficult: Some people might want a divided government that has a Democratic president and a Republican Congress, while others might want a divided government with a Republican president and a Democratic Congress, but unless things work out extremely well, they all might end up with the same party controlling both branches. Some political scientists have offered explanations for divided government that rely on structural features of elections, but these explanations, unfortunately, are rather abstract and do not have the intuitive pull that preference-based explanations do.

Whatever the cause, at least for the past decades voters have produced divided government. In doing so, however, the electorate has reduced the importance of parties as institutions. On the preference-based account, voters do not identify themselves as Democrats or Republicans; they cannot do so and still create divided government. But, as we will see in chapter 3, if divided government results from preferences, presidential leadership can reshape preferences and produce unified—and now, ideologically coherent—government.

Polarization among the candidates and in the electorate also contributes to divided government. As political scientist Morris Fiorina puts it, party activists "demand[ed] a choice, not an echo, [and] pulled their candidates toward more extreme positions. But preferring the echo to the choice, an increasing number of voters split their tickets. Activists tried to impose principled programmatic government; voters responded with divided government."[67] In an era of *voter* dealignment, political elites reconstituted the parties at the elite level. Presidents have always had platforms to run on, and those platforms provided a signal to voters about what they would get if they voted for one or the other candidate. Voters seeking divided government, however, might not know what, other than opposition, they were getting when they voted for members of Congress.[68] During Ronald Reagan's presidency, the New Deal–Great Society Democratic coalition was in a process of extended decay, but the fact that a person ran as a Democrat in the North at least conveyed some information about her political commitments. The Contract with America provided congressional Republicans with the equivalent of an opposition platform to signal the positions they would take as part of a divided government.[69] Then, the voters having decided in 1994 to divide the government, they decided to continue with divided government by reelecting Clinton in 1996.[70]

Dealignment affected the parties themselves. As I have argued, the New Deal–Great Society regime allocated positions in the nation's bureaucracies to different constituencies. And "[e]ntrenchment in governmental institutions provides modern political parties and interest groups with access to public resources without requiring them to engage in full-scale electoral mobilization."[71] The interest groups can bypass the congressional parties and deal directly with the bureaucracies. At the same time, interest group entrenchment makes regime transformation increasingly difficult, as Reagan's difficulties in dismantling the national executive structure demonstrated.

Lacking control over the resources of the national government, the national political parties changed from organizations seeking to mobilize the electorate to service organizations aiding candidates who conducted their own campaigns.[72] Such parties are basically interested in electing whoever gains the party's nomination: "[P]arty organizations . . . are constrained to make winning, rather than ideological purity their primary, if not exclusive, goal."[73] As one party worker describes the Democratic House Campaign Committee, "Our only interest was in Roll Call One [the party-line vote for House Speaker that opens each Congress]. What happened in the House after that was somebody else's responsibility."[74] As the candidates selected at the local level became more ideological, the parties at the national level gained institutional resources that they devoted to winning above all.

The effects of this transformation have been complex. National party organizations may not participate in governing, but they have increased their financial resources as they came under the control of elite professionals skilled at fund-raising, designing campaign messages, and the like.[75] Campaigns are run by "professionals who build ad hoc campaign organizations for each candidate . . . on the ballot. When election day is over, these ad hoc organizations of pollsters, strategists, fundraisers, field-operations specialists, and so on dissolve into thin air."[76] Voters, who no longer have any permanent organization they can contact about their problems, find this situation "alienating and demeaning."[77] "[B]ecause *voters* abandoned their party allegiances . . . *politicians* wanted stronger party organizations" to provide the resources voters used to offer politicians.[78] Fiscally stronger national parties, in turn, made it less necessary for politicians to rely on grassroots mobilization, and thereby reinforced the trend to lower voter turnouts.[79] And service-oriented parties, though devoted to electing *anyone* who runs under a party's label, indirectly contribute to partisan polarization because mobilizing core ideological constituencies is easier than appealing to broader ones. Thus, "[t]he emergence of parties of administration strengthened the national party organization and created more discipline among party members in Congress, but at the cost of weakening party loyalties among the electorate."[80] According to presidential scholar Sidney Milkis, "The new party system could muster a significant polarizing of politics within the Washington beltway, but . . . [may lack] the capacity . . . to build popular support for political principles and programs."[81]

In the new constitutional order, parties have become "coalitions of public officials, office seekers, and political activists."[82] National poli-cymaking is the product of "a fully developed political and policy net-work outside of the regular political process."[83] Parties "drop[] away," no longer "entities capable of sustaining and promoting their programs,"[84] individual campaign organizations have replaced parties as intermediaries between citizens and candidates,[85] and presidential candidates run "per-sonalistic" campaigns focused on their personalities rather than on their party's programs.[86] The result, in political historian Joel Silbey's terms, is that "[w]e have empowered chaos."[87]

These polarizing effects were themselves reinforced by changes *within* Congress. Individual candidates may run more or less independently of national direction, although they may choose to affiliate themselves with national agendas like the Contract with America. Paradoxically, however, the candidate-centered nature of individual elections creates incentives to strengthen party leadership inside Congress.[88] Members who have run independently of each other face a collective action problem in getting anything done, but they need to accomplish something if they are to present themselves to voters at the next election as successful legislators. Authorizing party leaders in the House and Senate to exercise substantial power solves the coordination problem.[89] Common platforms like the Contract with America have the same effect, but perhaps more important is the leadership's ability to compose legislative packages that members vote for as a whole, and prescribe the rules authorizing—or, more impor-tant, restricting—votes on amendments to proposals.[90] Packages, in turn, increase the cover potentially dissident members get, as they can explain to their constituents that the leadership forced them to vote on a group of measures, some of which the constituents like but others of which the constituents dislike.[91] And, of course, "[a]s intraparty homogeneity in-creases, the costs of policy leadership decrease and its benefits increase."[92] As political scientist David Rohde puts it, "Legislative parties today are characterized by fairly broad internal agreement on policy and by intense policy disagreements with the opposite party. As long as that remains true, members of the majority will be willing to grant significant powers to their leadership to pursue their common political and policy goals."[93]

Various internal changes, such as rules limiting the number of major committees on which members could serve and limiting the terms of committee chairs, dispersed power among members of Congress,[94] and made it more important for "the party's only central agent, the party leadership, to advance the party majority's legislative objectives."[95] So, for example, party leaders now have greater power to select committee chairs, to determine which committees will consider particular items of legisla-tion, and to structure floor action in the House through the adoption of rules governing which amendments and alternatives can be considered.[96]

The leadership chooses the participants when obstacles to legislation lead to "summit meetings" between the president and Congress. Leaders have developed so-called leadership PACs, through which party leaders raise money and distribute it to individual candidates,[97] thus linking members' campaign treasuries to their willingness to follow the directives of the parties' leaders.[98] As a result, party leaders have more weapons with which to discipline recalcitrant party members. These changes reinforce partisan polarization by pulling members who might otherwise dissent from the positions taken by the party's caucus back into the fold. The parties within Congress are "organizations that . . . [specialize] in coordinating action on shared policy goals, . . . identif[ying] the common ground among autonomous partisans and forg[ing] coalitions on the basis of these shared preferences."[99]

In sum, the new constitutional order consists of a public that does not participate in politics and weak parties but highly partisan institutions in a divided government.

A NOTE ON THE MEDIA

The role of the media in the new constitutional order is complex, and I am unaware of substantial scholarship, beyond the journalistic, that illuminates the structural relation between the media and the new order. There is, however, some agreement on important features of that relation.

The situation as seen from the politicians' side is rather simple. As two political scientists put it, "the decay of party organizations has made politicians ever more dependent upon favorable media coverage."[100] According to two analysts, politicians have learned to "craft" their messages "to attract media attention" and, perhaps more important, to obscure the points on which the policies the politicians are pursuing are inconsistent with their constituents' desires.[101] The politicians "manage the press" by "saturat[ing it] with their 'message,'" presented in "simple, attractive themes" that the politicians have pre-tested with focus groups to ensure that the audience would already be receptive to themes that might not accurately describe the concrete policies being offered.[102] "The combination of polarization, the emphasis on policy goals, the rise of political consultants, and the emergence of a new breed of media-savvy political leaders have dramatically widened the use of opinion manipulation strategies from presidents to members of Congress and interest groups."[103]

The situation as seen from the media's side is more complicated. The news media compete with entertainment for audiences. They have severe time constraints on producing stories and fitting them within the "newshole" each correspondent has available. For example, two political scientists have studied television coverage of the Supreme Court. They report "a dramatic decline in the extent and nature of the coverage" of the Court between the 1989 and the 1994 terms, with the number of stories dropping from 245 to 111.[104] They explain the reduction in coverage by the decline in the Court's caseload and the rise of "infotainment."[105]

News stories today must be "timely, terse, easily described, dramatic, colorful, and visualizable."[106] News reporting focuses on events rather than conditions, simplifies political proposals to fit the news-hole, and, importantly, tries to "personaliz[e] . . . events."[107] Political scientist Bartholomew Sparrow identifies "standard practices" such as the media's attention to the "'horse race' aspect of presidential campaigns," its commitment to balanced coverage, and a tendency "to take a critical view of political news . . . [in which] the news media are not merely umpires, but hanging judges."[108] He attributes these practices, in part, to the structural demands of the modern media, which face severe cost constraints and have discovered that they must rely on "soft news" and dramatic accounts of what otherwise might be dry events to attract the audiences that sponsors pay for.[109] As Sparrow puts it, "The job of producers and, increasingly, editors is to make the news into entertainment, in which drama is 'the defining characteristic of the news.'"[110] The result is straightforward: "Journalists and editors respond to economic pressures when covering politics by avoiding complexity in favor of simplicity, easy-to-sell stereotypes, and audience-grabbing plots. The marketing calculation . . . is that political conflict and the 'horse race' . . . will captivate and draw audiences addicted to titillating entertainment."[111] And, of course, politicians alert to media routines can respond by structuring their own presentations in ways that feed into the media's approach to the news.

Law professor Jack Balkin applies these ideas to law: "Television has created a world of law-related shows and legal commentators whose basic goal is to describe law in ways that are comprehensible to television audiences and that can hold their attention. This means, among other things, that law must become entertaining."[112] Political scientist Douglas Reed identifies a juridico-entertainment complex analogous to the military-industrial complex President Dwight Eisenhower described in his Farewell Address of 1961.[113] According to Reed, the juridico-entertainment complex "transforms legal proceedings and legal conflict into consumable commodities that purport to educate and enlighten but simultaneously titillate, amuse, and otherwise entertain a mass audience. This . . . gains political influence through a process of reinterpretation by professional analysts . . . [and] then forms the basis for policy-making in a more traditional sense."[114]

For present purposes the importance of Reed's analysis lies in its treatment of the electorate as passive consumers of constitutional policy. Rather than shaping policy, the electorate simply observes it being made, just as the viewing public observes entertainment shows on television. Those who interpret low voter turnout as an expression of voter alienation might contend that the juridico-entertainment complex contributes to alienation by treating voters as passive consumers, thereby making them so. As Reed puts it, "as this extra-legal . . . regime grows in power, the underlying legal institutions become[] increasingly irrelevant." Reed points out that the juridico-entertainment complex influences the policy agenda: To the extent that issues cannot be readily presented in an entertaining way, they find it difficult to force their way onto an agenda determined by policymakers' interpretation of public concern as evidenced by the material presented in the mass media.

All these features converge to make the politics of scandal "the weapon of choice for struggle and competition in informational politics."[115] Historian John H. Summers points out that the politics of scandal was a prominent feature of nineteenth-century U.S. politics and then disappeared for most of the twentieth century.[116] He attributes the disappearance of the politics of scandal to the insulation of national political elites through most of the century and, importantly, to "changes in the ideology and practice of professional journalism."[117] The politics of scandal revived when professional journalism changed again.

Of course, presidents are the most obvious focal points for the politics of scandal.[118] Judge Richard Posner describes the Clinton impeachment as "the most *riveting* chapter of recent American history" and the robes worn by Chief Justice William Rehnquist as part of the "theater" of impeachment.[119] Sociologist Manuel Castells offers a convenient summary that bears directly on the way some traditional constitutional issues might be handled in the new constitutional order:

> Judges, prosecutors, and investigative committee members enter into a symbiotic relationship with the media. They protect the media (ensuring their independence). . . . In exchange, they are protected by the media, they become media heroes. . . . Together, they fight for democracy and clean government, they control the excesses of politicians, and, ultimately, they seize power away from the society, diffusing it into the society. While doing so, they may also delegitimize parties, politicians, politics, and, ultimately, democracy in its current incarnation.[120]

Not everything Castells has to say here accurately describes the new constitutional order in the United States. Notably, the media overall did not treat Independent Counsel Kenneth Starr as a fighter for democracy. Rather, he became another character in the impeachment soap opera. Castells's fundamental insight into the symbiotic relation between courts and the media may account for part of the contemporary Supreme Court's enthusiasm for the First Amendment, however. Journalists present their inquiries into scandals as important to the nation's governance.[121] The public learns of Supreme Court decisions through newspapers, television broadcasts, and the like. The media have a fairly direct interest in maximizing the protection speech gets: The more protected speech is, the less they have to worry about. That means that as a general matter, a decision upholding a free speech claim will receive more favorable treatment in the media than a decision rejecting such a claim—not always, but generally. In a period of divided government justices can do pretty much whatever they want and need not be particularly sensitive to the public reaction to their decisions. But, to the degree that a justice is concerned about generating support for the Court, ruling in favor of free speech claims is a reasonably good way to do it.

Judge Posner's comment on Chief Justice Rehnquist's robes led Posner to conclude that "the appearance he presented makes it difficult to believe that the American people any longer expect their officials to be more dignified, aloof, and impressive than themselves."[122] Comedian Jay Leno was even more pointed about the impeachment: "We've reached the point where Congress does not affect anyone's life, so we look at it as entertainment."[123] In the new regime, the nation's constitutional aspirations have been reduced to the point that the public appears to regard elite manueverings in Washington as a soap opera of some modest entertainment value but without much effect on the lives of the American people.

IMPLICATIONS: THE SCOPE OF NATIONAL POLICYMAKING

Partisan polarization and divided government have obvious implications for the lawmaking process: Only initiatives that have bipartisan support are likely to be enacted, and polarization makes it difficult to assemble a bipartisan majority for major policy initiatives. Both points are important. Bipartisan support can be assembled under the right conditions, and divided government in itself "may lead either to 'stalemate' or to a 'bidding up' phenomenon, depending on the political and policy calculations made by policymakers."[124] David Mayhew's study of divided government finds that major legislation was enacted at roughly the same rate during periods of divided and unified government.[125] Later research has qualified Mayhew's conclusions by pointing out that divided government takes several forms and that Mayhew's conclusions may derive from the fact that the periods of divided government he examined were characterized by forms of party division that allowed for significant cooperation across party lines.[126] The new constitutional order is structured to produce more substantial partisan divisions, which make productive cooperation increasingly difficult. As Fiorina suggests, perhaps voters "choose[] split control of government so as to frustrate both parties."[127] Mayhew's measure of legislative productivity, after all, does not identify important laws that were *not* passed because of divided government.[128]

In addition, changes in legislative norms have increased the ability of the most partisan members of Congress to obstruct bipartisan cooperation. The case is clearest in the Senate, where the filibuster and other super-majority processes once were rarely invoked but now play a large role in structuring legislation.[129] According to Barbara Sinclair, writing in 1989, "[f]ilibusters are much more frequent than they used to be and are much less restrictive in their target bills. . . . A rare event in the 1950s, the filibuster had by the 1970s become quite common" and "threats to filibuster . . . are much more frequent than they used to be."[130] "In the 103rd Congress the filibuster was used as a partisan tool to an extent unprecedented in this century. In the first year of the 104th, Democrats, then in the minority, returned the favor. In 1995, 44 percent of major legislation encountered extended debate-related problems."[131] The rise in filibusters resulted from a convergence of factors: an increased workload in the Senate, which substantially increases the costs imposed by filibusters and similar obstructionist tactics, coupled with increasing partisanship.[132] In addition, senators have learned how to exploit the Senate's rules, creating the post-cloture filibuster, a form of extended debate that, though formally limited, can have severe effects as time pressure grows near the end of each legislative session.[133] Senate leaders must "accommodate the wishes of senators threatening to obstruct legislation—either by delaying consideration of the measure or making concessions to gain their support."[134]

The overall effect, in Sinclair's words, is to make obstructionism a "[s]tandard [o]perating [p]rocedure."[135] Other political scientists describe the rise of filibustering as "a parliamentary arms race" and suggest that "'[o]nce parliamentary strategies such as these have been unleashed, they—like the atom bomb—cannot be uninvented.'"[136] Routine filibusters, that is, characterize the new regime. More generally, obstructionism allows the minority party to block the adoption of their opponents' policies and create a legislative record defining their own program even though they cannot enact it either.[137]

A strategy of assembling a minimum winning coalition by attracting only a few votes from the opposing party may fail in the new constitutional order. The opposing party's leadership can use its assets to discipline and reward members to keep them in line, and individual members can "use[] obstructionist tactics to undermine . . . [major] policy initiatives."[138] And, although budget bills are exempt from the rules allowing extended debate, both the Senate and the House of Representatives have adopted rules that require super-majorities on some important budget issues.[139] The overall effect of these rules and norms has been to impose an effective requirement that nonbudget bills must have the support of sixty senators if they are to pass.[140] And, it seems likely for the foreseeable future, any bill that can attract sixty votes is likely to attract a much larger number: Once the threshold of bipartisanship has been crossed, large majorities from both parties will sign on.[141] In an evenly divided Senate, for example, any proposal supported by Republicans effectively requires sixty votes to pass, but any proposal likely to attract ten Democratic votes is likely to attract thirty.[142]

The effects of super-majority requirements on legislation's content are complex.[143] Super-majority requirements weaken the power of committees to dominate the agenda, as legislation must accommodate those who would engage in extended debate or otherwise obstruct enactment. By increasing the influence of members on the floor, super-majority requirements enhance the incentives for strong leadership, which itself has important implications. Super-majority requirements may increase the power of moderates in a narrowly divided and polarized body.[144] However, increasing homogeneity decreases the number of moderates and the general centralization of power in the leadership places the moderates under greater control by an ideologically guided leadership chosen by each party's partisan majority. Thus, super-majority rules may simply make it more difficult to enact legislation outside the context of omnibus budget bills.[145] Legislative gridlock results as much from arrangements *within* Congress, including increasing partisan polarization and the application of internal rules of procedure, as it does from disagreement between the president and one or both houses of Congress.[146]

Fiorina points out as well that the form of legislation appears to change in divided government. Delegation of lawmaking authority to executive agencies occurred in the New Deal–Great Society constitutional regime because they were essential to accomplishing that regime's programmatic goals. But Congress will be reluctant to delegate broad authority to an executive branch controlled by a different party.[147] A recent study shows "an overall downward trend" of delegation since the New Deal, which the authors find resulted in part from a reluctance to delegate during periods of divided government.[148]

But avoiding delegations in enacted statutes will be difficult. Legislation that spells out details is harder to enact because it requires agreement at the outset, and in any event takes more time to enact, a real cost to a Congress already facing severe time pressures. A reluctance to delegate when another party controls the executive branch, coupled with the difficulties of securing agreement on detailed legislation in a highly partisan Congress, will check the scope of any new programs.

Partisan polarization and obstructionism do not mean that Congress is inactive in the new constitutional order. After all, members come to Congress to do something, either to enact new initiatives or to scale back old ones. But the thickening of governmental institutions and the residual though substantial power of interest groups make it difficult to accomplish substantial programmatic change.[149] As Fiorina points out, "the struggle for political credit sometimes makes both parties as likely to compromise behind some legislation as to allow the process to stalemate."[150] The legislative product is likely to be policy initiatives that, while sometimes interesting and experimental,[151] are rather small in scope.[152] Looking at the process from the president's point of view, one scholar concludes, "President[s] have most control over *small pet projects* that they personally identify with and push early in their administration."[153] The conclusion seems apt with respect to legislation more generally.[154]

Bipartisan agreement can be reached, however. Sometimes it will be on smaller programs, consistent with the reduced scope of national government in the new constitutional order. Sometimes it will be on legislation that has largely symbolic meaning, albeit with real effects.[155] And sometimes bipartisan agreement can be reached on important programs, such as welfare reform and budget policies that briefly produced a budget surplus by constraining federal expenditures in an era of substantial economic growth. Notably, the *content* of these policies is precisely to reduce the national government's scope.

The policies produced by the national government in the new constitutional order, then, conform to the idea that our constitutional aspirations have been reduced.

IMPLICATIONS: PRESIDENTIAL ADMINISTRATION

Reflecting on her experience as a senior staff member in the Clinton White House, law professor Elena Kagan identified a new mechanism for controlling administrative agencies, which she called "presidential administration."[156] Kagan describes the methods of controlling agencies in prior constitutional orders. Sometimes Congress would prescribe the rules agencies were to enforce; sometimes Congress supervised through legislative oversight hearings, chastising agency officials for what members of Congress thought were their misdeeds. Agencies were also controlled by the professional norms of the experts who were supposed to run them and ultimately by the courts reviewing the agencies' decisions.

Presidential administration, which Kagan dates to the Reagan presidency, is the new constitutional order's distinctive method of controlling agencies. The most important early manifestation was the administration's attempt to impose cost-benefit analysis on all agency rules. The

New Deal–Great Society's interest groups fought the cost-benefit requirement on various legal grounds, with some success.

Presidential administration suited the political interests of presidents in the new constitutional order, and it persisted and, Kagan argues, was expanded in the Clinton administration. Divided government means that a president's *legislative* agenda may fall by the wayside. But, as Skowronek emphasizes, a president has to accomplish something to be regarded as a successful political leader. With the legislative agenda hard to enact, presidents will use any tool they have to implement the programs they favor. Presidential administration describes the tools available.[157]

Kagan argues that Clinton "convert[ed] administrative activity into an extension of his own policy and political agenda."[158] Clinton directed agencies under his supervision to start rule-making proceedings and prodded nominally independent agencies to do so as well, and then he associated himself with the rules when they were issued. Kagan shows how wide-ranging presidential administration was, involving extensive programs dealing with firearm regulation and health care regulation after the collapse of the president's effort to secure the adoption of a national health care plan.[159]

Kagan observes that these techniques have obvious limits. An ideologically divided Congress, even if controlled by the other party, may be unable to block the president's administrative actions.[160] But a president can administer only within the range of discretion given agencies by existing law. So, for example, President Clinton's effort to regulate tobacco advertising through the Food and Drug Administration was thwarted when the Supreme Court ruled that the statutes dealing with the FDA and tobacco barred the agency from acting.[161] The lawsuit itself illustrates another limit—the continuing role of interest groups as political actors placing constraints on all government action in the new constitutional order.

Presidents would undoubtedly like to do more than maneuver to advance their programs within the limits of existing law; they would like to define a new legislative agenda and have it enacted. Divided government makes it unlikely that they can be as effective as they would prefer. In the new constitutional order, presidential administration serves a president's political interests about as well as can be imagined, notwithstanding the limits imposed by existing law and interest group pressure. As Kagan argues, we can expect it to be an enduring feature of the present regime.

IMPLICATIONS: IMPEACHMENT

The institutions of the new constitutional order produced President Clinton's impeachment. A highly partisan House of Representatives voted to impeach the president even after an election that seemed to show that the nation's people did not want the impeachment process to go forward.[162] Republicans in safe districts were insulated from retaliation and attracted larger campaign contributions.[163] The leadership used its power to hold moderates in line.[164] Many observers have suggested, as Professor Cass Sunstein does, that the impeachment events were constitutionally destabilizing because "[t]here are grave systemic dangers in resorting to impeachment except in the most extreme cases."[165] One interpretation of the impeachment is that the outcome has established that impeachment should be available only in such cases.[166]

There is another way of looking at the impeachment and its outcome, however. As we have seen, President Clinton appropriated the themes of the new constitutional order even though he was the candidate of the party that had opposed the new regime's creation.[167] Writing shortly after Clinton's election in 1992, Stephen Skowronek foresaw the possibility of impeachment because of the structure of the constitutional order. According to Skowronek, the "hallmarks" of a "politics of preemption" of the sort Clinton practiced "have been the cultivation of independent political identities, the exploitation of ad hoc coalitions, and *the high risk of suffering the ultimate disgrace of impeachment.*"[168] A president in Clinton's position makes those in his own party uneasy because he has appropriated the other party's themes, and infuriates those in the other party for precisely the same reason. The chance that a misstep will lead to impeachment is not small.

But, as the Clinton impeachment and its outcome show, impeachment need not be anything major. The impeachment of President Clinton seems to have had little effect *qua* impeachment.[169] Within six months of President Clinton's acquittal, a leading Republican was quoted as observing, "We have a president rolling the Congress, getting everything he wants."[170] Rather than a constitutional crisis, we might see the impeachment as a "no harm, no foul" event: Anticipating an acquittal, a highly partisan and polarized House of Representatives could satisfy its majority's partisan interests *without* destabilizing the constitutional order.[171] And, similarly, a president observing the outcome of Clinton's impeachment might conclude that there is no serious risk in practicing the politics of preemption: Impeachment might occur, but without serious consequences.[172]

If government is divided in precisely the way it was in 1998—with a president of one party, a House majority of the other, and more than one-third of the Senate of the president's party—we might expect a normalization of impeachment, in which a House of Representatives, highly partisan for structural reasons, impeaches a president with no expectation that the Senate will remove the president from office. And, if impeachment is normalized in this way, it may have no large destabilizing effects.[173]

We might draw a somewhat broader lesson from the Clinton impeachment. Presidents who practice the politics of preemption are likely to be out of step with many members of Congress in their own party because, as we have seen, those members will be more partisan than most of the electorate and, in particular, more partisan than the voters who supported the preemptive president. This suggests that even a nominally unified government may sometimes be divided in practice, with the president and the congressional members of the president's party responding to quite different constituencies. The conditions for unified government, that is, may be even more severe than we might think were we to look solely at partisan affiliations in Congress and the presidency.

IMPLICATIONS: STATE GOVERNMENTS

The New Deal–Great Society constitutional order had little place for state and local governments. The national government had responsibility for securing economic stability and guaranteeing rights of civic participation and a safe and healthful environment. States were either obstacles to accomplishing the regime's goals or handy vehicles for administering national programs. The role of state and local governments in the new constitutional order might be a bit larger, but not as much as one might think at first. Two developments on the state and local levels during the 1980s and 1990s now appear to be settled characteristics of the new constitutional order: limits on the ability of these governments to impose taxes, which constrains their ability to pursue substantive programs, and term limits for elected officials. Both developments place limits on what state and local governments can do and make it likely that state legislatures will adopt some programs that courts will be inclined to hold unconstitutional.

Tax limitations spread rapidly after the adoption in 1978 of California's Proposition 13. Tax limitations arise from two sources. The first is the mobility of capital, which will leave jurisdictions that tax capital at too high a rate and will be attracted to jurisdictions that offer it tax breaks. Capital mobility produces local economic instability, which "foster[s] anxiety and discontent" and thereby produces the political conditions that lead to the adoption of the second source of tax limitations, constitutional and statutory provisions "that cripple the ability of local governments to function, much less invest in human capital development."[174] These effects occur, however, primarily on the *local* level. The overall effect of tax limitations has not been to limit the amount of money raised by *state* governments, but rather to centralize the collection—and redistribution—of tax revenue.[175] State governments collect the money that local governments did earlier, and then send it back to the local governments, but this time pursuant to standards defined in the state capitol.

The most dramatic effects have been in the area of education, where longstanding traditions of local control have been displaced, first by fiscal centralization and then by the centralization of education policy in the state governments.[176]

Legislators searched for new revenue sources to replace the funds lost due to tax limitations. They found them in fees and charges.[177] The most interesting of these fees are imposed on people who cannot vote easily or at all on the question of imposing them: hotel occupancy fees imposed on visitors from out of town, but also business licensing fees imposed on businesses that operate throughout the state or nation. The flow of revenue-raising power upward reduces the accountability of legislators to local constituents; the use of fees and charges reduces their accountability to the people on whom the fees are imposed.[178]

The term-limits movement of the 1980s and 1990s appears to have crested.[179] Until recently, there was more speculation than evidence about the effects of term limits, because it was not until around 2000 that entire legislatures were composed of members elected to limited terms. The evidence that is now available indicates that some of the speculations were right.[180] Term limits make legislators less powerful and increase the power of governors—even those facing term limits themselves—and the state bureaucracy, including the legislative staff. Bureaucracies, staffs, and lobbyists gain power because they have access to information and expertise that newcomers to the legislature lack—and in term-limited legislatures, almost everyone is a newcomer. Newcomers have to make names for themselves, and they do not have much time to do so. Term limits "force legislators . . . to push their policy priorities more quickly" and thereby "stimulate legislative initiatives."[181] Those initiatives, however, often have little support from other legislators. As one legislator put it, "I don't know who those guys are" and so he does not have much reason to trust that their policy proposals make sense.[182] Individual reputations cannot count for much in term-limited legislatures, but party affiliations can. Legislators use party membership as a cue to decide which way to vote on a proposal: Democrats vote for proposals by other Democrats, and similarly for Republicans. The effect is partisan polarization in state legislatures.[183]

Term limits have another effect: Legislators start looking for new jobs pretty quickly—a position in some *other* legislature. Members of the lower house in a state government start running for the state senate; members of the state senate start running for the House of Representatives or for some statewide elected office. To do that in the time they have, though, they have to make names for themselves. This leads them to "stak[e] out highly visible positions on issues salient to voters, without regard for progress on a viable legislative agenda."[184]

The substance of state legislative policy in the new constitutional order may focus on doing what is needed to preserve revenue sources. Investments in human capital—in education programs—might seem attractive. The difficulty is that such investments may be like pouring water into a leaky bucket: States will invest resources in educating people who will leave shortly after they have acquired the human capital they need.[185] States may also develop programs that satisfy the wishes of highly educated workers, who may be willing to trade off some taxes for improvements in lifestyle, such as a better environment or shorter commuting times.[186]

Taken together, the effects of term limits on the policymaking process are not terribly attractive. Proposals are "poorly thought out," and legislators have less ability, relative to governors and lobbyists, to supervise the implementation of state policies.[187] As Canadian law professors Michael Trebilcock and Ron Daniels note, "Good ideas are scarce," and working out the details of even the best ideas requires a fair amount of careful attention.[188] When all these effects are put together, the picture seems to be this: Legislators will thrash around to develop policies that seem politically attractive. No one will think seriously about whether those policies make much sense. Many of the policies will impose costs on people who had no say in adopting them. Most will be badly designed in purely technical terms. This is a prescription for a system with activist courts, even courts whose members think that their job is to strike down only laws that go far beyond the bounds of reason.[189]

IMPLICATIONS: INDIVIDUAL RIGHTS

The nation needed a Second Bill of Rights, according to the constitutional vision of the New Deal–Great Society regime, because combining background rules of property rights with the provisions of the first Bill of Rights and the Reconstruction amendments failed adequately to promote human flourishing.[190] Racial segregation had to be overcome by aggressive policies of national support for the aspirations of African Americans; economic inequality had to be addressed through a War on Poverty; the travails of old age had to be reduced by providing health care to the elderly through the Medicare program.

The chastened constitutional aspirations of the new constitutional order adopt a somewhat different view of the prerequisites of liberty and flourishing. To some extent the new constitutional order accepts a more libertarian definition of liberty and flourishing than the New Deal–Great Society order did. Background rules of property rights need be combined only with minor adjustments around the edges, the small-scale programs of the new constitutional regime, to guarantee liberty and flourishing.[191] Some proponents of the new order agree that there may be problems with the provision of health care, but they are to be dealt with by market-focused solutions. Poverty is to be alleviated by ensuring that the poor obtain education and training to allow them to participate actively in the labor market.

The new constitutional order thus continues to accept the older view that background rules of property are not enough, because its political institutions are structured to generate incremental adjustments in the larger programs of the prior regime, such as social security, but not to repeal them. Finally, the structures of the new regime make large-scale regulatory initiatives quite unlikely.

Taken together, these features suggest that the new order may back into a form of moderate libertarianism without making libertarianism one of the regime's organizing principles: Moderate libertarianism prevails because the government in the new order simply cannot do very much, and so it leaves people alone.

IMPLICATIONS: JUDICIAL REVIEW

As I have argued, the political institutions of the new constitutional order will continue to generate laws that courts will strike down. State legislatures will be constitutionally irresponsible because of their members' inexperience and political needs. The candidate-centered politics of Congress may produce laws that have little real policy justification but serve only the political interests of the members of Congress. Courts might be inclined to invalidate these laws, and they would face little risk of retaliation in doing so. Judicial review in connection with such laws, however, is not a terribly important institution precisely because the laws themselves are hardly important.

Divided government might make a stronger form of judicial review possible and even attractive to politicians. With neither party sure that it would continue to retain power to legislate, each would hope that the courts would persist in pursuing the out-of-power party's program after the party lost control of the legislature.[192] Courts, that is, "provide[] a form of insurance" for politicians.[193] As political scientist Cornell Clayton puts it, "Without a stable coalition controlling the elected branches, the Court has less fear of institutional retaliation if it makes unpopular decisions. Unlike in earlier periods, recent presidents and Congresses have not just been unwilling to coordinate an assault on the Court, but parties controlling each have acted to protect the Court's independence from threats mounted by the other."[194] On some issues, such as those dealing with the Constitution's allocation of power between the president and Congress, the Court automatically generates a supporter whichever way it rules.

Note, however, that the politicians' calculation supporting judicial review makes sense only if the out-of-power party can hope to place on the courts judges sympathetic to its concerns once the party regains the power to determine policy. One reason for Democratic discomfort with the outcome of *Bush v. Gore* is that it substantially diminished that possibility. The next chapter examines the Supreme Court's position on judicial review today. Chapter 3 contains a discussion of how political institutions may affect the process of nomination and confirmation in ways that reduce the pro-judicial review effect of divided government.

CONCLUSION

Divided ideological government plays a large role in this chapter's analysis. But divided ideological government need not persist, and even brief periods of unified ideological government may have important long-term consequences. It is not difficult to end up with a unified government "by accident." As the 1992 elections demonstrate, coordinating the preference for divided government in a presidential election year may prove difficult as voters throughout the country choose their senators and House members independently of the choices others make.[195] Unified government may be more partisan than the typical voter prefers, because the districting structures and presidential incentives described earlier help polarize the parties. A unified government's policies may then provoke electoral reactions in the next election, but in the interim important public policy decisions may be made that are difficult to reverse thereafter.[196]

Perhaps the most important qualification is to clarify the sense in which the New Deal order has fallen. The New Deal is gone, but only in the sense that the aspirations of government have been chastened, not eliminated. One recent survey concluded that the American people were deeply ambivalent about government: They disliked government in general but strongly want the government to continue to do what it has been doing in implementing New Deal–Great Society programs.[197] The new constitutional order remains committed to preserving a baseline of New Deal–Great Society protections for some quality-of-life programs, such as environmental protection, some aspects of the social safety net, such as the social security program,[198] and a fair amount of pluralistic tolerance. The guiding principle of the new regime is not that government cannot solve problems, but that it cannot solve any more problems.[199]

Chapter Two

THE SUPREME COURT OF
THE NEW CONSTITUTIONAL ORDER

THE SUPREME COURT could do essentially anything its majority wanted in a regime of divided government. Consider statutory interpretation: The Court's conservative statutory interpretations could be overturned if they were more conservative than a conservative president wished (because the president would then sign a new statute modifying the Court's decision sent to him by a Congress more liberal than he), *or* if they were more conservative than the most conservative one-third of both the House or the Senate (because then Congress could override a presidential veto).[1] But, given sharp ideological divisions in Congress, it is quite unlikely that a Supreme Court decision would be more conservative than the right wing of the congressional Republican Party or more liberal than the left wing of the congressional Democratic Party.[2]

The Court's constitutional interpretations are even less vulnerable: A conservative decision can be overturned only if it is more conservative than the most conservative third of either the House or the Senate, a liberal one only if it is more liberal than the most liberal third of those bodies. The ideological divisions in Congress in the new constitutional order make it possible for the justices to do basically whatever they want.[3] Or, more precisely, the Court can do whatever the justice closest to the middle of the Court's ideological divisions—the median justice—wants to do.[4]

The median justice on today's Court—perhaps Justice Sandra Day O'Connor, perhaps Justice Anthony Kennedy—pretty clearly wants to do something different from what happened during the New Deal–Great Society constitutional order. But what, exactly, does the median justice want to do? It is easy enough to find people describing the Court's decisions as revolutionary. Those who think the Court is engaged in a constitutional revolution see the Court repudiating long-settled constitutional understandings and threatening to return the nation to the constitutional universe of the 1920s or even earlier. The purported revolution would restore a constitutional world in which the Supreme Court can invalidate state and national laws in the service of a vision of restricted, almost libertarian government.[5]

The present Court's majority would almost certainly disclaim revolutionary ambitions, pointing out that they have not overruled *any* decisions at the heart of the New Deal–Great Society constitutional order. Rather, they would assert, they seek to restore the Constitution's true meaning, particularly with respect to its division of authority between the nation and the states. According to the restorationist, the vision that prevailed in the 1960s and 1970s simply abandoned the vision of federalism embodied in the original Constitution. The Supreme Court had unfortunately come under the influence of these innovators for about a generation, but the Court's majority is now in a position to restore the proper relation between the nation and the states. Similarly, the restorationist claims, the Court is restoring a proper balance between regulation and economic liberty in other doctrinal areas.

I offer a different perspective on the Court's actions. The modern Court's *agenda* might indeed be that of the pre–New Deal era. That is, the issues of primary concern to the modern Court are the same issues— federalism and property rights—that concerned the pre–New Deal Court. But the modern Court's resolutions of the issues on that agenda differ substantially from earlier resolutions. The Court's decisions do not portend further radical restructurings of the national government. Nor are they best understood as returning the Constitution to some imagined— and uncontroversial—original understanding, or even as returning it to some place we have been before. Instead, the current Court is developing constitutional doctrine appropriate to the new constitutional order, in which our constitutional aspirations have been chastened.

We can best discern where the Court is by taking on the challenge of those who assert that the Court is a revolutionary one. I begin by examining what the Court has done in three areas central to the pre–New Deal/Great Society constitutional order: federalism, economic liberty, and the delegation of authority from Congress to the executive. In each area, I show that the Court's actions are certainly susceptible to relatively narrow readings. Under those readings, government must be scaled back a bit, but the government's expansion in the New Deal–Great Society constitutional order remains substantially unimpaired. The exposition of this point requires some technical detail, but much can be seen even in a relatively broad-brush portrait.

I then take up the constitutional developments regarding individual rights and civil liberties during the New Deal–Great Society order. Here, I argue, there has been a significant transformation in some areas, particularly free expression, some retrenchment in other areas, and an expansion of civil liberties in others, which would be surprising were the Court engaged in a revolutionary repudiation of the New Deal–Great Society constitutional order.

After that, I describe some important statutes that are truly vulnerable under current doctrine extended at most only modestly. But, to complete a revolution the Court would have to explore major areas—involving Congress's power to give money to states with strings attached, for example—in which it has expressed little interest so far.

I do not deny that an aggressive Court *could* move in a revolutionary direction, or that the Court's recent decisions can be given broader readings than the ones I present. My point here is only that the Court has not made revolutionary moves or treated its own doctrine expansively. The doctrines the Court has articulated are, taken at face value, relatively modest in their impact on the New Deal–Great Society constitutional order. I defer to chapter 3 the obvious challenge to my analysis: Perhaps the *present* Court is not revolutionary, but a single new justice committed to constitutional transformation could push the Court in a quite radical direction: Justice Antonin Scalia could become the median justice, not Justice Kennedy or O'Connor. Drawing on the analysis in chapter 1 and on recent scholarship examining the nomination and confirmation processes, that chapter explains why the other institutions in the new constitutional order make it unlikely, though not certain, that such a justice will take a seat on the Supreme Court.

Today's Court and the Constitutional Doctrine of the 1920s

Before the New Deal the Supreme Court restricted government power by limiting the national government's power to regulate economic activity, by enforcing a constitutionally protected liberty of contract, and—during its consideration of New Deal legislation itself—by occasionally insisting that national regulation be done by Congress itself rather than by executive officials acting under delegations of power from Congress.[6] As those who constructed the New Deal–Great Society constitutional order saw things, the Court before the New Deal treated as constitutionally mandatory an economic order governed solely by traditional common law protections of property and contract. The common law did not establish a regime of complete laissez-faire in the economy, and the Court actually tolerated some important departures from common law rules. The pre–New Deal Court allowed states to exercise general regulatory power as part of what the Court called the states' police power over health, safety, and morals. And it allowed rather extensive regulation of what the Court called businesses affected with a public interest, which was not an extremely narrow category. But some businesses were ordinary ones, and the police power did not extend to laws seeking to equalize economic power between workers and employers.

The constitutional order before the New Deal had another important characteristic. The Supreme Court believed both that a discernable line separated constitutional law from politics and that its distinctive job was to discern—and police—that line, ensuring that legislatures stayed within the bounds of politics.

The New Deal–Great Society constitutional order involved far more substantial interventions in the economy than had occurred before. The Court essentially abandoned the idea of a restricted category of businesses affected with a public interest and decided that anything a government could do to any business it could do to them all. It also recognized government power to redistribute economic bargaining power. And it all but abandoned the idea that it had some special role in enforcing a line between constitutional law and politics. Has the present Supreme Court started down a path that leads back to the 1910s and 1920s, when businesses could invoke a wide range of constitutional protections against regulation? Probably not. But the Court has repudiated the assumption that there was no real line between constitutional law and politics. The Court may not have adopted *substantive* principles that regulated the constitutional order before the New Deal, but it has returned to the earlier vision of its own role.

FEDERALISM

The Supreme Court before the New Deal imposed serious limitations on Congress's power to regulate commerce, relying on the Constitution's limitation of congressional power to commerce "among the several States." Its reason for doing so was *federalism*: The more power to regulate Congress had, the less power states would have—at least in the sense that state power to develop distinctive regulatory policies would be limited, and displaced, by whatever Congress decided to do. According to the Court before the New Deal, for example, Congress did not have power to regulate manufacturing because "[c]ommerce succeeds to manufacture, and is not part of it."[7] Similarly, Congress could not require coal-mining companies to bargain with their employees, because "the incidents leading up to and culminating in the mining of coal do not constitute" commerce.[8] And, at the other end of the chain, Congress could not set up a system that ended up prescribing rules for the sale of poultry by slaughterhouses to butchers who dealt directly with consumers because "[t]he interstate transactions . . . [had] ended" when the slaughterhouses sold the chickens to the butchers.[9]

One of the rules in this last case required butchers to purchase entire "runs" of chickens, including any that might be ill. The "sick chicken" case was one of the centerpieces of the New Deal attack on the prior era's doctrine, because the Court had used its old doctrine to invalidate what New Dealers regarded as an important component of their program and, perhaps more important, because the old doctrine deployed in the "sick chicken" and the coal-mining cases indicated that the National Labor Relations Act might be held unconstitutional.

The Court retreated from that threat and in the process began to construct the federalism doctrine for the New Deal–Great Society order. It upheld the National Labor Relations Act, for example. The Court's 1942 decision in *Wickard v. Filburn* was its most important.[10] Congress had enacted a statute authorizing the secretary of agriculture to set quotas for wheat production. Filburn had a dairy farm on which he raised wheat for his cows to consume and for making bread at home. Filburn exceeded his quota and then argued that Congress could not regulate the production of wheat for on-farm consumption, because that activity had nothing to do with "interstate" commerce. The Court disagreed. The rather small effect Filburn's own production had on interstate commerce was irrelevant; what mattered, according to the Court, was whether the effect of activities like Filburn's, when aggregated, was significant.

The New Deal–Great Society Court applied the "aggregate effects" test to the point that it seemed that Congress could do anything. That might have seemed inconsistent with the very idea of federalism, in which there has to be *some* division of power between the states and the nation. Constitutional theorists supplied the New Deal–Great Society order with a justification for judicial abdication in this area. They argued that the question was not really whether there was a constitutionally prescribed line dividing what the national government could do from what it could not do. Of course there was such a line, they said. The real question, however, was which institution—Congress or the Supreme Court—was in a better position to determine whether some congressional action overstepped the line. The modern economy's complexity and the wide range of public goals the national government could pursue—according to the principles structuring the New Deal–Great Society constitutional order—limited the contributions the Court could make. And, conversely, the political structure of Congress, in which states had substantial representation, made Congress better than the Court in determining whether any particular proposal crossed the line dividing national power from state power—even taking into account Congress's self-interest in expanding its own regulatory reach.[11] The Supreme Court endorsed this "political safeguards" theory in 1985, when it upheld the application of federal maximum-hours laws to state and local governments.[12] That was the last significant federalism decision made during the New Deal–Great Society constitutional order.

Wickard and the case applying national wage laws to state governments illustrate two somewhat different dimensions of federalism doctrine. *Wickard* is about whether there are some things states can regulate—home-growing of wheat or, in more modern examples, violent crime, education, and family law—that the national government cannot regulate. The case involving national wage laws deals with states not as regulators of their own citizens but as sovereign governments, operating the institutions that make a government a government. The new constitutional order has addressed both these dimensions of federalism doctrine in four sets of cases: involving Congress's power to regulate interstate commerce; Congress's power to regulate the activities of states as sovereigns; Congress's power to enforce the Fourteenth Amendment; and the Eleventh Amendment, which provides that "[t]he Judicial power of the United States shall not . . . extend to any suit . . . commenced or prosecuted against one of the United States by Citizens of another State." Understanding the new constitutional order's federalism doctrine sometimes requires a fair amount of detail about the Court's holdings.

INTERSTATE COMMERCE

In 1996, for the first time since the New Deal, the Supreme Court found a national statute unconstitutional on the ground that the commerce clause did not give Congress the power to act as it had.[13] *United States v. Lopez* involved the Gun Free School Zones Act of 1990, which prohibited the possession of guns near schools. The Court began, it said, "with first principles," the most important being that "[t]he Constitution creates a Federal Government of enumerated powers."[14] After reviewing the New Deal–Great Society commerce clause cases, the Court identified three "broad categories of activity that Congress may regulate": "the use of the channels of interstate commerce," "instrumentalities of interstate commerce, or persons or things in interstate commerce," and the category implicated by the Gun Free School Zones Act, "activities that substantially affect interstate commerce."[15]

The United States argued that the act did regulate activities that substantially affected interstate commerce: "[T]he presence of guns in schools poses a substantial threat to the educational process by threatening the learning environment. A handicapped educational process, in turn, will result in a less productive citizenry. That, in turn, would have an adverse effect on the Nation's economic well-being."[16] That argument clearly was drawn from *Wickard*, where a similar chain of economic consequences was enough to support the statute. Chief Justice William Rehnquist's opinion in *Lopez* responded with the observation that, were the Court to accept the government's argument, Congress could do much more than regulate guns near schools. It could, for example, "regulate the educational process directly" by "mandat[ing] a federal curriculum for local elementary and secondary schools because what is taught in local schools has a significant 'effect on classroom learning,' and that, in turn, has a substantial effect on interstate commerce."[17] Second, the Court read the New Deal–Great Society precedents to mean that Congress could rely on *Wickard*'s "aggregate effects" theory only when it was regulating *commercial* activities. The Court acknowledged that determining whether an activity was commercial may not be easy, but "[t]he possession of a gun in a local school zone is in no sense an economic activity that might, through repetition elsewhere, substantially affect any sort of interstate commerce."[18]

Justice Kennedy wrote a concurring opinion in *Lopez*, which Justice O'Connor joined. He said that the sad history of the Court's efforts to enforce federalism limits on congressional power gave him "some pause" but thought that the Court's holding was "necessary but limited."[19] Justice Clarence Thomas also concurred, but he indicated a willingness to go much further in repudiating the New Deal–Great Society decisions. As he saw it, the term *commerce* should be confined to "selling, buying, and bartering, as well as transporting for these purposes" and should not include, for example, manufacturing or agriculture.[20] The majority opinion's concluding paragraph demonstrates the Court's understanding of *Lopez*'s significance:

> To uphold the Government's contentions here, we would have to pile inference upon inference in a manner that would bid fair to convert congressional authority under the Commerce Clause to a general police power of the sort retained by the States. Admittedly, some of our prior cases have taken long steps down that road, giving great deference to congressional action. The broad language in these opinions has suggested the possibility of additional expansion, but we decline here to proceed any further.[21]

Lopez may have involved a minor provision in the federal criminal code, adopted perhaps simply to show that Congress was trying to do something about gun violence rather than truly trying to accomplish significant policy goals. The Court's next decision in this line involved a provision of the Violence Against Women Act (VAWA), an important national initiative. Again, however, some justices might have thought the specific provision at issue was not all that important.

United States v. Morrison involved a provision in VAWA that authorized victims of violent gender-motivated crimes to sue their assailants in federal court.[22] (Other initiatives under the act include significant federal funding for programs aiding victims of gender-motivated violence. The Court's decision in *Morrison* does not suggest in the slightest that these additional, and arguably more important, federal programs are unconstitutional.) The Court's opinion in *Lopez* noted, almost in passing, that Congress had made no findings about the effects that guns near schools had on interstate commerce, and the supporters of VAWA's civil remedy provision took the hint. They developed a substantial record showing that "gender-motivated violence affects interstate commerce 'by deterring potential victims from traveling interstate, from engaging in employment in interstate business, and from transacting business, and in places involved in interstate commerce.' "[23] It turned out, though, that the findings were irrelevant. The Court did not say that the findings were inaccurate or speculative. Instead, it invoked *Lopez*'s doctrine: Congress could rely on the "aggregate effects" theory only when it regulated commercial or economic activity, and violence against women was not a commercial or economic activity. Thus, Congress's findings were "weakened by the fact that they rely so heavily on a method of reasoning that we have already rejected as unworkable if we are to maintain the Constitution's enumeration of powers."[24] Chief Justice Rehnquist's opinion for the Court again emphasized that the theory under which VAWA's civil remedy provision would be constitutional would allow Congress to regulate essentially everything, including violent crime, "the suppression of which has always been the prime object of the States' police power."[25]

What are we to make of these decisions? Undoubtedly they leave much open, including the possibility that they portend a revolutionary transformation in the national government's regulatory power. The Court said that the Gun Free School Zones Act and the Violence Against Women Act were constitutionally troublesome because the theories under which they were constitutional might just as readily support the constitutionality of national laws prescribing a national curriculum or a national law prescribing the conditions under which divorces could be obtained. This might suggest that the Court's project might be to identify substantive areas of state regulatory power into which the national government may not enter, such as education, family law, land-use planning, or street crime. That project would indeed threaten large portions of Congress's ordinary business.[26]

There are reasons to think, however, that the Court's project is more limited. The Court might have seen the statutes in *Lopez* and *Morrison* as particularly egregious exercises of truly expansive views of national power. The Gun Free School Zones Act might have been "feel good" legislation, a statute grandstanding members of Congress could vote for without seriously thinking it would have any important policy consequences.[27] As the legislation was pending, Chief Justice Rehnquist repeatedly said that the civil remedy provision at issue in *Morrison* was unsound policy that would drag prestigious federal judges into adjudicating the merits of domestic disputes of a sort typically handled by lower prestige state judges.[28]

Second, the Court's official theory in *Lopez* and *Morrison* was not that the national statutes invaded some substantive area of regulatory authority reserved to the states. The Court's stated concern was with what two scholars have called the "non-infinity" principle: No justification for congressional power is acceptable unless its proponents can identify *some* statute that could not be justified by that justification.[29] So, for example, Chief Justice Rehnquist wrote in *Lopez*:

> We pause to consider the implications of the Government's arguments. . . . [U]nder the Government's "national productivity" reasoning, Congress could regulate any activity that it found was related to the economic productivity of individual citizens: family law (including marriage, divorce, and child custody), for example. Under the theories that the Government presents, . . . it is difficult to perceive any limitation on federal power, even in areas such as criminal law enforcement or education where States historically have been sovereign. Thus, if we were to accept the Government's arguments, we are hard-pressed to posit any activity by an individual that Congress is without power to regulate.[30]

The Court's official theory has been that *Wickard*'s "aggregation" principle can be applied only when the activity Congress seeks to regulate is fairly described as commercial. Huge swathes of existing law involve such activities, even if we concede that sometimes it may be hard to decide whether the regulated activity really is commercial. Notably, the Court in *Lopez* actually endorsed *Wickard* as correctly decided, albeit without much enthusiasm, stating that the case, "perhaps the most far reaching example of Commerce Clause authority over intrastate activity, involved economic activity in a way that the possession of a gun in a school zone does not."[31]

Third, in addition to affirming *Wickard* when commercial activities are involved, the Court has indicated that Congress has the power to regulate even noncommercial activities when "the channels of interstate" commerce are used.[32] The trick, apparently, is to create a "jurisdictional hook" upon which Congress hangs its regulation. The obvious hook is a requirement that some aspect of the regulated activity have some unquestionable contact with interstate commerce. Congress inserted a jurisdictional hook into the Gun Free School Zones Act after *Lopez* by making it a national crime to possess within a school zone a gun that once had traveled across state lines.[33] No one can be confident that the Court would uphold the amended statute: The Court might be offended by such a transparent effort to evade the Court's decision in *Lopez*, just as it was offended in a related context involving the Fourteenth Amendment, as we will see. Justice Stephen Breyer's dissent in *Morrison* offered a somewhat more attractive example of using a jurisdictional hook. According to Justice Breyer, the Court's doctrinal concerns would be eliminated if Congress passed a statute providing a civil remedy for violence against women when it occurred in workplaces or public accommodations or colleges (described as places using lots of material that once had traveled in interstate commerce, or as places preparing people for employment in the national economy).[34] More generally, all Congress needs to do to satisfy the Court's non-infinity principle is to show that characterizing a particular activity as commercial does not mean that all activities are commercial. This should prove to be no problem for lawyers attentive to the Court's doctrine.

Justices O'Connor and Kennedy have repeatedly indicated their belief that large changes in the Court's federalism doctrine lead back to the pre–New Deal era and that they do not want to end up there.[35] As the Court said in *Lopez*, the case's outcome represented the Court's decision to refrain from going beyond the boundaries it understood had been set during the New Deal–Great Society constitutional order. Whether or not that is a fair characterization of the older regime's governing principles, the Court's language does not suggest that it has taken as a project a radical revision of prior understandings about the scope of Congress's power (though it has revised, probably radically, the old order's assumptions about the role of the Court itself). The Court's commerce clause cases do show that we are in a new constitutional order. They do not portend a return to the pre-New Deal–Great Society constitutional order, however. The holdings in *Lopez* and *Morrison*, understood as limited, show that the Court is willing to pare back what it regards as the excesses of legislation adopted by Congresses that accepted the principles of the New Deal–Great Society constitutional order. The Congresses of the new constitutional order are far less likely to engage in what the Court regards as excesses, in part because they will learn the lesson of *Lopez* and *Morrison* but, more important, because they themselves do not accept the older order's principles.

REGULATING THE STATES AS SOVEREIGNS

The modern Supreme Court has limited congressional power to regulate states in their capacity as sovereigns even when Congress has unquestionably been regulating interstate commerce. The Court started down the path in a case nominally involving only a question of statutory interpretation. *Gregory v. Ashcroft* presented the following question: Does the national Age Discrimination in Employment Act apply to state laws requiring state judges to retire when they reach the age of seventy?[36] The statute defines employees broadly but exempts "appointee[s] on the policy-making level." Missouri's judges are initially appointed by the governor, then run in retention elections to stay in office. Are they "appointees"? Do judges simply interpret the law, or do they make policy? One could plausibly interpret the statute to cover Missouri's judges. Justice O'Connor, writing for the Court, refused to do so.

Technically merely an opinion about the statute's proper interpretation, Justice O'Connor's opinion actually was an essay about what sorts of protection against national regulation states needed if they were to be sovereigns within a federal system. For our federal system to work, she wrote, states and the national government must exist in "proper balance. . . . In the tension between federal and state power lies the promise of liberty."[37] And establishing qualifications for judges was "a decision of the most fundamental sort for a sovereign entity. Through the structure of its government, and the character of those who exercise government authority, a State defines itself as a sovereign."[38] The Court would not lightly conclude that Congress had intruded on such an important sovereign function, and so it interpreted the statute as not covering Missouri's judges.

Justice O'Connor converted her position on the preservation of a state's governmental structure into a constitutional holding in *New York v. United States*.[39] The case involved a national statute dealing with the disposal of low-level nuclear waste, the residue of uses of radioactive materials in hospitals and smoke detectors. The problem arose because no one wants to be near a site where even low-level radioactive waste is stored. These wastes accumulated, and Congress wanted to solve the problem by getting states to agree on regional disposal sites. Congress set up a system under which a recalcitrant state would have to acquire all the nuclear waste generated in the state or, alternatively, create waste disposal sites that conformed to congressional requirements. In effect, Congress required states either to subsidize waste producers by absorbing the costs of nuclear waste generation or to regulate waste generators according to standards Congress prescribed.

Justice O'Connor wrote that this scheme violated a fundamental principle of federalism, one that barred the national government from commandeering state legislatures to do national business. Commandeering reduced the accountability of national and state officials, she said: "Where the Federal Government directs the States to regulate, it may be state officials who will bear the brunt of public disapproval, while the federal officials who devised the regulatory program may remain insulated from the electoral ramifications of their decision."[40] Justice O'Connor's opinion indicated that the Court could not find any other statute that "offers a state government no option other than that of implementing legislation enacted by Congress."[41]

Justice O'Connor summarized the Court's holding by saying that Congress could not compel states "to enact or administer a federal regulatory program."[42] This formulation both limited and extended the principle the

Court announced. It limited the principle to *regulatory* programs, by which the Court meant programs under which state governments did something to ordinary citizens. This limitation protected a state's exercise of its sovereign powers over its citizens but did not protect the state from national regulation of its internal operations, those that did not directly affect ordinary citizens.

The formulation extended the holding in another direction, however. At issue was a statute that directed a state to enact a regulatory program, not one that directed its executive officials to administer a national regulatory program. The Court proved it was serious in saying that Congress could not commandeer either state legislative *or* executive officials when it invalidated a temporary provision in the Brady Handgun Violence Prevention Act in *Printz v. United States*.[43] The Brady Act requires that people who sell guns check on their purchasers to see if the buyer has a criminal record or is otherwise barred from owning a gun. Today the national government performs these background checks, but the national system was not in place when the Brady Act came into effect. To fill the gap until the national system came on-line, Congress required the chief law enforcement officer in each jurisdiction to do the background checks. The Court again invoked the anti-commandeering principle to hold this portion of the Brady Act unconstitutional. Stressing that, as it viewed the historical record, "enlistment of state executive officers for the administration of federal programs is . . . unprecedented," the Court observed that "[t]he power of the Federal Government would be augmented immeasurably if it were able to impress into its service—and at no cost to itself—the police officers of the 50 States."[44] Justice Thomas concurred, suggesting that the Second Amendment might bar Congress from regulating "purely intrastate sale or possession of firearms."[45]

How important are these anti-commandeering decisions? Less important than they might seem at first. As Justice Kennedy, a supporter of the decisions, put it, they involve "the etiquette of federalism."[46] Ordinarily one would not think that an activity described as *etiquette* would be an important one. Even more, rules of etiquette are usually followed unthinkingly. To the extent that the anti-commandeering principle is such a rule, we might expect that Congress would rarely violate it. And, indeed, Justice Scalia's emphasis in *Printz* on how novel were attempts by Congress to force state officials to carry out its programs suggests that the New Deal–Great Society's theory that politics limited what Congress could do to the states has some force. The anti-commandeering principle can of course contribute to the political restraints on Congress: Citizens in states free of commandeering might come to see their states as important governing bodies, come to value strong state governments, and elect only members of Congress and senators who will respect state governments.[47]

That depends, however, on the scope of the anti-commandeering principle. The Court has suggested that it is limited to congressional decisions regulating states in their sovereign capacities, and even then that category might have a relatively narrow scope. *Reno v. Condon* upheld the national Driver's Privacy Protection Act, which regulates the disclosure of personal information in the records of state motor vehicle departments.[48] The act requires disclosure in some circumstances, and regulates the sale and resale of drivers' personal information. The Court unanimously held that the act did not violate the anti-commandeering principle. The act, according to the Court, did not "require the States in their sovereign capacity to regulate their own citizens. The DPPA regulates the States as the owners of databases."[49] In addition, the Court held that the act was "generally applicable"—that is, did not apply only to the states—because it regulated everyone who participated in the market for information derived from licenses, including private resellers of that information.[50]

Compiling information for licensing purposes certainly looks like a sovereign activity. Selling it to private parties for their own use, of course, is not. But it seems like something of a trick to say that Congress imposed a *general* regulation because it regulated people who resold information they could have obtained only from the state.[51]

More important, recall the Court's decision in *Garcia* upholding the application of national wage-and-hour legislation to state and local governments. Dissenting from that decision, both Justice O'Connor and then Justice Rehnquist said that they hoped to overrule it at the earliest opportunity.[52] That has not happened. Doing so would force the Court to face a number of quite uncomfortable problems. The Missouri judges case says that choosing who is to be a state employee is as central to state sovereignty as is deciding what wages to pay the employee. Does that imply that Congress could not require states to refrain from discriminating in employment against disabled workers, or that states refrain from discriminating on the basis of age when they make decisions about whom to promote in civil service positions? The Court devised the anti-commandeering principle and its exception for laws of general application as a better way to protect state sovereignty. States cannot discriminate on the basis of disability or age in their employment practices, because Congress has imposed anti-discrimination requirements on private employers as well.[53] States must comply with national wage-and-hour requirements, because everyone else must do so. Limiting the anti-commandeering principle to statutes that single out states for regulation preserves the constitutionality of a great deal of New Deal–Great Society legislation.

Finally, the Court in *New York v. United States* noted two devices Congress could use to encourage states to do what Congress wanted. Congress could use the conditional spending power: In *Printz*, for example,

Congress could give the states money to hire police officers, on the condition that the states have law enforcement officials do Brady Act background checks. It can use what has been called the conditional preemption power. That is, it can say to the states, "Federal officials will take over regulation of this area unless your officials do what we want." Congress could ban the sale of guns in any state whose law enforcement officials did not do the background checks. Politicians may find it more difficult to use one of these devices than to commandeer state officials directly. Conditional spending requires Congress to appropriate money, although sometimes it would appropriate the money anyway. Conditional preemption is something of an atomic bomb, a threat that can almost never be used, because supporters of gun sales would mount a huge political campaign against the prospect of stopping gun sales in one or two states and because Congress would be unable to hire enough federal bureaucrats to supervise sales that satisfied Congress's desire for background checks.[54] Still, these possibilities, coupled with the exclusion of generally applicable laws from the coverage of the anti-commandeering principle, substantially reduce the impact of that principle on programs Congress would like to implement.

Enforcing the Fourteenth Amendment

The Fourteenth Amendment's first section says, "No State shall make or enforce any law which shall abridge the privileges or immunities of citizens of the United States; nor shall any State deprive any person of life, liberty, or property, without due process of law; nor deny to any person within its jurisdiction the equal protection of the law." Section 1 identifies a number of individual rights. Section 5 of the same amendment gives Congress "the power to enforce, by appropriate legislation, the provisions of this article." What power does Congress have under section 5? Obviously, section 5 authorizes Congress to enact statutes giving the national courts the power to enforce the rights identified in section 1. Does it give Congress any more power than that?

The Court during the New Deal–Great Society constitutional order thought that section 5 did give Congress more power, by giving Congress the last word in defining the rights identified in section 1. *Katzenbach v. Morgan* upheld a provision in the Voting Rights Act of 1965 that barred states from denying the right to vote to any person who had completed elementary school in Puerto Rico, even if that person could not read English.[55] The provision's primary effect was to override a New York state statute that required English-language literacy as a prerequisite to voting, and thereby denied the right to vote to a large number of people who had migrated from Puerto Rico to New York. The problem was that the Supreme Court had already held in 1959 that statutes requiring English-language literacy for voting did not violate section 1 of the Fourteenth Amendment.[56] Where did Congress get the power to enact this provision, in the face of the Court's earlier decision? After all, section 5 gives Congress the power to enforce "the provisions of this article," that is, the ban on denying equal protection and the like. But how could a statute barring an English-language literacy requirement be "enforcing" a ban on denying equal protection when such a requirement did not deny equal protection?

The Supreme Court offered several answers. First, and most important, it suggested, without quite holding, that section 5 gave Congress the power to define substantive constitutional rights beyond those the Supreme Court itself recognized, at least as long as the newly defined rights did not infringe on other rights the Court enforced. Giving people educated in Puerto Rico the right to vote was generally consistent with the idea of equality with respect to voting and did not push anyone's rights below a judicially determined floor. Second, the Court suggested that Congress could enact bans that went beyond the rights the Court recognized to guard against *other* constitutional violations. Perhaps, it suggested, New York's legislators would provide fewer public services to districts with many nonvoters who were educated in Puerto Rico because they would not have to fear electoral retaliation. Third, the Court suggested in a related case that Congress could protect "rights" beyond those the Court recognized to guard against direct violations of judicially recognized rights, if enacting such a broad ban was a good way of ensuring that direct violations would not occur. For example, the Court believed that it was a direct violation of the right to vote to deny someone the vote because of her race, and the courts were perfectly ready to order voting officials to stop doing that. The problem, however, was that voting officials might use subterfuges: In administering literacy tests, for example, they might give easy equations to white voters and hard ones to African-American ones. Detecting these subterfuges can be quite difficult. Congress responded by outlawing "tests or devices" that had been widely used in such a racially discriminatory way. The Court upheld the ban, not because every such test was itself a denial of the right to vote, but because the tests had been administered so badly that a broad ban was an effective way of ensuring that direct violations would not occur.[57]

Congress responded to what it regarded as the Supreme Court's improper narrowing of religious liberty by relying on the first, "substantive," theory of section 5. The Court had held that states could enforce their general laws against religious practices, even if the impact on the practice was substantial and the state's justification for enforcing the law was not strong, unless the state had targeted religious practices for suppression.[58] So, for example, Oregon could bar the use of peyote in religious rituals under its general anti-drug laws. A broad coalition of supporters of religious liberty came together to overturn that decision, believing that it would allow states too much authority over religious practices. They persuaded Congress to enact, by broad margins in both houses, the Religious Freedom Restoration Act (RFRA) of 1993. That act prohibited governments from imposing substantial burdens on religious practices, even under general laws, unless the government had a compelling justification for doing so.

The case that gave the Supreme Court the opportunity to decide whether section 5 gave Congress the power to enact RFRA began when the Catholic bishop in Boerne, Texas, sought a building permit to expand a church to accommodate a rapidly growing congregation.[59] The city denied the permit, and the bishop filed suit, invoking RFRA. The Supreme Court held that section 5 did not give Congress the power it sought to exercise in RFRA. The Court's decision contained two major elements. First, the Court decisively rejected the "substantive" theory of section 5: Congress could not "enforce" constitutional rights other than those the Court itself recognized:

> If Congress could define its own powers by altering the Fourteenth Amendment's meaning, no longer would the Constitution be "superior paramount law, unchangeable by ordinary means." . . . Shifting legislative majorities could change the Constitution and effectively circumvent the difficult and detailed amendment process contained in Article V.[60]

The Court's equation of "the Constitution" with its own decisions interpreting the Constitution has been controversial[61] and, as I argue later in this chapter, is a significant element in the new constitutional order.

Second, the Court agreed that Congress could use section 5 to support statutes that guarded against difficult-to-detect constitutional violations. But, the Court said, Congress could use this "remedial or preventive power" only if the remedy was congruent with and proportional to the underlying judicially recognized violations. So, for example, the Voting Rights Act was constitutional because Congress had before it a substantial record showing that voting officials did in fact administer apparently fair tests in a racially discriminatory way. But, the Court said, there was no similar record of constitutional violation before the Congress that enacted RFRA. RFRA's supporters had produced a large number of anecdotes about the ways in which zoning and other *general* laws adversely affected religious practices but almost nothing showing that local officials had singled out religious institutions for bad treatment. RFRA could not be remedial because there was nothing to remedy.

The Court applied its requirement of proportionality in other cases.

Discrimination by public bodies on the basis of age is, according to the Court, unconstitutional only if the discrimination is irrational.[62] The federal Age Discrimination in Employment Act (ADEA) flatly bars age discrimination, even if the employer might have some plausible reason for the discrimination. The Supreme Court held that section 5 did not give Congress the power to apply the ADEA to state governments.[63] (Under section 5, Congress would not have power to apply the ADEA to anyone, but the commerce clause is enough to support the ADEA's application to private parties.) As in the RFRA case, there was no substantial record of *unconstitutional* employment discrimination against older people by state governments. The ADEA's application to state governments was "an unwarranted response to a perhaps inconsequential problem."[64] The "evidence" Congress had, the Court said, "consist[ed] almost entirely of isolated sentences clipped from floor debates and legislative reports," including newspaper articles and letters from constituents.[65]

Some applications of the Americans with Disabilities Act also fell without support from section 5. The act requires employers to provide reasonable accommodations to their disabled employees who remain qualified to perform their jobs. In *Board of Trustees v. Garrett*,[66] a nurse at a state hospital had an operation for breast cancer and then was denied the opportunity to return to her old job, and a security officer with chronic asthma was denied a smoke-free car to work from. The Court held that neither could recover damages under the Americans with Disabilities Act for failure to accommodate their disabilities.

The Americans with Disabilities Act resulted from a long legislative effort, which included the accumulation of substantial accounts of discrimination against the disabled presented to a congressionally appointed task force that held hearings throughout the nation. Again, however, for the Court the question was whether the "powerful evidence," as dissenting Justice Stephen Breyer referred to it,[67] identified enough *unconstitutional* discriminatory acts by state governments to trigger the "remedial" section 5 power. The Court's analysis in *Garrett* began by asserting that discrimination against the disabled was unconstitutional only if it was irrational, based *solely* on "negative attitudes" or "fear": The presence of "such biases . . . alone does not a constitutional violation make":[68]

> States are not required . . . to make special accommodations for the disabled, so long as their actions towards such individuals are rational. They could quite hard headedly—and perhaps hard heartedly—hold to job qualification requirements which do not make allowance for the disabled.[69]

The Court then turned to the record before Congress to see whether the act's requirements for accommodation might be defended as remedial or preventive. Going through the record with a fine-tooth comb, the

Court first set aside evidence of irrational discrimination by *city* governments, then noted that almost all of the remaining evidence showed discrimination by private employers. Only a handful of incidents—"half a dozen"—involved state governments, and some showed unwillingness to accommodate but perhaps not irrational discrimination. Responding to Justice Breyer, the Court's "close review" of his examples showed "unexamined, anecdotal accounts" of adverse treatment that might not have been unconstitutional anyway.[70] "Only a small fraction . . . relate[d] to state discrimination against the disabled in employment," perhaps around fifty, "and most of them are so general and brief that no firm conclusion can be drawn."[71] The Court noted as well that the "accounts . . . were not submitted directly to Congress" but to the congressionally appointed task force, "which made no findings on the subject of state discrimination in employment."[72] In short, the broad accommodation requirements of the Americans with Disabilities Act were not, to the Court, remotely congruent with and proportional to the actual constitutional violations Congress knew about.

The modern Court's section 5 decisions plainly have a larger impact than its other federalism decisions do. True, much that Congress has sought to accomplish using its section 5 power might be done by using other powers, including the power to regulate commerce and the conditional spending power. For example, Congress enacted a less sweeping version of RFRA in 2000, the Religious Land Use and Institutionalized Persons Act, which directed courts to use the "compelling interest" test in evaluating state zoning laws as applied to churches and state restrictions on the religious practices of prisoners.[73] The new statute applies where the religious practice affects interstate commerce or occurs in a facility or program that receives federal funds.

Even though Congress might accomplish many of the same results by using powers other than section 5, the Court's decisions do show that the new constitutional order is regulated by new principles. As Professors Robert Post and Reva Siegel have argued, Congress and the Court cooperated in developing substantive constitutional rights in the New Deal–Great Society order.[74] The Supreme Court invited Congress to participate in defining substantive constitutional rights after *Brown v. Board of Education*, and the Court took Congress's responses into account in its own decisions.[75] Sometimes the effort to promote collaboration failed, as in some of the Court's criminal procedure decisions, including *Miranda v. Arizona*, where the Court invited Congress to develop equally effective alternatives to the famous warnings.[76] By the 1990s a generalized culture of rights had come into existence, making the rhetoric of rights a powerful engine driving much legislation. Republican president George H. W. Bush, for example, saw the enactment of the American with Disabilities

Act as one of his administration's most important accomplishments.[77] Law professor Stephen Griffin has described the United States in the 1990s as a "democracy of rights,"[78] in which Congress and the president have large roles in identifying and enforcing what the public regards as fundamental rights. Section 5, along with international human rights (discussed in chapter 5), might be a favored source of congressional authority in such a democracy. But, *Garrett*'s skeptical examination of Congress's fact-finding processes is particularly illuminating in suggesting that the Court regards Congress not as a partner but as something of a recalcitrant subordinate whose actions have to be looked at with great care so that the Court can assure itself that Congress is acting responsibly. The modern Court's section 5 decisions show that it no longer regards cooperation in constructing such a democracy as a fundamental regime principle.

THE ELEVENTH AMENDMENT AND STATE SOVEREIGN IMMUNITY

Someone not attuned to the niceties of constitutional law might wonder why the Court had to deal with Congress's section 5 power in *Kimel* and *Garrett*. Both cases, after all, involved employment discrimination, and Congress pretty clearly has the power to apply its general anti-discrimination laws to states as employers, using the commerce clause. Section 5 mattered, though, because the plaintiffs in those cases sought to recover damages from the state for the injuries they had suffered. And states have a special constitutional immunity from monetary liability, which was triggered in *Kimel* and *Garrett*. Explaining that immunity is no easy task, however.

To begin at the beginning: During the Revolutionary War many state governments incurred substantial debts. When the war ended they were concerned that war "profiteers" who had not supported the war effort would unfairly collect the debts. They could take some comfort, however, in traditional notions that sovereigns like the states could not be sued. They could be confident about winning suits filed in their own courts to collect debts, because their courts would recognize their sovereign immunity. The Constitution reawakened concerns about collection of states' wartime debts. The new national government was clearly a superior sovereign to the states, and perhaps membership in the new union diminished the states' immunity from suit, at least in the national courts. One constitutional provision opened the new national courts to suits "between a State and Citizens of another State" and between "Citizens of different States," and the national courts might allow suits against states under these so-called diversity of citizenship provisions. The states' fears were realized when the Supreme Court upheld federal court jurisdiction over a suit for a wartime debt brought against Georgia by a South Carolina citizen.[79] Congress immediately proposed a constitutional amendment, which was quickly ratified.[80] The Eleventh Amendment dealt with the problem in the Georgia case, saying that "[t]he Judicial power of the United States shall not be construed to extend to any suit . . . commenced or prosecuted against one of the United States by Citizens of another State, or by Citizens or Subjects of any Foreign State."

The Eleventh Amendment had two limitations. It applied only when a citizen of one state sued another state, not when a local citizen sued her own state. And it probably did not apply when the plaintiff invoked not the diversity provision but another provision opening the national courts to suits "arising under th[e] Constitution [or] the Laws of the United States," the so-called federal question jurisdiction. After the Civil War states issued bonds to support railroad and other commercial development and then found themselves unable to repay the money they had borrowed. Debtors once again sued the states. The Supreme Court sometimes allowed the suits to go forward, particularly when the debtors managed to figure out ways of getting compensated that did not require state legislatures to enact laws appropriating money. The Court was reluctant, though, to allow suits that were in form against the states themselves.[81] The Court's struggles with the issue ended in 1890, when it held that a state citizen could not sue her own state in federal court.[82]

What if Congress attempted to eliminate the states' immunity from suits by their own citizens for violations of the Constitution or national statutes? The Eleventh Amendment's terms do not expressly address this problem. A decision at the end of the New Deal–Great Society constitutional order said that Congress could eliminate that immunity, if its intent to do so was clearly expressed, because the states had given up their immunity from suits by agreeing to participate in the national government.[83] The Court was sharply divided, however, and Justice Byron White, who cast the deciding vote, wrote cryptically that he agreed with the conclusion that Congress could subject the states to suit, but not with the reasoning offered in support of that conclusion.

With the arrival of the new constitutional order came a new set of decisions about states' immunity from suit. *Seminole Tribe of Florida v. Florida* involved a federal statute that regularly generated local controversies, by authorizing Indian tribes to set up gambling casinos, requiring states to negotiate with the tribes over the terms of gambling concessions, and authorizing suits in federal courts against states that did not negotiate in good faith.[84] Relying on "the background principle of state sovereign immunity embodied in the Eleventh Amendment,"[85] the Court held that the Constitution's original provisions giving Congress legislative power in article 1 did not authorize Congress to override the states' immunity from suit.

The Court's holding in *Seminole Tribe* is probably best understood as relying not on the Eleventh Amendment itself but on the proposition that state sovereign immunity was so deeply ingrained in eighteenth-century legal theory that it literally went without saying that provisions giving Congress legislative power would not give it power to override state sovereign immunity. The Court adopted that proposition in its 1999 decision in *Alden v. Maine*.[86] *Alden* was another wage-and-hour case. The state's probation officers claimed that the way the state calculated their hours violated the treatment of overtime in the national wage-and-hour statute. The state eventually agreed with the plaintiffs' interpretation of the statute and started paying them the higher wages they sought. But the plaintiffs continued to seek the wages they contended had been wrongfully withheld from them. After their federal suit was dismissed when *Seminole Tribe* was decided, they filed a new action, this time in state court. Of course the Eleventh Amendment was completely inapplicable in state court, because the amendment refers only to "the Judicial power *of the United States.*" The question in *Alden* was whether Congress could insist that state courts entertain suits against their own states. The Court said no. States' immunity from suit was a presupposition of the Constitution and was not displaced by the original Constitution's provisions giving Congress legislative power. In this sense, *Seminole Tribe* and *Alden* are restorationist decisions.

Presuppositions can change, of course, and the modern Court has held that the Fourteenth Amendment did indeed change the assumptions about national and state power with respect to the constitutional rights that amendment creates. As Justice Potter Stewart put it, the Reconstruction amendments worked "a vast transformation from the concepts of federalism that had prevailed in the late eighteenth century."[87] The Fourteenth Amendment allows Congress to eliminate a state's immunity from suit when Congress exercises its power under section 5.[88] That is why the Court had to consider in *Kimel* whether the Age Discrimination in Employment Act and in *Garrett* whether the Americans with Disabilities Act were supported by section 5. Once the Court concluded that section 5 did not authorize those statutes, only the commerce clause was left, and *Seminole Tribe* meant that the plaintiffs had to lose. But, the concession that Reconstruction transformed federalism is an important one, because it shows that a truly revolutionary Court would have to develop some account of the place of the states in a constitutional order that acknowledged the transformation wrought by Reconstruction. The Court has not begun to do so, again suggesting that its project is to chasten the national government, not to transform it.

These sovereign immunity decisions, while important, are also limited. First, only states, not local governments, can invoke the protection the Supreme Court has said the Constitution provides. Plaintiffs can recover lost wages and other damages from cities and counties that discriminate against the disabled or that fail to pay their employees what the national government says they should.

Second, the Court has emphasized that states remain obliged to follow the dictates of national law despite their immunity from suit. In *Alden*, Justice Kennedy pointed out that states can consent to suit, either in federal court or in their own courts,[89] and often have good reasons—rooted in political pressure from constituents like advocates for the disabled or their own state employees unions, or in the simple desire to conform to national law—for doing so. States also have no immunity from suits brought by the United States to enforce national laws giving citizens rights against the state. The Fourteenth Amendment was aimed at restricting state power, and states cannot claim an immunity from suits under statutes validly enacted under Congress's section 5 power.

The most important limitation on these decisions substantially reduces their importance. The aim of suits against states is not really to get a judgment for the plaintiffs but to ensure that the states comply with national law. In 1908 the Supreme Court created a remedy that works reasonably well to provide that guarantee. In *Ex parte Young* the Court held that a plaintiff could sue not the state but a state official to obtain an order directing that the state official comply with national law thereafter.[90] So, for example, in *Alden* the state workers could sue the director of the state probation agency in his or her official capacity and get the federal courts to order the director, and anyone who followed in office, to pay the federally required wages from the day the order was entered on.[91]

The one hitch in this story is that the Court in the new constitutional order might restrict the availability of *Ex parte Young* injunctions. Probably the largest threat to *Ex parte Young* comes from a decision saying that *Ex parte Young* injunctions could not be used to enforce state law.[92] The Court said that *Ex parte Young* rested on a fiction that a suit against a state officer was not really a suit against the state itself. That fiction was necessary, according to the Court, to guarantee that states would comply with *national* law, which under the nation's constitutional theory overrode state disagreement with that law. But no such fiction was necessary to ensure that state governments comply with *state* law. The Court said that the national law of remedies had to accommodate competing concerns, "the need to promote the supremacy of federal law" and "the constitutional immunity of the states."[93] It would not take much to refine this formulation to say that the overriding need was to guarantee state compliance with the Constitution, and that the balance changed when mere federal statutes were involved. That is, the Court could say that *Ex parte Young* injunctions could not be used to enforce statutes like the Americans with Disabilities Act.

Still, the only threat yet raised against *Ex parte Young* was decisively beaten back in 1997. Two justices expressed a desire to limit the circumstances under which federal courts can issue *Ex parte Young* injunctions, but the other seven insisted in the same case that *Young* should be preserved in its full scope.[94] Even the justices urging a revision of the doctrine thought that it would be important in deciding whether to eliminate the *federal* remedy that a parallel remedy would be available in state courts.

Injunctions under *Ex parte Young* are a pretty good device to get compliance with national law going forward.[95] They do nothing, of course, to provide a remedy for violations of national law that have already occurred—the lost wages in *Alden*, for example. In some, though limited, circumstances, people whose constitutional rights have been intentionally violated by individual state officials can get damages from those officials as individuals. In theory, the officers in *Alden* could have sued their supervisors for damages (their lost wages), but the Court's doctrines on recovering damages from individual officials would almost certainly defeat such a lawsuit.

To assess the overall impact of the modern Court's decisions, consider a state government that simply does not want to pay federally prescribed wages, or that does not want to accommodate its disabled employees. It can pretty much guarantee itself a free ride for a while. The United States might sue on the employees' behalf and recover the lost wages, but the national government devotes relatively few resources to this type of enforcement action. Eventually, though, the state is going to have to comply with national law, because eventually an employee is going to bring an *Ex parte Young* suit and get an injunction against the state's unlawful conduct.[96] The Court's sovereign immunity decisions undoubtedly reduce the incentives states have to comply with national law, and the decisions eliminate some remedies that Congress thought important in securing state compliance. Even so, the reduction in incentives does not ultimately undermine the national government's ability to enforce its law, even in the federal courts, against recalcitrant states.

Modern Nationalism

The modern Court does not always side with the states. It has begun to develop a notion of national citizenship that has some force. As we saw in chapter 1, the 1990s saw a substantial movement to limit the number of terms elected representatives could serve. Having achieved significant successes on the local and state levels, the movement's supporters hoped to impose similar limits for members of the House of Representatives and the Senate. The Supreme Court turned back those efforts in *U.S. Term*

Limits, Inc. v. Thornton.[97] The technical ground of the decision was that the Constitution specified the qualifications for members of the national legislature, and neither the states nor Congress itself could add a new qualification, for example, that the representative not have already served four terms. Underlying the decision, though, was the idea that the national Congress represented the nation as a whole, where representatives "owe primary allegiance not to the people of a State, but to the people of the Nation."[98] Notwithstanding our federal organization, we are, to the Supreme Court, the people of a single nation.

That idea may counter the localist urges that the Court's other decisions seem to promote. The Court relied on its vision of nationalism when it invalidated a state law, which Congress had authorized, limiting the public assistance benefits a new arrival could receive to the level the person would have received in the state the newcomer had left.[99] The Court invoked the Fourteenth Amendment's "privileges or immunities" clause. That clause, the Court said, requires each state to treat citizens of other states as "welcome visitor[s]" when they are present for short periods, and as equal to local citizens when they decide to become permanent residents. As in the term-limits case, the Court invoked a sense of the nation as a single entity, bound together in a common enterprise that could not be defeated by local programs that effectively treated other U.S. citizens as foreigners.

• • •

Professor Edward Rubin has termed the modern Court's vision *puppy federalism*: "[L]ike puppy love, it looks somewhat authentic but does not reflect the intense desires that give the real thing its inherent meaning."[100] That may be a bit overstated, but the limited scope of the Court's decisions shows that Rubin is closer to the truth than those who describe the Court's work as revolutionary. The Court's federalism decisions are about the nature of American constitutional identity as some combination of state and national orientations and power, but the Court's present members have as yet failed to articulate what they understand that identity to be.[101] The Court's present members know what an unconstitutional statute is when they see one, but they have not offered a larger theory to explain why one statute is constitutional and another is not. Justice Kennedy came as close as anyone in his opinion concurring in the Court's term-limits decision. The Constitution's framers, Justice Kennedy said, "split the atom of sovereignty," assigning some tasks to sovereign states and some to the sovereign nation.[102] But so far that remains only a metaphor, not a theory.

Puppy federalism allows the Court to imagine that it is upholding constitutional arrangements with a firm foundation in history when it is actually engaged in defining the regime principles of a chastened national government that has not abandoned the expansionist accomplishments and bureaucratic transformations of the New Deal–Great Society constitutional order.

Economic Liberties

The story about economic liberties in the present constitutional order is slightly less complicated. The Court has used three constitutional doctrines to protect economic liberty: the contracts clause, which bars states (but not the national government) from impairing the "Obligation of Contracts"; the takings clause, which precludes both state and national governments from taking private property without compensation; and a generalized notion of economic due process. In addition, the free speech clause, discussed later in this chapter, has come to protect not simply commercial speech at large but more particularly the interests of media conglomerates, which in today's economy may be the equivalent of the coal and steel companies that were the targets of New Deal–Great Society regulation.

The Contracts Clause

Before the New Deal the Court had occasionally invoked the contracts clause to limit state regulation of the economy. In 1934, however, the Court drained the contracts clause of any real meaning. *Home Building and Loan Association v. Blaisdell* involved a Minnesota statute enacted in response to the Depression's impact on homeowners' ability to make their mortgage payments.[103] The statute suspended lenders' rights to foreclose on mortgages with overdue payments. The contracts clause was put into the Constitution to deal with exactly this sort of statute: The framers knew that economic straits would tempt states into providing relief to debtors, and they wanted to stop the practice. Nonetheless, the Supreme Court upheld Minnesota's mortgage moratorium act. *Blaisdell* defined the contracts clause's meaning during the New Deal–Great Society constitutional order: It had none of any significance.

As that order decayed the Court toyed with reviving the contracts clause. In 1977 it suggested that the clause would be applied more vigorously when a government attempted to change its *own* contractual obligations,[104] and a year later it invoked the contracts clause to invalidate a state law forcing private employers to restructure their pension plans as applied to existing pensions.[105] The Court has given no indication of interest in proceeding beyond the quite modest limits set by those cases, and indeed some later cases suggest a return to the lax standards defined in *Blaisdell*.[106]

The contracts clause never was promising as a broad constraint on government's regulatory power in any event: From almost the beginning the Court interpreted the clause as its terms suggest, to preclude some regulations of *existing* contracts but having no effect on a government's power to prescribe terms to be included in contracts that people made after the regulatory statutes took effect. The contracts clause in the new constitutional order, then, is much like that in the prior one, placing no limits on government's power to enact significant regulatory legislation.

LIBERTY OF CONTRACT

The Court before the New Deal invoked a generalized liberty of contract with some vigor. In a classic case, for example, it held that liberty of contract meant that states could not enforce statutes limiting the hours worked by ordinary bakers: Liberty of contract meant that the government could not interfere with whatever agreements the bakers and their employers voluntarily found acceptable.[107] One of the key decisions establishing the New Deal–Great Society constitutional order specifically rejected any broad constitutional liberty of contract as a restriction on government power.[108] During the New Deal–Great Society era the Supreme Court never held that a regulation of economic activity violated a general liberty to work as one chose.

The idea of a general right to economic liberty was modestly revived in 1998. Justice Anthony Kennedy provided the decisive vote to invalidate the application of the Coal Act of 1992, a statute aimed at providing support for medical care for mineworkers, to Eastern Enterprises, a company that had abandoned the coal business years before the act took effect.[109] Justice Kennedy stressed the retroactive nature of the Coal Act as it applied to Eastern Enterprises. Coalminers might have come to expect the medical benefits supported by the Coal Act's provisions, but that expectation "was created by promises and agreements made long after Eastern left the coal business," and "Eastern was not responsible for the resulting chaos in the funding mechanism caused by other coal companies." Again, the narrowness of the protection Justice Kennedy would afford economic liberty is more important than the fact that he invoked a doctrine that had become moribund during the New Deal–Great Society constitutional order.

THE TAKINGS CLAUSE

In contrast, the Court has invoked the takings clause in ways that many environmentalists find particularly troubling. Takings clause cases fall into two categories, with the second having several subdivisions. A government can take a person's property by physically appropriating it—what the Court calls a "permanent physical occupation" of the property. Or, more important in the new constitutional order, it can take property by imposing such severe restrictions on the owner's ability to use the property that the property owner has only an extremely small range of choice about what to do with the property, a range that might not include much economically productive use. The modern Court has developed doctrines restricting the government's power to work such regulatory takings well beyond the limits imposed in the New Deal–Great Society constitutional order, and even beyond some limits that seemed settled before 1937.

The "permanent physical occupation" cases are largely uncontroversial but also largely insignificant because governments typically do pay people when they move onto their land. A 1982 case involved a New York statute requiring apartment-house owners to allow cable television operators to install receiving equipment on their buildings.[110] The Court held that this did indeed amount to a permanent physical operation and sent the case back to the lower courts to determine what compensation was required. (Not much, it turned out: The lower courts found that $1.00 was "just compensation" for the permanent physical occupation at each apartment building.)[111]

The regulatory takings cases are more important and controversial. The Court has devoted sustained attention to regulatory takings in the context of modern land-use regulations, aimed at environmental preservation (as with wetlands), historic preservation, and "smart growth." These programs are clearly important components of the political agenda of major interest groups, and constitutional doctrines that placed serious limits on modern environmental protection programs might well be described as revolutionary. The Court's doctrines do limit the ability of governments to protect the environment and promote smart growth, but not yet in ways that severely constrain such programs.

Before examining the Court's land-use takings decisions, though, it is worth mentioning that the modern Court has essentially confined its takings clause doctrine to land-use cases even though people have property rights to much more than land: We speak of intellectual property, for example, and restrictions on how a power company can use its power plants—for example, banning the plants from burning high-sulfur coal— can easily be described as takings of the right to use one's property as one chooses. And, of course, taxes quite literally take a person's property.

The modern Court has seriously applied takings doctrine beyond land-use regulation, though. The Court has discussed the takings clause in three cases outside the land-use area and found a violation in two. Those cases involved efforts by Congress to figure out some way to ensure that land distributed to Indians would not over time become so fragmented that it could not produce any real economic benefit to its owners: Congress said that once the land had been divided among too many owners, the fractional shares would automatically revert to the tribe as a whole. The Court held this unconstitutional. The owners of the fractional shares would have to be compensated for their land.[112] But, of course, precisely because the fractional shares were so small, the amount of compensation each owner would have to receive would be quite small.

A third case involved an innovative Great Society–era program. Lawyers frequently handle money for their clients: They hold funds in escrow prior to a house purchase, or temporarily hold onto damage awards their clients have received before disbursing the money to the clients. Ordinarily the funds held by any individual lawyer are too small to generate interest if they are placed in savings accounts because the administrative charges banks impose for maintaining individual accounts exceed whatever interest the money would earn. Texas, and every other state, required lawyers to pool these trust fund accounts into a single account into which *all* money held by lawyers in trust for clients would be placed, which ensured that the amounts would be large enough for banks to pay interest that exceeded the administrative charges. Then, it said, the interest earned on the accounts—interest that would not otherwise have been paid at all—would be used to support legal aid programs for low-income clients. The Supreme Court held that the interest was the "private property" of the owners of the money in the trust accounts.[113] But, notably, the Court did not decide whether the program constituted a taking of that property. (The difficulty the Court avoided was figuring out whether a state program in one of its aspects could "take" property that would not have even existed without another aspect of the very same program.)

Rent-control statutes are prime candidates for takings clause analysis for those who think it desirable to return to the constitutional order that prevailed before the New Deal. But the Court has shied away from dealing with such statutes. Its most important rent-control case involved an ordinance that placed substantial restrictions on the ability of owners of mobile home parks to increase their rents, with the effect, the park owners contended, of guaranteeing that anyone already occupying a mobile home could stay there permanently. The Court decisively rejected the argument, finding that nothing actually compelled the park owners to continue to rent to any particular tenant.[114]

The most robust application of the takings clause beyond the land-use setting occurred in the Coal Act case mentioned earlier. Four justices in the Coal Act case concluded that the Coal Act was a regulatory taking. The act provided a complex mechanism for assessing what amounted to taxes on businesses that had once engaged in mining. Justice O'Connor, writing for four justices, said that the Coal Act was a taking. Her reasons were as limited as Justice Kennedy's: The opinion described the background of the Coal Act in great detail, then explained Eastern Enterprises' corporate structure and its relation to the business of coal mining. The act took Eastern Enterprises' property, according to Justice O'Connor, because it "impose[d] severe retroactive liability on a limited class of parties that could not have anticipated the liability, and the extent of that liability [was] substantially disproportionate to the parties' experience."[115] No close reading of the opinion is necessary to see how limited its scope is: The outcome might be different if the retroactive liability was not "severe" (but how much does it take to be severe enough?), or if the class on whom liability was imposed was not "limited" (but how small does the class have to be to qualify?), or if the class's members could have anticipated the liability (but what sort of industry history would be needed to show that industry members should have anticipated liability?), or if the liability, while disproportionate, was not substantially so (but how disproportionate does it have to be before it becomes disproportionate?). More important, perhaps, is that five justices explicitly rejected the proposition that taxes—or their equivalent, as with the charges imposed on businesses by the Coal Act—could *ever* constitute a taking of property.[116]

The modern Supreme Court has decided more cases involving takings and land-use regulations than any other category of economic regulation. The cases are complex, but the bottom line is fairly easy to describe: The Court's decisions raise the cost to governments of imposing land-use regulations, particularly regulations designed to improve or preserve environmental quality or to encourage "smart growth," but place few direct limits on government's powers. The effect is to allow governments to continue to regulate land use for environmental and other reasons, while discouraging them from being as aggressive about regulation as they might otherwise be.

The modern Court has held that sometimes granting a permit to build but only on the condition that the landowner do something for the environment will be a taking of the landowner's property. In one case a homeowner wanted a permit to build an extension to the house. The extension would have obstructed the view of the beach from a nearby highway. The state said that it would issue the permit, but only if the homeowner agreed to let people walk along the beachfront on what was otherwise the homeowner's land. The state's theory was never entirely clear, but its best version is something like this: The obstructed view might reduce the number of people who realized that there was a *public* beach flanking the beach directly below the house and so reduce the number of people who used the public beach, and letting people walk along the beachfront would compensate for that reduction. The Supreme

Court held that the condition—requiring an easement allowing people to walk along the beachfront—had essentially nothing to do with the reduced *visual* access to the beach from the highway.[117] The state could not impose a condition on issuing a permit without what the Court called a "nexus" between the condition and the purpose for which it was imposed. The state's argument that there was indeed a connection between the denial of visual access and the requirement of physical access was implausible, according to the Court.

Another "nexus" case involved a "smart growth" initiative. The owner of a hardware store wanted to expand her store and pave her parking lot. The city planning commission said that she could, but only if she dedicated some of her land to a bike path to relieve traffic congestion in the city's central business district and some other land to a greenway along a nearby creek to minimize the risk of flooding resulting from run-off from the paved parking lot. The Court held that there might be a nexus between these requirements, which involved turning over about 10 percent of the property to the bike path and greenway, and the business owner's planned development but that the conditions were not "roughly proportionate" to the increases in traffic and flood risk from the expansion.[118] According to Chief Justice Rehnquist, "No precise mathematical calculation is required, but the city must make some effort to quantify its findings in support of the dedication for the pedestrian/bicycle pathway beyond the conclusory statement that it could offset some of the traffic demand generated."[119]

Land-use regulations are unconstitutional, the Court has said, if they "go[] too far."[120] When does that happen? The modern Court's doctrine has two branches. In one, regulation goes too far when it deprives a landowner of "all economically beneficial use" of the land.[121] The facts of the case in which the Court stated that test were, as presented to the Court, seemingly egregious. David Lucas bought two lots on some coastal islands near Charleston, South Carolina, where he planned to build two houses. Two years after he bought the land, South Carolina enacted a statute changing the way it regulated construction in the state's coastal zones, which included the island with Lucas's property. The state was concerned that erosion in the coastal zone endangered the state's environment. The new statute led to a regulation that barred Lucas from building the houses. As the litigation developed, the state conceded, probably unnecessarily, that if Lucas could not build the houses, the land had no economic value.

The tricky part of the Lucas case involves identifying the precise parcel of property that is deprived of *all* economically beneficial uses. Suppose, for example, that the lots Lucas bought were large enough that he could have built *one* house far enough back from the water to comply with the state's coastal zone regulation. Would he have been deprived of all economically beneficial use of the rest of the property? Or would the fact that he could do something with the property imply that his property, understood to mean the entire parcel, had not been taken? The Court provided some guidance in another wetlands regulation case. Anthony Palazzolo bought eighteen acres of a marshy waterfront in Rhode Island. He planned to build a beach club on eleven acres but could not do so because of the state's wetlands regulations. He could, however, build a house worth $200,000 on a portion of the eighteen acres not subject to wetlands regulation. That meant, according to the Court, that Palazzolo had not been deprived of all economically beneficial use of the parcel taken as a whole.[122] (The Court did note, though, that the case had been litigated on the assumption that Palazzolo was challenging the wetlands regulation as a taking of all eighteen acres, and refused to address what the outcome would have been had Palazzolo challenged the regulation as a taking of only the eleven acres.)

The Lucas decision might be a sport after *Palazzolo*. How often, after all, does a regulation make it impossible for a landowner to do *anything* productive with his or her property? Even a marsh might be converted into a site for eco-tourism. Still, the value of the marsh used for eco-tourism might be substantially less than its value as a beach club after being transformed by landfill. As Justice John Paul Stevens observed in the Lucas case, it would be quite odd to compensate someone who lost 100 percent of an investment because of a regulatory taking but give nothing to someone who lost only 95 percent.

The Court's response is the second branch of regulatory takings doctrine. *Penn Central Transportation Co. v. City of New York* involved the city's historic preservation program, which was typical of many throughout the country.[123] The city designated Grand Central Terminal as a historic landmark. The designation barred the terminal's owners from altering its outside appearance without permission from the Landmarks Preservation Commission. Penn Central wanted to build an office on top of the terminal, but the Commission denied permission. Penn Central then challenged the landmarking as a regulatory taking.

The Supreme Court rejected Penn Central's challenge. It said that there was no "set formula" for deciding when a regulatory taking had occurred and that the inquiry was necessarily "ad hoc" and "factual."[124] When some economically beneficial uses remain for the property, the courts must consider a number of factors to decide whether a regulatory taking has occurred: "[t]he economic impact of the regulation on the claimant and particularly, the extent to which the regulation has interfered with distinct investment-backed expectations," and "the character of the governmental action," including whether the "interference arises from some public program adjusting the benefits and burdens of economic life to promote the common good."[125]

The *Penn Central* test pretty clearly does not tell us much about when the government's regulations go too far. Probably courts should take into account how important the government's program is, as part of their assessment of the "character" of the action. But do we really want courts to decide that a wetlands program is truly important, a historic preservation program less so? A similar problem infects the question of determining the degree to which a regulation interferes with "investment-backed expectations." Some courts had tried to get a handle on the problem by saying that people who bought land *after* a regulatory scheme was in place could not have reasonable expectations that they could use the land in ways barred by the regulatory system. The Court in *Palazzolo* rejected that simple rule but did not say what should replace it. Justices Scalia and O'Connor both agreed that the prior existence of a regulatory scheme does not automatically defeat a takings claim, but a spirited exchange between them shows that the problem persists. Justice Scalia thought that the prior existence of the scheme should be entirely irrelevant to determining whether a regulatory taking had occurred, while Justice O'Connor said, "Courts properly consider the effect of existing regulations under the rubric of investment-backed expectations in determining whether a compensable taking has occurred."[126] Four dissenting justices agreed that at a minimum, Justice O'Connor's analysis should be followed, which means that it states the current law. What exactly it states, though, is quite unclear. Under what circumstances would an investment-backed expectation be reasonable when a preexisting regulation barred the use the investor planned? Justice O'Connor said, "[T]he nature and extent of permitted development under the regulatory regime vis-à-vis the development sought by the claimant may also shape legitimate expectations without vesting any kind of development right in the property owner." Why *shape* and not *determine*? Further, suppose there is a discrepancy between the "shape" of the investor's expectations and what the regulation permits. If the discrepancy is large, the investor's expectations would not be reasonable; if the discrepancy is small, how could the regulation go too far in defeating the investor's expectations?

The upshot of the substantive law of regulatory takings is that governments can engage in substantial regulation, which will be tested, if challenged, under a rather amorphous balancing test and in lawsuits where the government will have to develop extensive factual records. Governments face substantial litigation costs, and their lawyers will tell them that they also face some litigation risk when they are contemplating imposing some regulatory scheme—some possibility that the regulatory scheme will be held unconstitutional.[127] The Court, that is, has increased the cost of imposing regulation without directly barring it. The "smart growth" decision actually called land-use planning "commendable," while noting that there were "outer limits to how [it] may be done."[128] Programs that push aggressively beyond what we have now may or may not be specially vulnerable, but the combination of litigation cost and litigation risk may induce governments to be somewhat more restrained in exercising regulatory power than they would have been under the New Deal–Great Society constitutional order.

How does the law of economic liberty in the new constitutional order compare with the same law in the New Deal–Great Society order? Put briefly, in the New Deal–Great Society constitutional order, governments could regulate economic activity any way they wanted, while in the new constitutional order governments can regulate that activity quite extensively[129] but must avoid what the Court regards as extreme forms of regulation. The goal of the constitutional law of economic regulation in the new constitutional order is to chasten the most aggressive forms of regulation, not to revolutionize the regulatory state or restore some imagined era of laissez-faire.

The Nondelegation Doctrine

With the growth of modern government came new institutions. Unable to act with all the detail needed to regulate a complex economy, Congress delegated substantial rule-making authority to administrative agencies and to the executive branch. In general the Supreme Court accepted the constitutionality of administrative rule making. Nominally, though, the Court insisted that Congress give significant guidance to administrators by providing them with what the Court called an "intelligible principle" directing the administrators' actions.[130] The Court found that Congress had delegated lawmaking authority unconstitutionally in only two cases, both involving provisions of the National Industrial Recovery Act, a centerpiece of the New Deal's first phase.[131] No constitutional challenges based on the nondelegation doctrine succeeded during the New Deal–Great Society constitutional order.[132]

Hints of concern could be found, however. Many modern regulatory statutes use quite broad standards. The Occupational Safety and Health Act, for example, says that standards should be "reasonably necessary or appropriate to provide safe or healthful employment," and that the secretary of labor should set standards "which most adequately assure[], to the extent feasible, on the basis of the best available evidence, that no employee will suffer material impairment of health." Similarly broad delegations characterize other modern regulatory statutes. The Supreme Court construed the OSH Act narrowly, to avoid finding that Congress had delegated too much authority to the executive without providing sufficient guidance about which "hard choices" should be made.[133] The Court also invalidated the Line Item Veto Act, which could have been understood as a statute granting unconstrained authority to the president— although the Court expressly disclaimed relying on the nondelegation doctrine to support its decision.[134] Academics also criticized the broad delegations characteristic of New Deal–Great Society legislation.[135] As they saw the situation, delegations arose from the interest group structure of the New Deal–Great Society constitutional order. Congress could respond to pressure from interest groups by enacting a statute broadly granting authority to the executive branch and claim credit for addressing the problem. And, when other interests complained about the regulations the executive branch issued, Congress could blame the executive.

All this led some to predict that the Supreme Court in the new constitutional order would revive the nondelegation doctrine. A lower court relied on an unusual form of the doctrine in invalidating clean air regulations adopted under a statute saying that "the attainment and maintenance of [standards] . . . are requisite to protect the public health" with "an adequate margin of safety." The Supreme Court promptly reversed the lower court, in an opinion written by Justice Scalia.[136] The structure of the Court's opinion was striking. After describing the Clean Air Act's provisions, Justice Scalia said, in essence, that the standards in the act were not significantly different from those in many other modern regulatory statutes. As Justice Thomas put it in a concurring opinion, the Clean Air Act's provisions were "no less an 'intelligible principle' than a host of other directives that we have approved." Justice Scalia asserted that "in sweeping regulatory schemes we have never demanded . . . that statutes provide a 'determinate criterion' for saying 'how much [of the regulated harm] is too much.'"[137]

At least in this part of the territory occupied by the pre–New Deal Court, then, the present Supreme Court has indicated essentially complete agreement with the principles articulated during the New Deal–Great Society constitutional order.[138] No revolutionary return to the past seems likely.

•   •   •

The modern Supreme Court has revived constitutional doctrines that the New Deal–Great Society constitutional order treated as insignificant. Today, for example, utility companies facing deregulation can make credible, though ultimately unpersuasive, arguments that they should be compensated for the losses they face on investments they made while they assumed they would have protected monopoly status.[139] A decade ago the idea that there could be such "deregulatory takings" would have been laughable; today it is not.

The revival of old doctrines has not restored them to the more robust condition they enjoyed before the New Deal. Still, the revived doctrines increase the risk that innovative regulations will be challenged on constitutional grounds and expose Congress to increased expense in defending and implementing such regulations. The new doctrines thereby decrease Congress's incentives to adopt new regulations and, in that way, contribute to the chastening of the regulatory state.

INDIVIDUAL RIGHTS IN THE NEW CONSTITUTIONAL ORDER

I have developed the principles—chastened, not revolutionary—animating the new constitutional order's treatment of federalism and economic liberty by comparing the modern Court's work with that of the Court before the New Deal. Now I compare the modern Court's treatment of individual rights to what the New Deal–Great Society Court did. Professor James Fleming has offered the best summary in his comment on the Court's refusal to find that people suffering intense pain and nearing death did not have a constitutional right to obtain assistance in committing suicide.[140] The Court's precedents provided substantial support for finding that the Constitution did guarantee such a right, but the Court refused to push its precedents to that conclusion. Fleming observes that the Court said, in essence, "this far and no further."[141] With some qualifications, that is a good summary of the modern Court's position regarding the individual rights recognized during the New Deal–Great Society constitutional order. Rather than providing a detailed history of how the New Deal–Great Society's constitutional protections for individual rights were transformed, I provide quick summaries, whose aim is to support Professor Fleming's conclusion.[142] Set into my larger argument, his conclusion suggests that the new constitutional order has nearly reached the limit of its understanding of individual rights. Earlier decisions have been scaled back in some directions, extended in others. Some earlier commitments—notably, to racial integration as a constitutional project—have been repudiated, although those commitments may not have been firm even when they were made. The overall effect is to create a constitutional order with a chastened vision of what the Constitution requires in connection with individual rights, but no radical alternative to or general repudiation of the prior order's accomplishments.

RACE

Brown v. Board of Education, holding state-sponsored segregation unconstitutional, was the heart of the Warren-Brennan Court's constitutional
project. Many free speech cases arose from the civil rights movement that
Brown helped foster; the Court's criminal procedure decisions were animated by the justices' awareness that the enforcement of the criminal law
implicated race relations as well; and economic inequality had a strong
racial component.

In one of its most expansive phrases, the Court once said that its task
in desegregation cases was to eliminate segregation "root and branch."[143]
Doing so required school boards and courts to focus on results: The
requirement was "to convert promptly to a system without a 'white'
school and a 'Negro' school, but just schools."[144] School boards and
courts were authorized to use expansive remedies to ensure that desegregation actually occurred. The Court appeared to have taken the Constitution to require not simply the elimination of legal barriers to integration, but integration itself.[145]

The history of desegregation efforts is familiar and need not be repeated here. The Court struggled with the anomaly that it required results in the South, where segregation had been imposed by law, but apparently tolerated identical degrees of racial separation in the North,
where segregation arose from housing patterns that were themselves
shaped more subtly by legal requirements. Newly appointed justices
thought that "remedies" for segregation that imposed high costs on
whites, such as assignment of students to schools to which they had to be
bused, were unfair. The Court gradually dismantled the apparatus of desegregation. It refused to uphold a decision including suburban districts
in a desegregation plan.[146] By the 1990s the Court's decisions dealt primarily with defining the circumstances under which school districts that
once had been under court order could release themselves from judicial
supervision.[147] The Court had by then abandoned the constitutional project of integrating the nation's schools: If white and minority children
were to attend the same schools, that would result from decisions by
individual parents and school boards pursuing what they believed to be
desirable policies, not from some imperatives found in the Constitution.

The Supreme Court's affirmative action decisions actually placed some
limits on what school boards could voluntarily do.[148] The New Deal–
Great Society's constitutional vision combined two themes in a sometimes uncomfortable tension. First, it held that segregation was wrong
because it resulted from color-conscious decision making. Color blindness was to be the constitutional norm. Second, the New Deal–Great
Society vision also sought to achieve actual integration of society's insti-

tutions. The new constitutional project pursues color blindness alone, with a fairly strong presumption that any policies that take race substantially into account were unconstitutional.[149]

Here the term *chastened* precisely characterizes the new constitutional order's ambitions. The lesson today's justices have drawn from the desegregation experience is that the Constitution is not a suitable vehicle for driving the nation toward racial integration.[150] What is left are some mopping-up operations—defining more precisely the circumstances under which the presumption against race-conscious action can be overcome—and addressing the possibility that diversity might be sufficient to justify affirmative action programs in higher education. Those residual issues are important, but it seems worth emphasizing as well that affirmative action programs, which have strong opponents and almost equally strong proponents, have also become firmly embedded in institutions throughout the nation. Eliminating affirmative action "root and branch" might prove to be as difficult as eliminating segregation was. The modern Court might apply its sense of its own limited abilities, derived from the experience with desegregation, to any campaign against affirmative action.

FREE SPEECH

The New Deal–Great Society constitutional order provided substantial protection for speech by political and social outsiders. The modern Supreme Court provides almost the same degree of protection to corporate interests and has been uninterested in extending protection to nontraditional forms of political protest, even as such novel forms become more important in dissenters' efforts to get the public's attention.

The Court began its reexamination of the protection commercial speech would receive in a case involving a state's ban on price advertising for prescription drugs.[151] Justice Harry Blackmun's opinion for the Court observed that a consumer's "interest in the free flow of commercial information . . . may be as keen, if not keener by far, than his interest in the day's most urgent political debate."[152] Gradually the Court developed a stronger stance regarding commercial speech. Responding to a perceived energy crisis, New York's public utilities commission adopted a regulation barring public utilities from advertising designed to stimulate electricity use. The Supreme Court held the ban unconstitutional, setting up a four-part test: The advertising had to concern a "lawful activity and not be misleading"; the government's interest in regulation had to be "substantial"; the regulation had to advance the government interest directly; and the regulation could not be "excessive" when more limited methods of achieving the government's goals were available.[153]

The Court used this test in 2001 to invalidate restrictions on the advertising of tobacco products near schools. After states settled a nation-wide suit against the tobacco industry, Massachusetts's attorney general, as "one of his last acts in office," promulgated regulations that barred billboards advertising tobacco products within one thousand feet of any schools or public playgrounds.[154] A Court that fractured along many lines held this restriction unconstitutional. A majority examined the evidence about the relationship between advertising and children's use of tobacco products with some care, and concluded that there really was a problem. But, the Court concluded, the regulations were excessive because the attorney general had not engaged in a careful calculation of the costs and benefits of barring billboard advertising. The primary difficulty was that the regulations prohibited billboard advertising in a very large geographic area, particularly in the state's largest cities, in effect "nearly a complete ban on the communication of truthful information . . . to adult con-sumers."[155] The Court's formulation of the constitutional problem is of some interest as well: "The breadth and scope of the regulations, and the process by which the Attorney General adopted the regulations, do not demonstrate a careful calculation of the speech interests involved."[156] The Court went on, "The Attorney General *did not seem to consider* the im-pact of the 1,000-foot restriction on commercial speech in major metro-politan areas," and "the range of communications restricted *seems* unduly broad."[157] The Court appears to require deliberative processes of some significance before the government can restrict commercial speech.

To those who think it obvious that exposing children to tobacco adver-tising is a social problem, even the Court's careful examination of the importance of regulating tobacco advertising would suggest the Court's sympathy for commercial advertisers. The Court before the New Deal did express some skepticism about claims that economic regulations served important public ends; perhaps the Court's commercial speech decisions are moving the direction of reviving such skepticism. Even though the Court *accepted* the government's arguments about the importance of its goals, the tobacco advertising decision suggests that governments will have increasing difficulty in regulating commercial speech. Indeed, there is some reason to believe that the modern Court will treat commercial speech as indistinguishable from the speech by political dissenters and outsiders around which free speech doctrine developed. Justice Thomas has ex-pressly urged that the Court abandon the distinction between commercial and other types of speech and give commercial speech the same degree of protection it gives political speech, and others on the Court have expressed similar views.[158]

The commercial speech decisions deal with *what* gets protected. An-other line of important decisions deals with *where* it gets protected. Start-ing early in the New Deal–Great Society constitutional era the Supreme Court developed what has come to be known as the "public forum" doctrine. According to that doctrine, governments must make some public spaces available to people who want to use them for speech purposes, such as demonstrations and protest marches. Over the years the issue became *which* public spaces had to be made available. Relying on what are now old-fashioned notions of where the public congregates, the Court held—and continues to hold—that governments must make the public streets and parks available for demonstrations and speeches.

The world has changed since the high point of the New Deal–Great Society constitutional era. Now, demonstrators must do something different, and go somewhere new, to have access to people who would have seen them on the streets and in the parks a generation ago. The modern Court has not been sympathetic to the extension of the public forum doctrine. It upheld the National Park Service's ban on sleeping overnight in ordinary national parks, applied to advocates for the homeless who thought that having a group of homeless people sleep overnight in the park across the street from the White House would be a particularly pointed demonstration of what the nation's housing policies were doing to the homeless.[159] Other cases deny access for demonstrators to military bases, the fairgrounds for the state fair, and post office sidewalks.[160] The Court did require air terminals to be open for the distribution of literature,[161] but in perhaps its most important "public forum" decisions the Court held that privately owned shopping malls, the modern equivalent of a city's downtown shopping area, are not public forums.[162] Modern free speech law protects traditional forms of political expression carried out in traditional venues—but that may not be enough to make dissenting political speech visible to the public under contemporary circumstances.

Of course free speech law continues to protect many political and social outsiders. The modern Supreme Court has decided relatively few cases involving the kinds of restrictions its predecessors dealt with (the suppression of expressly political speech in public places),[163] but this is probably because the culture of free expression has become so deeply entrenched that people rarely think about imposing those kinds of restrictions on that kind of speech.[164] The Court's commercial speech decisions, though, do not contribute to free speech law alone. By restricting the government's ability to regulate commercial speech, the modern Court has given commercial interests another weapon against regulation. Indeed, to the extent that commercial interests receive constitutional protection for their speech, they may be strengthened in their efforts to avoid new regulation in the first place.

EQUALITY BEYOND RACE

Franklin Roosevelt's "Second Bill of Rights" would have protected social welfare rights. The Supreme Court began to lay the constitutional foundations for such rights in scattered cases in the 1960s but made little progress on the project. The Court held that states had to subsidize appeals by criminal defendants even though the defendants had no constitutional right to appeal in the first place, because, the Court said, allowing rich people to appeal (because they could pay their lawyers) but not allowing poor people to do so (because they could not) violated the equal protection clause.[165] The Court's doctrinal formulation was that access to appeals was a fundamental—although not constitutionally guaranteed—interest, and the equal protection clause required close judicial examination of laws that treated poor people differently from rich ones with respect to fundamental interests.

The idea that some interests might be fundamental even if not guaranteed by the Constitution could have been developed to support strong social welfare rights. People have an interest in housing and food that easily could be described as fundamental, for example. Welfare rights advocates tried to push the law toward recognizing the Second Bill of Rights. They failed. The Court conclusively turned its back on the implications of the wealth-discrimination cases in *San Antonio Independent School District v. Rodriguez*.[166] The case challenged the widespread use (at the time) of property taxes to finance public education by arguing that education was a fundamental interest and that property tax financing treated rich districts differently from poor ones. Justice Lewis Powell's opinion for the Court held that the only truly fundamental interests were those protected explicitly or implicitly by the Constitution. His opinion had its own doctrinal problems—in explaining the earlier cases and in explaining what the equal protection clause added to the careful judicial examination required by laws restricting constitutionally protected rights—but it ended the Court's foray into creating a Second Bill of Rights. Notably, with the exception of the residency requirement case I discussed earlier, no serious constitutional challenges were even mounted against the transformation of the nation's system of public assistance by the Personal Responsibility and Work Opportunity Reconciliation Act of 1996 (the welfare reform statute of the new constitutional order).

The modern Court has not abandoned the ideal of equality, of course. It has pushed doctrine into new areas, following important social changes. The New Deal–Great Society Court did little to protect women's rights and nothing to protect gay rights. The modern Court has treated laws distinguishing between men and women with almost as much suspicion as it has for statutes that treat the races differently.

The Court's two most important gay rights cases point in opposite directions. The Court upheld state laws making sodomy between homosexuals a crime, in an opinion stating almost expressly Professor Fleming's thesis.[167] Acknowledging that its precedents could be read to support a right of privacy expansive enough to make anti-sodomy laws unconstitutional, the Court abjured any "inclin[ation] to take a more expansive view of our authority to discover *new* fundamental rights" in the Constitution and expressed "great resistance to *expanding* the reach" of the due process clause.[168]

A decade later the Court sounded very different. In an opinion opening with a quotation from the opinion dissenting from the Court's decision a century before upholding segregation, the Court overturned Colorado's Amendment 2, which denied "protected status" to gays and lesbians, thereby precluding city governments from adopting ordinances barring discrimination against gays and lesbians.[169] The Court said that "laws of this sort" were "not within our constitutional tradition,"[170] although it never explained exactly why a state could not discourage homosexual activity by denying gays the protection of anti-discrimination laws rather than by making the activity a crime directly.

Justice Scalia's dissent in the Amendment 2 case began by saying, "The Court has mistaken a Kulturkampf for a fit of spite."[171] Justice Scalia apparently thought that he could give a patina of intellectualism to his opinion by translating "culture war" into the German from which it came, insensitive to the historical context—a vicious anti-Catholic campaign in 1880s Germany—of the term *Kulturkampf.* His perception that the case was part of a cultural conflict was, of course, accurate. He also noted that "[w]hen the Court takes sides in the culture wars, it tends to be with the knights rather than the villeins."[172] Accurate enough. Justice Scalia's observation, though, treats the Court as lagging behind cultural transformations that elites lead—which is to say, almost every transformation, because the ability to lead such a transformation is what makes an elite an elite. The main point to note about the protection of gay rights is that it occurs at a level unthinkable when the New Deal–Great Society constitutional order was at its height.

The Court gave up on creating a Second Bill of Rights before the new constitutional order was consolidated. It has supported the extension of individual rights to some new categories, but only after substantial cultural change had already occurred. That is not the way a bold Court would behave—and, of course, it is not what critics have in mind when they describe the modern Court as leading a revolution.[173]

THE RELIGION CLAUSES

As we have seen, the New Deal–Great Society constitutional order enforced the rights of religious minorities against state laws that hit them harder than they did others, even though the laws did not single out the minorities for adverse treatment. The Court's most notable cases allowed a Seventh Day Adventist who could not accept work on Saturday to get unemployment compensation, and allowed members of the Amish denomination to keep their children out of high school.[174] And, as we have also seen, the modern Court has rejected the earlier approach. Today states do not have to accommodate religious believers when the states apply their general zoning, drug, or other laws.[175] In doing so, however, the Court preserved the *results* in the earlier cases: It said that states might have to make accommodations when they had administrative mechanisms already in place to make individualized determinations, as in the unemployment insurance system, and that the Amish case involved a "hybrid" of rights, combining religious rights with the parents' right to control their children's education.

The other religion clause says that governments shall not establish religion. What that means is of course a matter of great contention. The politics of the establishment clause during the New Deal–Great Society era centered on suspicion of Catholics and on the public schools.[176] Members of mainline Protestant denominations were politically dominant and structured the public schools to reflect their denominations' support for a secular public sphere. The Supreme Court came closer to endorsing the separationist position than to accepting any coherent alternative. The Court found it unconstitutional for states to sponsor prayers in public schools and to provide direct and substantial financial assistance to religiously affiliated schools. The transition to the new constitutional order saw the erosion of Protestant support for separationism, particularly in conjunction with the creation of private religiously affiliated academies designed to allow parents to continue to send their children to segregated schools, and the diminution of anti-Catholic feeling.

The Court's position in the new constitutional order is only partly a subject of continued contestation. The Court continues to find troublesome manifestations of symbolic connection between religion and the public schools, particularly in its decisions barring schools from having prayers at graduation ceremonies or, where football is a major civic preoccupation, at football games.[177] One of the Court's concerns has been that in the circumstances, observers—and particularly members of groups that are religious minorities in the school—will take the government to be endorsing the religious expressions.

The situation is quite different with respect to public assistance to religious institutions, including religiously affiliated schools. Voucher programs involve grants of public money to individuals who then can use the money for specified social services, including education. It has been reasonably clear since the 1980s that voucher programs that allow the use of vouchers at religiously affiliated institutions are constitutional, and the Court confirmed that judgment in 2002.[178] The only really interesting constitutional question is whether governments that create voucher programs can *exclude* religiously affiliated institutions from the programs. Voucher programs that exclude religiously affiliated institutions might themselves violate the Constitution—not either of the religion clauses, but the Free Speech Clause. According to the Court, governments must not create programs that discriminate against speech based on its viewpoint. The government does not have to build a public auditorium, but if it builds one it cannot rent the auditorium only to Republicans and Democrats but not the Reform Party. On the other hand, it can discriminate against speech based on its subject matter. The government can rent the auditorium only for entertainment and not for political rallies (although it probably has to adopt a rather generous interpretation of entertainment).

The question then arises, When a government seeks to exclude religion from some program it has voluntarily created, is it discriminating on the basis of subject matter, which it can do, or on the basis of viewpoint, which it cannot? One case involved a university program that provided financial support to student publications. Citing its desire to avoid establishing religion, the university refused to provide funds to a student magazine that was devoted to proselytizing in the context of discussions presenting a Christian perspective on questions of general interest such as racism and pregnancy. The Supreme Court held that this was an exclusion based on viewpoint rather than subject matter.[179] Truly religious people might think it somewhat odd to characterize their beliefs as (mere) viewpoints, but presumably they will take what they can get from the Supreme Court. And, it would seem to follow pretty easily that a voucher program that excluded religiously affiliated institutions would be excluding on the basis of viewpoint.

Decisions upholding voucher programs and, perhaps, even programs of direct financial assistance to religiously affiliated institutions when those institutions engage in valuable social service activities do not, however, completely define the new constitutional order. Evaluating that order requires looking at more than the courts. The scope of public assistance to religious institutions is likely to remain small in a world of divided government with encrusted interest groups that include public employee unions.[180]

• • •

Everyone knows that "the Warren Court is dead."[181] That does not mean that the modern Supreme Court has undone that Court's work. It has added new shadings to earlier doctrine and, more important, has drained the most expansive decisions of any generative significance. Its doctrinal innovation in the gay rights case invalidating Amendment 2 seems quite self-consciously limited in scope.[182] As one political scientist puts it, "The contemporary effort . . . may succeed where it is confined to what can now be at least argued as doctrinal excesses that were the product of time-bound ideologies."[183] I believe that the modern Court *has* succeeded in moving to a new constitutional order, but it is one that trims what the Court believes to be excesses without completely repudiating what has gone before.

AT-RISK STATUTES

Of course the Supreme Court will continue to find unconstitutional statutes whose constitutionality would have been unquestionable during the New Deal–Great Society constitutional order. That is what it means to say that we are in a *new* constitutional order, after all. Former solicitor general Seth Waxman, who argued and lost many of the recent federalism cases, observed: "[M]odern federalism doctrine is being developed at the expense of a series of enactments that Congress passed at a time when another paradigm—a paradigm of greater national power—prevailed."[184] This observation actually makes two points. As we saw in chapter 1, legislatures in the new constitutional order may enact few statutes that the Court in the new order would find unconstitutional. The other is directly relevant here. The Court has invalidated statutes adopted by Congresses that accepted the constitutional presuppositions of the New Deal–Great Society order, but—with the exception of the civil remedy provision of the Violence Against Women Act and the Religious Freedom Restoration Act—none was, in my judgment, a central component of the Great Society social vision at its most expansive. Perhaps, though, there are some important statutes that are indeed truly vulnerable in the new constitutional order.

I believe we can identify four such statutes that the Court could invalidate without substantially extending the doctrines it has already developed. According to *Lopez* and *Morrison*, Congress can invoke the commerce clause to regulate local *commercial* or economic activities whose aggregate effects on interstate commerce are substantial. One might speculate about the meaning the Court will give *commercial*. Consider, for example, the important national statutes making it unlawful to discriminate on the basis of race in providing public accommodations. Clearly the restaurants and hotels that are covered by the statutes are commercial activities. But is the regulated activity their *general* provision of services, or their acts of discrimination? And, if the regulated activities are the acts of discrimination, are such acts truly commercial or economic? No one thinks that the Court is about to use *Lopez* and *Morrison* to invalidate the Great Society's major civil rights acts, which will constrain the definitions the Court can give *commercial* in its interpretation of *Lopez* and *Morrison*.

The Endangered Species Act rests on Congress's power to regulate interstate commerce.[185] But no matter how the Court makes sense of the term *commercial* in connection with anti-discrimination statutes, it seems difficult to describe the regulation of *some* endangered species as commercial in the sense apparently required by *Lopez* and *Morrison*. Some endangered species cross state lines, which might be enough. The act's supporters sometimes cite the economic benefits of eco-tourism to show how the Endangered Species Act is indeed commercial in the relevant sense. That claim might be plausible with respect to some endangered species, but I doubt that anyone other than the most devoted environmentalist actually travels anywhere to look at the Delhi Sands Flower-Loving Fly, which is the focus of one of the most interesting commentaries on the Endangered Species Act and the commerce clause.[186] Probably the strongest argument supporting the Endangered Species Act is that biodiversity in itself has economic value, because species that go out of existence might have produced something of real economic value (as yet, however, unknown), and that the courts should focus on the level of biodiversity itself rather than on the level of the Delhi Sands Flower-Loving Fly in determining whether the Endangered Species Act does regulate commercial activity. Perhaps so, but the chance that the Court will look at the specific rather than the general level seems substantial. Environmentalists criticize the Court's focus on commerce anyway, because in their view the *problem* with human relations to the environment is that we think of it as something for us to use, something of commercial value, rather than as something of intrinsic worth. In some of its applications, the Endangered Species Act is now itself endangered.

Another at-risk statute is Title II of the Americans with Disabilities Act. Title II requires state governments to accommodate their programs to people with disabilities. Its constitutional basis is the commerce clause and section 5 of the Fourteenth Amendment. We know from *Garrett*, however, that the record of constitutional violations Congress found was insufficient to justify imposing a requirement of accommodation as a remedy for Fourteenth Amendment violations as an exercise of Congress's power under section 5. Many state activities covered by Title II do involve activity that can fairly be described as commercial, as do the prohibitions on employment discrimination contained in Title I of the act. Maintaining sidewalks with curb cuts seems fairly described as a commercial activity. Perhaps, though, holding elections or operating courthouses to which the disabled have unimpeded access is not commercial in the Court's sense. If so, some applications of Title II would be outside the scope of the commerce clause and vulnerable to challenge as insufficiently justified to be section 5 legislation.[187]

A more substantial problem for Title II may be the anti-commandeering principle. The statute directs state executive officials to pursue policies prescribed by the national government, which is precisely what the anti-commandeering principle condemns. And it does so with respect to many core functions of state governments, including the delivery of services to the public. Title II regulates commercial activities by state governments, but it also regulates their activities as sovereigns.

If anything saves Title II, it is the fact that the Americans with Disabilities Act imposes parallel obligations on private businesses. One theme in the anti-commandeering cases is that Congress cannot single out state governments for regulations not imposed more generally. That is why the anti-commandeering cases do not, by themselves, threaten the application of national wage-and-hour laws to state government employees, and why the restrictions on disclosure of private information in the Driver's Privacy Protection Act were not unconstitutional. The general requirements of reasonable accommodation imposed on private businesses by the Americans with Disabilities Act are, however, less extensive than the obligations imposed by Title II, and the Court might well find that Title II did impermissibly single out and commandeer states in their sovereign capacities.

Third, section 2 of the Voting Rights Act of 1982 may no longer be constitutional. In 1980 the Supreme Court held that the Fifteenth Amendment prohibited only those voting schemes that intentionally deprived African Americans of their right to vote.[188] Congress responded by amending Section 2 to make it clear that in certain circumstances, practices that had a disparate impact on African Americans were unlawful. Those practices are not themselves unconstitutional. Section 2 can therefore be justified as remedial legislation only if Congress has a record showing that actual constitutional violations were sufficiently widespread that a remedy reaching beyond actual constitutional violations is congruent with and proportional to practices that are actually unconstitutional. Section 2 was amended at a time when Congress did not know that it had to develop a strong record showing intentional constitutional violations as a predicate for making it unlawful to engage in practices that had a disparate impact. In light of the Court's treatment of Congress's efforts to compile a record in *Garrett*, it seems unlikely that the present Court would find the record made in 1982 sufficient. And even if the 1982 record was sufficient, another question must be answered: Must the actual constitutional violations occur at the time the broader remedial legislation is applied? That is, suppose there were enough intentional exclusions from the vote in 1982 to make a prohibition on practices with a disparate racial impact proportional to the constitutional violations then existing. In 2002, a state says, "No longer are there enough intentional exclusions for the broader ban on disparate impact to be proportional to the constitutional violations now occurring." Whether a statute constitutional at the time it was enacted might become unconstitutional as time goes by is an interesting theoretical question.[189] It will lurk in the background if section 2 is challenged today. The Court's skepticism about records attempting to identify actual constitutional violations is enough to put Section 2 at risk.

Before examining the final area where the Court's new doctrine places statutes in danger, it may be worth stepping back a bit. The constitutional vulnerability of the Endangered Species Act and the Americans with Disabilities Act illustrates a broader problem with the Court's approach to determining when Congress has the power to enact legislation affecting interests traditionally regulated by state governments. Both statutes resulted from changes in the way Americans thought about what mattered to us as Americans—that is, from changes in what we regarded as matters of truly national interest. The Court's approach may impede the development of new understandings of the national interest independent of commerce and traditional notions of equality.

Finally, the Court's decision finding that New Jersey violated a constitutional protected right of expressive association when it required the Boy Scouts to refrain from discriminating against a gay Scoutmaster might have quite broad implications, although it seems unlikely that the present Court is committed to reading the decision expansively. According to the Court, the right of expressive association protects associations that "engage in some form of expression, whether it be public or private."[190] Second, the courts must "defer[] to an association's assertions regarding the nature of its expression."[191] That is, the values an association seeks to transmit simply *are* what the association asserts them to be; the courts should not examine the values, or the views expressed, to determine whether they are "internally inconsistent" or otherwise problematic as long as they are sincerely held.[192] Third, the right of expressive association is impaired if the government's requirement "affects in a significant way the group's ability to advocate public or private viewpoints."[193] Finally, just as the courts must defer to an association's statements about its own views, so too they must defer "to an association's view of what would impair its expression."[194] In particular, some entities entitled to the protection of the right of expressive association are protected against "[t]he forced inclusion of an unwanted person" because such inclusion would "force the organization to send a message . . . to the world" that is inconsistent with the organization's own message.[195]

The precise scope of the right of expressive association remains to be determined, and my discussion is therefore both more extended and more speculative than my discussion of other at-risk statutes. As the

Court put it, the entity "must engage in *some form of expression*, whether it be public or private."[196] Consider an ordinary commercial enterprise owned by a group of devoutly religious friends, who place expressions of their religious beliefs throughout their place of business.[197] One can readily imagine a charge that the pervasiveness of those expressions constitutes harassment of employees on the basis of religion,[198] or that the displays discriminate against potential customers who adhere to other religions or none at all. Would the owners be protected against such charges by the right of expressive association?

It is tempting to think that the right of expressive association extends only to entities organized for the purpose of expression, or perhaps more broadly to entities that engage primarily in expression. *Dale* shows that entities entitled to claim the protection of the right of expressive association need not devote themselves entirely to expression or, more generally, even to the transmission of values. The Boy Scouts engage in a lot of activities other than expression or the transmission of values, including some commercial activities. As the Court said, "associations do not have to associate for the 'purpose' of disseminating a certain message" to be protected by the right of expressive association.[199] Richard Epstein has pointed out that nearly every commercial entity has a "corporate culture" that is the entity's expression of its basic commitments.[200] As Epstein puts it, "every organization engages in expressive activity when it projects itself to its own members and to the rest of the world."[201] Under that analysis, *Dale* might provide constitutional protection to all associations.

Extending the right of expressive association to ordinary commercial enterprises owned and operated by people with deeply held beliefs, religious or political, might be quite troubling. The owner of Ollie's Barbeque may have had political or moral objections to serving African Americans in the restaurant he owned,[202] and Lester Maddox, who became governor of Georgia, came to public attention when he vehemently objected to "associating" with African Americans by providing them with service at his restaurant.[203] The right of expressive association might threaten the enforcement of anti-discrimination laws quite broadly were purely commercial entities owned by people with strong convictions entitled to claim the right's protection.

The Court's language in *Dale*—"must engage in some form of expression"—tends to support a broad application of the right. The very act of discriminating, one might say, *is* expression sufficient to bring the right of expressive association into play.[204] Alternatively, one might analogize the association forced by non-discrimination laws to coerced expression in the free speech context. Perhaps the best one can do is to say that a line must be drawn somewhere, noting only that size, the amount of expression relative to the amount of commercial activity, and the degree to which an entity is under the personal supervision of individuals who really do espouse particular views will affect the line-drawing exercise. That is, the larger and more fully commercial the enterprise, the less likely it is that it will be able to claim a right of expressive association.[205] Even so, taking the right of expressive association seriously places some pressure on existing anti-discrimination law as applied outside its traditional core.

If large commercial enterprises pose one problem for efforts to define the coverage of the right of expressive association, extremely small ones pose another. Here the model is the individual landlord renting a room, or the half of a duplex in which he or she does not reside, to tenants. The landlord may have religious objections to cohabitation by non-married people and may want to refuse to rent the room to a cohabiting couple. Enforcing an ordinance prohibiting discrimination on the basis of marital status might indeed force something reasonably called association on the unwilling landlord. Yet, as Herbert Wechsler notoriously pointed out, the government forces association on unwilling people all the time.[206] The landlord's case may differ from the general case of forced association for two reasons. First, the setting seems somehow more intimate, more tied to the landlord's definition of his or her own identity, than in the general case of forced association through anti-discrimination laws.[207] The landlord, that is, may be able to assert a right to intimate association as the basis for finding unconstitutional this particular type of "forced association." Second, society may be more willing to accept as sincere claims that forced association in relatively small-scale interactions would send a message to the world that is inconsistent with the messages the objector wishes to send. In this way the claim of forced association takes on a specific expressive component. My intuition is that a landlord who is physically present near the leased premises should be able to claim the protection of the right of expressive association.

The second problem with the right of expressive association that deserves attention is the Court's conclusion that the right is violated when a statute has the effect of requiring an entity covered by the right of expressive association to "send a message to the world" inconsistent with the entity's own beliefs. In *Dale* enforcing the state's anti-discrimination laws would not require the Boy Scouts actually to send a literal message. Rather, as the Court put it, "Dale's presence" sends the message.[208] Action, not words, sends the message that impairs the Boy Scouts' own message. A person or entity covered by the right of expressive association might claim that complying with some government directive would similarly send a message, for example, that the person does not so severely disapprove of the people he or she is not allowed to discriminate against. *Dale* holds that the courts must defer to the claimant's own characterization of its beliefs, which, I would think, would have to include beliefs about what constitutes a message that the claimant does not want to send.

UNEXPLORED TERRITORY

The Supreme Court would have to explore new territory if it sought to carry out a revolutionary transformation of constitutional doctrine. Here I examine three of those areas: the power of Congress to give money to states with strings attached; the power of Congress to displace state policies by enacting statutes that clearly fall within Congress's powers—a power that might be seen as a form of negative commandeering—and the question of stare decisis, that is, the Court's obligation to adhere to precedents with which its members currently disagree.

CONDITIONAL SPENDING

The Court's first step toward the anti-commandeering principle came in the Missouri judges case, where it said that Congress had to be really clear about its intentions when it enacted statutes that might be interpreted to regulate important aspects of state sovereignty. The Court has taken the same step in dealing with the conditional spending power, insisting that Congress state quite clearly its desire to force states to comply with national standards if they accept money from the national government.[209] The substantive standards governing conditional spending programs were established relatively recently, in a 1987 decision upholding a national law that reduced federal funding for highway construction by 5 percent in states that did not enact laws raising the drinking age to twenty-one.[210] Chief Justice Rehnquist wrote the Court's opinion, which said that conditions on spending were constitutional if they were related to the federal interest embodied in the spending program itself and if they were not so substantial as to deprive states of a real choice about forgoing the money or taking it with the strings attached.

Justice O'Connor dissented, saying that the connection between the federal interest in building safe highways was not closely enough related to the drinking-age condition. Scholars have observed, correctly, that states depend so much on grants from the national government that we can have no real transformation in federal-state relations unless the Court revises its conditional spending doctrine, perhaps along the lines Justice O'Connor suggested.[211]

So far, however, the Court has declined to begin exploring revisions in the conditional spending doctrine. It declined the opportunity to examine the question in 2001 when it denied review in a case enforcing a federal requirement that state facilities be accessible to the handicapped when states accepted federal money for their programs.[212] Invoking federalism principles to limit the conditional spending power might be particularly awkward, because the conditional spending power is the means by which the national government has become involved in determining substantive education policy, requiring states to test elementary and secondary school children if they accept federal funds. Such programs have strong bipartisan support, and yet the Court has repeatedly used substantive education policy as an example showing why the non-infinity principle is important.[213]

The Court's reluctance, at least so far, to take on the question of conditional spending suggests that its federalism decisions may be driven less by some general view of the proper division of power between the states and the nation and more by concerns going to judicial prerogatives. Put simply, the Court's commerce clause decisions keep cases out of the federal courts, whereas conditional spending statutes have no direct impact on caseloads.[214]

PREEMPTION

The most important things states do, most people would say, is enact regulatory programs, like the ban on tobacco advertising discussed earlier in this chapter. In addition to the free speech issue already discussed, the Court invoked another doctrine to bar Massachusetts from regulating cigarette advertising. Congress passed a statute in 1965 and again in 1969 directing that cigarette packages carry the now famous surgeon general's warning about the risks of smoking. Another provision of the statute says that states may not impose any requirements "based on smoking or health . . . with respect to the advertising or promotion of cigarettes." The Court held that this provision preempted the state's ban on billboard advertising for cigarettes.

I suspect that most ordinary people would say that Congress interfered more with their state's sovereign authority when it barred states from regulating cigarette advertising than when it required local police officers to do Brady Act background checks. Preemption directly stops voters in a state from getting their legislatures to do what the voters want; commandeering has a much less direct effect, as it displaces political energy from locally preferred programs to nationally required ones. Preemption, that is, can be seen as a sort of negative commandeering, interfering with a state's exercises of its sovereign prerogatives.

If affirmative commandeering is constitutionally impermissible, perhaps the Court ought to rethink its preemption doctrine. To show how preemption might be treated as a form of negative commandeering, I must develop doctrinal and analytic arguments that are significantly more detailed than what I have presented so far. The reason is precisely that we are here entering territory that has been unexplored because it is a swamp.

At least in form, the Court has begun to rethink preemption doctrine. Justices regularly state that national laws displacing state authority in areas traditionally regulated only by the states ought to be interpreted narrowly. Modern cases are filled with references to a presumption against preemption of the states' ordinary police powers, to the point where the Court can now refer to "the normal presumption against preemption."[215] And yet, in case after case the Court has found this presumption overcome. In practice, then, preemption doctrine has not been affected more than rhetorically by the Court's new federalism doctrine.

Preemption, or negative commandeering, does have significant effects on the states' ability to do what their voters want.[216] How can it be distinguished from the impermissible affirmative commandeering? The Court's decisions suggest some possibilities.[217] As we have seen, Justice O'Connor argued that political responsibility would be diffused when Congress directs a state legislature to enact a statute or a state executive official to enforce a national law. The problem, according to the Court, is that the state's citizens will feel the brunt of the law and may attribute the problems they face to the officials with whom they deal most directly, their legislators and executive officials. The Brady Act, for example, required state law enforcement officials to run background checks on people who sought to purchase handguns, and no handgun could be transferred to a purchaser until the background check was completed. A person seeking to buy a handgun and faced with the delay in transfer would become annoyed with the local sheriff, the most readily identifiable person causing the delay, not with Congress, the entity truly responsible for the delay.

In this form, the "diffusion of political responsibility" argument is clearly vulnerable. The sheriff could post a large sign (or could require gun sellers to post a large sign) saying, "Don't blame me for the delay; write your Senators and members of Congress, because it's their fault, not mine."[218] Developed a bit more carefully, however, the argument may have some force. What is needed is to identify some area in which state officials have some discretion. Here *New York v. United States* provides a better example than *Printz*. The statute at issue in *New York* required states that did not develop other forms for disposing of low-level nuclear waste to take title to the waste generated within their borders; as the owners, the states would have to find some place to put the waste. Picking a site within the state is clearly discretionary, and when the people who find a nuclear waste site in their neighborhood ask, "How come this material is our backyard rather than somewhere else in the state," the state's legislature cannot say, "Don't blame us, blame Congress." Congress did not tell the state where to put the waste site, but only to find one.[219]

Political responsibility, that is, might be diffused when Congress commandeers state officials in an area where they have some discretion.[220] It might seem as if negative commandeering would not have that same effect. Consider here a decision we will examine in more detail in chapter 5. A repressive military regime took power in Burma in 1962.[221] International human rights groups, and governments, have sought ways to put pressure on the military government to restore democracy in Burma. Massachusetts adopted a law in 1996 that barred state agencies from purchasing goods or services from businesses doing business in Burma. Three months after the state adopted its law, Congress enacted a statute imposing some sanctions on Burma and authorized the president to impose others. The Supreme Court held that national statute preempted the state one.[222]

In light of the "diffusion of political responsibility" argument, what might Massachusetts respond to protestors who object to the purchase of goods made by a company that does business in Burma? Its officials might say, "We had no choice; Congress made us do it."[223] Unfortunately, the protestors have two obvious ripostes. First, they might say, the state did not have to design its program in a way that required purchasing *that* good rather than some other. Buying from a company that did business in Burma was in fact discretionary, not with respect to the purchase itself but with respect to the program of which the purchase was a part. Second, the protestors might point out that the state might have avoided the purchase by abandoning its "low bid" process. The chance that a company doing business in Burma would get a state contract might drop dramatically if state purchasing agents had complete discretion to award contracts.[224] Showing that the "diffusion of political responsibility" argument is inapplicable to negative commandeering will therefore require some distinction between the discretionary processes displaced by affirmative commandeering and those displaced by negative commandeering.[225]

The Court's second functional argument for the anti-commandeering principle is a somewhat more focused version of the first. State legislators and executive officials have limited time to accomplish things. Their constituents have policy priorities to which public officials respond. When Congress commandeers the officials, Congress forces them to spend time on programs that Congress wants rather than on programs that the officials' constituents want. Again *New York* provides a good example. One can readily imagine that the legislative battle over locating a nuclear waste disposal site would be politically contentious and time-consuming. Not only would New York's legislators lose time they could use to develop programs to improve the state's education system, for example, but the strains of the site-location battle, forced on the legislature by Congress, might make it more difficult for legislators to achieve compromises on other issues.

The problem here is that negative commandeering is in some sense clearly *worse* than affirmative commandeering, with respect to changes in legislatures' priorities and responsiveness to constituent demands. Affirmative commandeering puts a new and undesired element on the legislative and executive agenda. Everything below it on the legislature's priority list shifts down a bit and, given limited time and political resources, some things drop off the list entirely. Notice, though, that the things that drop off the list are, necessarily, low-priority ones anyway. In contrast, negative commandeering can remove from the legislative and executive agenda the policy that constituents want more than anything else. (Suppose that the Burma Law was, by all political accounts, the single most important statute enacted by the Massachusetts legislature that year.)

Probably the strongest argument in favor of such a distinction is that negative commandeering, that is, preemption, has been common and uncontroversial in constitutional history, while affirmative commandeering has been rare and, when it occurred, controversial. Arguments from history depend crucially on the characterization of the relevant history. One can concede that, taken at its broadest, the power to preempt has unquestionable historical roots and still wonder whether there might be a narrower principle denying Congress the power to commandeer negatively in some discrete areas.

The constitutional text is silent, and constitutional history can be made ambiguous. Does structure tell us anything more about the possibility of a constitutional immunity from preemption? Here, I think, the Court's functional arguments in its federalism cases return to view. Do the political processes at the state and national level differ with respect to affirmative and negative preemption? If not, the constitutional immunity states have from affirmative preemption perhaps should be extended to afford them immunity from negative preemption as well.

We should consider the question on both the state and national levels. At the state level, recall that affirmative and negative commandeering seem almost indistinguishable when the state actually purchases goods. The state can introduce a distinction by blurring what it is doing: Instead of having a system that requires it to accept the lowest bid, it can have a completely discretionary system for awarding contracts. Similarly, in the affirmative commandeering context, Congress can introduce ambiguity by shifting to conditional commandeering: Instead of directing state executive officials to enforce the Brady Act, Congress could enact a statute barring all sales of handguns in states whose executive officials did not perform background checks that conformed to national standards. The examples indicate the problem with the suggestion that policymaking processes at the state level differ with respect to affirmative and conditional or negative preemption. The pressure on state governments to adopt low-bid contract award systems and to allow handgun sales is so great that we cannot reasonably expect the states to resist. They will enact a low-bid system and be required to purchase from low bidders who do business in Burma; they will allow handgun sales and have their sheriffs do background checks.

If the political process on the state level is the same with respect to affirmative and conditional or negative commandeering, what of the process on the national level? As suggested earlier, the issue here is whether Congress is more likely to adopt problematic statutes that affirmatively commandeer state officials than it is to adopt statutes that conditionally or negatively commandeer them. At least intuitively, one might think that conditional commandeering would be at least as attractive to Congress as affirmative commandeering and that preemption might be *more* attractive. In light of the practical pressures on state governments to succumb, conditional commandeering is equivalent to affirmative commandeering from Congress's point of view. Negative commandeering might be more attractive, however. Affirmative commandeering requires that some taxpayers foot the bill; Congress escapes responsibility by passing the costs off to state taxpayers. Negative commandeering in the Burma Law case and perhaps others, in contrast, costs taxpayers nothing. Indeed, it might even save them money, as the state is required to accept a lower bid than it would otherwise accept.

Roderick Hills has developed the most careful argument supporting the conclusion that Congress is indeed more likely to attempt to commandeer affirmatively than conditionally.[226] Hills's argument does establish that the national political process does differ in some circumstances depending on whether Congress is contemplating using affirmative or negative commandeering. Even that conclusion supports the development of *some* doctrine banning negative commandeering for the reasons that support the ban on affirmative commandeering.[227]

Hills argues that states are in a stronger bargaining position when Congress uses conditional preemption because the states can realistically threaten to refrain from engaging in the activity to which the condition is attached.[228] Desiring to accomplish its policy goals, Congress will restructure the statute to make the conditional preemption program more attractive to states. In doing so, however, Congress will inevitably compromise on the achievement of the goals it initially sought. Conditional preemption, that is, is costly to Congress, sometimes in dollar terms but always in terms of policy achievements forgone.[229] With affirmative commandeering, in contrast, Congress can simply impose its own program at no cost to the policy goals Congress had in view when it designed the program.

Hills's argument goes no further than showing that affirmative commandeering is more likely than conditional commandeering where states can make credible threats to refrain from engaging in the underlying activity. He also shows that states can make such threats more often than enthusiasts of national power might think.[230] Still, conditional commandeering remains attractive for that subgroup of matters where states cannot make credible threats.

Further, Hills's argument has no purchase if Congress's policy goals can be fully accomplished by displacing a state's power to regulate. Sometimes the threat to preempt, standing alone, would not be credible, because Congress lacks the will or resources to use national resources to implement a regulatory program.[231] Perhaps Congress cannot realistically threaten to impose a regime in which *nothing* could be done—as suggested above, no gun sales in states whose officials do not perform background checks.[232] State officials might realistically find no threat in such a proposal, because they should know that the prospect of actually enacting the proposal is minuscule. Again, however, the argument preserves the possibility that negative commandeering will be more attractive than affirmative commandeering in circumstances where negative commandeering coupled with a regime of nonregulation fully accomplishes Congress's policy goals.[233] The Burma law is a good example: It takes the investment of no national resources to accomplish the nation's policy goals by forcing Massachusetts to buy goods from companies that do business in Burma.[234]

Hills offers a final argument that might support a distinction between affirmative and negative commandeering. State officials will often cooperate in implementing national policy. But, Hills points out, state politicians are often competitors of national ones. They may want to claim credit for the national policies, sometimes as a springboard for a campaign against a sitting member of Congress.[235] Affirmative commandeering allows Congress to weaken the political position of these elected state officials. By commandeering them, Congress may direct that a state's elected officials refrain from interfering with bureaucrats, nominally employed by the states, who are actually engaged in implementing federal programs. Individual members of Congress can then deploy their personal resources to supervise the state's bureaucrats, "through telephone calls . . . [and] casework for individual constituents."[236] Negative commandeering in the form of preemption does not give individual members of Congress that opportunity. I believe that this argument, while probably correct, is not strong enough to withstand the pressure that comes from trying to align doctrine dealing with affirmative and negative commandeering.

On neither the subnational or the national levels, then, does the across-the-board operation of the political process make it less likely that Congress will employ negative rather than affirmative commandeering. If a ban on affirmative commandeering is necessary to preserve the structure of U.S. federalism, so is some sort of ban on negative commandeering.[237]

Two possibilities for defining a domain of state immunity from preemption immediately suggest themselves. First, one might construct a doctrine barring Congress from displacing a state's policy choices when it acts as a market participant. The intuition underlying the market-participant doctrine is that states may reasonably use the tax revenue they have raised from their own citizens for the benefit of those citizens[238] by discriminating against out-of-state commerce in the states' commercial activities. Negative commandeering requires the states to spend their tax revenues in ways that the revenue source, the citizens, dislike. The same policies that justify the market-participant doctrine might justify a constitutional immunity from preemption with respect to market participation.

Second, either alone or in conjunction with the first, constitutional doctrine might distinguish between state actions taken for commercial reasons and those taken for other reasons, and give states immunity from preemption of their actions in the latter category. Here the idea would be that national actions preempt state ones to ensure that we have a national community that nonetheless preserves an important domain for citizens to choose, in their states, the policies they prefer. The theory of the Constitution underlying this idea is that the national community is to be attained by commercial intercourse unrestrained by parochial state legislation, while states may pursue varying policies with respect to noncommercial activities.

Obviously I have designed the proposed doctrine of a state immunity from preemption with the Burma Law case in mind. My point is not that the historical sources compel us to accept this doctrinal proposal, or indeed any other for a constitutional immunity from preemption. Rather, my point is that recharacterizing the scope of the power to preempt that emerges from constitutional history leaves the way open to developing such a doctrine.

What is notable is that the Court has not been inclined to develop preemption doctrine in a way that would reconcile preemption with the anti-commandeering principle. Justice O'Connor sidled up to the anti-commandeering argument in a passing comment in the Massachusetts cigarette advertising case. Justice Stevens, in dissent, noted an "ironic" tension between the advertising decision, which stopped states from banning cigarette advertising on billboards within one thousand feet of a school and thereby "protecting children from dangerous products," and *Lopez*, which barred Congress from "imposing a similarly motivated ban" on guns near schools.[239] Justice O'Connor replied, correctly, that the legal issues were different and that, in any event, the state had not challenged the constitutionality of the federal statute that preempted its own. Such a challenge would rest on *Printz* and the anti-commandeering principle, not *Lopez*. Perhaps the Court should confront the constitutional question when someone raises it and develop a ban on negative commandeering that would harmonize well with *Printz*. That *Crosby* refused to do so, in a case presenting perhaps the strongest case for such a doctrine, suggests that the modern Court's federalism doctrine is limited, or that a real change in federalism doctrine can occur only if the Court begins to apply its anti-commandeering principle in preemption cases.

STARE DECISIS

Supreme Court decisions overruling prominent holdings from the prior constitutional order signaled that the New Deal constitutional revolution had been completed. Notably, the present Supreme Court has done nothing remotely similar to decisions central to the New Deal–Great Society constitutional order. The federalism decisions insist that they are doing no more than interpreting earlier decisions in light of "first principles."[240] The RFRA decision noted that "language in" *Katzenbach v. Morgan* "could be interpreted as acknowledging a power in Congress to enact legislation that expands the rights contained in § 1 of the Fourteenth Amendment," but, the Court continued, "[t]his is not a necessary interpretation . . . or even the best one."[241] *Seminole Tribe* went to great lengths to demonstrate that the opinion it repudiated had not actually represented the considered views of the justices who decided the case. In revising free exercise doctrine, the Court carefully preserved the outcomes of the cases most dramatically in tension with the Court's new rule.

A revolutionary change in constitutional doctrine would require the Court to overrule prior decisions, and to do so it would have to develop a theory of stare decisis, specifying the circumstances under which overruling earlier decisions is acceptable. The theory of stare decisis the present Court has developed is not easily used in a revolutionary enterprise.

Roe v. Wade and *Miranda v. Arizona* are centerpieces of the Supreme Court's actions during the New Deal–Great Society constitutional order. Yet, the modern Supreme Court declined the opportunity to overrule *Roe* and *Miranda*. Its reasons combine a strong theory of judicial supremacy, according to which the Court *must* insist on adhering to its own decisions in the face of disagreement offered by other political institutions, with an endorsement of the *cultural* impact of the Court's decisions. The Court's theory of stare decisis impedes its ability to transform constitutional doctrine on its own: Large-scale changes can occur, the Court's theory holds, only *after* the larger political culture has changed in a similar large-scale way. But, as I argued in chapter 1, that has not happened. The Court's theory of stare decisis, that is, commits it to maintaining, however grudgingly, the central decisions it made during the New Deal–Great Society constitutional order.

Consider first *Roe v. Wade*. The sustained political campaign against *Roe* resulted in the appointment of Supreme Court justices by Republican presidents who probably assumed that, given the opportunity, these justices would vote to overrule *Roe*. And, indeed, *Roe* appeared to be on its last legs after 1989, when the Court upheld several provisions of a Missouri law that seemed to make access to abortions quite difficult.[242] Three years later the Court faced the question of overruling *Roe* and refused to do so. The details of the statute challenged in *Planned Parenthood of Southeastern Pennsylvania v. Casey* are unimportant for my purposes.[243] Four justices would have overruled *Roe*, and two would have affirmed it without qualification. The decisive votes were cast by the median justices—Sandra Day O'Connor, Anthony Kennedy, and David Souter. Their joint opinion did not, however, say that *Roe* had been correctly decided. Instead, it relied on a theory of stare decisis.

That theory had several components. First, the recognition of a constitutional right to choose an abortion was not "unworkable."[244] Second, legal changes between *Roe* and *Casey* had not made *Roe* a "doctrinal anachronism."[245] Third, nothing had changed regarding the "factual premises" of *Roe* that made its holding "somehow irrelevant."[246] Fourth, and of central importance here, abandoning *Roe* would result in "serious inequity to those who have relied upon it or significant damage to the stability of . . . society."[247] The notion of reliance at work in *Casey* is quite important. Perhaps some people engage in sexual intercourse relying on the availability of abortion if pregnancy results. Presumably, announcing that states could make abortions illegal again would change people's behavior from that moment on. That was not the notion of reliance the joint opinion emphasized. Reliance did not involve "specific instances of sexual activity." Rather, the Court had to "face the fact that for two decades of economic and social developments, people have organized intimate relationships and made choices that define their views of themselves and their places in society, in reliance on the availability of abortion in the event that contraception should fail. The ability of women to participate equally in the economic and social life of the Nation has been facilitated by their ability to control their reproductive lives."[248] That is, *Roe* had become so embedded in the nation's culture that overruling it would disrupt understandings not about abortion alone, but about the role of women in society. Stare decisis precluded a decision so inconsistent with the understandings that prevailed outside the courts.

The joint opinion in *Casey* relied as well on a strong theory of judicial supremacy. The "sustained and widespread debate" about *Roe* led the authors of the joint opinion to expound on the relation between political controversy and stare decisis.[249] The Court's legitimacy, the acceptability of its decisions in the public's eyes, rested, according to the *Casey* opinion, on the public perception that the Court acted according to principle and not in response to political pressure. "[T]o overrule under fire in the absence of the most compelling reason . . . would subvert the Court's legitimacy beyond any serious question."[250] The very political controversy *Roe* had provoked, that is, was a reason for the Court to stick with its earlier decision. The Court in *Roe* had "call[ed] the contending sides of a national controversy to end their national division by accepting a common mandate rooted in the Constitution,"[251] and it was important that the people involved in that controversy accept the Court's resolution and move on. This vision of the Court's role in highly political controversies is itself quite controversial.[252] It is not hard to understand why justices would adhere to it, though: The Court's role under a theory of strong judicial supremacy is about as large as it could be.

The Court's next confrontation with stare decisis reiterated its commitment to a cultural theory of stare decisis. Congress responded to *Miranda* in the Crime Control Act of 1968, which directed federal courts to admit into evidence voluntary confessions even if they had been obtained when the *Miranda* warnings had not been given. For decades government prosecutors refrained from asking courts to admit such confessions into evidence, believing that the statute was unconstitutional. The courts therefore did not have a chance to decide the constitutional question. Charles Dickerson's prosecution for bank robbery gave them the chance, because a court of appeals took an aggressive stance: The trial court suppressed Dickerson's confession because he had not received the *Miranda* warnings; the government appealed, arguing that the circumstances were such that the police had no duty to give the warnings; the court of appeals agreed with Dickerson that *Miranda* required that warnings be given but that the confession was admissible anyway because of the federal statute. Dickerson then asked the Supreme Court to hold the statute unconstitutional, and it did.[253]

Chief Justice Rehnquist's opinion for the Court reviewed *Miranda* and the Court's subsequent case law and concluded that the decisions showed that the *Miranda* warnings were required by the Constitution, despite some indications to the contrary in some opinions. The federal statute was unconstitutional under *Miranda*, and the remaining question was whether the Court itself should overrule *Miranda*. Chief Justice Rehnquist devoted two paragraphs to explaining why it should not. The first paragraph said, "*Miranda* has become embedded in routine police practice to the point where the warnings have become part of our national culture."[254]

Treating culture as a constraint on overruling places substantial limits on the Court's ability to take a leading role in changing one constitutional order into another.[255] For culture, in some of its dimensions, affects what the other institutions of the constitutional order are willing to do. A cultural theory of stare decisis will stop the Court from doing much until the other institutions repudiate the regime principles built upon the prior order's cultural understandings.

THE SUPREME COURT AND THE CONGRESS OF THE NEW CONSTITUTIONAL ERA

One reason for skepticism about the prospect of a revolutionary Supreme Court imposing its will on a Congress committed to a course different from the Court's is structural. The Supreme Court can aggressively exercise the power of judicial review only when its members think that government's power is narrow (relative to the views of legislators) and members of legislatures think that broader exercises of power are both good public policy and constitutionally permissible. Only under such conditions will legislatures enact statutes the justices think unconstitutional.

A legislature committed to a government of small scope—or immobilized by partisan divisions—will enact no legislation that a Court with similar commitments could invalidate, and neither will it give a Court committed to an expansive view of national power any opportunity to endorse expansive exercises of national power.[256] Only when a Court with a limited view of national power confronts a legislature with an expansive one will the Court have any real chance of developing a distinctive constitutional vision. And, as I argued in chapter 1, the likelihood seems small that Congress will soon return to the New Deal–Great Society's expansiveness.

This does not mean that the Court will have nothing to do. The *present* Congress and president are unlikely to offer the Court opportunities to invalidate their own legislation. But what about laws enacted earlier? The justices can basically do whatever they prefer. In particular, the Court can eliminate laws that could not be enacted under present circumstances and yet that cannot be repealed either. Some of these laws will lack substantial contemporary support, but, given the distribution of power in a divided government, some of them might have the support of a legislative majority unable to reenact the invalidated laws.[257]

To summarize: The political branches of the national government are unlikely to give the Court many opportunities to invalidate major new statutes that have substantial contemporary support. The Court might invalidate new "feel-good" statutes, but precisely because such laws are designed merely to claim credit and not to accomplish significant public policy goals, these statutes are unlikely to be important ones. As noted in chapter 1, the Court might also find opportunities to invalidate some probably ill-considered innovations that state legislatures adopt. The Court *could* pursue the revolutionary path by invalidating statutes enacted in prior decades that lack the super-majority support needed to reenact them over the Court's objection. The Court, that is, might be revolutionary as to old statutes but passive as to new ones.[258] But, the Court runs some risk in invalidating even old statutes. The risk arises because decisions act as precedents, and the justices may find that they— or their successors—take the doctrine articulated in decisions invalidating old statutes seriously enough to produce invalidations of *new* statutes.

WHY THE COURT IS MODEST

Most of the Court's decisions invalidating statutes seem to be a grab-bag of items that happen to come to the Court's attention. The Court seems attracted to the idea of purely formal equality in its affirmative action decisions, many of its free speech decisions, and its treatment of the free exercise clause. But even formal equality does not provide a consistent thread in the Court's actions.

One theme does runs through the modern Court's decisions. It is not substantive, however, nor is it that the constitutional order needs to be transformed or some pristine original understanding restored. Rather, the theme is suspicion of a legislative process in which, as the Court sees it, politicians engage in grandstanding for their constituents, adopting legislation that seems "good" in the abstract but that has no decent policy justification, and in which, again as the Court sees it, new forms of interest groups, labeling themselves as serving the public interest, push legislation forward.[259] As two scholars put it, the Court's favorite activity is "dissing Congress."[260] And, whether *Congress* deserves respect or not, recall my argument in chapter 1 that contemporary state legislatures are likely to produce ill-considered, grandstanding laws with some regularity.

Skepticism about the political process pervades the Court's section 5 decisions, which insist that Congress follow quasi-judicial procedures in making and adopting appropriate factual findings. It crops up in the Court's disparaging references to the inadequacies of the processes followed by the Massachusetts attorney general in the tobacco advertising case and in its oblique reference to his defeated political ambitions. And, most notably, it provides the best explanation for the Court's willingness to intervene in the 2000 presidential election: The most cogent defenses of the Court's action argue that the Court acted correctly to forestall what the justices and their defenders believed to be the unruly political process that would otherwise have dealt with the problem.[261]

The Court's strong theory of judicial supremacy meshes reasonably well with its generalized suspicion of legislators, interest groups, and politics because it explains to the Court why *it* is the proper forum for deciding again questions already addressed by politicians. The Court's theory of judicial supremacy echoes the pre–New Deal idea that the Court could enforce the line between constitutional law and politics. Unfortunately, a Court that refrains from governing everything cannot operate on the basis of a generalized suspicion of politics. Consider, for example, voucher programs. A judge with a generalized suspicion of politics could readily see such programs as the product of base interest group politics, in which self-serving institutions donning the mantle of religion overcame the resistance of equally self-serving public employee unions, or—worse—overcoming the principled resistance of those committed to a historically rooted separationism. Generalized suspicion of politics, that is, gives a court no basis for sorting unacceptable from acceptable statutes, because all statutes result from the suspicious political process. What is needed, and what the pre–New Deal Court had, was a theory about where the line between constitutional law and politics was. The present Supreme Court's generalized suspicion of politics provides it with no similar theory.

What a generalized suspicion of politics *can* support are decisions that discipline what the justices think are "obvious" excesses.[262] And, these excesses are likely to be precisely those statutes that push at the margins of existing doctrine, that is, statutes that are arguably justified by straightforward readings of existing doctrine but that are somehow innovative. To invalidate such statutes, the justices will have to tinker with existing doctrine, to ensure that it provide no support for these innovations, and will not have to take on major initiatives of either the prior or the present constitutional order. In short, actually implementing a generalized suspicion of politics means adopting a chastened rather than a revolutionary vision of the Court's own ability.

●   ●   ●

At the peak of the New Deal–Great Society constitutional order, the Supreme Court heard argument in about one hundred forty cases per term. Today it hears argument in fewer than one hundred cases.[263] This downsizing has many sources,[264] but here I end by noting the way in which administrative downsizing is compatible with the characteristics of the new constitutional order.[265]

Chapter Three

BEYOND THE NEW CONSTITUTIONAL ORDER?

SO FAR I have described the characteristics of the new constitutional order. But, as I defined *constitutional order* in the introduction, such orders have to be reasonably stable. I believe the descriptions I have given accurately characterize political arrangements and judicial decisions over the past decade. Why, though, should we think that those arrangements are sufficiently stable to be called a new constitutional order?

This chapter briefly examines some challenges to the argument I have made.[1] The first section notes the possibility that what I have described as a new order is merely the present version of a longstanding pattern of low—rather than chastened—constitutional ambitions. Then I describe how a unified government might come into being, albeit briefly, and have lasting effects. I also discuss the possibility that the Supreme Court itself might be transformed into an agent leading the nation into a different constitutional order. Then I turn to analyzing ways in which existing arrangements might become unstable or move into a new, more stable system different from the one we had in the 1980s and 1990s. Here I take up the possibility of presidential leadership, concluding the chapter with a discussion of the constitutional principles that might guide a newer constitutional order created by presidential leadership, including leadership giving the Supreme Court a prominent role in advancing the regime's principles.

In the end, I do not contend that I have established that our present governance arrangements are stable enough to be described as a new constitutional order. The ability of the American people acting collectively to change things pretty much whenever we want makes it impossible for anyone to demonstrate conclusively—except in retrospect—that the arrangements are indeed stable. All I really claim is that thinking about the possibility that we are in a new constitutional order illuminates our current condition in a way that thinking that we are in a period of aimless drift or in a period foreshadowing a true transformation does not.

LOW AMBITIONS BETWEEN CONSTITUTIONAL ORDERS

Presidential historian Robert Dallek summarizes the course of American political history in writing that our political development "has traditionally depended on periods of stasis as a preparation for any new forward surge."[2] The word *stasis* could describe what I have called chastened constitutional ambitions, and so what I have called a new constitutional order might simply be the ordinary experience that occurs *within* constitutional orders. Yet, although the principles guiding policy might be those of a constitutional regime in place since the New Deal, the institutional structure of politics seems quite different: Interest group bargaining characterized the New Deal–Great Society order, while divided government and ideologically distinct parties characterize the present one.

We can begin by returning to Bruce Ackerman's idea of constitutional moments, short periods during which one constitutional order replaces another. Ackerman's idea captures what happened in earlier constitutional transitions, with the establishment of the United States in 1789, the era of Reconstruction after the Civil War, and the New Deal. As one political scientist summarizes the scholarly consensus, "[I]mportant political change in the United States tends to be punctuated with historically limited moments of turmoil and rapid reform followed by much longer periods of incremental adjustment and consolidation."[3] But, as noted in chapter 1, there was no such moment of turmoil or critical election associated with the creation of what I have called our new constitutional order. So, perhaps, we should understand the present as one of those periods of incremental adjustment.

Writing specifically about public policy on race, Philip Klinkner and Rogers Smith offer a succinct description of what policy looks like during such periods.[4] Klinkner and Smith argue that progress in eliminating racial discrimination has occurred only when three conditions coalesce: "a large-scale war requiring extensive economic and military mobilization of African-Americans for success"; "the nature of American's enemies has prompted American leaders to justify such wars and their attendant sacrifices by emphasizing the nation's inclusive, egalitarian, and democratic traditions"; and "the nation has possessed domestic political protest movements willing and able to bring pressure upon national leaders to live up to that justificatory rhetoric."[5] Without those conditions, the nation reverts to its inegalitarian norms. As Klinkner and Smith point out, the course of public policy on race during the 1980s and 1990s is consistent with their interpretation of the larger course of American history.

Klinkner and Smith's focus on a particular issue of public policy may obscure larger patterns. Recall that constitutional orders combine institutions and principles. On the level of principles, Klinkner and Smith clearly identify the possibility that public policy on issues other than race might be characterized by a reversion to a conservative norm once periods of intensified liberalism pass. Their focus on policy regarding race limits the utility of their analysis on the institutional level, particularly because the

precise conditions they identify are plainly not relevant to substantial re-
direction of public policy in a conservative direction.

Ackerman has tried to describe another large pattern by dividing the
nation's constitutional history into constitutional moments and longer
periods of what he calls normal politics.[6] For Ackerman, constitutional
moments are periods when people devote a great deal of their political
attention to fundamental principles for ordering society. But, doing so
is exhausting, and in any event no well-designed constitutional system
would require its citizens to focus so much of their lives on high politics.
The system should work reasonably well if, after these occasional out-
bursts of principled deliberation, people have put in place institutions
that allow them to reduce their attention to politics and spend more time
on the rest of their lives—working, being with their families, and the
like—while implementing the principles developed during the constitutional moment. Normal politics occurs when political attention is reduced to this lower level.

Ackerman describes normal politics (at least during the modern era) as
the arena for traditional interest group bargaining. Such bargaining occurs within the institutional structure developed as the result of the preceding constitutional moment and take as a given the ordering principles
of that moment. Political scientist Robert Dahl, writing when the New
Deal constitutional order had been firmly entrenched, put the point well:
"[W]hat we ordinarily describe as democratic 'politics' is merely the
chaff. It is the surface manifestation, representing superficial conflicts. . . .
[D]isputes over policy alternatives are nearly always disputes over a set of
alternatives that have already been winnowed down to those within the
broad area of basic agreement."[7] On this view of politics, what I described in chapters 1 and 2 as a new constitutional order with chastened
ambitions is actually normal politics, which is always characterized by
ambitions that are chastened relative to the principles articulated in constitutional moments.

I cannot dismiss the possibility that I have misdescribed normal politics
as a new constitutional order. Yet, treating the current state of affairs as a
new constitutional order does bring out some features of our current
system—principles and institutions—that the alternative account might
lead us to overlook.

Consider first the tension between the idea that typically politics reverts to a conservative norm and Ackerman's account of normal politics.[8]
Reversion to a conservative norm would mean that the fundamental
commitments of New Deal liberalism would be matters central to political debate. On Ackerman's account, without a new constitutional moment since the New Deal (and the Great Society), political contention
should be about the implementation of the New Deal's governing princi-

ples. Here Ackerman's account seems more accurate. The conservative center of the Republican Party presents its policy prescriptions as *better* ways of ensuring environmental quality, retirement security, and even racial equality. The Republicans who have taken office have not repudiated the New Deal–Great Society commitment to some government role in achieving the goals sought by the New Deal–Great Society order. Liberal Democrats typically think that the conservative position is simply a smoke screen concealing Republicans' true intentions. But, at present, what we have are conservative Republicans offering contested policies they defend as implementations of existing regime principles. A unified Republican government might move more substantially to repudiate those principles. In Ackerman's scheme, such a repudiation would demonstrate that we had moved into a new constitutional order. For now, his approach suggests, we are experiencing normal politics.

Ackerman's description of the principles that animate today's public policy debates is compatible with my account of a new order's chastened aspirations. To that extent we might be unable to choose between my account and his. On the institutional level, though, Ackerman's account seems at best incomplete.

Ackerman's normal politics after the New Deal is interest group bargaining. And, of course, a great deal of public policy involves interest group lobbying and the like. This is what I called in chapter 1 the residual effect of the New Deal's creation of a government in which interest groups were deeply embedded. Taking interest group bargaining to define today's normal politics, however, is misleading. Interest groups try their best, but in a world of divided government with ideological parties public policy is made primarily by compromises between ideological positions, not by satisfying the demands of competing interest groups. I find myself unable to locate systematic studies that capture this difference, and so ask readers to consult their "feel" for the situation: My sense is that the contemporary legislative process rarely succumbs to the feeding frenzy characteristic of the New Deal–Great Society order at its height, in which legislators offered every interest group something.[9]

Chastened constitutional aspirations may indeed characterize periods between constitutional orders, either because of a reversion to a conservative norm or, as I think more likely, because of the exhaustion of political energy that Ackerman emphasizes. Such chastened aspirations could characterize a new constitutional order as well. Whether I am right in describing the current regime as a new constitutional order depends on my argument in chapter 1 that the institutional arrangements we have in today's politics differ significantly from those of the New Deal–Great Society order. In part to provoke consideration of an overlooked possibility, I have tried to make the case that our institutional arrangements are indeed new and distinctive. Here as elsewhere, much depends on the judgments one reaches after considering the evidence.

A BRIEFLY UNIFIED GOVERNMENT?

Much of the argument so far has rested on the proposition that divided government characterizes the new constitutional order. But, of course, unified government remains possible. The difficulties of coordinating choices to bring about a divided government when we elect a president, a House of Representatives, and one-third of the Senate make unified government a real possibility. Such a government might last only two years—or, as the defection of Senator Jim Jeffords from the Republican Party in 2001 shows, even less—but the unified government might engage in policy initiatives that would be difficult to overturn once government became divided again.

The U.S. political parties are unified internally and sharply divided from each other ideologically. As noted in chapter 1, divided government might result from preferences among the American people or from electoral structures. In either case, control over each branch might be quite narrow, with a president winning election by a hair's breadth, with control of the Senate turning on control of one or two seats, and with control of the House of Representatives turning on control of a half dozen. Under these circumstances, random events—the death of a popular candidate, the sudden eruption of a localized scandal, and the like—might have a dispositive effect on partisan control of the government. If everything is aligned correctly, one highly ideological party might gain control over the presidency, the House, and the Senate—and, through the presidency and the Senate, the Supreme Court. This unified government might not persist, precisely because it would have resulted from the confluence of a large number of essentially uncorrelated factors. But it could have large long-term effects.

Ackerman, writing with a different aim, has identified why.[10] He contrasts parliamentary systems with separation-of-power systems. He argues that parliamentary systems make large policy swings possible as control over a unified government is transferred from one party to another, at least where the parties (or party coalitions) are strongly ideological. In contrast, he argues, separation-of-powers systems conduce to gradual shifts in policy, because a party (or coalition) has to gain control over all branches of government in a series of elections. That may be true of separation-of-powers systems in general but may not be true when the political system is closely divided. Under the conditions I have described, which may characterize the present constitutional order, a large shift in policy may be possible when a party gains narrow control of the presidency and Congress and uses its control to enact a strongly ideological program. Divided government may replace unified government soon enough, perhaps even before the next election. But, just as divided government makes it difficult to enact sweeping legislation, so it makes it difficult to repeal already enacted legislation. The present constitutional order may produce a ratchet-like effect: When government is divided, little happens without strong bipartisan support; when government is (briefly) unified, a great deal happens in advancing the ideological program of the party in power; when government is divided again, little happens again, leaving in place the achievements of the unified government.[11]

Briefly unified government might produce new governing principles without changing fundamental institutional arrangements. That, in turn, might indeed provoke a constitutional crisis. Ackerman offers the clearest account of why.[12] Suppose the briefly unified government made enough Supreme Court appointments to make the Court strongly sympathetic to the principles that animated the unified government. Now consider the possibility that a randomly unified conservative (or liberal) government might be replaced not by divided government but by a randomly unified liberal (or conservative) government, which might be able to repeal what its predecessor had enacted and enact laws driven by an ideology dramatically different from that of the prior unified government. The Supreme Court might well take this new ideological legislation to be inconsistent with what the Court's members believe to be constitutional principle. Invalidating central features of a government's legislative program is the kind of thing that provokes crises.

I believe this sequence of events to be quite unlikely, though possible. Two conditions have to be satisfied: The first unified government must have the opportunity to appoint enough Supreme Court justices to give the Court an ideological cast for the long term, and the first unified government must be replaced by a second one. Supreme Court nominations are themselves almost random events, although a government's ideological allies on the Court can sometimes time their retirements strategically. And unified governments come into being only through a conjunction of almost random events. The odds are low that everything will fall into place in a way that would produce a constitutional crisis.

A NEW MEDIAN JUSTICE?

One aspect of my argument for identifying a new constitutional order with chastened ambitions has been a description of the Supreme Court's cases, which some treat as revolutionary but which I treat as rather modest in aspiration. My characterization can be contested in two ways. First,

I have given the Court's decisions rather modest readings but, as I have repeatedly suggested, the decisions are clearly open to more expansive readings. The commerce clause decisions could be read by a future Court, or even by the present one, to cast serious doubt on a wide range of national anti-discrimination laws, for example, because those laws might be taken as regulating a noncommercial dimension—the discrimination—of a commercial activity. The decisions dealing with expressive and intimate association could similarly threaten state and local anti-discrimination laws. The Court might notice that no coherent vision of federalism will ever emerge until the Court limits Congress's power to give states money with strings attached. The list could go on: The Court's decisions can be given narrow readings that support my argument about a chastened constitutional order, but they can also be given broad ones that would indeed produce a revolutionary transformation. As Ackerman suggests, perhaps the Court has been particularly talented in allaying suspicion about its intentions by picking its targets carefully, refraining—so far—from invalidating "a major statute in a way that would catalyze a massive political reaction."[13] But, given the opportunities opened up by divided ideological government, why would the median justice care about picking targets carefully?

That observation suggests the second line of challenge to my argument. I have focused on the present Court, but its position, one might say, hangs by a thread. One or two new justices could shift the median from where it now is—a position perhaps compatible with a chastened constitutional order—to a more revolutionary position.

The argument that the Court might change in a revolutionary direction cannot be rejected out of hand. Evaluating it requires us to examine the processes of judicial nomination and confirmation in the new constitutional order.[14] Both stages are now strongly affected by the interaction of divided government and interest group attention to the courts, as political scientists David Alistair Yalof and Mark Silverstein have shown.[15]

The Warren Court era made the politics of judicial appointments an important part of politics generally because political leaders learned how courts can contribute to the extension and consolidation of their political programs. As the New Deal–Great Society political coalition decayed, some of its components sought to preserve or extend their gains by securing victories from the federal courts. Republicans responded by making judicial appointments an important theme in their political challenge to the New Deal–Great Society regime. Interest groups have added judicial nominations to their areas of concern, and some interest groups now take those nominations as a primary area of interest for both lobbying and fund-raising purposes, and "the greater the split between the Senate and the president, the greater potential such groups will see for an effective campaign against the nominee."[16]

As we saw in chapter 1, norms of deference within the Senate have eroded, giving individual senators the opportunity to take opposing a judicial nomination as a personal project.[17] Deference to presidential choices for the Supreme Court has also diminished since the New Deal–Great Society era. Ideological polarization in divided government means that it becomes more likely than before that a nominee's views about what the Constitution means will differ substantially from the views on the same question held by substantial numbers of senators. A nominee's opponents have sometimes searched out what they presented as personal failings to justify their opposition and sometimes presented what the nominee's supporters regarded as distorted characterizations of the nominee's views. As the new constitutional order has matured, however, this so-called politics of personal destruction has begun to change into one in which senators explicitly and unabashedly take a nominee's ideology into account.[18]

What sorts of judges are likely to be appointed to the federal courts in the new constitutional order of divided government and highly partisan and polarized Congresses? The run of Supreme Court nominations from Robert Bork through Stephen Breyer suggests the answer. A high-profile nomination is likely to be quite costly politically, at least when different parties control the presidency and the Senate.[19] The opposition party in the Senate may be able to convert a nomination into a political issue that can damage the president and his party even if the Senate and the president are from the same party. This is particularly true because, as Silverstein puts it, "The current reality is that the confirmation process now demands a calculation of political variables so complex that even the most experienced and electorally secure senators are often unable to predict the course and outcome of the proceedings."[20]

We can see something of a learning curve in recent appointments. The nomination of Robert Bork, a highly qualified, strongly ideological figure with well-known positions on many issues, failed and taught liberal interest groups how they could use judicial nominations as a means of more general political organizing. The nomination of Clarence Thomas, known to be ideological but with some special demographic appeal, succeeded, but the success imposed a fairly high political cost on the president who nominated him.[21] The nomination of David Souter, whose positions were unknown when he was nominated, succeeded, but Souter's performance as a justice taught conservatives that they could not rely on reassurances that a nominee without a substantial public record would be a conservative after appointment.

A reasonably risk-averse president and senators will strongly prefer bland nominees: "The constellation of political and legal forces at work in the nation virtually guarantees a potentially powerful *opposition* in response to any nomination, and thus the modern president is compelled to seek out nominees who present characteristics certain to forestall, or at least minimize, this opposition."[22] Yalof points out that the development of computerized research and databases has made it much easier for interest groups to locate information about prospective nominees.[23] Because "prominence facilitates the mobilization of opposition,"[24] the so-called stealth nominee, who lacks a substantial record that opponents can attack, should be the characteristic nominee in the new constitutional order. And yet the case of Justice Souter indicates that although stealth nominees may escape substantial challenge from the president's opponents, they may not be sufficiently reliable, at least openly so, to satisfy the president's supporters. Even worse, consider the reaction of the opposition party to a stealth nominee: The very fact that the president's supporters are willing to tolerate the nominee after the Souter experience will demonstrate to the opposition that the president's supporters must have enough information to reassure them in the face of a thin public record.

What is the best pool from which to choose a nominee? Sitting judges who, as Yalof puts it, "chart a course of moderation" in which any controversial decisions can be explained away by saying that the judge had to follow the Supreme Court's dictates.[25] A sitting judge nominated for the Supreme Court, and even more so the president, can suggest without quite saying so that the nominee's own views might be different from the Supreme Court decisions that forced the nominee to decide the case in a controversial way. Politicians and law professors, in contrast, achieve prominence by confronting highly controversial issues, which is precisely why presidents shy away from such nominations.

Nominating a sitting judge might minimize opposition. And yet in doing so the nominee may not satisfy the interest groups *within* the president's constituency: Opponents cannot be sure that the stealth nominee disagrees with them, but neither can supporters be sure that the nominee agrees with *them*. Silverstein summarizes the most likely outcome: "Experienced, competent, noncontroversial jurists with a restrained understanding of the role of the federal judiciary in the political system may be the best the modern system can offer."[26]

Supreme Court nominations are rare enough that generalizations about the nomination and confirmation processes in the new constitutional order are hazardous. A nomination of an older ideologue might attract less opposition than the nomination of a younger one; in the president's mind the weaker opposition might offset the inability to ensure that the nominee would serve a very long term. Some additional insight can be gained by examining the politics of lower-court nominations. There senators have become experienced in using "holds" and threats of filibusters to thwart nominations of those they find too far outside the so-called mainstream.[27] Eleanor Acheson, in charge of processing nominations for President Clinton, reportedly conceded that "the administration would be reluctant to name anyone to a judgeship who might be unable to command 60 Senate votes, the number needed to override a filibuster," even though filibusters on nominations have historically been rare.[28] Other techniques of delay—including scheduling hearings for nominees, a prerequisite to consideration by the full Senate, at a snail's pace—have now been well developed.

Further, the mainstream in the new constitutional order is more conservative than it has been even in the recent past. A study of the positions taken by district and court of appeals judges appointed by President Clinton on criminal justice and civil liberties issues shows that they have been more conservative than President Jimmy Carter's appointees, though—unsurprisingly—less conservative than judges appointed by Presidents Reagan and Bush.[29] These figures confirm that President Clinton is Reagan's successor, not Lyndon Johnson's. This has meant that a large number of appointments by a Democratic president has had the effect of institutionalizing the general approach to adjudication—and to substantive constitutional principles—taken in the new constitutional order.

Presidents may sometimes calculate that the benefits of making a controversial nomination, for example in satisfying an important constituency,[30] exceed the costs of attracting opposition, but those costs are likely to lead presidents to make such a nomination only rarely. Under the right circumstances, a Republican president supported by a Republican Senate and perhaps even one facing a Democratic Senate might be able to push through some strikingly conservative nominees to the federal courts, and even to the Supreme Court.

We can see the difficulties and possibilities by examining the suggestion that President George W. Bush could nominate a reasonably conservative Hispanic judge or former judge to the Supreme Court. Liberal interest groups learned from the Thomas nomination that they have to be quite careful about a nominee with specific demographic appeal, but they might be unable to muster enough opposition to block the nomination.[31] Even a Hispanic nominee could not have a publicly perceptible position in favor of restricting abortion rights. And yet the president's conservative supporters themselves are not comfortable with a stealth nominee, having taken as a slogan, "No more Souters."[32] The president must choose someone with no visible position on abortion and then assure his conservative supporters that the nominee is not another David Souter while simultaneously avoiding stirring up serious opposition precisely because, on the abortion issue, the nominee is indeed not another David Souter. This is a delicate political task, and even minor stumbles are likely to make the choice quite costly in political terms. Those high political costs may be worth bearing, particularly if the nomination occurs well before the president seeks reelection.[33]

The hypothetical nomination I have described deals with the political circumstances of a particular president, but its outlines arise from the general characteristics of the new constitutional order. Interest group attention to the Supreme Court coupled with divided government makes it unlikely—not impossible, but unlikely—that the new median justice will be interested in revolutionizing constitutional doctrine rather than chastening it.

THE POSSIBILITY OF PRESIDENTIAL LEADERSHIP

Regime transformations usually have occurred under conditions of severe crisis—the crisis of governance in the aftermath of the American Revolutionary War, the crisis posed by the threat of Southern secession over the issue of slavery, and the crisis presented by the Great Depression.[34] Another feature of regime transformation as a response to crisis is political leadership, usually by the president.[35] Typically elected precisely to deal with the crisis, presidents who guide the nation to a new constitutional order succeed in the short run on three levels and succeed in the long run on a fourth. Rhetorically, they articulate for the nation a new constitutional vision around which the nation can come together. Politically, they obtain from Congress laws that implement that vision. Programmatically, the statutes they put in place are seen to solve or at least substantially mitigate the problems to which they were addressed. For the longer term, successful political leaders begin to construct a new institutional structure within which day-to-day political contention occurs.

Political scientist Jeffrey Tulis stresses the importance of what has come to be known as "the vision thing," so named after President George H. W. Bush failed to get reelected in part because he acknowledged that he lacked it.[36] Drawing on examples from Franklin D. Roosevelt and Woodrow Wilson, Tulis identifies a number of characteristics of successful presidential rhetoric. In Tulis's view, rhetorically successful presidents articulate "public principles with sufficient clarity to educate, not simply arouse public opinion," and "state [their] case[s] in terms of principle, not detailed policy."[37] In addition, transformative political leaders "find a core of issues that . . . reflect[] majority will even if the majority was not fully aware of it," and "understand the true majority sentiment underneath the contradictory positions of factions and the discordant views of the mass."[38] We can couple these views with the argument, discussed in chapter 1, that contemporary political leaders use focus groups and other methods of identifying public sentiment to craft the presentation of the policies they propose.[39] Rhetorical leadership, that is, may be easier today than it was earlier because of developments in political technology.

Rhetorical success is not enough, however. The cases of President Ronald Reagan and Representative Newt Gingrich show that leaders who do indeed clearly articulate visions that many in the public find attractive may nonetheless fail to transform the political order as they hope. The reason for the incomplete transformation during the Reagan presidency is that rhetoric must be accompanied by political and programmatic success. As Dallek puts it, the most successful presidents "combined a clear sense of purpose with both a carefully judged assessment of what degree of change the country was ready to accept and a strategic sense of when to accommodate themselves to opponents who were ready to yield on at least some points."[40] Presidents must be ready to yield because the old constitutional order still retains institutional power when they seek to lead the nation to a new constitutional order and must be accommodated to some degree. The tension between visionary statements of new constitutional ambitions and pragmatic accommodation of the status quo is one that only the most accomplished political leaders succeed in dissolving. As Tulis says, "[I]t is difficult in practice . . . to be inspirational and highly specific at the same time."[41]

Even political success joined with rhetorical leadership may not be enough. The policies a president persuades Congress to adopt must be seen to be work, that is, to advance the nation in the direction the president's vision has identified. An example on a scale smaller than regime transformation may help here. Presidents have routinely deployed the rhetoric of war to justify their programs: the war on drugs, the war on crime, the war on cancer. These programs are not of course transformative, and policies implementing the programs resulted at least as much from the interest group bargaining characteristic of the New Deal–Great Society order as they did from presidential leadership. What matters at this point, however, is that the policies did not visibly succeed in reducing the drug problem or eliminating cancer.[42]

The final component of political leadership in regime transformation is the hardest to observe as the process occurs. This is the development of novel institutional forms supportive of the new constitutional order, like the combination of professional bureaucracy and interest group power in the New Deal–Great Society constitutional order. One might have seen hints of these institutional features in the early 1940s, but an analyst would have to have been extraordinarily prescient to identify them as the characteristic features of the emerging constitutional order.[43]

These observations have obvious implications for the possibilities opened up by the terrorist attacks of September 11, 2001. What role might President George W. Bush play in shaping a new constitutional regime? He could take as his guide Abraham Lincoln's message to Congress in December 1862:

> The dogmas of the quiet past are inadequate to the stormy present. The occasion is piled high with difficulty, and we must rise with the occasion. As our case is new, so we must think anew, and act anew. We must disenthrall ourselves, and then we shall save our country.[44]

President Bush occupied the office in a period of crisis under several disadvantages. Unlike Lincoln, he was not elected by a public aware that his selection was likely to provoke a crisis with which the public expected him to deal. There is a crisis, but it is not the one—of economic stagnation—that produced the initial successes of the Reagan Revolution, and it is not something that was the focus of public attention at the time of President Bush's election. Of course partisan Democrats have misgivings about the manner in which he came to occupy the office. Perhaps most problematic, he became the Republican candidate for the presidency precisely because he did *not* articulate a strong ideological vision, but rather because he was seen as the Republican candidate most likely to blur ideological differences with the Democrats, who themselves had succeeded in blurring their disagreements with the new regime principles of the chastened constitutional order.

Chapter 1 discussed the analysis of presidential leadership developed by Stephen Skowronek, which distinguishes between reconstructive presidents and affiliated ones. Reconstructive presidents initially articulate principles different from those of the constitutional order they confront, begin to dismantle that order, and start developing a new one. Affiliated presidents "extend and consolidate what they have inherited."[45] Within this framework, Ronald Reagan was the reconstructive president, George W. Bush the affiliated one. But, as I have argued, the Reagan Revolution dismantled the New Deal–Great Society constitutional order but did not implement the strongly conservative alternative principles President Reagan articulated. The result, I have argued, was the creation of a new constitutional order with chastened, not reconstructive, ambitions. In Skowronek's framework, then, President Bush is a president affiliated with the chastened constitutional order. And, for Skowronek, affiliated presidents, at their best, are acolytes of the reconstructive presidents they follow. Their political dilemma, for him, lies in developing a distinctive political position and thereby asserting their personal political leadership while adhering to the principles given them by their predecessors.

I am comfortable with that conclusion. But, there is another possibility, not readily accommodated by Skowronek: It is that President Bush will implement the reconstruction that President Reagan envisioned but could not put in place. President Bush could be an affiliated president to the degree that he is a successor to Ronald Reagan and Newt Gingrich with a vision embodied in the regime principles they initially put forth. He could be a reconstructive one to the degree that he does more than "consolidate and extend" what already was in place and actually institutionalizes the Reagan-Gingrich vision. President Bush's task is to rearticulate the Reagan-Gingrich principles for a public that did not fully accept them in their first incarnation.

Relying on President Bush's first State of the Union address, E. J. Dionne, Jr., a liberal columnist, suggested the direction in which President Bush might transform policy.[46] According to Dionne, Bush combined conservatives' defense of the free market with a traditionalist's interest in securing the conditions of moral development through the use of public power to nurture the institutions of civil society that help people understand their personal responsibility for personal and economic success. Tax cuts and reductions in the scope of existing regulation represent the first element, while faith-based public programs, improvements in education that include but are not limited to vouchers for use in private schools, and government programs that support volunteer activities represent the second.

The glimmerings of new institutional arrangements can be seen as well. Picking up on themes stated during the Reagan presidency, the Bush administration asserted its interest in establishing the constitutional independence of a strong presidency. It limited disclosure of presidential records and resisted disclosure of vice-presidential contacts with officials of energy-related companies. Its initial version of a proposal for military tribunals for noncitizens held for terrorist activities would have kept the ordinary courts out of the process entirely. The constitutional separation of powers is constructed through political struggles,[47] and early initiatives may fail or be transformed in ways that leave existing institutions substantially unchanged. Still, in at least this respect we can see the Bush administration's interest in developing a new institutional arrangement for a new constitutional order.

The crisis provides the opportunity for this rearticulation and shift in conservative principles and institutions, cast once again in the rhetoric of war and given structure by the process of crafting public appeals through political technology. At this writing it is of course too early to know whether President Bush's rhetoric will succeed, whether he will accommodate enough in politics to achieve his political goals, whether the policies that are enacted will be seen to succeed, and what the distinctive institutional characteristics of a newer constitutional order would be.

Still, if President Bush succeeds programmatically, in developing and implementing policies that are seen to respond well to the perceived crisis, and rhetorically, in articulating a grander ideological vision that explains why new regime principles are suited to the new situation, the U.S. constitutional order could be transformed into one committed in principle to a sharply reduced role for government in supporting economic growth and achieving economic and social justice.

How might that occur? Consider a scenario with two parts. A president who succeeds programmatically and rhetorically would be in a position to go to the country in the 2004 elections as the leader of a unified ideological party and might help his party gain solid control of Congress. A full-scale repudiation of New Deal–Great Society principles might then occur, symbolized by a substantial privatization of the U.S. system of pensions for the elderly. The second part of the scenario involves the Supreme Court. I have argued that under the conditions that prevailed before September 11, President Bush would face a difficult political choice when given the opportunity to nominate a Supreme Court justice. Under the circumstances immediately after September 11, his choice would be easy: select the uncontroversial, bland stealth nominee. Under the circumstances that might prevail if he becomes a transformational leader, his choice would also be easy but precisely the opposite: select the committed ideologue. The Supreme Court then could assist the new unified government by cleansing the statute books of legislation left over from the prior constitutional order.

Both scenarios I have described are more realistic now than they were when I began working on this project. They are, however, less realistic than the description of a new constitutional order already in place. Consider the keystone legislation of the New Deal–Great Society constitutional order: social security, the Civil Rights Act of 1964, the environmental legislation of the 1970s. I think it wholly unrealistic to imagine that even a unified conservative Congress would repudiate the national commitments those statutes represent. Of course there would be tinkering at the edges and substantially less enforcement by the national government, including the courts, than the most ardent environmentalists and civil rights advocates would like. And of course there would be serious contention over what precisely the normative commitments made by those statutes were: How clean must clean water be? Is affirmative action consistent with or contrary to principles of equal opportunity? But the normative commitments—to a livable environment and to equal opportunity—will, I believe, remain unquestioned. In short, we have and are likely to continue to have a constitutional order with chastened constitutional ambitions.

It is even less likely that a Supreme Court with several new conservative members would hold these statutes unconstitutional at their core. The Court's role might be to push policy in the direction of personal responsibility somewhat more quickly than the political branches. Chapter 2 described the first step of one possibility: The Court might hold that any education voucher system a government adopts may include vouchers for use at religiously affiliated schools. I can imagine a court taking the next step and holding that such systems *must* include those schools because excluding them would be discrimination on the basis on the content of the instruction they offer, a violation of free speech principles. And, I can imagine a third, more dramatic step, a holding that states must *establish* voucher systems. A sketch of the argument is that parents have a constitutional right to send their children to private schools, whether religiously affiliated or not, and that voucher systems are necessary to ensure that this option is truly available to parents. Another possibility is that the Court might hold it unconstitutional to have a social security system that does not provide individuals with some opportunity to determine how their retirement savings will be invested—that is, a partial privatization of social security as a constitutional requirement. Here the argument would develop from some of the modern Court's takings doctrine.

These are possibilities, but it would certainly take time for the lines of precedent to develop to the point where the Court could comprehensively implement a new constitutional vision. Indeed, in some ways it is easier to imagine a Court overruling the decisions that validated the New Deal–Great Society constitutional order than it is to imagine it moving in an entirely new direction. But, as I have argued, as a political matter it seems unlikely that even a newer constitutional order would repudiate the keystones of the earlier one.

CONCLUSION

When I began working on this project, I was reasonably confident in my evaluation of the regime principles and political structure of the new constitutional order. Political life is never stable, however, and the new opportunities presented by the current situation make a larger transformation of the constitutional order more possible than it had been before 2001. Were I forced to make a choice, I would still say that there is already a new constitutional order in place, that its political structure centers on a government divided between two ideologically opposed but internally unified parties, and that its governing principles are chastened versions of the principles of the New Deal–Great Society constitutional order. But the possibility that there is a quite different constitutional order around the corner is substantially greater than it was when George W. Bush was inaugurated. That new order, which could fairly be called the

Reagan-Gingrich-Bush constitutional regime, would have a political structure centered on a highly ideological unified government guided by the principle that the national government not only has no responsibility for achieving economic growth and economic and social justice, but actually lacks authority to do so except by providing the context within which private actors and market processes generate growth and produce justice according to their own standards.

Chapter Four

THE JURISPRUDENCE OF THE
NEW CONSTITUTIONAL ORDER

CONSTITUTIONAL ORDERS elicit theories of adjudication that explain and justify the Supreme Court's role in each particular order. This chapter examines several candidates for the jurisprudence of the new constitutional order, focusing primarily on Professor Cass Sunstein's arguments for what he calls judicial minimalism. The chapter begins by examining some aspects of the jurisprudence of the New Deal–Great Society constitutional order, including controversies among the justices over how they should understand their own role and, in more detail, the arguments offered by Professor Alexander Bickel for his own vision of the Court's role. Bickel's account of constitutional adjudication in *The Least Dangerous Branch* was a theory of adjudication appropriate to the New Deal–Great Society constitutional order. With an interpretation of Bickel's jurisprudence in hand, I turn to the constitutional jurisprudence of the present order, as represented in Professor Sunstein's discussion of judicial minimalism and a less well-developed cousin that treats constitutional law as, in its progenitors' terms, equilibrium. These approaches to constitutional adjudication descend from but also transform Bickel's in ways that illuminate the new constitutional order.

ANXIETY ABOUT THE SUPREME COURT'S ROLE,
AND ITS DISAPPEARANCE

During the early years of the New Deal constitutional regime the Court divided over identifying its proper role. At least as New Deal constitutional theorists came to understand the matter, the prior order rested on a theoretically indefensible legal formalism to justify the exercise of the power of judicial review. So, for example, New Deal theorists derided Justice Owen Roberts's wooden formulation in *United States v. Butler* that the Court's "only . . . duty" was "to lay the article of the Constitution which is involved beside the statute which is challenged and to decide whether the latter squares with the former."[1] They rejected Justice George Sutherland's originalist insistence that "[a] provision of the Constitution . . . does not mean one thing at one time and an entirely different thing at another time."[2]

With formalism and originalism rejected, however, the justification for judicial review was placed into question. As political scientist Martin Shapiro puts it, the New Deal justices had vanquished the previous constitutional regime and had taken over the fortress that had defended it.[3] They then faced a divisive choice: They could dismantle the weapons that had impeded them, or they could turn those weapons against their own enemies. To the extent that he had a coherent constitutional theory, Justice Felix Frankfurter urged the first course.[4] In his theoretical moments, though not entirely in his practice, Frankfurter proposed a generalized theory of judicial deference to decisions taken by democratic majorities.[5]

Justice Harlan Fiske Stone's "footnote 4" provided the theoretical basis for the alternative course.[6] Under footnote 4, the courts had responsibility for enforcing specific constitutional protections for civil liberties and, more important, would protect the channels of democratic government such as elections and free speech and "discrete and insular minorities" who faced discrimination in politics and society. The "footnote 4" jurisprudence was the Court's first effort to fit judicial review into the New Deal (and later, Great Society) constitutional order. It simultaneously authorized judicial review and limited the occasions for its exercise. It had the advantage as well of allowing the Court to deploy judicial review primarily on behalf of the political constituencies important in the New Deal constitutional order.

The Court's role in the New Deal–Great Society constitutional order was not fully worked out, however, until the Warren Court consolidated its position after Frankfurter's retirement in 1962.[7] By the mid-1960s the "footnote 4" jurisprudence was no longer enough. Instead the Court moved in the direction of taking the regime's programmatic liberalism as a constitutional mandate.[8] The equal protection clause was the primary vehicle for this movement. As we saw in chapter 2, several cases suggested that differential distribution of the goods provided by the activist welfare state would violate the Constitution.[9] These cases hinted at a new constitutional doctrine: Distribution of goods based on market criteria might be unconstitutional unless there was a strong justification for their differential distribution, where those goods were fundamental in some nonconstitutional sense.[10] This doctrine would have completed the constitutional foundation for the Second Bill of Rights and for the New Deal–Great Society's programmatic liberalism.

Chapter 2 pointed out that the Supreme Court never fully signed on to this new doctrine, and the 1996 welfare reform legislation shows that the new constitutional order rejects programmatic liberalism.[11] Perhaps more interesting, however, the justices in the new constitutional order do not seem to have the same anxiety over justifying judicial review that characterized the early years of the New Deal constitutional order and that continued to dominate scholarly concern through the Warren Court years. They have invalidated congressional legislation without seriously mentioning, or agonizing over, the fact that they were displacing decisions made by a presumptively democratic legislature.

The reason may be that the new constitutional order was established without dramatic confrontations between the Court and the political branches,[12] and the justices therefore had no need to rethink the Court's proper role. They could simply continue to take their role as it had been defined in the prior regime and merely change *what* they did. But they appear to have scaled back their aspirations.

PRINCIPLE AS AN INADEQUATE JUSTIFICATION FOR THE COURT'S ROLE

Bickel theorized about the Supreme Court's role in the New Deal–Great Society order. The Warren Court's defenders often thought Bickel dangerously wrongheaded and insensitive to the Court's programmatic agenda.[13] Bickel was, in part, a critic of the Warren Court because, I believe, he understood the way in which the Court's decisions contributed to the decay of the New Deal–Great Society constitutional order.[14] Even more, the work that began his trajectory in constitutional theory, *The Least Dangerous Branch*, was written well before the Warren Court came into its own after the retirements in 1962 of Felix Frankfurter, Bickel's mentor, and Charles Whittaker.[15] Further, the book was completed before Lyndon Johnson's Great Society programs confirmed that the New Deal–Great Society constitutional order should be thought of as blending interest group pluralism with a specifically liberal substantive program. Despite these qualifications, the conceptual underpinnings of *The Least Dangerous Branch* could be taken to support the Warren Court's programmatic liberalism, though the book's ambivalences and internal tensions mean that the work can also be taken as a partial critique of that program.

Bickel's account of the proper occasions for, and the content and scope of, substantive judicial review emerged from his reflections on two dimensions of the Court's history and current performance. First, his jurisprudence had to take into account the way in which the New Deal's justices, particularly Felix Frankfurter, understood the lessons of the Court crisis that preceded the Court's transformation by President Franklin D. Roosevelt. Second, the jurisprudence had to assimilate the Court's substantive commitments, especially the Court's insistence on achieving what the justices and their political culture understood to be racial justice in the aftermath of *Brown v. Board of Education*. These two dimensions reflected different aspects of the New Deal–Great Society constitutional regime—its commitment to interest group pluralism and to programmatic liberalism—and no jurisprudence that failed to take both into account could serve as the jurisprudence of that regime.

Frankfurter had responded to the New Deal crisis by articulating a general theory of judicial restraint, to which he did not always adhere. Such a theory responded directly to the events that provoked the crisis—the Court's refusal to treat legislation affecting the distribution of economic power as the product of ordinary interest group politics.[16] It was less suitable for the New Deal's programmatic elements, as was made clear by Frankfurter's discomfort with the Court's articulation of a theory under which some constitutional rights were said to have a preferred status.[17]

Frankfurter's difficulty, and derivatively Bickel's, lay in drawing the line between politics, the domain of interest group pluralism, and law, perhaps the domain of programmatic liberalism.[18] A generalized theory of judicial restraint failed to draw such a line, and even Frankfurter lapsed into programmatic commitments. Bickel himself had personal experience with Frankfurter's ambivalent embrace of judicial restraint when Frankfurter directed Bickel, at the time Frankfurter's law clerk, to prepare a memorandum describing the intent of the Fourteenth Amendment's framers with respect to school segregation.[19] Bickel concluded that the framing history was inconclusive on all the questions Frankfurter asked. Frankfurter then felt free to hold segregation unconstitutional, although it is quite hard to reconcile that determination with either a generalized theory of judicial restraint or an originalist analysis where the historical inquiry was inconclusive. And yet Frankfurter had no other resources with which to address those of the New Deal's programmatic commitments to which he, much less the Warren Court as a whole, adhered. To the extent that Frankfurter's jurisprudence incorporated a generalized stance of judicial restraint, that jurisprudence had been displaced by the time Bickel began to develop the argument that culminated in *The Least Dangerous Branch*.

An alternative approach, that of the Legal Process school, provided a better foundation for the New Deal–Great Society constitutional regime. Legal Process theory was founded on a concern that law could ensure stability, order, and social justice.[20] Law, according to the theory, could secure a stable social order by allocating different types of legal decisions to the institutions with the characteristics most suitable for developing results appropriate to the issues presented, and—somehow—the appropriate decisions would produce social justice. Legislatures had the capacity to address novel problems based on some degree of factual investigation. More important, however, they could develop policy based on the preferences and values of the people legislators represented. Democracy was valuable in promoting stability because it ensured that those who were represented had a stake in the governing process: Even if they were defeated on some particular issue, they still had a chance to raise it again, and in any event they might prevail on other issues of interest to them. In this dimension, the Legal Process school embraced and provided a jurisprudential rationale for the New Deal's commitment to interest group pluralism.

The Legal Process notion of *principle* sought to justify the emerging commitment to substantive rights. For Legal Process theorists, the courts' distinctive characteristic was the ability to articulate principled bases for the results they reached. The joint opinion in *Casey* echoed this idea. By *principle* Legal Process theorists meant reasons that transcended the particular conflict before the courts and in doing so provided guidance for the resolution of other conflicts that implicated the same interests as were at stake in the case at hand. In Legal Process terms, courts had a duty to take the implications of their actions for future controversies into account in a way that legislatures did not. Otherwise the *distinctive* contribution of courts to lawmaking in a stable social order would disappear.[21] Legal Process theorists gave no particular substantive content to the principles that courts should articulate, but their notion of principle was clearly compatible with programmatic liberalism understood as a set of substantive commitments.

Bickel attempted to meld a defense of the early Warren Court with the insights of the Legal Process school. Bickel's essay on the passive virtues, incorporated into *The Least Dangerous Branch*, pointed out that sometimes principle might undermine stability. A principled decision in a particular case might imply that some other controversy would have to be resolved in a way society was as yet unwilling to accept.[22] For Bickel, *Naim v. Naim* was a pivotal example of the threat principle posed to stability and the way courts could avoid excessive commitment to principle.[23] *Naim* was a challenge to Virginia's law prohibiting interracial marriage, which came to the Supreme Court in 1955, just after *Brown v. Board of Education*.[24] Whatever principle justified *Brown*, whether it be that statutory distinctions based on race were almost necessarily invalid or that statutory classifications that perpetuated racial subordination were unconstitutional or any other, that same principle would certainly invalidate laws against racial intermarriage. Taking his cue from Frankfurter's arguments to his Supreme Court colleagues, Bickel argued that applying principle in *Naim*—that is, acting in the distinctive way courts act—would contribute to domestic instability. The Court therefore had to avoid deciding the case.

Bickel's overall argument gained much of its force by emphasizing the discretion the Court had to decide which cases to decide on the merits.

His innovation was to point out that precisely because grants of certiorari were discretionary, the Court would not violate principles of legality in taking political considerations into account in determining whether to grant or deny review in such cases. What made *Naim* so striking was that it came to the Supreme Court as an appeal brought by the litigants from the Virginia Supreme Court. As a technical matter the U.S. Supreme Court was required to decide all appeals on the merits; that is, it had no discretion to avoid acting like a court, in contrast to the discretion the Court had in deciding whether to grant certiorari. The Court attempted to jawbone Virginia's Supreme Court into reconsidering its endorsement of the state's antimiscegenation law, but when that failed the Court dismissed the appeal for failing to present a federal question in the proper manner. As Herbert Wechsler put it, the Court's decision was "wholly without basis in the law."[25] It was an unprincipled decision in a context where Congress appeared to require principle.

As Bickel's endorsement of *Naim* showed, his solution operated mainly within Legal Process theory, but at points it took advantage of tensions within the theory. Bickel directed attention to the various justiciability doctrines the Court had—mootness, the requirement that a federal question be properly presented, and others—that allowed the Court to avoid decisions when invoking principle would promote instability. The justiciability doctrines posed no conceptual problems within Legal Process theory, however. As doctrines, they could be applied in a principled way, thereby reducing the number of occasions on which principled substantive doctrines might produce instability.[26] But Bickel went further. As his position on *Naim* showed, he would allow the Court to be unprincipled in avoiding decisions in these troublesome areas.

In law professor Gerald Gunther's words, Bickel insisted that the Court be 100 percent principled 20 percent of the time.[27] As Gunther's observation suggests, Bickel's approach was in deep tension with the Legal Process assumption that courts were different from legislatures in their commitment to principle alone.[28] As Bickel presented the Court's role, the justices were to be politically sensitive in *selecting* the cases they chose to decide and then were to abjure politics in *deciding* the cases they chose. How could a Court sustain that combination of approaches? In the end, the New Deal–Great Society Court did not do so, choosing instead to pursue politics at both stages.

The first part of Bickel's analysis, in which political judgment played a large role, made sense for the Court as it was constituted during the New Deal–Great Society regime. The long Democratic Party dominance of the national policymaking process had two important implications for judicial selection. Presidents could nominate justices who were personally committed to programmatic liberalism, knowing that those commitments would not become controversial in the confirmation process. In addition, they could nominate justices who had substantial national political experience or who satisfied the demands of typical interest groups, in part because the New Deal crisis had taught the New Deal–Great Society Democratic Party that political judgment was essential to sound constitutional decision making and in part because judicial appointments were a form of patronage compatible with interest group bargaining. Together, these aspects of the nomination and confirmation process meant that the New Deal–Great Society Court would be staffed by people who could be counted on to be sensitive to problems of identifying the occasions on which programmatic liberalism could be implemented by the courts, and distinguishing the occasions when programmatic liberalism should be relegated to legislatures.

Consider the Supreme Court appointments made by President John F. Kennedy. Byron White had played a large role in Kennedy's campaign for the presidency and held a high policy and managerial position in the Department of Justice, and Arthur Goldberg was a labor lawyer, close to the leadership of organized labor, and secretary of labor when appointed. These are appointments of the sort one would expect in the New Deal constitutional order, figures associated with the national political regime. But even President Dwight D. Eisenhower's were largely compatible with the regime characteristics of the New Deal constitutional order. Eisenhower made three major appointments and two minor ones. Earl Warren received the chief justiceship because Eisenhower had promised Warren a Supreme Court position as a reward for Warren's support at the 1952 Republican convention.[29] Warren was a major national political figure, the Republican candidate for vice president in 1948, governor of California, and a serious aspirant for the presidency himself. He was a leader of the progressive wing of the Republican Party, which accepted the New Deal's major programmatic elements. William J. Brennan was a state supreme court justice who was nominated in 1956, an election year, because Eisenhower thought that nominating an urban Catholic with Democratic Party ties would strengthen his electoral prospects.[30] John Marshall Harlan was a leading New York corporate lawyer serving on the Court of Appeals for the Second Circuit when he was nominated to the Supreme Court.[31] Harlan was close to Herbert Brownell and William Rogers, the Department of Justice's leaders, and themselves at the heart of the northeastern liberal internationalist wing of the Republican Party, which accepted the New Deal's domestic programs and enthusiastically embraced the internationalism that emerged during World War II. Potter Stewart was also associated with the "country club" wing of the Republican Party. Only the appointment of Charles Whittaker cannot readily be fit into an account that treats Supreme Court nominations as an aspect of the New Deal regime.

In the end, however, the very commitment to the proposition that judges could be politically sensitive enough to decide when they could properly be principled and when they had to avoid decision undermined Bickel's general approach. For him, judges should and could exercise political judgment in deciding whether to decide, but once they had decided to decide they should follow the principles they articulated to the conclusions that necessarily flowed from those principles. The Legal Process school's notion of what constituted a principled decision failed to take adequate account of some insights the legal realists of the 1930s and 1940s had. For the realists, conclusions did not flow from principles: In a mature legal system whose doctrinal space was thickly populated, a judge given a principle articulated in some prior case could faithfully deploy that principle along with others equally available in the doctrinal universe to reach whatever result the judge thought socially desirable. This doctrinal richness makes it possible for judges to deploy principle in ways that do not promote, but may indeed undermine, the stability sought by Legal Process theorists. Where such theorists might see ordinary interest group politics, judges invoking principle might insist that substantive liberal principles be advanced. Some Legal Process theorists developed criticisms of key Warren Court decisions as unprincipled, but the Warren Court's defenders readily devised responses that took the general form of demonstrating that the critics had misunderstood the true set of principles the Warren Court was pursuing. To turn Bickel's phrase against the Warren Court critics, and sometimes against Bickel himself, under the guise of asserting that the Warren Court was unprincipled the critics were simply expressing moral disapproval of the lines.[32]

But if judges could *always* satisfy the requirement that adjudication be principled in the Legal Process sense, there was no reason to insist on a sharp distinction between the political judgment exercised in deciding not to decide and the judgments of social value expressed in the fully principled decisions on the merits. Further, as a matter of judicial psychology it was implausible to think that judges who were politically sensitive at stage one would abandon their political sensitivity when dealing with the merits.

Again Frankfurter provides a model. During the deliberations over *Brown*, Frankfurter's real concern had always been not whether a decision that segregation was unconstitutional could be supported by originalist arguments but how the Court could effectively transform the South's system of race relations.[33] That concern led Frankfurter to focus on the remedy entailed by a holding that invalidated school segregation. Relying on well-established case law, Thurgood Marshall and his colleagues argued that constitutional rights were personal and present, which to them implied that orders should be entered requiring the immediate admission of African-American students to previously white schools. Frankfurter thought that such orders would lead to disaster for the Court and its anti-segregation holding. Eventually Frankfurter devised the famous formula that desegregation should take place "with all deliberate speed" and linked that remedy to the historic traditions of equity jurisprudence. That is, Frankfurter and his colleagues made a *political* judgment about the best course to pursue and found a *principled* basis in the law to justify the rule embodying that judgment.

The division between political judgment at stage one and principled judgment at stage two could not be sustained against the combination of legal realism's arguments, the background in politics of the Warren Court's justices, and the Warren Court's behavior. With the legal realist understanding of principle in hand, we can invert Gunther's critique by saying that in practice, the Warren Court was simultaneously one hundred percent principled and zero percent principled all of the time. It exercised political judgment both in deciding whether to decide and in deciding on the merits, and it was fully principled at both stages.

Commentators on Bickel's work have agreed that even he came to understand that his initial position could not be sustained. According to Dean Anthony Kronman, when Bickel's work is viewed as a whole, one sees that Bickel argued that courts "must exercise prudence in advancing principle." As Kronman interprets Bickel's ideas about prudence, prudential decision making involves "perceptual and judgmental powers [such as] the ability to size up people and situations, to draw an estimate of their varying receptivity to different ideas, and to see, with a kind of bifocal vision, how general principles operate, or ought to operate, in the full complexity of particular cases. A Justice must also possess considerable patience and be prepared to live with temporizing accommodations while the lines of a satisfactory arrangement gradually take shape."[34] Notably, Kronman treats prudence as a virtue to be exercised not only in deciding to decide but in deciding on the merits as well. Further, the qualities Kronman describes could easily be associated with people who pursued successful careers as national politicians in the New Deal–Great Society order, combining pursuit of programmatic liberalism with the "temporizing accommodations" required by interest group pluralism.

Legal Process theory proved inadequate as a constitutional jurisprudence for the New Deal–Great Society regime. In part its difficulties arose from the theory's foundational concern with social stability. The civil rights movement of the 1950s and 1960s pointedly raised the question: What is so desirable about stability when the social order rests on background conditions of injustice? John Hart Ely's elaboration of Legal Process theory went a long way toward addressing the particular concerns of the civil rights movement.[35] Legal Process theory accepted the civil rights critique insofar as it rested on the effective disfranchisement of African Americans in the 1950s and 1960s South. But the more general concern about stability against background injustice remained. As disagreement persisted over whether the background in the United States was one of justice with some exceptions or one of pervasive injustice with occasional bright moments, the Legal Process assumption that stability in itself justified legal decisions came under pressure. As law professor Jan Vetter observes, Bickel himself "had come to disbelieve in the possibility of resolving current constitutional controversies by rational argument" as a result of his reflection on the social disorder occasioned by the civil rights movement.[36]

In addition, Legal Process approaches were incompatible with some aspects of the programmatic liberalism of the Great Society. That liberalism had some substantive content that Legal Process theory simply could not incorporate.[37] And, finally, legal realism cast doubt on the claim that courts could be principled in the Legal Process sense. According to legal realism, no decision could project itself into the future in the way that principle in the Legal Process sense demanded. Courts were therefore *not* distinct from legislatures; both institutions could collaborate in pursuing programmatic liberalism.

The social and intellectual trends created two related processes within a generally Bickelian approach to constitutional adjudication. Retaining the insistence on principled adjudication, courts sensitive to political concerns could develop large-scale principles sweeping across a wide range of policy areas. As law professor Robert Burt put it, the Warren Court articulated an ambitious program that accepted the proposition that "the judiciary acts properly when, and only when, it can invoke abstract principles of sufficient generality and logical force to impose definitive resolution on social disputes."[38] Having been taught that adjudication must be principled, the Warren Court adopted programmatic liberalism as its guiding principle. This weakened the Court's attachment to the interest group pluralism that was another feature of the New Deal–Great Society constitutional order and introduced a tension within that order that eventually contributed to its demise.

Second, Bickel's approach required that judges have the capacity to make sound political judgments, whether in connection with decisions to avoid the merits or in connection with decisions on the merits. This might be true once a constitutional regime is in place, as judges might be chosen whose principled ambitions comport with those of the rest of that regime's institutions.[39] Times of regime transition, however, place the Court's principles under stress. What was sound political judgment under the old regime can become political folly under the new one, as holdover judges insist on implementing political principles no longer in harmony with the principles of the new regime. Indeed, the description of the new order's nomination and confirmation processes in chapter 3 suggests that today's judges are unlikely to be politically astute.

The jurisprudence of the new constitutional order must differ from Bickel's because the judges who make constitutional law in the new order are different in ways that matter from the ones for whom his jurisprudence was designed. I turn to three candidates for the new order's jurisprudence.

Constitutional Seriousness as a Replacement for Principle

Relieved of anxiety over providing elaborate justifications for the exercise of judicial review, the justices now present themselves not as theorists of constitutional law but as serious-minded adjudicators. The Court's recent substantive due process cases, and in particular the reaction of Justice Antonin Scalia to the Court's actions, provide the best illustrations of the current Court's self-presentation. Justice Scalia's concerns have been those central in controversies over the role of the Court in the New Deal–Great Society constitutional order. Deeply skeptical of the idea of substantive due process, he has nonetheless attempted to provide an analytic structure that would discipline the Court's substantive due process decisions. In his most sustained effort,[40] Justice Scalia argued that substantive due process decisions could rest only on the judgment that a statute was inconsistent with the traditions of the American people specified at an appropriately concrete level of generality. He thought that he had gained a majority for at least one important part of his proposed structure in the right-to-assisted-suicide cases, where Chief Justice William Rehnquist's opinion for the Court asserted that substantive due process rights could rest only on tradition, and that the Court could not take contemporary views into account in making substantive due process decisions.[41] As Justice Scalia saw it, the sort of structure he proposed would solve the problem of justifying judicial review in substantive due process cases in the terms set by discussions during the New Deal–Great Society constitutional order: It would authorize but constrain judicial review.

But, as it has turned out, the current Court is not committed to Justice Scalia's approach because, I believe, it does not take the problem of justification to be central.[42] His proposal to define tradition at the most concrete level of generality attracted only one additional vote. And only a year after the Court appeared to confine substantive due process to tradition, a majority reverted to a formulation in which contemporary views had a bearing on substantive due process cases.[43]

Justice Scalia was disturbed by what he saw as the majority's backsliding.[44] But he was even more upset by the joint opinion of Justices O'Connor, Kennedy, and Souter in *Planned Parenthood of Southeastern Pennsylvania v. Casey.*[45] The joint opinion relied on Justice Harlan's concurring opinion in *Poe v. Ullman,*[46] itself a predecessor of *Griswold v. Connecticut,* one of the New Deal–Great Society Court's central programmatic cases. According to the joint opinion, "adjudication of substantive due process claims may call upon the Court in interpreting the Constitution to exercise that same capacity which by tradition courts always have exercised: reasoned judgment."[47] But, the opinion continued, while reasoned judgment's "boundaries are not susceptible of expression as a simple rule,"[48] it did not authorize the Court to overturn legislative enactments simply because the justices disagreed with the legislature's policy choices. And, the justices concluded, reasoned judgment supported the proposition that the Constitution barred state legislatures from adopting laws that placed undue burdens on a woman's decision to obtain an abortion.[49]

Justice Scalia's dissenting opinion was laced with sarcasm, expressed in part through his use of excerpts from the joint opinion as headings for portions of the dissent. And the discussion of reasoned judgment was one of his targets. He simply could not see how something the joint opinion called "reasoned judgment" could lead to what was essentially the "value judgment" that in some circumstances a woman's interest in terminating a pregnancy overbalanced the state's interest in protecting potential life, much less the fetus's interest in life itself.[50] The joint opinion's "reasoned judgment," according to Justice Scalia, could support virtually any decision a majority of justices reached, because exercising it was ultimately an "empt[y]" process,[51] devoid of the constraining force that Justice Scalia believed essential to any method authorizing the Court to invalidate statutes.

Justice Scalia's criticism of the emptiness of reasoned judgment as a constitutional method can be deepened by noting that the joint opinion invoked the idea in one section of an opinion that pointedly refused to exercise it elsewhere. The authors of the joint opinion twice expressed doubt about the correctness of *Roe v. Wade* as an original matter, but refused to overrule *Roe.*[52] The joint opinion's discussion of stare decisis, examined in one context in chapter 2, deserves reexamination here. Among the joint opinion's reasons for refraining from overruling *Roe* was a concern for the Court's legitimacy, which, according to the joint opinion, rested on decisions "grounded truly in principle" and "perceived as such."[53] *Roe* had been the subject of severe criticism in the ordinary political process. Overruling it would be perceived as a "compromise[] with social and political pressures" that should have, "as such, no bearing on the principled choices that the Court is obliged to make."[54] Under such circumstances, "overrul[ing] under fire . . . would subvert the Court's legitimacy beyond any serious question."[55] Taken together with the joint opinion's unwillingness to endorse *Roe*'s correctness as an original matter, the import of this portion of the opinion is clear: Although the authors cannot, or are at least unwilling to, provide a reasoned argument that *Roe* was correctly decided, they nonetheless insist that people accept its outcome "to end . . . national division by accepting a common mandate rooted in the Constitution."[56] The role of reasoned judgment at work here is at least quite complex.[57]

A similar difficulty attends the Court's later formulation in the assisted-suicide case, which Justice Scalia joined. There the Court insisted that it could determine whether a statute violated substantive due process only after it provided a "careful description" of the interests at stake.[58] Justice Scalia and some academic commentators may have believed that "careful description" was equivalent to "narrow definition"[59] and thus that the Court had accepted Justice Scalia's approach to determining the appropriate level of generality at which competing interests should be identified. This seems plainly wrong. Applying the "careful description" test, the Court rejected what it characterized as a broad challenge to statutes prohibiting assistance in committing suicide. But five justices, some of whom accepted that test, appear to agree that in some circumstances a state would (or, in Justice Souter's case, might at some time in the future) violate the Constitution in barring assistance in suicide.[60] If careful description of the interests at stake can lead both to the conclusion that statutes outlawing assistance in suicide are unquestionably constitutional and to the conclusion that they are sometimes unconstitutional, the "careful description" test has much of the quality of emptiness that Justice Scalia found in the "reasoned judgment" approach.

Concern for doctrinal emptiness and constraint—that is, anxiety about performing the judicial role well—may characterize only the New Deal–Great Society constitutional order and not the new constitutional order. Doctrinal formulations that refer to *careful description* and *reasoned judgment* may be doing something more appropriate to the new order. Consider their rhetorical force: Given the choice between reasoned and unreasoned judgment, or between careful and careless description, who would choose the latter? The doctrinal formulations, that is, visibly demonstrate a certain seriousness about the task at hand, even if they do not provide rules or formulas that constrain the exercise of judgment or the outcome of the definitional process.

Perhaps we can say rather tentatively, then, that the new constitutional order has replaced the prior order's concern that judicial review be authorized and constrained with a concern that it be exercised with an appropriate degree of seriousness.[61] Its justices seek to show that they are technically competent lawyers who do small things very well. Why might seriousness matter? Seriousness may serve a strategic purpose in preserving the Court's position as it awaits the consolidation of a new constitutional order. But there may be more.

If Justice Scalia serves as the foil for characterizing the new order's judicial project, he may be the foil as well for understanding the importance of seriousness. His widely noted verbal cleverness attracts attention, and he is routinely referred to as the most stylish writer on the Supreme Court.[62] He is, in short, an entertaining justice. And entertainment does characterize one dimension of the new constitutional regime because, as we saw in chapter 1, the disconnection between the aspects of national political life that are presented to the public in the media and the daily lives of the American people has made observing national politics a form of entertainment. The Supreme Court too may be an institution of entertainment in the new regime.[63] But our entertainment outlets are varied. Justice Scalia might be the Fox Network of the judicial system, but the rest of the Court may see itself as National Public Radio, committed to a self-presentation as thoroughgoingly serious. Seriousness itself, that is, is one mode of entertainment.

There may be deeper points about seriousness. Professor Philip Bobbitt has argued, for example, that the practice of judicial review, understood as the dispositive choice among options made available by our modes of constitutional discourse, is justified because it makes possible the exercise of moral choice by a set of our public officials.[64] Seriousness, in this view, is embedded in the justified practice of judicial review. And Professor Frank Michelman has suggested that courts might attempt to obtain agreement to controversial results not by invoking any substantive criteria but by reverting to what Professor Charles Fried, harkening back to an older era, calls the "artificial reason of the law."[65] Judges might be able to secure assent by demonstrating their seriousness as lawyers.

Bickel once criticized a certain type of enthusiasm for particular Supreme Court decisions as resting solely on "the moral approval of the lines."[66] That was insufficient for his jurisprudence of the New Deal–Great Society order. Today, however, perhaps what we seek in the new constitutional order is "the moral approval of the justices," both in the sense that *we* seek to approve them morally and in the sense that we hope to obtain *their* moral approval. Yet what their defenders might describe as the justices' seriousness could also be described, I think, more accurately by Russell Baker's deflation of pomposity through the neologism "seriosity."[67]

METAPHORS OF SCIENCE

Law professors William Eskridge and Philip Frickey used the phrase "law as equilibrium" to describe their understanding of the contemporary

Court's jurisprudence.[68] The phrase suggests that science helps us understand the chastened role for constitutional law. Their article, published in a series in the *Harvard Law Review* that constitutional scholars take as exemplifying cutting-edge scholarship in constitutional law and theory, invokes legal process theory,[69] but it is more in the legal realist tradition in alluding to (social) science through the metaphor of equilibrium and in expressly injecting political calculation into the account of judicial behavior. The combination of jurisprudence with science, through metaphor and in the form of public choice theory, might be an attractive way of capitalizing on important cultural and academic trends, although the political dimension of the Eskridge-Frickey analysis undermines its scientific tone.

Eskridge and Frickey define equilibrium as "a state of balance among competing forces or institutions."[70] Their account of law as equilibrium vacillates between two positions. In the predominant one, the Court is one of the institutions that contributes independently to the equilibrium. Here they describe the Court as a strategic actor, "calibrating its actions in anticipation of how other institutions would respond."[71] The Court has "preferences" that it seeks to achieve through these strategic calculations.[72] In the less prominent position, the Court mirrors the forces expressed elsewhere. Here Eskridge and Frickey say that the Court "accommodat[es] apparent national equilibria."[73] Eskridge and Frickey use the language of science in asserting that their account of law as equilibrium is both "necessary" and "sufficient" to understand and explain the Court's actions.[74]

Their theory is only metaphorically scientific, however. First, Eskridge and Frickey never resolve the tension between the predominant position and the subordinate one in their own account. Sometimes the Court is an independent actor seeking to advance its preferences while taking into account the possible responses by other policymakers, but at other times the Court reflects the play of forces elsewhere. As indicated in chapter 3, however, in a world of divided government it is not at all clear why any justice should be concerned that Congress would be able to overturn decisions reflecting the justice's preference. Some political scientists argue that a justice might worry about even unsuccessful *attacks* on the Court, because attacks might damage the Court by "compromis[ing] its ability to make future constitutional decisions."[75] Again, however, divided ideological government changes the picture. Controversial decisions become zero sum: For every enemy the Court makes with a decision, it generates support from someone on the other side of the ideological divide. What we know about *Bush v. Gore* is suggestive, even though the full returns are not in. Survey evidence indicates that contrary to the views of some, mostly liberal, scholars, the Court as an institution did not suffer substantial damage to its reputation, at least in the short term, by giving the 2000 presidential election to George W. Bush. What did happen is more interesting: The Court suffered no *net* harm, because its losses among Democrats were offset by gains among Republicans.[76]

In addition, Eskridge and Frickey never actually provide an account of the Court's asserted preferences. Instead, they speculate: Taking a particular case outcome, they argue that a Court with certain imputed preferences would produce that outcome.[77] This analysis is almost entirely circular: We know the values the justices have because we see how they voted, and then we use those values to explain why their votes make sense within a model of law as equilibrium.

Confirming the model of law as equilibrium in a scientific way would be extraordinarily difficult.[78] We would have to have some measure of the justices' preferences antecedent to their decision in the case we are analyzing, for example. Political scientists attempting to develop this model have used two indicators of justices' preferences: the political party of the president who nominated them and newspaper comments at the time of the justices' nomination describing their ideologies.[79] These measures certainly get at something important, but they are too crude to provide a nuanced understanding of the justices' preferences in particular cases, or even in a run of disparate cases.[80] As political scientist Howard Gillman puts it, "Virtually everyone who studies law and courts agrees that to understand judicial decision making we should take into account the values, ideologies or worldviews of judges. . . . While most legal scholars would agree that the language of 'liberal' or 'conservative' is a useful shorthand for summarizing a judge's worldview, behavioralists tend to treat these as the only appropriate labels, and on occasion this leads them to adopt characterizations that some . . . might find too reductionist."[81]

One reason for the difficulty of using crude measures of preference is that cases present complex blends of issues: The Court's Eleventh Amendment decisions examined in chapter 2 raised stare decisis concerns, questions about federalism, and questions about the economic and social merits of different ways of compensating workers for overtime. It seems quite unlikely that we could come up with an appropriate antecedent measure to identify even a single justice's preferences on that complex of issues.[82]

Finally, the Court does not have preferences; justices do.[83] A scientific model of law as equilibrium would need an account of how individual preferences are aggregated into a "Court" preference. Only with such material at hand could we really work out a strategic account of the Court's behavior.

In fact Eskridge and Frickey use the language of science to dress up fairly standard Court-watching analyses—what political scientists committed to a particular understanding of science disparage as mere anecdotal accounts. Eskridge and Frickey attribute one decision to "the Court's general anti-regulatory, libertarian bent"[84] and assert in a related context that "[t]he current Court valorizes the free market."[85] Fair enough, but no model or theory seems necessary to generate such observations. Yet the use of the language of science is itself significant. It connects the jurisprudence of the new order to practices that are highly valued in the contemporary legal academy.[86]

Equilibrium has another connotation, of stability. As Eskridge and Frickey put it, "At any given time, most legal issues are in a state of stable equilibrium."[87] "Technological, social, or economic [change]" may make an equilibrium "susceptible to movement," and legal institutions, including the Court, can then "shift public policy to render it more reflective of [their] own preferences."[88] This creates a new equilibrium. For Eskridge and Frickey, "[L]aw that is a balance among three interacting branches is superior to law as it might be produced by a single institution."[89] The Court, they say, can play a "mediati[ng] role" by "accommodat[ing] the primary needs of each warring group."[90]

The interest in stability is apparent here, as is the tension between that interest and the scientific language that pervades their article. That tension is even clearer when Eskridge and Frickey identify a dynamic role for the Court. The Court, they say, "can contribute to tomorrow's equilibrium by destabilizing today's squalid consensus."[91] Yes, but only if the Court's preferences lie in that direction. For all we know, the Court can contribute to tomorrow's squalid consensus by destabilizing today's equilibrium if the array of technological, social, and economic forces leave justices so inclined room to do *that*.

Eskridge and Frickey are clearly strongly committed to the reformism they describe. Their reformism is not, however, at all grounded in the theory they offer. In this they resemble the proponents of Legal Process theory.[92] The connection to Legal Process theory has two elements, both important in a chastened constitutional universe. The first is the appeal to science for implicit normative support. The second is an interest in stability with an attendant metaphorical defense of the status quo. As with Legal Process theory, this version appeals to politics at a deep level. But it differs from Legal Process theory, and evokes Bickel's reliance on legal realism, in appealing to politics even closer to the surface—here, politics in the sense of the justices' preferences. The jurisprudence of the new constitutional order thus is more openly political than the Legal Process branch of the jurisprudence of the New Deal–Great Society regime. In this way the new regime's jurisprudence combines both aspects of the old regime's. Yet in bringing politics closer to the surface it fails to take into account the capacity of those who are likely to become justices in the new constitutional order to perform well, at least for those who think that the justices should pursue more than rather modest programmatic goals.

MINIMALISM AS THE NEW ORDER'S JURISPRUDENCE

I have argued that the justices of the new constitutional order may not have the degree of political adeptness that Bickel's jurisprudence required of them. But they may be astute *enough* to serve in the present constitutional regime. The reason is that the regime's programmatic commitments are indeed substantively modest, as we saw in chapter 1. This is not to say that particular political factions lack ambitious agendas, and indeed all factions might have such agendas. Nonetheless, the persistence of effectively divided government means that the principles advanced by the regime, taken as a whole, will be modest. With programmatic liberalism in retreat, the Legal Process concern for stability regains its importance. The judgment needed by a judge in the present constitutional regime need only be a cautious reluctance to take bold steps.

Cass Sunstein offers a constitutional jurisprudence well suited to the present constitutional order. If Bickel's jurisprudence was appropriate for the New Deal–Great Society constitutional regime, Sunstein's is equally appropriate for the present one. As one reviewer put it, "It is rare that a work of constitutional theory so precisely expresses . . . the mood of a particular Supreme Court."[93] Sunstein describes a style of opinion writing that he calls minimalism and defends that style as appropriate in those many situations in modern society where people disagree about fundamental propositions regarding the proper role of government but may agree about particular results. Sunstein's analysis derives from Bickel's, as he acknowledges, but transforms it as well: Where Bickel urged the Court to exercise political judgment in deciding which cases to decide and then to make fully principled decisions on the merits, Sunstein asks the Court to exercise political judgment at both stages.[94]

Sunstein distinguishes decision-making styles along two dimensions. First, he argues, opinions can be either *deep* or *shallow*. A deep opinion draws on some general theoretical account to defend its result.[95] In contrast, shallow opinions do not seek to defend their results by invoking general theories. Rather, they eclectically invoke principles or ideas common to many analytic approaches without defending either the analytic approaches on which they draw or the selection of principles from them on any ground other than the fact that taken together, the principles are widely shared in the society.[96]

The second dimension Sunstein identifies distinguishes between *broad* (or *wide*) and *narrow* opinions. This distinction is familiar: A broad opinion plainly governs a wide range of legislative activity beyond the case presently decided, while a narrow one resolves a particular case but does not have evident implications for many others whose facts might differ either substantially or even in small ways.[97]

The minimalist approach Sunstein defends seeks opinions that are narrow and shallow, at least with respect to constitutional controversies where the society as a whole remains substantially divided.[98] Here the ground for minimalism might be the persistence of divided government in the present constitutional regime because the division within the political branches may reflect parallel divisions in society more broadly. According to Sunstein, minimalist opinions are more likely than maximalist (broad and deep) ones to succeed in promoting the goals of the constitutional order as the courts identify them. A deep opinion will appeal only to those who share the entire set of implications of the deep principles it invokes; such opinions may be suitable for a regime that itself has deep principles widely shared. In contrast, the shallowness of minimalist opinions means that they appeal to a collection of principles each of which is shared by some segment of society and that taken together are rather widely shared. In addition, the narrowness of minimalist opinions reduces the risk that the public will resist them. A broad opinion might mobilize opposition because it casts constitutional doubt on a large number of statutes, each of which has some supporters. A narrow one can annoy only a small segment of society, those adversely affected by the statute before the Court.[99]

Sunstein argues as well that minimalist opinions promote democratic dialogue and deliberation on constitutional matters more effectively than maximalist ones do.[100] Maximalist opinions foreclose a large number of options, taking them entirely out of public dialogue. They might be thought to provoke public debate over the deep principles the courts invoke in them, in particular by bringing dramatically to the public's attention an issue of principle rather than fudging it in some muddled way. But such debate is fruitless, at least in the short run, because the debate can have no effects on outcomes even if the public ultimately concludes that the courts invoked the wrong deep principles.

For Sunstein, minimalist opinions can stimulate debate in two ways. First, they can raise constitutional questions about a range of statutes without, however, holding them unconstitutional. Those who would like to extend the minimalist opinion's result to other statutes will use arguments drawn from it to show that those statutes are unconstitutional, while those who disagree will be able to invoke competing constitutional principles in the statutes' defense. Second, the minimalist opinion's eclecticism makes a number of constitutional arguments available for public use. It allows those who are not originalists, those who disagree with economic analysis, and proponents of a variety of moral approaches to constitutional interpretation to participate in the debate. Minimalism in this way invites general public participation in constitutional discussions.

Without question, Sunstein has identified an important characteristic of many recent opinions. What is the relation between minimalism and the new constitutional regime? First, minimalism is not a different term for Bickel's passive virtues, for it is a technique courts can use in deciding the merits, and it therefore is responsive to the need, after the legal realist challenge to Legal Process, for an account of adjudication that allows courts to make substantive decisions. Second, Sunstein does not defend minimalism as a method fit for all occasions. Rather, minimalism is appropriate, he argues, when judges accurately assess political circumstances and discover a degree of social dissensus, and yet believe that some normative claims being urged on them should not be disregarded. In other circumstances, maximalist decisions are appropriate.[101] Political judgment, then, pervades Sunstein's prescription for the courts: The justices are to consider the degree of social consensus on the issue they are considering, the degree to which there is an ongoing democratic debate about it, and the like. Questions then arise that parallel those that arose in connection with Bickel's analysis seen in the light cast by legal realism. Can minimalist and maximalist opinions have the beneficial effects Sunstein says they can? Do the justices in the new constitutional regime have the background and political astuteness to engage in the political calculations Sunstein says they should?

Consider first the contribution minimalist decision making is said to make in promoting democratic deliberation. Shallow opinions drawing on a variety of principles to support a result resemble the compromises legislators make in working out the details of a statute. To that extent, Sunstein's analysis of courts weakens the distinction between courts and legislatures as, of course, does his insistence that courts engage in political analysis to determine whether their opinions should be shallow or deep, narrow or broad. Indeed, Sunstein reduces that distinctiveness even more by insisting that *legislatures* are forums of principle as well.[102] This immediately raises the question: Why should the courts ever invalidate legislation, even in minimalist opinions?[103]

Sunstein's answer is that such invalidations can be democracy promoting by forcing legislatures to consider problems they have been ignoring.[104] The difficulty here is that democracy promoting is unrelated to whether an opinion is minimalist or maximalist, because minimalism and maximalism are not intrinsic characteristics of opinions themselves.[105] Rather, they are characterizations the opinions receive in retrospect.[106] As Sunstein puts it, "Courts deciding particular cases have only limited authority over the subsequent reach of their opinions. . . . A court that is determined to be maximalist may fill its opinion with broad pronouncements, but those pronouncements may subsequently appear as 'dicta' and be disregarded by future courts. . . . A court may write a self-consciously minimalist opinion, but subsequent courts may take the case to stand for a broad principle that covers many other cases as well."[107] Sunstein argues, I think correctly, that the way a court formulates its opinion can do no more than provide structure for the disputes that might arise later over the opinion's proper characterization.

Sunstein concludes that "[t]he public reception of a judicial opinion may matter as much as the applicable theory of stare decisis."[108] Or, I would add, as much as the opinion's minimalism or maximalism: "Public officials may take an opinion as settling a range of issues . . . despite the Court's determined effort to proceed narrowly. . . . Alternatively, public officials may take an opinion to be narrow, or distinguishable, despite the Court's effort at breadth."[109] But if this is so, it is hard to see how an opinion's minimalism can be democracy promoting rather than democracy obstructing, or how its maximalism can be democracy obstructing rather than democracy promoting. Everything depends on the opinion's reception, over which the justices have little control, not its intrinsic character, which they might control.

A few examples may help.[110] Sunstein treats *Romer v. Evans* as a minimalist opinion.[111] There the Court held unconstitutional an amendment to the Colorado constitution that barred any official body from adopting regulations that protected gays and lesbians from discrimination. But the Court's account of *why* the amendment was unconstitutional was not at all well developed. As a minimalist opinion, *Romer* might open up democratic dialogue by providing an array of arguments, none conclusive, against efforts to enact anti-gay legislation. What it contributes to democratic dialogue by proponents of that legislation is less clear, but perhaps its very refusal to condemn anti-gay legislation in broad terms might be taken by them to validate their view that public evils are associated with homosexuality. *Romer* might obstruct democratic dialogue nonetheless, because it rhetorically associated proponents of anti-gay legislation with advocates of racial segregation,[112] and by attributing the particular anti-gay initiative involved in the case, and perhaps by extension all anti-gay proposals, to "animosity toward the class of persons affected."[113] It is not hard to imagine circumstances under which these aspects of *Romer* would suppress contributions to democratic dialogue by proponents of anti-gay legislation.[114]

Consider next a minimalist decision upholding legislation. Such a decision, as Sunstein says, is obviously democracy permitting.[115] So might be a minimalist or maximalist decision striking the very same legislation down. Sunstein uses the assisted-suicide cases to show why maximalism is sometimes undesirable.[116] The first question about the cases is whether they should be placed on the minimalism-maximalism continuum. Professor Michael McConnell regards them as a broad assertion of the absence of federal constitutional controls over state legislation in the area.[117] If so, they are an example of democracy-permitting maximalism.

The assisted-suicide decisions may not be maximalist in that way, however. Sunstein notes that five justices appear to have said that there are such controls under some circumstances, which they do not define entirely clearly.[118] That lack of clarity might promote democratic dialogue. Legislators must be concerned that if they fail to act, the courts will take up the issue again and refine the doctrine to invalidate restrictions on assisted suicide in circumstances where the legislators, on reflection, would perpetuate them. Democratic deliberation leading to a reaffirmation of existing restrictions might be enough to persuade the courts not to revisit the question.

It seems clear, however, that a minimalist decision identifying a narrow range of circumstances in which restrictions on assisted suicide are unconstitutional would have exactly the same effect.[119] More interesting, so could a narrow but deep invalidation. Such an invalidation would offer one principled ground for regarding the right to assistance in suicide as fundamental in a limited range of circumstances. It would then open up the possibility of discussing why the right was or was not nonfundamental outside that range, considering the principle the Court invoked and many others it did not.

But when a court invokes a deep principle, no matter how narrow it is, trouble may arise. The discussion about the principle's scope and its implications when other principles might come into play can occur inside courts as well as outside them. And on the Legal Process notion of principle, they *must* occur in courts. In the course of such discussions, the initially narrow decision might become broad, as the courts consider the implications of the principle they invoked. Consider, for example, Sunstein's suggestion that *Roe* could have been decided more narrowly as "a rape case."[120] What theory (or elements of diverse theories) supports the conclusion that abortions may not be barred in such cases? Opponents of choice with respect to abortion find it far from apparent that the wrongfulness of the rapist's conduct has any bearing on whether it is proper to override the state's interest in protecting the potential life of the innocent fetus, or on the woman's interest in autonomy with respect to the rape's consequences (as compared to other situations in which the woman wants to terminate the pregnancy).[121] So, it seems to me, whatever account the Court gave of *Roe* as "a case involving rape" would have to rest on some judgment about the relative weights of the woman's interest in autonomy and the state's interest in protecting the potential life of the fetus.

But that is precisely the account the Court gave in *Roe* itself. Allowing abortions when pregnancy results from rape might be an acceptable resolution in the unprincipled (in the Legal Process sense) legislative process but would be difficult to sustain in the principled judicial one.

Further, a wide but shallow invalidation could also promote democratic dialogue. Such a decision would conclude that a flat ban on assistance in suicide is impermissible, without clearly offering a single principle explaining why. In response, legislators might focus more clearly on the circumstances in which they believe assistance should be prohibited, or might devise procedures to regularize existing but subterranean practices of providing assistance.[122] Those responses might easily be found compatible with the initial wide but shallow invalidation.[123]

What, finally, of the truly maximalist opinion, the one that is both wide and deep? Sunstein discusses *Dred Scott v. Sandford*[124] and *Brown v. Board of Education*.[125] He also describes *Roe v. Wade*[126] as maximalist.[127] Sunstein regards *Dred Scott* as a disaster. He argues in connection with *Roe* that "the Court decided far too many issues too quickly" and that "the democratic process would have done much better with the abortion issue if the Court had proceeded more cautiously and in a humbler and more interactive way."[128] Finally, he suggests that *Brown*, understood as a maximalist decision, does not provide an example to emulate[129] and should be understood in less maximalist terms.[130] Maximalist invalidations, then, do not seem to have much going for them.

Even with these examples, I would suggest that maximalist invalidations can be democracy promoting in one important sense. Maximalist opinions often identify the moral heart of the matter. They can foster discussion among the public broadly both about the particular issue the Court purported to foreclose and about the deep theory on which the Court rested its judgment. This may contrast with minimalist opinions, which may focus discussion—among lawyers only, probably—about the precise technical distinctions the Court drew. *Dred Scott* may have contributed to the outbreak of the Civil War, but it did so by providing an impetus to the growth of the Republican Party and its campaign for the limitation of slavery's spread. *Roe* may have made it impossible to *enact* a range of restrictions on the availability of abortion, but I confess that it is not clear to me that the quality of public debate over abortion and privacy was better before *Roe*.[131] And, of course, the discussions fostered by maximalist invalidations may affect the Court's composition and ultimately constitutional interpretation itself, to the point where the Court repudiates or sharply limits its earlier decision. That seems to me the story of *Roe* and *Casey*.

Further, minimalist opinions purport to leave much open for resolution in the democratic process, but they have their own problems. They may encourage a certain kind of irresponsibility, as when a justice concludes that the law being made in the case at hand does not matter that much because the minimalist holding can always be distinguished the next time a related issue arises. As we will see, that may be one problem of the minimalism of *Bush v. Gore*.

In addition, the minimalist opinion may be inserted into a political environment where it will have precisely the same effect as a maximal one. The Canadian experience with the law of abortion is suggestive. The Canadian Supreme Court overturned a conviction for violating the nation's ban on performing abortions because the ban was accompanied by exceptions that were in fact unavailable in the real world.[132] Criminal laws could not be enforced if they offered such illusory defenses, according to the Court. This appeared to leave open the way for a substantial reenactment of the general ban on abortion. But the political terrain was such that *no* legislation could be enacted after *Morgentaler*, leaving Canada without any criminal laws dealing specifically with abortion.[133] As Sunstein points out, "The choice between minimalism and the alternatives depends partly on pragmatic considerations and partly on *judgments about the capacities of various institutional actors.*"[134] Positive political theory suggests that particularly in circumstances of divided government, a minimalist invalidation may well have maximalist effects: The legislature will be unable to come to agreement on *anything* to replace the invalidated statute, leaving the subject of the Court's action completely unregulated, just as would occur had the Court adopted a maximalist position.[135]

Minimalism, then, may not be democracy promoting or even minimal in its effects. Proponents of older Legal Process approaches would raise a second objection, arguing that the people we select as justices may not be competent to make the political assessments that Sunstein asks them to.[136] Here we can note several concerns.

How confident should we be that the justices can make good judgments about the readiness of the democratic process to accept a correct result (or about how complex institutions actually operate)? Confidence in their ability to do so might depend to some extent on their pre-judicial experience. Notably, the Warren Court's justices had much greater involvement in national politics than do today's justices.[137] And even they may have made errors when they sought to think politically. Some of the justices deliberating in *Brown v. Board of Education*, for example, expressly adverted to political calculations in explaining their positions.[138] These concerns led the justices to adopt the gradualist remedy in *Brown II*, which some have thought exacerbated rather than dampened resistance.[139]

Sometimes Sunstein suggests that maximalist judgments can appropriately be rendered by courts whose judges, otherwise divided, are quite confident in the correctness of their wide (or broad) and deep judgments.[140] Yet it seems quite likely that judges who render broad and deep decisions are themselves quite confident of the merits of their action. So, for example, the Court's Eleventh Amendment decisions reflect such confidence, and the majority expressed some exasperation with the dissenters' refusal to acknowledge that the majority was correct.[141] Perhaps, then, wide and deep decisions are appropriate only if a supermajority of the justices agree on them. For example, in *City of Boerne v. Flores* the Court found Congress's effort to define a right to religious liberty that went beyond the Court's earlier definition unconstitutional, with no justice disagreeing with the Court's analysis of Congress's power.[142] But perhaps that very agreement demonstrates a *lack* of the diversity (with respect to the problem at hand) that would justify a maximalist opinion—in *Boerne*, whether the Court should be absolutely supreme in identifying the content of constitutional rights. The obvious self-interest shared by all justices in giving an affirmative answer to that question makes it difficult to be confident that their maximalism deserves special respect.[143]

Further, Sunstein's analysis sometimes reflects his own contestable political judgment without a clear acknowledgment of the role that such judgment plays in the analysis. His comments on affirmative action provide the best example. Sunstein uses the arguably maximalist opinion in *Brown v. Board of Education* to suggest that maximalism might be appropriate when the courts have accumulated enough experience after rendering a series of minimalist opinions to be confident of their maximalist judgment.[144] He suggests, however, that the courts should continue to be minimalist in the area of affirmative action.[145] The differences between the Court's experience with segregation and its experience with affirmative action are small, however, and if maximalism was appropriate for the former, perhaps it is appropriate for the latter as well. The Court had decided four cases dealing with segregation in graduate and professional education when it considered *Brown*.[146] It had decided none dealing with elementary, secondary, or undergraduate education. The Court had decided six or seven cases dealing with affirmative action in public employment and contracting when it considered *Adarand Constructors, Inc. v. Pena*.[147] Its accumulated experience in that area would appear to be as great as it was in *Brown*. And, if the Court appropriately generalized from experience with professional and graduate education to elementary and secondary education in *Brown*, perhaps it could appropriately generalize from employment and contracting to education in the affirmative action area.

Finally, there may also be the more fundamental Legal Process questions about stability in the face of disagreement. Robert Burt suggested that Bickel's interest in principled adjudication drew on a vision of social order in which "violent conflict seemed the only plausible outcome unless some authoritative body, somewhere, somehow, would impose a conclusive end to the dispute."[148] Minimalism leaves things undecided while allowing for accommodations among contesting parties, thereby achieving a temporary solution to a permanent problem without imposing a conclusive end. But, according to Sunstein, courts must make political judgments in deciding when minimalism is appropriate and when it is not. Those judgments reflect the courts' assessment of the degree and depth of social division.

Those assessments, in turn, will sometimes themselves be controversial, particularly because one issue may be the level of abstraction on which to describe social practices. The abortion controversy provides one example: There may be little division over the abstract principle of personal privacy invoked by pro-choice advocates, but there obviously is great division over the appropriate characterization of that principle in the abortion setting. Sunstein's analysis asks the courts to interpret social practices with respect to disagreement on the level at which substantive disagreements are presented. But to do so they must take some position on the controversial question of characterization. If they can do that, perhaps they can resolve the underlying substantive issues on the merits, which is what Professor Sunstein's minimalism seeks to avoid. Or, perhaps the courts are not able to make the needed political determinations with much accuracy.

MINIMALISM AND JUDICIAL POWER: A JURISPRUDENCE FOR *BUSH v. GORE*

The Supreme Court's actions in the presidential election cases of 2000 provide a helpful example of many of the problems associated with minimalism. In *Bush v. Palm Beach County Canvassing Board* the Court asked the Florida Supreme Court to reconsider its interpretation of the state's statutes dealing with election protests, indicating that the U.S. Supreme Court was unsure of the extent to which the state supreme court had considered the relevance of a federal statute and constitutional provision in construing the state statutes.[149] Sunstein praised the unanimous decision as appropriately minimalist, "a triumph for good sense and even for the rule of law" because "unanimity can go a long way toward deflecting political passions."[150] In the context of the rapidly developing election litigation, however, the Court's intervention, nominally neutral between the parties, actually reinforced the claims of then Governor Bush. As one critic of Sunstein's column observed, Republicans took the Court's action as a criticism of the Florida Supreme Court, so that the Court's decision "unintentionally help[ed] confirm the intemperate attacks made on the state court and on judicial independence generally."[151] More generally, the political effects of minimalist decisions depend on their context. *Bush I* suggests that minimalist decisions can have larger political consequences than Sunstein's general characterization suggests.

Bush v. Gore, the decision in which the Supreme Court determined who the president would be, purported to be minimalist too. The Court found that the procedures adopted by the Florida Supreme Court for conducting a recount violated the equal protection clause. The Court tried to limit the reach of that holding, however, referring to the "special instance of a statewide recount under the authority of a single state judicial authority" and expressly asserting, "Our consideration is limited to the present circumstances, for the problem of equal protection in election processes generally presents many complexities."[152] Sunstein calls the decision "subminimal" because of its narrowness and the lack of substantial precedent supporting the Court's holding.[153] Subminimal holdings are, for Sunstein, improper because they are inconsistent with the most modest demands of a rule-of-law regime. As he puts it, the Court's attempt to minimize its decision in *Bush v. Gore* "seemed ad hoc and unprincipled— *a common risk with minimalism.*"[154] It bears noting, however, that the relation between acceptable minimalism and unacceptable subminimalism resembles the relation between the two stages of decision Bickel wrote about. Having authorized judges to think politically at stage one, Bickel had little ground to stand on when judges thought politically at stage two. Similarly, judges may find it easy to deploy the reasons Sunstein gives them for making a minimalist decision when they wish to make a subminimalist one. Even more, minimalist decisions are characterized by the narrowness of the principles they invoke, and a judge attempting to find a narrow principle to justify a minimalist decision may easily end up finding one that was too narrow, unintentionally producing an undesirable subminimalist decision.

In addition, *Bush v. Gore*, minimalist though it purported to be, did impose a conclusive end to the only real dispute that generated it: The equal protection issue remained open, but not the office of the presidency.[155] The consensus among legal commentators appears to be that the Court acted to avoid the continuation of what it believed to be a chaotic and perhaps lawless state of affairs in Florida. Its judgment about that state of affairs remains controversial, and the accuracy of its overall political judgment will be determined not by anything intrinsic to *Bush v. Gore* but by the success or failure of the Bush administration: A successful presidency will vindicate the Court's judgment, and an unsuccessful one will show that the Court was wrong. Again, minimalism's merits are closely tied to questions of political judgment.

Minimalism may not, therefore, have the characteristics Sunstein attributes to it.[156] But, as the term suggests, minimalism can be described as the form that doctrinal downsizing takes. Big courts issue big—maximalist—opinions, but a Court that is part of a smaller government should issue smaller—minimalist—ones. At the same time, however, minimalism enhances judicial power, as debates over the proper form of constitutional adjudication in the 1950s and 1960s showed. Then one side of the argument was taken by proponents of ad hoc balancing, who believed that the courts were to take every relevant detail of a case into account, carefully identify the precise interests that competed for vindication, and finally balance those interests.[157] Their critics, led by Justices Black and Douglas, argued that ad hoc balancing gave judges too much power, in part because the metaphor of balancing concealed the necessary elements of judgment that went into constitutional adjudication but in part because opinions justifying outcomes as the result of ad hoc balancing gave too little guidance to other lawmakers.[158]

As Sunstein suggests,[159] minimalism is subject to the same criticism. Perhaps the most pithy critique was offered by one of Justice Thurgood Marshall's law clerks in a memorandum explaining why it was hard to tell whether a lower court had followed the Court's affirmative action holding in *Wygant v. Jackson Board of Education*:[160] "[N]obody knows what that opinion stands for now that Justice Powell has retired."[161] That is, to know what a minimalist opinion means one must go to the source. In a world where minimalist opinions are the general rule, no one can be confident that a statute is constitutional until we ask the Supreme Court. Minimalist opinions thus make the Court the focal point with respect to *every* statute, hardly the position that a Court that aimed at reducing its role in public life would seek.[162] Minimalist opinions maximize the power of the courts that issue them because minimalist opinions have few discernable implications for other cases.

Nor is this accidental. It is only a slight overstatement to say that if Bickel asked the Court to be 100 percent principled 20 percent of the time, Sunstein hopes that the Court will be 5 percent principled 75 percent of the time, with the degree of and occasions for the use of principle determined by the judges' prudential assessment of political circumstances.[163] For Legal Process adherents, *principle* meant some verbal formulation used to justify a result in the case at hand that implied how other reasonably imaginable cases should be resolved. Minimalist opinions are not principled in that sense, in part because they are self-consciously narrow and in part because they may draw eclectically on a variety of deeper theories to demonstrate that people of diverse views may converge on a result in the case at hand.

Perhaps, then, we should consider whether, in regime terms, the reduced scope of recent opinions has a different source. Seen program-matically, the Court's minimalist invalidations enforce a reduction in the scope of national power. A Court firmly embedded in the new constitu-tional order might confidently develop doctrines, not necessarily mini-malist, that would define the new contours of national power.[164] That, however, is not what the present Court has done as yet. Instead, the Court, like the other institutions of the new constitutional regime, takes small steps. Minimalism might be a holding action for a Court uncertain about the direction the next constitutional revolution will take. The term, though, is precisely what one would use to describe the practices of courts in a constitutional regime whose aspirations had diminished.[165]

Chapter Five

GLOBALIZATION AND THE NEW
CONSTITUTIONAL ORDER

NO ONE REALLY knows precisely what globalization is, but nearly every-one thinks that it has some effects on domestic constitutional orders.[1] One prominent view is expressed clearly by international political econo-mist Susan Strange, who writes that "state authority has leaked away, upwards, sideways, and downwards. In some matters, it seems even to have gone nowhere, just evaporated."[2] Authority has moved upward to supranational organizations such as the World Trade Organization; it has moved downward as nations concede greater authority to the regions; and it has evaporated as transnational corporations use the threat of re-location to constrain every nation's ability to impose regulation.[3]

The effects of globalization on constitutional regimes are quite complex. Capital mobility means that individual nations lose a significant portion of their ability to regulate production and employment and—indirectly, as their tax bases are threatened by capital mobility—their ability to sustain extensive social welfare programs.[4] Yet, as urbanologist Saskia Sassen points out, even transnational organizations have local "incarnations," which means that individual nations have some regulatory power, though, as Sassen emphasizes (and as we will see in the conclusion), "it would require considerable innovation in the framework" for regulation to succeed.[5]

Some political scientists have developed models showing that globaliz-ation makes decentralization—the revival of federalism described in chapter 2—less costly. The basic idea, as one puts it, is that "international economic integration has . . . made smaller states more economically via-ble [because] trade between nations can substitute more easily for trade within nations."[6] Here the focus is on independent nations and the threat of secession. The general point, however, is that governing units smaller than nations can take on larger roles even as the nation's power evapo-rates.[7] One might say, though, that the American states might be gaining more and more power over less and less important subjects.

Sociologist Manuel Castells offers another perspective on the politics of decentralization. Drawing on European experience, Castells argues that personal identity is increasingly organized not on national lines but regionally (or, as we will see, transnationally). But, while "regional and national minority identities find their easiest expression at local and regional levels, . . . national governments tend to focus on managing the strategic challenges" of globalization. They let "lower levels of governance take responsibility for linking up with society by managing everyday life's issues, so to build legitimacy through decentralization."[8] The European perspective emphasizes identities that are less well developed in the United States, but again the general point seems applicable to the United States: The reduction in national regulatory power that globalization produces increases the likelihood that *other* forms of governmental power will be exercised at the state and local level.

All this suggests that the term *globalization* has become a buzzword with little content and a vehicle for grandiose claims about large-scale constitutional transformation. That transformation will occur seems to me quite likely, but how a nation's constitutional law will be transformed by globalization will vary widely. What matters is that *something* will happen. Law professor Harold Koh, who served as assistant secretary of state during the Clinton administration, has described processes by which international legal norms are incorporated into the domestic legal order.[9] I adapt his term to describe the incorporation of international *policy* concerns as well. After such concerns are incorporated and internalized in the policymaking process, they must be *integrated* with the remainder of constitutional law.[10]

This chapter begins by describing the New Deal–Great Society's treatment of norms associated with international affairs and providing some examples from trade law and human rights law to suggest how globalization may require integration of international norms with domestic constitutional law. It then examines several cases in which, one would think, integration might require changes in the New Deal–Great Society approach. The cases lead to a consideration of the scope of Congress's power to enter into treaties that might affect the distribution of power between the nation and the states. These federalism issues come in several forms, including a new version of the arguments about preemption and commandeering developed in chapter 2.

My focus is relatively narrow—primarily on problems of federalism and globalization—to restrain myself from speculating about what globalization *will* entail even though we see little effect so far. My view, consistent with my overall argument, is that we have seen little effects of globalization on constitutional doctrine because, in the new constitutional order, large-scale developments generally have small-scale effects. On analysis, it turns out that not much needs to be done to adjust constitutional doctrine to fit the new constitutional order—not so much because one cannot imagine serious problems that might arise from aggressive implementation of norms associated with globalization but rather because such aggressive actions are unlikely in the new constitutional order.[11]

NAFTA AND THE BURMA LAW

The conventional wisdom about the way in which foreign affairs were integrated into the New Deal–Great Society constitutional order can be easily stated. The United States came to play a major role in international affairs, initially in World War II and then as the leader of anti-communist forces during the cold war. A bipartisan consensus emerged supporting that role as traditionally isolationist segments of both major parties were displaced. The consensus was that the new U.S. role required maximum flexibility in developing international policies.[12] The nations power with respect to foreign affairs therefore had to be plenary.[13] As Martin Flaherty puts it, the New Deal, World War II, and "the emergence of the Soviet Union led to a rejection of formalist nineteenth-century understandings, fostering instead a regime that was executive-centered in terms of separation of powers, nationalist as a matter of federalism, and internationalist in general orientation."[14] Formalist doctrines, in which some matters might be categorically excluded from the foreign affairs power, were replaced by balancing tests that gave the government what seemed to be the appropriate degree of flexibility.[15]

With the collapse of the Soviet Union, "parochial doctrines reemerged. Domestically, 'states' rights' is no longer a segregationist slogan but once again constitutional doctrine."[16] The declining threat of international crisis removed one source of nationalizing pressure.[17] Consensus over foreign policy dissipated: The idea that politics stopped at the water's edge became a relic of the past. So, for example, law professor Jack Goldsmith uses the Massachusetts Burma Law case, described in chapter 2, to show that at least some of the international issues currently raising questions of domestic constitutional law "are from any perspective much less significant" than the ones arising from the cold war.[18] That he uses such an example is symptomatic of another feature of the modern constitutional order—the decay of consensus on what matters in international affairs. Supporters of the claim that international human rights matters a great deal in international affairs have significant political leverage within the Democratic Party and rather less in the Republican Party. Similarly, the parties seem to disagree systematically about the appropriate role in U.S. foreign policy of a generalized concern for human rights.[19]

The international lawmaking process changed in two important ways.[20] During the New Deal–Great Society constitutional order, international law was developed through bilateral and multilateral agreements that imposed obligations on the nations who signed. More recently multilateral treaties have begun to create free-standing lawmaking institutions: Created by agreement, these institutions then go on to make new law themselves. In addition, nongovernmental organizations (NGOs) have become increasingly significant in influencing public opinion and the positions nations take while negotiating international agreements and in lobbying with the new free-standing international institutions. Law professor Paul Stephan argues that international law in the new constitutional order "engages three antidemocratic tendencies": it strengthens the president against Congress; it "enhances the ability of concentrated interest groups to procure rules that benefit their own, rather than the general, welfare"; and it "bolsters the power of the bureaucracies of international institutions."[21]

The North American Free Trade Agreement (NAFTA) is a good example of the integration problem. NAFTA requires the United States, Mexico, and Canada to conform to free-trade principles. What if a dispute arises? In one interesting case a Mississippi jury told the Canadian-owned Loewen Group to pay $500 million to the owner of a local funeral home because, the jury concluded, Loewen Group had engaged in fraudulent practices aimed at driving the funeral home out of business.[22] Loewen Group settled with the funeral home operator for $175 million. Then, it turned to NAFTA. Loewen Group argued that NAFTA required the U.S. government to compensate it for what amounted to an unfair confiscation of its investments in the United States. Disputes under NAFTA are presented to an arbitration panel, with each side choosing one member and then those two choosing a third.[23] The arbitration panel has the power to decide whether the state court action violated the U.S. commitments made in NAFTA.

This dispute-resolution mechanism raises interesting questions of domestic U.S. constitutional law. The arbitrators provide the only authoritative interpretation of an agreement the United States entered, and under the Constitution that agreement, a treaty, is "the supreme Law of the Land." Ordinarily the only people who can provide such authoritative interpretations of U.S. law, including treaties, are federal judges. But under the Constitution, federal judges are nominated by the president and confirmed by the Senate, and they have life tenure. No institution with domestic U.S. constitutional status has any connection to the appointment of two of the three NAFTA arbitrators, and the arbitrators serve for one time only.[24]

The Burma Law case described in chapter 2 illustrates the role transnational NGOs play in modern international law[25] and how their actions raise questions about integrating international norms with domestic constitutional law in the new constitutional order.[26] The Burma Law resulted from the local actions of a transnational movement against the repressive regime in Myanmar. Political scientists have noted that such transnational NGOs monitor the international policies of the national governments where the NGO members live and act politically, and the NGOs serve as

internal interest or pressure groups.[27] These transnational NGOs differ
from most traditional interest groups, though. Typically, the latter have
some direct material interest in the legislation they seek,[28] while transnational NGOs typically assert only moral interests.[29]

Much domestic constitutional law responds to concerns about the role
interest groups play in politics. Integrating the new international law into
the new constitutional order will, as Stephan suggests, require thinking
through the role of transnational NGOs seen as interest groups. At the
most general level, the New Deal–Great Society constitutional order har-
monized foreign affairs to other provisions by giving foreign affairs primacy.[30] Ordinarily foreign affairs policies might express the U.S. national
interest narrowly understood. Sometimes, however, those policies would
adopt international norms. Even then the New Deal–Great Society constitutional order gave them primacy. The new constitutional order may
treat international norms as on roughly the same plane as other sources
of law.[31] The project of integration would then become more complex, as
the case studies that follow show.

BREARD, SOERING, AND THE BURMA LAW CASE

Angel Breard was a national of Paraguay who was convicted in a Virginia
court of capital murder and sentenced to death.[32] The Vienna Convention on Consular Relations provides that foreign citizens detained by officials in another nation must be informed promptly of their right to contact their embassy. Breard did not receive that information. After his
conviction Breard filed a petition for habeas corpus in federal court, arguing that the failure to comply with the Vienna Convention's requirements
entitled him to relief from his conviction. In addition, Paraguay filed suit
in the federal district court and in the Supreme Court against various
Virginia officials, seeking an injunction against the execution. And, finally,
Paraguay filed an action against the United States in the International
Court of Justice, which promptly issued an order directing the United
States to "take all measures at its disposal to ensure that Angel Francisco
Breard is not executed pending the final decision in these proceedings."[33]

All the suits failed. Breard's habeas corpus suit was rejected because he
had failed to present his claim under the Vienna Convention to the state
courts in an appropriate manner; he had, in the terminology used in habeas corpus cases, procedurally defaulted his claim. Paraguay's suits failed
because a foreign nation is not a "person" entitled by the relevant federal
statute to sue state officials for constitutional violations, because the convention did not clearly provide a private right of action in which a nation
could vacate a conviction, and perhaps because the Eleventh Amendment
barred suits against the state officials. Responding to the International

Court of Justice's order of provisional measures, the U.S. secretary of state wrote a letter requesting that Virginia's governor delay Breard's execution. The U.S. Department of Justice took the position in its briefs to the Supreme Court that such a request was the only "measure at its disposal" under U.S. constitutional law.[34] The U.S. Supreme Court, after citing that letter, concluded, "If the Governor wishes to wait for the decision of the ICJ, that is his prerogative. But nothing in our existing case law allows us to make that choice for him."[35] After the Breard litigation concluded, the U.S. government apologized to the government of Paraguay and distributed information about the Vienna Convention's requirement to police agencies throughout the country.[36]

The Breard litigation in the U.S. courts was followed by a claim brought by Germany against the United States in the International Court of Justice (ICJ). The pattern was the same as in *Breard*: Walter La Grand, a German national, was arrested, not informed of his rights under the Vienna Convention, and sentenced to death. On the eve of his execution, Germany filed its complaint with the ICJ.[37] As before, this action did not halt the execution. By the time the ICJ acted, the United States conceded that there had been a violation of the convention and had already sent a formal letter of apology to the government of Germany. The United States contended that its apology, and the "vast and detailed programme" it was implementing to inform law-enforcement officials of their duties, were all that the convention required. The ICJ disagreed.[38] With only one judge dissenting on this issue, it held that the procedural default rules applied by the federal courts in habeas corpus cases violated the convention by preventing "full effect [from being given] to the purposes" of the convention. The United States had to develop rules that would "allow the review and reconsideration of the conviction and sentence by taking account of the violation" of rights under the convention.

Virginia was also involved in the other case on which I focus. Jens Soering and his girlfriend conspired to kill her parents. He fled to Europe. Responding to a request for extradition, Soering obtained a ruling from the European Court of Human Rights that Virginia's method of administering the death penalty was "cruel, inhuman, [or] degrading treatment" in violation of the European Convention on Human Rights,[39] with the result that the British government could not comply with both the extradition request and the European Convention. The U.S. government then represented to the United Kingdom that Soering would not be prosecuted for capital murder in Virginia.[40] Soering was then extradited and was prosecuted without facing the risk of capital punishment.[41]

Finally, recall that the key doctrinal feature in the Burma Law case was the presence of two statutes regulating doing business with Burma: the state law that made it difficult for businesses that did business in Burma to obtain contracts with the state government, and a national statute that gave the president broad authority to impose sanctions on Burma and to negotiate with other nations to come up with a common plan of economic sanctions against the Burmese regime.

The Breard and Soering cases raise questions about the integration of international human rights norms and U.S. federalism. In particular, the cases implicate the two dimensions of the new constitutional order's federalism doctrine described in chapter 2: a restriction on the subject-matter scope of congressional power and a restriction on the methods Congress may use to carry out policies otherwise authorized by the Constitution.

Both the Breard and Soering cases indicate the ways in which a national obligation assumed under a treaty may have adverse effects on a state's ability to prosecute ordinary crime, an interest that the Court has occasionally invoked in explaining its subject-matter limitations on congressional power. In addition, the Vienna Convention appears to impose an obligation on state police officials to comply with a directive from the national government, in apparent tension with the anti-commandeering principle. Finally, the Burma Law case raises questions about the preemption of state law by a national one. How will the law of the new constitutional order respond to these challenges?

BREARD AND SUBJECT-MATTER LIMITS ON THE TREATY POWER

The Breard litigation was rushed and reached the Supreme Court in an extremely awkward procedural posture. In addition, Breard's argument that Virginia's failure to comply with the Vienna Convention entitled him to relief from his conviction may well have been flawed on the merits. More interesting than Breard's personal claims are the responses to the ICJ's order of provisional measures. The ICJ ordered the U.S. government to "take all measures at its disposal." What measures were at the national government's disposal? In particular, could the U.S. government direct that Virginia forgo its prosecution because of the state's failure to comply with the convention? To focus the discussion, suppose that Congress enacted a statute implementing the convention with two basic elements. First, Congress directs all state police officials to ask all persons whom they arrest whether they are foreign nationals and then to inform immediately those who are of their rights under the Vienna Convention. Second, Congress provides that no person entitled to such information can be prosecuted if the information was not given and that convictions obtained when the information was not given are void. Would such a statute be constitutional? Similarly, one can ask where the national government gets the authority to represent to foreign nations that state governments will not invoke their ordinary criminal processes, including the option of the death penalty.

Applying subject-matter limitations in the context of international relations is likely to prove quite difficult. A subject-matter limitation appropriate to the context of international relations would have to accommodate two concerns: the national interest in conducting international affairs and federalism. The Court's federalism doctrine provides only hints at what such an accommodation might look like. Those hints suggest that the accommodation might place in doubt national actions that go back to the early republic. Applying the anti-commandeering principle to international affairs would have similar effects. The Court has supported the anti-commandeering principle by pointing out that Congress has only recently attempted to direct state officials to enforce national policy. That argument seems unavailable with respect to national power over international affairs. Finally, the Court's articulation of the anti-commandeering principle allows a number of escape hatches, some of which are rather clearly applicable to the Breard and Soering litigation.

Subject-matter limitations will be difficult to develop in the context of Congress's power in international affairs, and so will be applying the anti-commandeering principle. One problem is that the Court's federalism decisions have been concerned with what it characterized as innovative exercises of congressional power. For example, the Court used the fact that Congress had only recently begun to commandeer state executive officials in support of the anti-commandeering rule.[42] But, treaties in which the U.S. government agreed to legal rules that according to contemporaneous understandings it could not otherwise enact go back to the nation's first years.[43] Even more, the Constitution unambiguously gives Congress the power to "define and punish . . . Offences against the Law of Nations,"[44] some of which might be the subject of ordinary state criminal law. Professor David Golove notes early treaties overriding state laws barring aliens from owning real property, which might fall within the present Court's area of "land use regulation," despite the fact that no one at the time thought that Congress had a general power, independent of its treaty-making power, to prescribe rules of real property law applicable in the states.[45] Professor A. Mark Weisburd, describing treaties upheld by the Supreme Court that overrode state laws regulating inheritance of lands by aliens, suggests that "regulation of . . . those subjects would even today be difficult to bring within the powers of Congress described in Article I of the Constitution."[46]

What shape might a doctrine limiting the treaty power take?[47] One might think that just as regulation premised on the commerce clause must target truly commercial activities, so regulation premised on the treaty power or other international affairs powers must target subjects truly appropriate for international agreement.[48] The problem with this suggestion is that it is quite difficult to identify subjects that are not appropriate for international agreement.

The difficulty comes in two forms. First, in a globalized world the line between domestic matters and international ones is increasingly difficult to draw—far more difficult than drawing the line between commercial and noncommercial activities.[49] As Professor Goldsmith puts it, the difficulty of identifying U.S. foreign relations interests "is exacerbated by the waning of the distinction between domestic and foreign affairs. . . . In truth there is no definitive way of divining the U.S. foreign relations interest in a particular context or the manner in which this interest would be best accommodated. The Constitution gives these tasks primarily to the political branches that have the expertise and structure to perform them relatively well."[50]

Second, and probably more important, determining what is a matter for international agreement is not a unilateral decision made by the United States; it is a bilateral or multilateral one made in negotiations with other nations not necessarily concerned about U.S. domestic arrangements. So, for example, U.S. negotiators could come to the table with proposals that in U.S. constitutional terms might deal solely with matters uncontroversially within the scope of the treaty power, such as international trade or the international rendition of fugitives from prosecution by the United States. The negotiating partners might see this as an occasion for raising other issues. For example, they might take the position that they will agree to extradite those charged with federal money-laundering offenses only if the United States agrees to prohibit the execution of juvenile offenders charged in both federal and state courts.[51] The U.S. treaty makers—the president and the Senate—might agree to this proposal because they think the trade-off worth it. Standing alone, the ban on the execution of juvenile offenders might not be a matter appropriate for international agreement, but the extradition issue clearly is.[52] It is hard to understand why U.S. negotiators' hands should be tied when they seek to accomplish what all would concede are appropriate foreign-policy objectives.

The foregoing example suggests the difficulty with the other approach to subject-matter limitations: carving out enclaves where only the states may regulate. One can readily devise scenarios in which the treaty makers can accomplish concededly national objectives only by trading off some matters otherwise within the control of the states. For example, in the middle of a trade negotiation one of the trading partners says, "Well, we'll concede to you and allow the distribution in our country of food products from the U.S. in which biotechnology was involved, although our people are going to be pretty upset about that. To offset their concern, though, in exchange you've got to stop executing juvenile offenders anywhere in the United States." As Professor Weisburd puts it, the United States enters negotiations with other nations "because it wants something from the other party or parties to the treaty, not because it seeks to use the treaty as a mechanism for domestic regulation," but "[d]omestic effects may be inevitable."[53] It is implausible to impute to the Framers, or to any reasonable manner of constructing a national government, an interest in creating a structure that bars the national government from achieving national objectives in a manner that interferes with state prerogatives, when compelled to do so by its negotiating partners.[54]

The preceding argument also responds to the Court's expressed concern that constitutional doctrine must not authorize Congress to do whatever its members think wise policy without regard to the source of their power to do good things. The Court's concern arises from the perception that Congress may act on its own, to do what it wants. The treaty context comes close to eliminating the possibility of unilateral action by Congress or the treaty makers: National lawmakers cannot do whatever *they* want but only what other nations require them to do in order to extract an agreement from those other nations to do something in the U.S. national interest. The bargaining context, that is, sets the limits on Congress's unilateral action that the Court has sought through constitutional doctrine in the purely domestic context.

Professor Curtis Bradley has suggested one final subject-matter limitation. Under his proposal, Congress's power in international affairs, in particular the treaty power, would not be an *independent* source of national authority.[55] That is, no law could survive a federalism-based challenge unless its defenders could identify some source of congressional power other than the treaty power that is sufficient to authorize the statute. Professor Bradley's proposal is reminiscent of controversies in an earlier era over whether the spending clause was an independent source of national power, or whether instead Congress could appropriate money to achieve objectives determined only by some other enumerated power. The Supreme Court rejected the latter proposition,[56] thus avoiding the problem that the alternative interpretation would have rendered the spending clause redundant. Redundancy is something of a problem in connection with Professor Bradley's proposal as well, because it would not authorize the national government to do anything domestically that it could not do anyway.[57] Professor Bradley points out, however, that his proposal would not make the treaty power completely redundant because it would authorize the national government to enter into agreements that would bind it internationally, that is, would create obligations that, if breached, would subject it to international sanction. Note, however, that

Professor Bradley's proposal means that the United States simply cannot comply with some provisions in international agreements the Constitution allows it to make. It is only a slight exaggeration to say that under his proposal, the nation would be in violation of its international obligations at the moment it entered the agreement. Again, it is difficult to understand why one would design a constitution having that shape.

A requirement that international agreements deal with matters truly appropriate for international agreement, or a rule that the treaty power was not an independent source of domestic authority, might bar what might be called sham treaties. Such treaties are agreements ginned up by the U.S. treaty makers simply to accomplish something they could not accomplish under any other power.[58] One must imagine U.S. officials approaching some foreign partner saying, "Look, could you do us a favor? We want to do something—regulate land use, eliminate the death penalty for juveniles—that the Supreme Court won't let us do on our own. But if you sign on to an agreement that obligates us to do it, then everything would be hunky-dory under our Constitution." Perhaps there is a reason to construct constitutional doctrine to guard against such a remote possibility.[59] Doctrines, though, have a tendency to expand beyond their rationales, and the risk of doctrinal creep probably exceeds the risk that the United States would negotiate sham treaties, in which case it would be better not to create a doctrine whose sole function is to bar sham treaties.[60]

In sum, it is quite hard to devise a reasonable subject-matter limitation on Congress's power in the international domain. Even in the new constitutional order, an agreement to eliminate the juvenile death penalty should be upheld.[61] But, as I argue later in this chapter, in that order the United States is unlikely to make such an agreement.

THE ANTI-COMMANDEERING PRINCIPLE AND INTERNATIONAL AFFAIRS

There is an obvious objection to the argument so far. Suppose the negotiating partners demanded that the U.S. government enact not a law impermissible for federalism reasons but a law violating the First Amendment.[62] The New Deal–Great Society order accepted the proposition that the foreign affairs power was limited by the Constitution's protections of liberty.[63] But, if the United States can override federalism concerns to achieve its foreign policy goals, why can it not override the Bill of Rights for the same reason?

One answer may simply be that the New Deal–Great Society constitutional order accepted a sharp distinction between individual liberties, enumerated in the Constitution, and what Justice Oliver Wendell Holmes called the "invisible radiation" of the Tenth Amendment.[64] Another answer may be that the treaty power is indeed limited by federalism concerns, conceptualized as arising independent of the substantive scope of the treaty power.[65] The issue then becomes one of identifying an appropriate federalism doctrine limiting not just the Treaty Power but all enumerated powers. At present the only candidate for such a doctrine is the anti-commandeering principle.

The Soering case raises an anti-commandeering question that appears to have gone unnoticed. The U.S. secretary of state made representations to the United Kingdom about what the state of Virginia would do. Where does it get the power to make a commitment that would bind Virginia? The answer international lawyers would give is the doctrine known as *speciality*. The doctrine of speciality permits post-extradition limitations on the power to prosecute. Most reported speciality cases appear to involve limitations on the U.S. government's power to prosecute after extradition, but state courts assume that they must enforce limitations pursuant to. representations by the U.S. government.[66] It seems to be assumed as well that the doctrine applies to limitations on post-extradition punishment, or at least to representations that the death penalty will not be invoked. Further, a federal statute provides, "Whenever any person is delivered by any foreign government to an agent of the United States, for the purpose of being brought within the United States and tried for any offense of which he is duly accused, the President shall have power to take all necessary measures . . . for [the accused person's] security against lawless violence."[67] Although the context clearly suggests a concern for protecting against mob violence, the term "lawless violence" might reasonably be interpreted to refer to a state government's refusal to comply with the doctrine of speciality. In addition, the extradition of a particular individual after a representation by the United States that triggers the doctrine of speciality might be regarded as an executive agreement made pursuant to the overarching extradition treaty, and as an executive agreement would bar states from acting in a manner inconsistent with the agreement.[68]

All the foregoing rests on assumptions with which the New Deal–Great Society constitutional order was comfortable. Has anything changed in the new constitutional order? Perhaps the new order's toleration of commandeering with strong historic roots is sufficient to explain why the representations made in *Soering* should bind Virginia.[69] Perhaps the explanation is that the doctrine of speciality is available as a defense to a criminal prosecution and is therefore applied by state courts even though the representations made are about what executive officials will do. According to the Supreme Court, the anti-commandeering principle does not bar the national government from imposing obligations on state judges.[70] Perhaps Virginia's governor would not violate the law in directing that Soering *face* the death penalty in court, but the Virginia state courts would be obligated to invoke the doctrine of speciality and relieve Soering of the risk of execution.

The Vienna Convention's requirement that police officials advise foreign nationals of their rights under the Convention seems a straightforward example of commandeering pursuant to a treaty.[71] Other treaties might direct state officials to comply with international human rights norms in ways requiring that they act rather than refrain from acting.[72] Similarly, treaties might require that effective remedies be provided for violations of human rights. Creating such remedies might require legislation.[73] Do these possibilities raise constitutional questions?

The Court's anti-commandeering decisions describe a quite limited exception that might be applicable to the Vienna Convention problem, though not to the others. The exception, described by Justice O'Connor and not disclaimed by the Court, would allow Congress to require state officials to compile information and report that information to federal officials.[74] The decisions do not provide a justification for this exception.[75] The Court asserted that it lacked the capacity to determine whether congressional requirements were too burdensome,[76] so it cannot be that information compilation does not impose real burdens on state officials. The most prominent functional reason the Court offered for the anti-commandeering doctrine is that commandeering diffuses political responsibility by making it unclear to citizens whether they should complain to local officials or to their representatives in Congress about some action they dislike. As we saw in chapter 2, commentators have questioned the cogency of this argument,[77] but perhaps it explains why Congress may require state officials to compile information. The Court might believe that few citizens are likely to complain about state officials' efforts to obtain the information Congress requires, or that Congress has asked state officials merely to assemble in a form Congress requires information they already have obtained for their own purposes. I have my doubts about these factual propositions, but something like them must underlie a functional explanation of the exception to the anti-commandeering doctrine.

Perhaps Congress might require notification as well as information compilation.[78] Notification is, in one sense, simply information compilation in reverse: Instead of asking someone for information, the police officials provide information to that person. And yet, the Court's functional concerns seem to come into play here. Providing the required information might be burdensome, particularly when the police officials must locate a consular official who might be far away.[79] Obviously the person receiving the information is unlikely to complain. But what about the victims and their families? Notifying a criminal suspect of his or her Miranda rights is controversial when the notification is required by the Court's interpretation of the U.S. Constitution because, critics think, it interferes with the ability of the government effectively to enforce the criminal law. Might not notification required by a treaty be at least as controversial? Describing the problem *after* a failure to notify has occurred, one commentator observes that executive officials face "a difficult decision . . .—whether to adhere to an international obligation that most of their constituents probably did not know of or understand, or whether to adhere to their states' criminal justice concerns."[80] The public might well project the same conflict back to the time when notification is actually given. The argument from diffusion of political responsibility in controversial settings seems no less powerful here than in the cases the Court decided.[81]

Perhaps one might conceptualize a notification requirement somewhat differently. As noted earlier, the Court's anti-commandeering doctrine applies to efforts by Congress to commandeer state legislative and executive officials, but the Court allows Congress to commandeer state judicial officers. The doctrine thus implicates the separation of powers on the state level. Modern separation-of-powers doctrine has two competing strands.[82] In one, the three branches are sharply separated. According to this strand, a notification requirement would clearly be imposed on state executive officials and would be subject to the anti-commandeering requirement. In the other strand, however, the lines are blurred, largely for functional reasons. This strand might support an argument locating the notification requirement somewhere on the edges of the judicial branch because notification is closely bound up with criminal prosecutions heard by the courts.[83]

Once again history might justify some degree of commandeering pursuant to the treaty power. According to Professor A. Mark Weisburd, "early treaties included topics that apparently required action by local executive officials."[84] One might read the Court's anti-commandeering decisions to mean that commandeering that lacks a decent historical pedigree is impermissible, leaving open the possibility that long-established forms of commandeering, such as consular notification, are constitutionally permissible.

The Court has offered another, substantially more expansive way of working around the anti-commandeering principle.[85] The analysis is deceptively simple. Assume that Congress may preempt state action, directing the states to do nothing about a particular problem. Then, according to the Court, Congress can restore authority to the states on condition that they enact legislation Congress wants or on condition that their executive officers do something that Congress wants.

Professor Carlos Vázquez defends the Vienna Convention's requirements by invoking the conditional preemption doctrine.[86] According to him, the convention says to state officials, "Of course you don't have to arrest foreign nationals, but if you do, you have to notify them of their rights under the convention."[87] Professor Vázquez's argument is entirely compatible with the Court's articulated doctrine, but it has the effect of trivializing the anti-commandeering rule. As Professor Vázquez points out, the statutes the Court invalidated as commandeering state officials could readily be recast—and even merely reinterpreted—as conditionally preempting state law.[88] A broadly construed doctrine authorizing commandeering by means of conditional preemption would make the anti-commandeering principle one truly of form alone.

That said, the power to commandeer through conditional preemption would seem expansive enough to encompass virtually any imaginable international agreement that would effectively require states to comply with international human rights norms. Consider again the death penalty for juvenile offenders. Recall that I have argued that it is nearly impossible to devise a doctrine that would take some subject matter off the table for international negotiation. If that argument is right, there can be no subject-matter limitation barring the national government from agreeing by treaty to regulate ordinary crime. Pursuant to a treaty, then, Congress could enact a statute making every capital crime committed by a juvenile in states with the juvenile death penalty exclusively a federal offense, punishable by something other than death. With the power to preempt, Congress can then exercise the conditional-preemption power and authorize states to prosecute juvenile offenders but only on condition that they not be subject to capital punishment.[89]

Perhaps the intuition behind the anti-commandeering principle can be salvaged by transforming the Court's concern with the diffusion of political responsibility. As Professor Weisburd puts it, the early treaties "do not purport to bring about *fundamental* changes in state governmental structures."[90] As noted above, Congress's self-serving purposes and impulse to aggrandize its power at the expense of the states might be constrained at least a bit in the treaty context because the other nations with whom the treaty makers deal may have no interest in helping Congress become more powerful. In this context, then, a rule more limited than the anti-commandeering one might be defensible: The treaty makers cannot enter into agreements that would fundamentally change state governments.

The Burma Law and Preemption Doctrine

Preemption law raises questions about the relative scope of national and state power. A national statute that preempts a state law displaces the state's authority to accomplish the goals sought by the state legislature and, ultimately, by the state's voters.[91] The more broadly the *power* to preempt is construed, the smaller the scope for state authority, and similarly the more broadly *statutes* are construed as preemptive, the narrower the scope of state authority. Preemption law should therefore be integrated with the law dealing directly with the relative scope of national and state power, that is, with the constitutional law of federalism, if the nation is to have a coherently unified law of national and state power.

As we have seen, the new constitutional order has reduced the scope of national regulatory power somewhat. One might expect a parallel development in the law of preemption. The Court's decisions on the scope of national power limit Congress's ability to displace states' judgments about the policies they can pursue. Preemption law is *about* Congress's power to displace such judgments. As the Court restricts Congress's power to displace state policy judgments in one area, it might do the same in the other. And, the Court may indeed have done so, at least in the arena of domestic policy.[92]

Preemption law operates on three levels. On the highest and most general level, we have broad principles about preemption; on the next, we have specific tests for determining when a national statute displaces state law; and on the lowest, we have the application of those tests to particular statutes. Focusing on the most general level provides the best illumination of the relation among globalization, national power, and state law.

I think it helpful to describe the possibilities for preemption law as lying along a continuum ranging from maximum national power at one end to maximum state power on the other. For present purposes, it is sufficient to identify five points: preemption *in* the Constitution; a presumption in favor of preemption; neutral statutory interpretation; a presumption *against* preemption; and constitutional immunity from preemption. As we will see, the opinion in *Crosby*, the Burma Law decision, is written in a way that rules out only the proposition that Massachusetts's statute is immune from preemption because of federalism concerns. The opinion is self-consciously written as an exercise in neutral statutory interpretation, but it leaves the other three possibilities open.[93]

The Constitution preempts state law when it gives Congress exclusive power to prescribe the rules dealing with some subject.[94] Preemption in the Constitution might be thought to be rare because it creates a troublesome risk: The subject matter may be one as to which there ought to be regulation, according to some policy views, and yet Congress may not enact any regulation at all, not because it makes a conscious decision to reject those policy views but because Congress uses its limited time and political energy to deal with other problems. The area goes unregulated, despite the possibility that the area is one in which regulation is desirable, if Congress's power is exclusive and Congress fails to act.

Still, preemption in the Constitution is more common than one might initially think. Historically the proposition that Congress's power to regulate interstate commerce was exclusive had a fair amount of support in the Supreme Court. Justice William Johnson's separate opinion in *Gibbons v. Ogden* specifically endorsed that proposition,[95] and Chief Justice John Marshall's opinion for the Court conceded that the proposition had "great force."[96] The *Gibbons* Court did not adopt Justice Johnson's view, however, because it did adopt a broad definition of the scope of the power to regulate interstate commerce.[97] With such a definition the risk was too high that there would be large areas of subjects that ought to be regulated but were not.[98]

Foreign affairs might be one place we could find preemption in the Constitution, and the Court came close to doing so in its controversial decision in *Zschernig v. Miller*.[99] There the Court invalidated an Oregon statute that barred nonresident aliens from inheriting property from an Oregon resident if the alien lived in a country that might confiscate the inheritance. The Court found that statutes like Oregon's "radiate[d] some of the attitudes of the 'cold war,' where the search is for the 'democracy quotient' of a foreign regime as opposed to the Marxist theory."[100] Justice Douglas, writing for a unanimous Court,[101] found that the statute was "an intrusion by the State into the field of foreign affairs which the Constitution entrusts to the President and the Congress."[102] He did so notwithstanding a representation by the Department of Justice that the specific application of Oregon's statute did not "unduly interfere[] with the United States' conduct of foreign relations."[103] According to the Court, "As one reads the Oregon decisions, it seems that foreign policy attitudes, the freezing or thawing of the 'cold war,' and the like are the real desiderata. Yet they of course are matters for the Federal Government, not for local probate courts."[104] Justice Stewart, concurring, was even more explicit: The Oregon statute "launch[es] the State upon a prohibited voyage into a domain of exclusively federal competence."[105] Preemption in *Zschernig* arose from the Constitution itself.[106]

State power might be displaced somewhat less if the Court adopted a presumption in favor of preemption. Again the foreign affairs field provides the best examples. States have attempted to tax the activities of multinational corporations in ways that place some of their non–United States business in the states' tax base. Not surprisingly, the corporations object and frequently influence their home nations to place pressure on the United States to reduce the tax burden. These foreign relations complications of state tax policy might support a presumption in favor of preemption. For, as Justice Blackmun put it in *Japan Line, Ltd. v. County of Los Angeles*, "In international relations and with respect to foreign intercourse and trade the people of the United States act through a single government with unified and adequate national power."[107]

The Court effectively rejected the proposition that there should be a presumption in favor of preemption in *Barclays Bank PLC v. Franchise Tax Board*.[108] *Barclays Bank* involved a highly controversial application of California's corporate tax.[109] Executive officials with foreign affairs responsibilities had repeatedly expressed concern about the state's tax system.[110] But the Court found that *Congress* had the constitutional power to regulate interstate commerce and knew of the foreign affairs problems California's tax system was causing, and Congress had not enacted any statutes restricting California's ability to apply its tax system as it chose.

Barclays Bank applies ordinary preemption standards in the foreign affairs context. It amounts to more than a movement away from the stronger position taken in *Zschernig*, because cases like *Japan Line*, with their emphasis on the need for the nation to speak with a single voice, seemed to suggest that there might be a presumption in favor of preemption in matters affecting foreign affairs.[111] Consistent with the broader view articulated by Castells, law professor Peter Spiro has suggested that the rationale for a presumption in favor of preemption in such matters has been weakened by globalization.[112] The "one voice" rationale rested on the view that the position of the national government would be compromised and its diplomacy made unnecessarily complicated unless the entire nation stood behind the positions taken by the national government. But, according to Spiro, globalization has enhanced the ability of non–U.S. nations to distinguish between actions taken by the United States and those taken by its subnational units and to target only the latter for retaliation.[113] The entity called the United States might still have to speak with one voice, but the presence of other voices, Spiro argues, need not compromise what that one voice is saying.

Still further along the continuum is the position in which preemption questions are ordinary matters of statutory interpretation, with no presumption that national statutes either override or preserve state authority.[114] *Geier v. American Honda Motor Co., Inc.* can be taken to illustrate this position.[115] There the issue was whether a federal safety standard preempted state tort law. The case involved an accident in which a car collided with a tree. The plaintiff sued the car's manufacturer, alleging that a car without an airbag was negligently designed. The relevant federal statute authorized the Department of Transportation to issue safety standards. The department's standard required some but not all pre-1987 cars to have airbags, and the standard did not require that the plaintiff's car have an airbag.

The federal statute had two provisions dealing with preemption. One provision expressly preempted state "safety standards applicable to the same aspect of performance" different from the federally prescribed standard. The manufacturer argued that state tort law established standards of conduct and was therefore preempted. The Court found it unnecessary to address that claim because of the statute's second provision. This one provided that compliance with a federal standard did not "exempt" anyone from liability under tort law. In effect, the savings provision canceled out the express preemption provision.

But, the Court held, that left matters as they would have been without any statutory provisions addressing preemption: "The two provisions, read together, reflect a neutral policy, not a specially favorable or unfavorable policy, towards the application of ordinary conflict pre-emption principles."[116] The Court thus held that it should apply the ordinary preemption principle that a national statute preempts state rules that actually conflict with the national law. Justice Stevens, writing for four dissenters, argued that the savings clause showed that the manufacturer should carry a "special burden" in attempting to establish preemption.[117] The Court rejected that proposition, however. Justice Breyer asked, "Why . . . would Congress not have wanted ordinary preemption principles to apply where an actual conflict with a federal objective is at stake?"[118] Allowing a state to enforce a rule that actually conflicted with federal law "would take from those who would enforce a federal law the very ability to achieve the law's . . . objectives."[119]

The Court in *Geier* invoked ordinary principles of statutory interpretation, rejecting the dissent's claim that there ought to be a presumption against preemption.[120] It is possible to reach the same point on the continuum even if one recognizes a presumption *against* preemption. Sometimes something will offset such a presumption, not in the sense of giving a reason to conclude that national law preempts state law notwithstanding the presumption but in the sense of nullifying the presumption, thereby allowing the Court to apply ordinary principles of statutory interpretation.[121]

The Court's decision in *United States v. Locke* provides a useful illustration.[122] The case involved a state law regulating the design and operation of oil tankers, which the Court found preempted by national law. The Court emphasized the pervasive national interest in the regulation of navigation. The international implications of navigation regulation suggested that it was truly important that in this area the nation speak with one voice, that is, through Congress.[123] Analyzing the most important precedent, the Court concluded, "an 'assumption' of nonpre-emption is not triggered when the State regulates in an area where there has been a history of significant federal presence."[124] There should be "[n]o artificial presumption" as the Court went about the job of interpreting the preemptive effect of national law.[125]

Locke is more representative of modern preemption law than *Geier*, at least in the sense that it implicitly acknowledges the *general* availability of a presumption against preemption even though it finds that presumption offset by the need for uniform national policy in an area traditionally regulated primarily by national law. As we saw in chapter 2, the modern cases refer to "the normal presumption against pre-emption." The formulations vary. One, dating from 1947, is that "we start with the assumption that the historic police powers of the States were not to be superseded by the Federal Act unless that was the clear and manifest purpose of Congress."[126]

Crosby suggests that this "normal" presumption might be inapplicable in the area of foreign affairs. But *Crosby* was careful to "leave for another day" the possibility that there still might be a general presumption against preemption, finding that, even assuming that "some presumption against preemption is appropriate," the Massachusetts Burma Law was preempted.[127] And *Locke* suggests the difficulties of characterization that are likely to attend any effort to distinguish among subjects for purposes of deciding whether presumptions in favor of or against preemption should be invoked. *Locke* itself presented a conflict between an interest in preserving the local environment, fairly characterized as a police power interest, and an interest in ensuring the easy operation of trade across national borders, fairly characterized as a matter on which the nation must speak with a single voice. The Court attempted to avoid that difficulty by invoking a different distinction, between "a field which the States have traditionally occupied"[128] and "an area where the federal interest has been manifest since the beginning of our Republic and is now well-established."[129] Difficulties with this distinction are obvious. First, surely there are large areas in which the contrast the Court draws is not nearly as stark as this: where the states have done some legislating, but not all that much, and where Congress too has acted, but only intermittently. Indeed, one more familiar than I with shipping, oil tankers, and the environment could almost certainly explain why the contrast the Court drew was too stark even with respect to the subject at issue in *Locke*. That is, the distinction the Court draws relies on what are likely to be readily contestable characterizations of the history of state and national regulation of the area.

Second, the distinction between areas that states historically have regulated heavily and those they have not evokes memories of the Court's unsuccessful attempt to identify areas of core state concern under the doctrinal regime of *National League of Cities v. Usery*.[130] The Court abandoned that effort when it realized the impossibility of devising a stable distinction between areas in which states have historically operated and those where their intervention was relatively recent. The distinction drawn in *Locke* seems likely to succumb to similar pressures.

The final difficulty is a more general problem of characterization. Whether something is a matter of domestic affairs or foreign affairs is not written in the book of nature; it is a characterization adopted by lawyers for particular purposes. Perhaps *shipping* is part of foreign affairs; perhaps *purchasing goods from multinational companies* is. But then again, perhaps *the environment* is part of domestic affairs; perhaps *respecting human rights* is too, in light of the legacy of the Reconstruction amendments.[131]

Crosby leaves open nearly every possibility for preemption in the area of foreign affairs.[132] Although the Court's opinion does not mention constitutionally based preemption or a presumption in favor of preemption, the case's result is consistent with either position; the opinion expressly invokes ordinary principles of statutory interpretation; and the opinion notes that the Court would reach the same result even if it invoked a presumption against preemption. The only possibility *Crosby* rules out is a constitutionally based *immunity* from preemption with respect to the subject of the Burma Law.[133] The Court adverted to such a possibility in noting that a prior opinion had "rejected the argument that a State's 'statutory scheme . . . escapes pre-emption because it is an exercise of the State's spending power rather than its regulatory power.' "[134] Although the Court did not put it this way, it in effect held that there was no "market participant" exception to Congress's power to preempt state law analogous to the "market participant" exception to the judicially developed rule that states may not discriminate against out-of-state commerce.[135]

In all three of the preemption cases described here, which I believe to be representative of the contemporary Court's approach, the Court effectively limited the reach of *state* regulatory authority. As Justice Stevens noted in his dissent in *Geier*, preemption cases are "about federalism."[136] But when the Court has addressed federalism issues directly, it has limited the reach of *national* authority precisely to preserve the ability of states to pursue autonomously developed policies. There seems to be some tension between the Court's federalism decisions and its preemption cases. In the main, there is no direct conflict between the Court's solicitude for federalism in cases involving the scope of national power and the lack of regard it gives state authority in some preemption cases.[137] The preemption cases all involve statutes that clearly fall within Congress's power to regulate interstate and foreign commerce. The tension may be resolved in the future if the Court develops the idea of negative commandeering discussed in chapter 2. Or, perhaps more consistent with the general idea that the new constitutional order is a less ambitious one, the Court might continue to invoke ordinary principles of statutory interpretation in pre-

emption cases rather than engage in a substantial reconstruction of preemption doctrine.

THE POLITICS OF INTERNATIONAL AGREEMENTS
IN THE NEW CONSTITUTIONAL ORDER

Much existing discussion of U.S. federalism and international human
rights proceeds by hypothesizing that the United States has entered into
some international agreement that requires national action that intrudes
on matters of state concern, whether by taking over a subject matter
ordinarily regulated by state governments or by commandeering state
officials. So, for example, authors ask whether the U.S. Constitution
would preclude the nation from entering into an international agreement
to ban the imposition of death sentences on those who were juveniles
when they committed their crimes. Proceeding by hypothetical may be
particularly misleading in the new constitutional order because such
agreements are exceedingly unlikely to be adopted.

I begin with what should be obvious: Over the past generation the
treaty makers have been quite reluctant to endorse expansive exercises of
the treaty power. They have routinely added a "federalism" understanding to international agreements dealing with human rights and sometimes expressly disclaim the applicability of particular treaty provisions.[138]
The understanding attached to the Senate's ratification of the International Covenant on Civil and Political Rights asserts that "the United
States understands that this Covenant shall be implemented by the Federal Government to the extent that it exercises legislative and judicial
jurisdiction over the matters covered herein, and otherwise by the state
and local governments; to the extent that state and local governments
exercise jurisdiction over such matters, the Federal Government shall take
measures appropriate to the Federal system to the end that the competent authorities of the state or local governments may take appropriate
measures for the fulfillment of the Covenant."[139] As the Breard litigation
showed, what the United States regards as "appropriate measures" might
include deference to the domestic constitutional law of federalism, and,
as the La Grand decision shows, international interpreters might disagree.
If anything, the practice of attaching federalism understandings is likely
to strengthen in the new constitutional order.

The political origins of these "federalism" limitations are reasonably
clear. The basic features of the national governing process over the past
generation have been divided government and increasingly hostile divisions between the Democratic and Republican Parties. Acceding to the
international agreements in question has been a priority of the human
rights and internationalist wings of the Democratic Party.[140] They picked

up some support from the residual internationalist wing of the Republican Party. But Republicans have been significantly more skeptical of international institutions than Democrats. Treaties require agreement from two-thirds of the Senate, a level that cannot be reached without substantial bipartisan support in a Senate that has become increasingly divided along partisan lines even on foreign affairs issues. The federalism understandings are the price Democrats have to pay to obtain enough votes from Republicans to adopt the treaties.[141] Even Democrats, however, appear to believe that the United States, as the world's dominant power, need not respond too substantially to suggestions that it may not be meeting international standards.[142] The sharper partisan divisions in the new constitutional order make it unlikely that the United States will enter into treaties or international agreements raising serious federalism questions.[143]

New, problematic agreements may be rare. What of *existing* agreements? Some agreements made during the New Deal–Great Society constitutional order might raise questions that were not taken seriously at the time they were entered but would be taken seriously in the new constitutional order. This could occur in two ways. First, the existing agreements might be interpreted expansively. The Supreme Court's actions in the Breard litigation suggest that the Court is unlikely to provide such interpretations. Its opinion was shot through with skepticism about the claim that the Vienna Convention should be interpreted to provide *any* of the many grounds for relief Paraguay and Breard found in the convention. Nor is it likely that today's Congress would seize upon an existing treaty as the basis for legislation it could not otherwise enact.[144] Second, the existing agreements might be unambiguous.[145] The Vienna Convention, for example, really does command state police officials to take particular actions; the ambiguities the Court found in the convention concerned the remedy, not the underlying obligation. As we have seen, however, the unambiguous agreements raising serious federalism questions have a rather strong pedigree. The Court could enforce federalism limitations only by engaging in a revolutionary transformation of constitutional doctrine. But it need not do so. The existing agreements that unambiguously raise federalism questions are, I believe, rather few in number; these exceptional cases can be preserved without threatening any serious federalism concerns the Court might have in the new constitutional order.[146]

In the new constitutional order, then, the Supreme Court is not likely to have any *need* to develop constitutional doctrines dealing with power to regulate international affairs that limit national power in the name of federalism. Modesty, not revolution, is the order of the day.

REGULATION IN THE NEW
CONSTITUTIONAL ORDER

WELFARE REFORM and tax cuts: How can a government that manages to enact such programs be fairly described as having chastened constitutional ambitions? So far I have described the New Deal–Great Society as having substantive commitments to an otherwise unspecified programmatic liberalism. Law professor Richard Stewart, who oversaw the Department of Justice's environmental programs during the first Bush administration, describes two propositions established by the New Deal: "[T]he federal government ought to take responsibility for the overall productivity and health of the economy at the macro-economic level [and] . . . had a basic responsibility for protecting individuals and families against the economic risks of an industrial market economy through various means of social insurance and assistance."[1]

Welfare reform and tax cuts do not fundamentally repudiate those commitments, however. Instead, both respond to perceived failures of the *strategies* used during the New Deal–Great Society regime to achieve that regime's programmatic goals. Welfare reform and tax cuts provide incentives to individuals to do what the government thinks desirable without direct regulatory coercion. Programs like vouchers for education or social services are even more continuations of earlier programmatic commitments through new strategies. Political scientist John Coleman observes that "Republicans of the 1990s did not withdraw the federal government from major areas of responsibility initiated in the 1930s and 1940s. They rearranged and restructured these areas and introduced new approaches but did not radically restrict federal responsibility in economy, society, and culture."[2] The revived interest in federalism led to devolution of welfare state functions to lower levels of governments but not to their evaporation. As three political scientists note, "[T]he Republican advocates of privatization hoped that by shifting public functions to state and local authorities there might also be an absolute reduction in those functions, but part of the reason for this shift was that there was no constituency for eliminating the welfare state entirely."[3] An observer of international trends puts the point more generally: "[L]iberalization, deregulation, and privatization have not reduced the role of state intervention overall, just shifted it from decommodifying bureaucracies to marketizing ones."[4]

Having focused on the Supreme Court in most of the book, I return to where I began—the operation of the political institutions of the new constitutional order—for two reasons. I want to end by emphasizing that the *constitutional* order extends beyond the Supreme Court, and I hope to identify the mode of welfare state regulation that may be characteristic of the new order. We can see the distinctive characteristics of the new constitutional order best by examining briefly the way in which its institutions carry out the continued programmatic commitments it has inherited from the New Deal and Great Society. First, consider environmental, consumer protection, and similar regulatory endeavors. The initial point to note is that complete deregulation is not a realistically foreseeable outcome of politics in the new constitutional order. Some strong conservatives will continue to advocate complete deregulation, but the political forces sustaining continued government involvement in these areas are strong enough to forestall the abolition of the Consumer Product Safety Commission or the Environmental Protection Agency.[5]

Whenever some regulatory problem arises there are today two near-consensus policies: disclosure and output measures.[6] Information—about what a factory is discharging into the atmosphere or the local waters, about the risks associated with a toy—can be a commodity, of course. A strong deregulatory regime would leave disclosures to the market for information just as it would leave the design of products to the market. The contemporary consensus that finds mandated disclosures attractive rests on arguments about failures in the market for information that parallel precisely the arguments accepted during the prior regime about failures in the markets for products. That parallel suggests that the near consensus on mandated disclosures rests more on political principles defining the chastened scope of the new constitutional order's ambitions than on economic principles about market failure.

The case for output measures accepts the prior regime's programmatic commitments as well. The typical regulatory method in the New Deal–Great Society constitutional order was "command and control." Congress, either directly or through administrative agencies, would specify the operating methods businesses had to use—the technologies for reducing air pollution, the width of slats in baby cribs, and the like. These command-and-control methods became increasingly discredited. That happened in part though a clever rhetorical move that associated the regulatory method with the command-and-control methods of the failed socialist economies. Another perhaps more important reason for the political failure of command-and-control regulation was its combination of intrusiveness and arbitrariness. Command-and-control regulations specify what businesses must do in great detail. Sometimes the prescriptions are inapt for some of the businesses to which they apply. Businesses faced with regulations requiring them to do one thing when they were reaching the goals the government wanted—reducing air pollution by their own methods rather than by the ones the government prescribed—complained about unnecessary government regulation. Even more, the government really had no ability to inspect every business to determine whether it was complying with the command-and-control regulations. The number of inspectors was simply too small. Enforcing command-and-control regulations came to have the quality of lightning striking: One business would be hit with a fine while a neighbor, doing exactly the same thing, was not.

The consensus alternative to command-and-control regulations is output measures. Such measures involve the government saying, "Here's where we want you to be in a year—reduce discharges of pollutant Z by 15 percent, cut the number of injuries to consumers using your products by 50 percent, and the like. All we care about is results. We don't care what you do to get them." Two features of output measures deserve emphasis. First, and most obvious, the government does care about the results. That is, the near consensus on using output measures reflects a continuing commitment to government supervision of economic behavior and, like the near consensus on disclosure, decisively rejects the strongest possible deregulatory agenda. Second, the government does have to specify the desired level of output. Politics does not disappear from the regulatory process, but its focus changes from identifying which command-and-control methods should be prescribed to selecting the desired level of output.

The movement from the New Deal–Great Society regime to the present one has of course been a movement toward the right. One consequence is that conservatives have done relatively little theorizing about regulatory policy in the new constitutional order. Having seen the system move in their direction, they hope that it will continue to do so, that is, that the new regulatory regime will be one of strong deregulation and privatization. And, of course, they have political reasons for continuing to insist that deregulation and privatization should be extended. Probably the most prominent alternative to conservative theorizing about deregulation is the "Third Way" theory associated with European social democrats.[7] However, because the European political, economic, and social setting within which Third Way ideas developed differs so much from the U.S. setting, programmatic suggestions emerging from Third Way theorists provide little help in thinking about regulation in the new U.S. constitutional order.

Scattered initiatives undertaken by the Clinton administration had a Third Way flavor to them, but they were not brought together into a systematic set of principles that theorists could explain as part of the new constitutional order's regime principles.[8] The Environmental Protection Agency developed a number of projects that offered alternatives to command-and-control regulations.[9] Some involved "negotiated regulation," in which the agency sat down with representatives of various interest groups—or "stakeholders"—to develop command-and-control regulations that everyone could live with. Probably the most prominent initiative was Project XL, which invited companies to submit plans for achieving environmental goals. If the EPA approved the plans after consulting other stakeholders, the companies would be exempted from complying with various regulatory requirements.[10]

The Clinton administration developed a similar program in the area of workplace safety, which it called Maine 200.[11] The two hundred companies in Maine with the worst safety records were given a choice between facing intensified enforcement through more frequent inspections or cooperating with the Occupational Safety and Health Administration's experts to develop effective safety programs. They would drop to the bottom of the enforcement list if they choose cooperation. Workers themselves sometimes participated in the consultation process, helping OSHA and their employers identify problems and potential solutions.

Charles Sabel and his colleagues describe a longstanding program for cleaning up the Chesapeake Bay.[12] The EPA and the governors of several states signed an agreement setting up an executive council to develop plans to restore the bay's ecosystem. After several years of experience, a new agreement was negotiated, which created specific monitoring plans. The next step involved revising the plans to include specific goals aimed at particular tributaries flowing into the bay. The program began as a project developed almost entirely by government officials, but as it developed public participation grew. Beyond mere public education, the program's participants began to enlist the public as monitors of discharges into the bay and eventually as members of teams that could draw on intensely local knowledge about particular tributaries to design implementation plans for each tributary.

Sabel, working with other scholars from the fields of law, sociology, and political science, has identified these initiatives as a distinctive regulatory form, which he calls "democratic experimentalism." Democratic experimentalism has several characteristics.[13] Instead of focusing on the macro-economic problems that preoccupied the New Deal–Great Society regime, democratic experimentalism deals with practical problems and almost always on a scale that allows ordinary, nonexperts to be involved and draw on their local knowledge to suggest solutions. At the same time, however, the central government does more than accept the solutions arrived at locally, as it might in a purely federalist arrangement. Instead, the central government's institutions, including administrative agencies like the EPA and OSHA, monitor the local solutions and try to identify which ones seem promising for use elsewhere. That is, it treats the local decision-making processes as experiments that produce results that can be transferred to other communities. Drawing on experience in the private sector, proponents of democratic experimentalism describe it as involving several stages: benchmarking (identifying processes used elsewhere that are both better than the ones currently in use and achievable by the organization); concurrent engineering (the repeated adjustment of ends and means as experience accumulates); and monitoring to detect and correct errors.[14] Adapted to government, they write,

> The model requires linked systems of local and inter-local or federal pooling of information . . . so that actors scrutinize their initial understandings of problems and feasible solutions. These principles enable the actors to learn from one another's successes and failures while reducing the vulnerability created by the decentralized search for solutions.[15]

The affinities between democratic experimentalism and the regime principles of the new constitutional order are apparent. The smaller scale of the experiments fits well with the new order's chastened ambitions. Its emphasis on local decision making fits well with the new order's interest in federalism "understood as experimentalist collaboration between the states and the federal government,"[16] as does its focus on empowering ordinary people and deflating expert claims to knowledge. Perhaps most important for my purposes, Sabel and his colleagues stress that democratic experimentalist initiatives emerge when there is a consensus that something needs to be done but the array of political forces makes it impossible for the political system to produce results consistent with the wishes of any particular side.[17]

One should be cautious about democratic experimentalism as the regulatory theory for the new constitutional order. What follows is a short list of some of the obstacles that stand in the way of implementing democratic experimentalism in a vigorous form.

As its proponents acknowledge, we really have only a few experiments with democratic experimentalism, and the results are not yet in.[18] Some of the most interesting programs exist merely as descriptions or as proposals that for accidental reasons never were implemented.[19] Democratic experimentalism should be an iterative process, with central agencies learning from local ones, then encouraging local agencies to adopt the best practices that have emerged, only to learn more, modify the suggestions, and so on—almost literally. Almost no iterations have occurred yet, however: We know what the process is supposed to look like, but we do not know whether in practice the back-and-forth between central agencies and local ones will occur or be effective.

Localized deliberations might be less participatory than proponents of democratic experimentalism hope. The deliberations may be localized, but they are unlikely to be all-inclusive; the principles by which someone chooses who can participate—if only by deciding the times and places at which meetings occur—can affect the degree of real participation.[20] Further, any system giving deliberation a central role risks domination by the articulate. And, of course, participants may bring other types of power to the deliberations as well.[21] Deliberations may break down or, more damaging to the case for democratic experimentalism, may end with an apparent though false consensus, elicited by the participants' agreement, often unstated, to take some possible solutions off the table as unreasonable or unachievable.[22]

Central decision makers might impose premature closure on a set of experiments, mistakenly concluding that they have acquired enough information to impose a single solution nationwide. An example might be national education reform. A number of states began to use output measures—performance of students as measured by standardized tests—to evaluate the effectiveness of individual schools. Congress and the president agreed that output measures should be used[23] but may have selected badly designed measures as the national standard. The 1996 welfare reform statute might be another illustration of premature closure: Congress prescribed rigid time limits beyond which recipients of public assistance would be cut off and dictated that by 2002 half of all recipient families include an adult working at least thirty hours a week.[24]

Social experiments run a special hazard known as the "Hawthorne effect." The effect was discovered when specialists in industrial relations thought they could improve productivity by changing the lighting conditions at a Western Electric plant. Productivity did indeed increase. On further examination, though, it turned out that productivity increased not because of the improved lighting conditions—it increased no matter how the experimenters changed the lighting—but because the workers knew they were participating in an experiment.[25] One interpretation of the Hawthorne effect is that social experiments work *because* they are experiments.[26] Once made routine, the innovations proposed by democratic experimentalism might degenerate into the ordinary ways that contemporary bureaucracies operate.[27]

The political and legal environment for democratic experimentalist programs also poses some problems for those programs.[28] They are the liberal alternative to the more expansive unregulated devolution and deregulation favored by conservatives. Conservatives may try to obstruct their implementation for precisely that reason. The U.S. Chamber of Commerce successfully sued to block the expansion of Maine 200 nationwide.[29] The risk that experimentalist programs will collapse into the programs conservatives favor is not trivial. Appointment of a proponent of unregulated devolution as the administrator at the center would transform the program from experimentalist to mere devolution, at least for a while. Environmentalists have been quite suspicious of Project XL. One critic writes, for example, that Project XL's criteria "could result in projects that save compliance costs but are harmful to the environment, projects that deliver benefits for the environment but do not save significant costs, or projects that will have ambiguous and unpredictable effects on both compliance costs and the environment," and that "Project XL became a regulatory free-for-all, with companies requesting lengthy lists of exemptions in their initial applications that bear little if any relationship to the environmental improvements they pledged to achieve."[30] Others have been more receptive to these initiatives,[31] but the persistence of encrusted interest groups in the new constitutional order places democratic experimentalist proposals under sustained threat.

More generally, democratic experimentalism's proponents argue that democratic experimentalist projects get off the ground when there is widespread agreement that some problem requires solution yet no solution seems available. But the definition of precisely what the problem is may impose some constraints on what the experiments can show. Local deliberation occurs within a framework of existing laws, not all of which will be changed when a democratic experimentalist project begins, and the framework may restrict the choice of programs with which to experiment, thereby depriving the process of some potentially valuable innovations.

These difficulties are legal as well as practical. Divided government means that legislation authorizing innovation on a large scale, including authorization of experimentalist programs, is unlikely. That, in turn, makes experimentalism an aspect of presidential administration, which as we saw in chapter 1 can be challenged for operating outside the limits of law. In the Chamber of Commerce lawsuit, for example, the court agreed that the Clinton administration could not expand the program without going through the laborious procedures required for substantial changes in regulatory programs, procedures—it should be noted—that were designed primarily with command-and-control regulations in mind. Sabel and his colleagues, while enthusiastic about the Chesapeake Bay program, observe that some of its important components are "of dubious legal pedigree and status."[32] A widely quoted observation about Project XL indicates a broader problem that democratic experimentalist programs may face: "If it isn't illegal, it isn't XL."[33] The possibility of premature closure allows regulated businesses to claim that they are being asked to do the impossible.[34]

All this said, democratic experimentalism remains the most promising candidate for a theory of government activity in the new constitutional order. Democratic administrations will do a little more of it, Republican ones with stronger impulses to complete deregulation will do a little less. Developing experimentalism as a practical theory of government, however, might require courts willing to collaborate with Congress and the president in pushing the limits of legality.[35]

The courts are the wild card in the new constitutional order. Low voter turnout, the decline of parties as institutions to mobilize voters around programs, personalized candidacies, the stultifying effects of accumulated interests groups, divided government, ideologically polarized parties in Congress: the prospect of all these features of the new constitutional order changing seems small and the prospect of "continuing policy stasis" seems large, unless some unanticipatable crisis intervenes.[36] The Supreme Court, though, might be different, primarily because there small numbers can have large and lasting effects.[37] Still, nothing like the New Deal confrontation between the Court and the political branches seems likely because divided government will give the Court strong allies no matter what it does and, more important, because divided government will give the Court very little material out of which it could construct a crisis.

NOTES

INTRODUCTION

1. Clinton, "State of the Union 1996."

2. The regime concept has been developed primarily by students of international relations. One prominent definition is that "[r]egimes . . . [are] sets of implicit or explicit principles, norms, rules, and decision-making procedures around which actors' expectations converge." Krasner, "Structural Causes and Regime Consequences," at p. 186. Another defines a regime as "an ensemble of patterns that determines (a) the forms and channels of access to principal governmental positions, (b) the characteristics of the actors who are admitted to or excluded from such access, (c) the resources or strategies that these actors can use to gain access, and (d) the rules that are followed in the making of publicly binding decisions. To produce its effect, the ensemble must be institutionalized; that is, the various patterns must be habitually known, practiced, and accepted by most, if not all, of the actors. Increasingly, this has involved their explicit legalization or constitutionalization, but many very stable regime norms can have an implicit, informal, prudential, or precedential basis." Schmitter, *How to Democratize the European Union*, at p. 3. These formulations differ in detail, and in some contexts the differences might be significant, but they can serve my purposes by orienting readers to the general idea of a constitutional order or regime. My presentation in this book provides the details of my particular understanding of the idea of a constitutional order.

3. The principles that animate a constitutional order may come to be implemented by the courts in reviewing the constitutionality of legislation, but judicial review predicated on such principles is not a prerequisite to identifying a new constitutional order.

4. Roosevelt, "Annual Message to Congress, January 11, 1944."

5. For a discussion of the gradual nature of regime construction, see Orren and Skowronek, "Regimes and Regime Building", at pp. 698–99. Orren and Skowronek conclude that a "regime may hang together for a time, but it never really fits together, and the contentious interaction of old and new elements keeps it in a more or less constant state of transformation" (792). See also Whittington, "Dismantling the Modern States?" at p. 527 ("The constitutional order is . . . an emergent architecture that operates within and through politics itself.").

6. Bobbitt, *The Shield of Achilles*, develops an account of regime transformation that is at least a cousin to the one I develop, although Bobbitt focuses more than I do on the role of war and international affairs in creating and providing structure to constitutional orders, and although he agrees that a new constitutional order may have arisen at the end of the twentieth century, he argues that that regime replaced one that originated not in the New Deal and the Great Society but in the Civil War.

7. See Ackerman, *We the People: Foundations*; Ackerman, *We the People: Transformations*.

8. Balkin and Levinson, "Understanding the Constitutional Revolution."

9. See also Halpern and Lamb, "The Supreme Court and New Constitutional Eras" (developing a model in which "a convulsive historical event or force" precipitates a regime change).

10. Balkin and Levinson provide a detailed account of how recent Supreme Court decisions could be expanded in what they describe as a revolutionary way. Chapter 2 below provides an alternative account of those decisions.

11. Ackerman, "Discovering the Constitution," at pp. 1045–49.

12. Ackerman's claim might be a normative one about constitutionalism in general or, as I think it is, a descriptive one about the conventions of U.S. constitutionalism. The descriptive claim would then be that the American people happen to treat decisions made during constitutional moments as having greater normative weight than decisions made at other times.

13. My normative position is developed in some detail in Tushnet, *Taking the Constitution away from the Courts*.

14. I should note as well that to some extent Ackerman's formal criteria for identifying constitutional moments have a partisan motivation: He wants to show that the New Deal constitutional crisis, in which Franklin Roosevelt confronted and transformed the Supreme Court, was a constitutional moment, but that the Reagan Revolution—and its successors—was not. See Ackerman, "Revolution on a Human Scale," at pp. 2286, 2290 (noting that "none" of the New Deal's "fundamental commitments" have been "fundamentally revised *thus far*" [emphasis added] and foreseeing "an extended period of normal politics—punctuated by more failed efforts of would-be revolutionaries to shift the system into transformative mode"); Ackerman, "A Generation of Betrayal?" at pp. 1534–36 (asserting that "things did not turn out that way" in describing the possibility that the Reagan Revolution could have been consolidated by a series of pro-Republican elections); Ackerman, "Off Balance," in Ackerman, ed., *Bush v. Gore*.

15. See chapter 1 for a brief discussion of the theory of critical elections.

16. The March 2000 issue of *PS: Political Science and Politics* contains a number of articles describing the successes and failures of these voting models.

17. Cf. R. Kent Weaver and Bert A. Rockman, "Assessing the Effects of Institutions," in Weaver and Rockman, eds., *Do Institutions Matter?* at p. 39 ("Political institutions are best thought of as creating risks and opportunities for effective policymaking. Whether these risks and opportunities are realized depends upon whether the specific conditions that facilitate or limit those institutional effects are present.").

18. Balkin, "*Bush v. Gore*," at p. 1446.

CHAPTER I

1. The structural preconditions for a regime transition may have been in place earlier, but I believe that the transition was crystallized by Reagan's articulation of new regime principles.

2. The characteristic institutional form of the New Deal–Great Society regime

was the so-called iron triangle in which interest groups, the bureaucracies about which each had special concern, and congressional committees set policy in particular areas, with no institution exercising substantial control over the aggregate policies that resulted. The basic general description of the "iron triangle" political order is Ripley and Franklin, *Congress, the Bureaucracy,* and Public Policy.

3. My discussion omits any consideration of the institutions and principles of foreign policy and focuses on national-level policymaking, with only a short discussion of state and local government.

4. The classic statement of the critical election theory is Burnham, *Critical Elections and the Mainsprings of American Politics.* Arguing for longer term cycles lasting sixty to seventy years, and perhaps linked to long-term economic trends is A. James Reichley, "The Future of the American Two-Party System after 1996," in Green and Shea, eds., *The States of the Parties,* at pp. 10, 20–22. For a historian's skeptical view of claims about the importance of party realignments at least for the nineteenth century, see Formisano, "The 'Party Period' Revisited."

5. Political scientists disagree about the characterization of the new constitutional order. Some see it as the precursor of a new system in which voters have permanently realigned, while others see it as a new and distinctive party system with its own characteristics, including loose voter affiliation with the parties. For a recent overview of the former positions and a presentation of the latter one, see Aldrich, "Political Parties in a Critical Era." Here and throughout I rely on arguments made by political scientists and acknowledge that other political scientists have offered alternative arguments. I have relied on arguments that seem to me rather widely accepted even though sometimes challenged and that seem to me accurate.

6. For example, one observer wrote in 1983, "Reagan succeeded in unraveling in 1980 the political class coalition that Franklin Roosevelt has put together in 1934." Sundquist, *Dynamics of the Party System,* at p. 424.

7. An important partisan shift did occur over the past generation, as Southern white males moved from the Democratic to the Republican Party, with significant effects discussed in more detail below, text accompanying notes 42–75 below. See John Ferejohn, "A Tale of Two Congresses: Social Policy in the Clinton Years," in Weir, ed., *The Social Divide,* at p. 71 ("Racial and social conservatives have largely deserted the congressional Democratic party, which means that the principal source of internal party division has mostly evaporated, producing a much more liberal and homogenous party than ever before. The replacement of conservative southern Democrats by very conservative Republicans has also transformed the Republican party in two ways: it has made it more homogeneously conservative than it was, and the influx of southerners has increased the party's attachment to social conservatism.").

8. One index of dealignment is the seriousness with which third-party candidates John Anderson and Ross Perot were taken by the electorate. For evidence on dealignment, see Shea, "The Passing of Realignment and the Advent of the 'Base-Less' Party System," at pp. 34–40 (summarizing evidence through the 1990s); Wattenberg, *The Rise of Candidate-Centered Politics,* Presidential Elections of the 1980s at pp. 31–46 (chapter titled "Dealignment in the Electorate"); Paul Allen Beck, "The Changing American Party Coalitions," in Green and Shea,

eds., *The States of the Parties*, at p. 28 (describing creation of two electorates, one highly partisan and the other dealigned, nonpartisan, and volatile in its preferences). For evidence on the loss of Democratic Party predominance, see Meffert, Norpoth, and Ruhl, "Realignment and Macropartisanship."

9. See Pomper, "The 2000 Presidential Election," at pp. 205–6 (reporting that "[f]ewer than one of every thirteen Republicans considered themselves liberal, and fewer than one in eight Democrats were conservatives").

10. Skowronek, *The Politics Presidents Make.*

11. Franklin Roosevelt played this role for the New Deal–Great Society constitutional order and Ronald Reagan for the present one. It is important in Skowronek's argument that presidents are most effective "as an instrument of negation, . . . dislodging established elites, destroying the institutional arrangements that support them, and clearing the way for something entirely new." *The Politics Presidents Make*, at p. 27. It is therefore unimportant in Skowronek's analysis whether a new constitutional order is created within any individual president's term of office. In an observation relevant to my argument, for example, he notes that Ronald Reagan "close[d] off a prior course of development" but did not establish a new set of possibilities" (428). For additional discussion, see chapter 3.

12. See Landy and Milkis, *Presidential Greatness*, at p. 200 ("Republican presidents from Eisenhower to Nixon . . . provided no alternative public philosophy on which to base a party realignment. Initially, Reagan seemed to provide one, but . . . [a]t the critical moment, he . . . content[ed] himself with stalling the further expansion of the administrative state without challenging its fundamental tenets.").

13. According to one analysis, 69 percent of the Contract's promises were achieved "in large measure," some rather quickly and others over a longer term. Gerald M. Pomper, "Parliamentary Government in the United States?" in Green and Shea, eds., *The States of the Parties*, at pp. 258–60. The Contract's provisions included a balanced budget (achieved) and the line-item veto (enacted but held unconstitutional by the Supreme Court, *Clinton v. City of New York*, 524 US 417 [1998]), substantial changes in habeas corpus procedures and the possibility of challenges by prisoners to their conditions of confinement (enacted in the Antiterrorism and Effective Death Penalty Act, Pub. L. 104-132, 110 Stat. 1214 [1996]), and the Prison Litigation Reform Act, 42 U.S.C. § 1997e[d][3] [1994 ed., Supp. II]), increases in federal support for prison construction (enacted), welfare reform (enacted, Personal Responsibility and Work Opportunity Reconciliation Act of 1996, Pub. L. 104-193, 110 Stat. 2105 [1996]). (I should note, in anticipation of the argument in chapter 2, that the Court's invalidation of parts of the Contract with America's program is not inconsistent with my argument that the Court is part of a new constitutional order. The overall principles of that order are what matter, not the detailed programs promoted as part of the political effort to consolidate the regime.) Substantial tax cuts were finally enacted in 2001. Substantial increases in defense spending were authorized in 2002. Provisions of the Contract that have not yet been adopted include congressional term limits (which the Supreme Court held could not be imposed by statute, *U.S.*

Term Limits v. Thornton, 514 US 779 [1995]). The provisions dealing with federal regulation of environmental matters provide perhaps the largest exception to
the claim that the Contract's provisions were substantially enacted.

14. This is not to assert that the statutes identified with the Contract with
America are in some sense intrinsically major pieces of legislation. They are, however, what proponents of the new regime sought to enact. That they were enacted supports the proposition that a new regime has been established.

15. Skowronek, *The Politics Presidents Make*, at pp. 429–42.

16. Ibid., at p. 43.

17. Dwight Eisenhower's acceptance of the general outlines of the New Deal
regime is exemplary here.

18. See John J. Coleman, "Clinton and the Party System in Historical Perspective," in Schier, ed., *The Postmodern Presidency*, at p. 152 (describing Clinton as
"[t]he [p]rototypical [p]reemptive President"). For a historian's similar evaluation, see Kennedy, "Bill Clinton in the Eye of History."

19. Margaret Weir, "Political Parties and Social Policymaking," in Weir, ed.,
The Social Divide, at p. 27 (describing New Democrats' principles).

20. See David R. Mayhew, "Clinton, the 103d Congress, and Unified Party
Control," in Geer, ed., *Politicians and Party Politics*, at pp. 270, 271 (describing
Clinton's programs as extensions of prior ones). The third major initiative, health
care reform, obviously was not appropriated from the Republicans; nor was it
enacted. One reason for its failure was its New Democratic insistence on a
market-based system of health insurance, which forced the program to become
bureaucratically awkward and politically vulnerable. For analyses of the health
care initiative, see Hacker, *The Road to Nowhere*; Skocpol, *Boomerang*. Mayhew
lists eleven major pieces of legislation enacted during Clinton's first two years in
office: deficit reduction; NAFTA; the Family & Medical Leave Act; the Motor
Voter Act; the National Service Act; reform of college-student loan financing; the
Brady Act; national education goals; the omnibus crime act; California desert
protection; and legislation dealing with the World Trade Organization. Mayhew,
"Clinton, the 103d Congress, and Unified Party Control," in Geer, ed., *Politicians and Party Politics*, at pp. 264–65.

21. Cf. Sidney M. Milkis, "Political Parties and Divided Democracy," in Shull,
ed., *Presidential Policymaking*, at p. 91 (noting that Clinton's health care proposals "enraged conservatives" and "dismayed the ardent liberals of his party").
Michael Foley, "Clinton and Congress," in Hernnson and Hill, eds., *The Clinton
Presidency*, at p. 39, provides a good summary: "President Clinton's relationship
with the Congress revealed the problems of a New Democrat in mobilizing legislative support both within his party and across party lines when the agenda was a
nuanced hybrid that had to combine fiscal restraint and a recognition of the end
of 'big government' with the maintenance of the positive state and the acceptance of small yet conspicuous interventions in targeted areas of social concern."

22. For a discussion of triangulation, see Morris, *Behind the Oval Office*, ch. 5.

23. Woodward, *The Agenda*, at p. 165, quoted in Dilys M. Hill, "The Clinton
Presidency: The Man and His Times," in Hernnson and Hill, eds., *The Clinton
Presidency*, at p. 18, and in Ribuffo, "From Carter to Clinton," at p. 20. I should

note that the full quotation, provided by Ribuffo but not Hill, may be read to have an ironic tone. It continues: "We stand for lower deficits and free trade and the bond market. Isn't that great?"

24. See Berke, "Following Baby-Size Issues into Voters' Hearts" (asserting that "[i]f President Clinton transformed the Presidency . . . from a well-spring of grand ideas to one of itsy-bitsy proposals, his Vice President has gone further," and noting that "the smaller-is-better movement threatens to infiltrate American political discourse" "well beyond Mr. Gore").

25. Dorf and Sabel, "The Constitution of Democratic Experimentalism," at p. 344n. 172.

26. See also Olson, *The Rise and Decline of Nations* (arguing from public choice premises that all political regimes gradually accumulate interest groups that eventually obstruct economic growth until they are destroyed in some usually convulsive transformation like war).

27. Milkis, *The President and the Parties.*

28. For a general discussion of the relation between the New Deal and state party organizations, see Patterson, *The New Deal and the States.*

29. See Amenta, *Bold Relief,* at p. 19 (concluding that "a patronage-oriented party system" obstructed the development of "modern social spending policy" and was replaced by a "programmatic . . . political party system").

30. For a discussion of the role of progressivism in modern American liberalism, see Ribuffo, "From Carter to Clinton," at pp. 5–6. For a summary of the role of professionalism, see Whittington, "Dismantling the Modern State?" at pp. 490–93.

31. See Whittington, "Dismantling the Modern State?" at p. 492 (referring to "the replacement of locally rooted party regulars with nationally oriented experts, rooting out decentralizing ties and commitments as well as inefficiency and corruption"). See also Milkis, *The President and the Parties,* at pp. 134–36; Ginsberg and Shefter, *Politics by Other Means,* at p. 79 (asserting that bureaucratic networks centered in the institutions of the welfare state supplanted party organizations). For a discussion of later developments in staffing the president's executive office, supporting the argument that the staff has become a source of policymaking within the White House and independent of the bureaucracies, see Shirley Anne Warshaw, "Staffing Patterns in the Modern White House," in Shull, ed., *Presidential Policymaking,* at p. 131.

32. See Milkis, *The President and the Parties,* at pp. 163 (describing Eisenhower's continuation of the practice); at p. 179 (describing Lyndon Johnson's "assault" on the Democratic Party apparatus).

33. Ibid., at p. 243.

34. Theda Skocpol, "Advocates without Members: The Recent Transformation of American Civic Life," in Skocpol and Fiorina, eds., *Civic Engagement in American Democracy,* at p. 461.

35. Ibid., at p. 487.

36. Ibid., at p. 503.

37. Skowronek, *The Politics Presidents Make,* at p. 31.

38. See Wattenberg, *The Rise of Candidate-Centered Politics,* at pp. 1–2.

39. Cf. Milkis, *The President and the Parties*, at p. 263 (noting the "revival of party politics" under Reagan).

40. See Thomas H. Little, "The 1996 State Legislative Elections: The Fate of Responsible Parties in America," in Green and Shea, eds., *The States of the Parties*, at p. 306 (arguing that the Contract with America formed the platform in state and local elections as well).

41. For an overview, see David W. Brady, Robert D'Onofrio, and Morris P. Fiorina, "The Nationalization of Electoral Forces Revisited," in Brady, Cogan, and Fiorina, eds., *Continuity and Change in House Elections*, at p. 130.

42. Ginsberg and Shefter, *Politics by Other Means*, at pp. 2–3.

43. Compare Hall and Lindholm, *Is America Breaking Apart?* at p. 120 ("Lack of participation also can signify widespread relative satisfaction with things as they are. The widespread and rapid appearance and disappearance of single-issue groups makes it clear that when confronted by matters they feel are personally relevant, Americans do become politically active. But when nothing particular concerns them, voters are content to remain quiet, occupying themselves with more pleasurable and more edifying non-political activities"), with Lipset, *American Exceptionalism*, at p. 282 (attributing the decline in turnout to a "precipitous and stead[y]" decline in public confidence in U.S. institutions), and Keefe, *Parties, Politics, and Public Policy in America*, at p. 181 ("Indifference, alienation, declining party loyalness, and a generalized distrust of government combine to cut the turnout rate in elections.").

44. See, e.g., Piven and Cloward, *Why Americans Don't Vote*.

45. See Kornbluh, *Why America Stopped Voting* (arguing that the decline occurred at the turn of the twentieth century and stayed low thereafter).

46. For an overview of the reasons for polarization, see Jacobson, "The Electoral Basis of Partisan Polarization in Congress."

47. Compare Ansolabehere and Iyengar, *Going Negative*, at pp. 112–13 (arguing that negative advertising reduces the numbers of independents who vote in general elections), with Gant and Lyons, "Democratic Theory, Nonvoting, and Public Policy" (concluding that voters are more likely than nonvoters to form preferences based on policy grounds, but that the two groups differ very little in their preferences for president). Perhaps the differences result from focusing on legislative and presidential choices respectively.

48. See, e.g., Shea, "The Passing of Realignment and the Advent of the 'Base-Less' Party System," at p. 43 (noting that increased partisanship "might be a product of declining turnout, something service-oriented parties could be contributing to by mobilizing only the most partisan voters").

49. See Jacobs and Shapiro, *Politicians Don't Pander*, at p. 5 (reporting findings that "candidates' ideological responsiveness to opinion within their district was weak prior to the 1930s, steadily rose between 1934 and [reached] its peak in the early 1970s, then declined into the 1990s [precipitously among Republican candidates]".

50. See Pomper, "The 2000 Presidential Election," at pp. 205–6 (noting that in 2000, "[f]ewer than one of every thirteen Republicans considered themselves liberals, and fewer than one in eight Democrats were conservatives"); Hethering-

ton, "Resurgent Mass Partisanship" (concluding that "[g]reater partisan polarization in Congress has clarified the parties' ideological positions for ordinary Americans, which in turn has increased party importance and salience on the mass level").

51. Wattenberg, *The Rise of Candidate-Centered Politics*, at pp. 22–23.

52. Cameron, *Veto Bargaining*, at p. 259.

53. See Cohen, "A Congress Divided" (reporting that in the 1999 Senate, for the first time since the magazine began compiling statistics in 1981, "every Democrat had an average score that was to the left of the most-liberal Republican's. [Or, depending on your perspective, every Republican was to the right of the most-conservative Democrat.]"). Cameron, *Veto Bargaining*, at pp. 247–49, provides another statistical measure of increasing polarization in the 1990s. See also Watson and Stookey, *Shaping America*, at pp. 180–81 ("In 1968 the ideological centers of the two parties were separated by 36 on the [authors'] scale. . . . By 1991 that separation had grown to 70 points. . . . At the same time, both parties exhibit much less diversity in their ideological makeup. . . . There are simply fewer moderates and liberals within the Republican party and fewer moderates and conservatives within the Democratic party.").

54. Salant, "Fewer congressional candidates means less campaign spending." See also Ginsberg and Shefter, *Politics by Other Means*, at pp. 3–4 (describing the increasing number of noncompetitive districts).

55. See Calmes, "House Divided" (describing "computer-driven mapping capabilities . . . [w]ith precision down to the block level"). For a court's description of (and comment on) the computer programs, see *Johnson v. Miller*, 864 F Supp 1354, 1363 (S.D. Ga. 1994) ("Ms. Meggers provided the Court with an enlightening demonstration of state-of-the-art redistricting on her computer, 'Herschel.' Only Georgians truly understand the depth of respect that is accorded to this equipment by such an appellation. When fed geographic and demographic data [including black voting age population data], it allows the user to map voting districts at the census bloc level with the greatest of ease.") See also *Vera v. Richards*, 861 F Supp 1304, 1318 (S.D. Tex. 1994) (describing the REDAPPL program).

Sometimes the increasing homogeneity is attributed to apportionments made in response to litigation under the Voting Rights Act of 1965. Cf. Pildes, "The Politics of Race," at pp. 1384–90 (citing studies showing that Democrats' overall prospects are reduced by such apportionments, although those Democrats who are elected are likely to be more liberal). Epstein and Sharyn O'Halloran, "Majority-Minority Districts and the New Politics of Congressional Elections," in Brady, Cogan, and Fiorina, eds., *Continuity and Change in House Elections*, at p. 87. The overall effects at issue are too large to result primarily from these apportionments. See David A. Bositis, "The Future of Majority-Minority Districts and Black and Hispanic Legislative Representation," in Bositis, ed., *Redistricting and Minority Representation*, at p. 19n. 5 (citing studies showing that these apportionments led to a loss of between eight and thirteen seats for Democrats in 1992, when overall the Democrats lost fifty-four seats); Bernard Grofman and Lisa Handley, "Estimating the Impact of Voting-Rights-Related Districting on

Democratic Strength in the U.S. House of Representatives," in Grofman, ed., *Race and Redistricting in the 1990s*, at pp. 51, 61–62 (concluding that "[t]hrough 1994, Democrats did not suffer greater levels of decline in those states where black majority districts had been drawn than in those states where they had not been," and that "[g]iven the national scope of the Republican 1994 tidal wave, even had no new black majority seats been drawn in the 1990s districting round, the Republicans would still have gained control of the House").

56. Tilove, "The New Map of American Politics," at p. 35 (arguing that "migration choices . . . reinforce the political and cultural characteristics [in-migrants] came looking for").

57. Gimpel and Schuknecht, "Interstate Migration and Electoral Politics."

58. The effect on Republicans is complex, because incoming Republicans may be more moderate than those already in place. The newcomers might then make the state's Republican Party less conservative than it had been. And, the authors point out, inmigration that is disproportionately Republican, but less Republican than the state already was, would weaken Republican strength in the state. Ibid., at p. 213.

59. In 1976 the number of states with mixed Senate delegations peaked at twenty-seven. Segura and Nicholson, "Sequential Choices and Partisan Transitions in U.S. Senate Delegations," at p. 86. In 2001 only fourteen states had mixed delegations.

60. For a candidate-centered explanation of the rise of partisanship in the House, see Lucas, "Voters, Parties, and Representatives."

61. See Rohde, *Parties and Leaders in the Post-Reform House*, at pp. 166–67 (describing increasing party homogeneity in the 1980s); Sinclair, *Legislators, Leaders, and Lawmaking*, at p. 50 (describing the increase in voting cohesion in the House from 1982 through the early 1990s); Gimpel, *Legislating the Revolution*, at pp. 13–14 (noting that the trend was extended through 1994).

62. Representative Jack Tanner (D-Tenn.), quoted in Gimpel, *Legislating the Revolution*, at pp. 122–23. See also Calmes, "House Divided" (quoting Roger Davidson, "a leading congressional scholar," as asserting that "[t]he divisions between the two parties are probably larger than they've been at any time in the modern era at least").

63. Hetherington, "Resurgent Mass Partisanship."

64. Fiorina, *Divided Government*, at p. 72. Fiorina's general argument is that voter preference for divided government better accounts for the phenomenon than other explanations. To establish this argument, it is sufficient that enough voters prefer divided government, even though most voters do not split their tickets.

65. For survey evidence supporting this account, see Layman, Carsey, and Rundquist, "The Causes and Effects of Preferences for Party Government."

66. For an overview of the disagreement, see Burden and Kimball, "A New Approach to the Study of Ticket Splitting," at p. 538 (distinguishing between "intentional" and "unintentional" theories). In support of Fiorina, see, e.g., Mebane, "Coordination, Moderation, and Institutional Balancing in American Presidential and House Elections," at p. 51 (concluding that in recent elections, "a small but significant proportion of voters have been motivated to vote a split

ticket in order to increase the chances of institutional balance"). For some structural accounts, see, e.g., Jacobson, *The Electoral Origins of Divided Government* (arguing that divided government occurs because voters have different expectations for House members and the president); Ingberman and Villani, "An Institutional Theory of Divided Government and Party Polarization"; Sigelman, Wahlbeck, and Buell, "Vote Choice and the Preference for Divided Government" (finding no correlation between preferences for divided government and ticket splitting); Grofman et al., "A New Look at Split-Ticket Outcomes for House and President."

67. Fiorina, *Divided Government*, at p. 77. Fiorina also points out that ticket splitters play a role similar to that played by supporters of third parties (121). Here too the Anderson-Perot phenomenon, see note 8 above, confirms the general argument.

68. Ibid., at pp. 68–69 (pointing out that creating divided government is easier with respect to executives than legislatures because changing the composition of the legislature requires coordination across districts).

69. See Gimpel, *Legislating the Revolution*, at p. 7 (describing the Contract as "a ready-made platform" that "inject[ed] party responsibility into the campaign").

70. Writing before the 1996 election, Fiorina observed that "the Republican victories in the 1994 Congressional elections have raised the probability that President Clinton will be reelected in 1996." Fiorina, *Divided Government*, at p. 156. Born, "Policy-Balancing Models and the Split-Ticket Voter, 1972–1996," generally disagrees with Fiorina's policy-balancing analysis but concludes that the results of the 1996 election provide support for Fiorina's approach.

71. Ginsberg, Mebane, and Shefter, "The Presidency, Social Forces, and Interest Groups," at p. 368.

72. Shea, "The Passing of Realignment and the Advent of the 'Base-Less' Party System," at pp. 41–50.

73. Briffault, "The Political Parties and Campaign Finance Reform," at p. 646. I suspect that ideological concerns might affect decisions on the margin. For example, faced with two candidates with equal chances of winning, the party campaign committees might allocate a bit more to the one more likely to "fit" with the party's congressional majority. But that effect is, I think, likely to be small overall.

74. Menefee-Libey, *The Triumph of Campaign-Centered Politics*, at p. 131.

75. Shea, "The Passing of Realignment and the Advent of the 'Base-Less' Party System," at p. 42.

76. Menefee-Libey, *The Triumph of Campaign-Centered Politics*, at p. 218.

77. Ibid.

78. Menefee-Libey, *The Triumph of Campaign-Centered Politics*, at p. 45. John F. Bibby, "Party Networks: National State Integration, Allied Groups, and Issue Activists," in Green and Shea, eds., *The States of the Parties*, at pp. 70–75 (describing the centralization of power in national parties acting as service organizations for candidates and for state parties as well).

79. Shea, "The Passing of Realignment and the Advent of the 'Base-Less' Party System," at p. 48. An interesting side effect is that it has become more

difficult for political parties to mobilize new voters, specifically naturalized citizens, who can no longer rely as they did in the past on assistance from local party organizations in the Americanization process. For a discussion, see Peter Skerry, "The Racialization of Immigration Policy," in Keller and Melnick, eds., *Taking Stock*, at pp. 81–82, 89–92, 94–96.

80. Milkis, *The President and the Parties*, at p. 87.

81. Milkis, *Political Parties and Constitutional Government*, p. 141.

82. Ginsberg and Shefter, *Politics by Other Means*, at p. 10.

83. Milkis, *Political Parties and Constitutional Government*, at p. 187.

84. Landy and Milkis, *Presidential Greatness*, at p. 199.

85. Menefee-Libey, *The Triumph of Campaign-Centered Politics*, at pp. 33–34.

86. Landy and Milkis, *Presidential Greatness*, at p. 224.

87. Silbey, *The Partisan Imperative*, at p. 36.

88. This paragraph follows the argument of Sinclair, *Legislators, Leaders*, and *Lawmaking*, as expanded in Sinclair, *Unorthodox Lawmaking*. The mechanisms for leadership control may differ between the parties, and for obvious reasons the scholarship is more extensive with respect to the Democrats. In addition, the depth and pace of change has been greater in the House of Representatives than in the Senate. Nonetheless, as Sinclair argues, there are structural reasons for increasing centralization, and changes in Senate rules do parallel those in the House. See John Ferejohn, "A Tale of Two Congresses," in Weir, ed., *The Social Divide*, at p. 68 ("Everyone agrees that Congress has gradually changed from a loosely structured locus of committees and subcommittees operating fairly independently, with party leaders serving largely as 'traffic cops,' to a more coherent, collegial, partisan, and sometimes even centralized institution, where significant policymaking activity sometimes takes place in the offices of party leaders, in party caucuses, and on the chamber floors. These changes have gone farther and happened faster in the House of Representatives than in the Senate, but they have been visible in both chambers to varying extents."). In the preface to her 1995 book, Sinclair suggested that "[a]ny alterations Republicans make in House rules can at most marginally affect the process." Sinclair, *Legislators, Leaders*, and *Lawmaking*, at p. xi. In 1997 she observed that the new Republican majority did not alter "internal rules . . . very much." Sinclair, *Unorthodox Lawmaking*, at p. 100. Ferejohn observes that "the Republican procedural reforms of the 104th Congress . . . served to increase majority party influence in committees." Ferejohn, "A Tale of Two Congresses," at p. 69.

89. As Sinclair observes, these new rules invoke the "standard response" to collective action problems of "plac[ing] in the hands of leaders selective incentives that can be used to induce institution-regarding behavior." Sinclair, *The Transformation of the U.S. Senate*, at p. 210.

90. On the use of rules, see Farrar-Myers, "Controlling the Floor."

91. Barbara Sinclair, "Do Parties Matter," Center for the Study of Democracy, UC Irvine, Research Papers (1998), available at *http://www.democ.uci.edu/democ/papers/sinclair.htm*, emphasizes this role of the leadership.

92. Sinclair, *Legislators, Leaders*, and *Lawmaking*, at p. 15. Sinclair, writing in 1995, refers primarily to decreased ideological heterogeneity among Democrats; see, e.g., at pp. 6, 44, 50, 182. The point seems valid with respect to Republicans as well.

93. Rohde, "The Gingrich Speakership in Context," at p. 7. This statement summarizes a position about which "something of a consensus" has developed. Cox and McCubbins, "Toward a Theory of Legislative Rules Changes," at p. 1376. Emphasizing party polarization and finding little effect of homogeneity alone is Schickler, "Institutional Change in the House of Representatives, 1867–1998."

94. See Sinclair, *Legislators, Leaders, and Lawmaking*, at pp. 34–36 (describing the reforms in the House of Representatives).

95. Ibid., at p. 34.

96. For an overview of the changes, see Aldrich and Rohde, "The Transition to Republican Rule in the House," at pp. 548–56. For a case study, see Aldrich and Rohde, "The Republican Revolution and the House Appropriations Committee." Some analyses of even recent legislation continue to rely on older scholarship about congressional organization. See, e.g., BeVier, "The Communications Assistance for Law Enforcement Act of 1994," at p. 1096 (describing enactment of CALEA in 1994 as "a product of the committee process in general, and of the work of . . . subcommittee chairmen in particular, to which subcommittee members and other members of Congress might have been expected in the ordinary course of the legislative day to have given considerable deference," and relying on works describing congressional processes published in 1985 and 1977). The account may be accurate as to a single piece of legislation, but older scholarship must be used with caution when we deal with recent legislation, produced under the processes put in place in the 1980s and 1990s.

97. See Wayne, "Congress Uses Leadership PACs to Wield Power" (describing use of funds created by Sen. Trent Lott and Rep. Newt Gingrich); Pomper, "Parliamentary Government in the United States?" in Green and Shea, eds., *The States of the Parties*, at p. 262 (noting that Representatives Gingrich and Armey "did their best to aid loyalists—but only loyalists—through fund-raising and strongarming of ideological allies among political action committees"). Money from the national congressional campaign committees, in contrast, does not appear to increase party discipline. See Ansolabehere and Snyder, "Soft Money, Hard Money, Strong Parties," at pp. 611–13.

98. See Ferejohn, "A Tale of Two Congresses," at pp. 75–76 ("Individual constituents increasingly expect their representatives to behave as partisans and are increasingly inclined to evaluate them in terms of whether they agree with them. It is becoming more difficult for members to insulate themselves from national tides by providing services to the district. . . . As a consequence, members are coming to see their fates as more bound up with issues and how their parties are doing nationally. Over time these tendencies should produce an increased sorting of members into ideologically congenial districts."). Of course the fact that leaders have greater power under the rules does not mean that they will actually exercise it. I do note, however, that the degree of party discipline exhibited in the impeachment process was widely regarded as unusually high, particularly with respect to moderate Republicans in the House of Representatives.

99. Jacobs and Shapiro, *Politicians Don't Pander*, at pp. 37–38.

100. Ginsberg and Shefter, *Politics by Other Means*, at p. 25.

101. Jacobs and Shapiro, *Politicians Don't Pander*, at pp. 7, 27.

102. Ibid., at pp. 49, 63, 106, 272.

103. Ibid., at p. 46.

104. Slotnick and Segal, *Television News and the Supreme Court*, at pp. 165, 187.

105. Ibid., at pp. 64–67.

106. Cook, *Governing the News*, at p. 113. Even print media are affected by these requirements, though obviously some are more important for television.

107. Castells, *The Power of Identity*, at p. 322.

108. Sparrow, *Uncertain Guardians*, at pp. 47–51. See also Jacobs and Shapiro, *Politicians Don't Pander*, at p. 158.

109. Sparrow, *Uncertain Guardians*, at pp. 96–97, 109–10.

110. Ibid., at p. 109.

111. Jacobs and Shapiro, *Politicians Don't Pander*, at p. 57. The authors go on to note studies suggesting that "[t]he extent to which audiences are in fact drawn by 'horse race' coverage is open to dispute."

112. Balkin, "How Mass Media Simulate Political Transparency," at p. 397.

113. Reed, "A New Constitutional Regime." (Reed's focus is somewhat different from mine, but I believe that my argument is consistent with his.)

114. The juridico-entertainment complex includes trial courts. For a discussion of the politics associated with celebrated criminal trials, see Fox and Van Sickel, *Tabloid Justice*.

115. Castells, *The Power of Identity*, at p. 337. See also Balkin, "How Mass Media Simulate Political Transparency," at pp. 404–7 (describing "the culture of scandal"). Castells draws on evidence from around the world. For a somewhat more skeptical view with a similar transnational evidentiary base, concluding that "political institutions increasingly are dependent on and shaped by mass media but nevertheless remain in control of political processes and functions," see Mazzoleni and Schulz, " 'Mediazation' of Politics: A Challenge for Democracy?"

116. Summers, "What Happened to Sex Scandals?"

117. Ibid., at p. 826.

118. See Fitts, "The Legalization of the Presidency," at pp. 733–34 (1999) (noting that "the rise of a diverse and hypercritical media . . . has impacted upon the presidency disproportionately").

119. Posner, *An Affair of State*, pp. 1, 168 (emphasis added).

120. Castells, *The Power of Identity*, at p. 338.

121. In Balkin's words, "Journalists . . . have adapted the rhetoric of political transparency to defend their emerging investigative practices, to rationalise greater sexual frankness in reporting of news stories, and to justify their sense of greater entitlement to investigate and report on the private lives of public officials, including their infidelities, their sexual orientations, and their sexual habits." Balkin, "How Mass Media Simulate Political Transparency," at p. 400.

122. Posner, *An Affair of State*, at p. 168.

123. Quoted in Kurtz, "Americans Wait for the Punch Line on Impeachment." See also Rich, "All the Presidents Stink" (describing a "disconnect" between the Washington political elite and the American people).

124. Harvey Feigenbaum, Richard Samuels, and R. Kent Weaver, "Innovation, Coordination, and Implementation in Energy Policy," in Weaver and Rockman, eds., *Do Institutions Matter?* at p. 101.

125. Mayhew, *Divided We Govern,* at p. 76.

126. See Jones, *The Presidency in a Separated System,* at pp. 19–23 (distinguishing among partisanship, co-partisanship in which parties compromise at the enactment stage, bipartisanship in which they cooperate in formulating legislation, and cross-partisanship in which segments of each party form alliances). Other research is summarized in Fiorina, *Divided Government,* at pp. 162–66.

127. Fiorina, *Divided Government,* at p. 128.

128. See ibid., at p. 89 (observing that Mayhew's methods do not measure the "demand" for legislation); Binder, "The Dynamics of Legislative Gridlock, 1947–96," at p. 520 (a measure of "potential enactments . . . is needed to test theories of political stalemate").

129. For a discussion of the methods of extended debate, see Fisk and Chemerinsky, "The Filibuster," at pp. 203–6.

130. Sinclair, *The Transformation of the U.S. Senate,* at pp. 94, 95. For more recent evidence and examples, see Sinclair, *Unorthodox Lawmaking,* at pp. 47–49; Fisk and Chemerinsky, "The Filibuster," at pp. 182–83.

131. Sinclair, *Unorthodox Lawmaking,* at p. 49.

132. Binder and Smith, *Politics or Principle?* at pp. 14–15.

133. Sinclair, *The Transformation of the U.S. Senate,* at pp. 128–29. Sinclair also describes the rise of "nearly absolute" holds on legislation, requests by individual senators to delay consideration of a particular bill, nominally for a short period but increasingly as a way of permanently derailing the process (130–31).

134. Binder and Smith, *Politics or Principle?* at p. 40.

135. Sinclair, *The Transformation of the U.S. Senate,* at p. 125.

136. Binder and Smith, *Politics or Principle?* at p. 16 (quoting a "Senate observer").

137. Evans, "The House That Governs Least, Governs Best." Thorson, Maxwell, and Nitzschke, "Strategic Decision Making and the Invoking of Cloture in the United States Senate," find "some limited evidence that cloture voting rules at least occasionally promote the majority party to offer concessions and moderate bills that are otherwise unacceptable to members of the minority party" (13).

138. Hernnson, "Reflections on Clinton's First Term," in Hernnson and Hill, eds., *The Clinton Presidency,* at p. 168 (describing the Republican response to Clinton's "reliance on minimum winning coalitions").

139. For a discussion, see Garrett, "A Fiscal Constitution With Supermajority Voting Rules," at pp. 478–82. These rules are formally subject to waiver, sometimes by majority vote and sometimes by a supermajority requirement (which, however, could itself be displaced by yet another majority vote). But Garrett suggests that the rules have not been "toothless" (482).

140. Fisk and Chemerinsky, "The Filibuster," at 213; Sinclair, *Unorthodox Lawmaking,* at p. 77 ("passing legislation that is at all controversial increasingly required sixty votes"). Applying the analysis to budget bills is more complicated. In a divided government the president's program can be enacted with simple majority support, although procedural rules may make it difficult for the president to obtain a straight up-or-down vote on that program. The opposition's program, in contrast, can be enacted only with two-thirds support in both houses, sufficient to override a veto.

141. *See* Sinclair, *Unorthodox Lawmaking*, at p. 49 ("If legislation reaches the point of a passage vote, it almost certainly will pass.").

142. For an analysis showing an increase in the number of bills enacted with more than two-thirds support during divided government periods, see Covington and Bargan, "The Effect of Divided Government on the Ideological Content of Bills Enacted by the House of Representatives."

143. For a discussion, see Fisk and Chemerinsky, "The Filibuster," at pp. 217–20.

144. Ibid., at pp. 221–22.

145. See Sinclair, *Unorthodox Lawmaking*, at p. 96 ("Party leaders, responding to their members' demands for legislative success, sought ways of coping with the problems. They began to use omnibus legislation more frequently; summits were developed as a last resort means of reaching agreements between Congress and the president."). See also Thorson, Maxwell, and Nitzsche, "Strategic Decision Making and the Invoking of Cloture in the United States Senate" (concluding that cloture voting rules, as an aspect of supermajority decision making, have some effect on moderating bills). For a formal model showing that supermajority rules make legislative gridlock probable, see Krehbiel, "Institutional and Partisan Sources of Gridlock."

146. Sinclair, "Bipartisan Governing," provides a good summary of the problems facing Republicans controlling the House, the presidency, and (at the time it was written), the Senate.

147. Fiorina, *Divided Government*, at p. 168, describes a formal model in which "the legislature grants broader discretion when its preferences are more similar to the executive's." For a more elaborate presentation, see Epstein and O'Halloran, *Delegating Powers*.

148. Epstein and O'Halloran, "The Nondelegation Doctrine and the Separation of Powers," at pp. 978–80.

149. See Skowronek, *The Politics Presidents Make*, at p. 413 (describing "an ever thicker government that can parry and deflect more of [innovators'] repudiative thrust").

150. Fiorina, *Divided Government*, at p. 90.

151. For a description of some initiatives of this sort, see the conclusion.

152. Sinclair, "Structure, Preferences and Outcomes: Explaining When Bills Do—and Don't—Become Law," concludes that the legislation that occurs during periods of divided government has a different form from that which would have occurred had control been unified.

153. Pfiffner, "Presidential Constraints and Transitions," in Shull, ed., *Presidential Policymaking*, at p. 32 (emphasis added).

154. For a journalist's comment on the scope of policy proposals, see Berke, "Following Baby-Size Issues into Voters' Hearts."

155. For an analysis of the habeas corpus and prison litigation legislation of 1996 making this argument, see Tushnet and Yackle, "Symbolic Statutes and Real Laws."

156. Kagan, "Presidential Administration."

157. For Kagan's analysis of the causes of presidential administration's rise, see ibid., at pp. 2310–12.

158. Ibid., at p. 2282.

159. Ibid., at pp. 2303–06.

160. See ibid., at p. 2314 (explaining Congress's inability to thwart President Clinton's initiatives).

161. *FDA v. Brown and Williamson Tobacco Corp*, 529 US 120 (2000). Kagan discusses general constitutional objections to presidential administration in Kagan, "Presidential Administration," at pp. 2319–31.

162. One analysis suggests that the impeachment occurred because lame ducks who had been defeated or had chosen to leave the House of Representatives voted contrary to the wishes of the voters who had been, but would no longer be, their constituents. Rothenberg and Sanders, "Lame-duck Politics."

163. See Abramowitz, "It's Monica, Stupid"; Morris, "Conventional Politics in Exceptional Times."

164. Drawing on the general accounts relied on earlier in this chapter, Hurwitz, Moiles, and Rohde, "Distributive and Partisan Issues in Agriculture Policy in the 104th House," at p. 912, use the Clinton impeachment to illustrate how, "[w]hen the majority party is relatively (but not perfectly) homogeneous in its beliefs on an issue salient to its members, and those beliefs are different from the floor median, the majority will use its influence over the rules and structures of the body to attempt to steer the outcome away from the center of the floor and toward the median of the majority party."

165. Sunstein, "Impeaching the President," at p. 281.

166. Cf. Ackerman, "Revolution on a Human Scale," at p. 2347 ("Constitutionalists of all parties should work together to build a consensus that establishes the Clinton case as a negative precedent for future constitutional development.").

167. Judge Posner, appointed to the bench by President Ronald Reagan, comes close to seeing the point but does not grasp the degree to which Clinton appropriated Reagan's themes: "From the standpoint of policy, Clinton is pretty indistinguishable from a Nelson Rockefeller Republican, even a George Bush, Bob Dole, or Gerald Ford Republican. It is a little as if the Democratic Party had disappeared and the Republican Party has fissioned into a left (Nelson Rockefeller, William Weld) wing led by Clinton and a right (Dan Quayle, Jesse Helms) wing led by Trent Lott and Tom DeLay." Posner, *An Affair of State*, at p. 202.

168. Skowronek, *The Politics Presidents Make*, at p. 444 (emphasis added).

169. I mean by this to reserve the possibility that the events underlying the impeachment may have had permanent effects.

170. Dewar and Eilperin, "GOP Fears Agenda Drift as 2000 Elections Near" (quoting Rep. John Edward Porter, R.-Ill.).

171. The House's actions did place their partisan allies in the Senate in the uncomfortable position of going through the motions of a process that would almost inevitably lead to an acquittal. In other circumstances, for example, where divided government involved a Republican House and a Democratic president and Senate, going forward with a partisan impeachment would have little cost to the House majority.

172. Indeed, the impeachment resulted in at least one increase in the president's power, when Congress let the statute creating the independent counsel mechanism lapse. Spitzer, "Clinton's Impeachment Will Have Few Consequences

for the Presidency," supports its thesis by noting that the grounds for impeachment had almost nothing to do with the ordinary exercise of presidential power.

173. Perhaps it is worth noting that the structural source of President Clinton's difficulty is that he practiced the politics of preemption. But even a president from the Republican party might face a normalized impeachment under the right circumstances. As Skowronek argues, successor presidents nonetheless must do something to distinguish their leadership from that of the president who established the regime. And as they do so, they may make the kinds of missteps that can be the occasion for a normalized impeachment.

174. Clarke and Gaile, *The Work of Cities*, at p. 33.

175. See, e.g., Joyce and Mullins, "The Changing Fiscal Structure of the State and Local Public Sector," at p. 252 (concluding that "local [tax expenditure limitations] have resulted in movement away from local taxes toward . . . a greater expenditure role for states"); Sokolow, "The Changing Property Tax and State-Local Relations," at p. 165 (concluding that these limitations "add to state centralization in several ways: [1] giving statewide voters and state legislators control over local-tax rates and other property-tax rules; [2] encouraging states to increase levels of fiscal aid to local governments; and [3] reducing the proportion of locally raised taxes in the state-local revenue mix").

176. See Sokolow, "The Changing Property Tax and State-Local Relations," at pp. 175–77 (describing the centralization of education funding). Sokolow points out that state court decisions requiring more equal expenditures on schools throughout the state also impelled this centralization.

177. For some statistics, see Pagano, "State-Local Relations in the 1990s," at p. 94.

178. For an analysis, see Stark, "The Right to Vote on Taxes."

179. *See* Doron and Harris, *Term Limits*, who show that successful movements to impose term limits on legislators ended in the mid-1990s.

180. For what follows I draw heavily on Carey, Niemi, and Powell, *Term Limits in the State Legislatures*.

181. Ibid., at pp. 49, 50.

182. Ibid., at p. 44.

183. Rader, Elder, and Elling, "Motivations and Behaviors of the 'New Breed' of Term Limited Legislators."

184. Carey, Niemi, and Powell, *Term Limits in the State Legislatures*, at p. 44.

185. See Clarke and Gaile, *The Work of Cities*, at pp. 193–94 (describing this problem).

186. See Boeckelman, "The American States in the Postindustrial Economy," at p. 185 (providing some evidence to this effect).

187. Clarke and Gaile, *The Work of Cities*, at pp. 45, 93.

188. Michael J. Trebilcock and Ron Daniels, "Journeys across the Institutional Divides: Reinterpreting the Reinterpreting Government Movement," unpublished manuscript in my possession. They develop their ideas in more detail in Trebilcock, Daniels, and Thorburn, "Government by Voucher."

189. The difficulty legislatures have had in enacting tort reform statutes that state courts find constitutionally acceptable may be an indication of this problem. See Berkman, "After the Hype, Tort Reform Moves Slowly"; Glaberson, "State

Courts Sweeping away Laws Curbing Suits for Injury." Sometimes this difficulty is attributed to the campaign contributions trial lawyers make to judicial campaigns, but business interests that support tort reform have learned to make offsetting contributions.

190. In this sense legal realism was the jurisprudence of the New Deal–Great Society constitutional order.

191. These adjustments, however, might consist of incursions on what proponents of the prior regime regard as fundamental human rights, such as free expression and the right to reproductive liberty. The new constitutional order therefore need not be an entirely libertarian one. It does contain principles that incline in the direction of libertarianism and institutions that may indirectly advance libertarian goals by making it difficult to enact any new restrictions of liberty understood in libertarian terms.

192. For formal presentations of the point, see Hansen, "Is There a Politically Optimal Level of Judicial Independence?"; Ginsburg, "Economic Analysis and the Design of Constitutional Courts."

193. Ginsburg, "Economic Analysis and the Design of Constitutional Courts," at p. 5.

194. Cornell Clayton, "Law, Politics, and the Rehnquist Court: Structural Influences on Supreme Court Decision Making," in Gillman and Clayton, eds., *The Supreme Court in American Politics*, at pp. 155–56.

195. One version of the collective action problem is this: A rational voter who believes it advantageous for his or her district to be represented by a member from the president's party, but also prefers divided government, may cast a straight ticket, expecting that enough voters in enough other districts will split theirs. The result may be a unified government even though in the abstract we might find that voters, when asked, preferred divided government. Mebane, "Coordination, Moderation, and Institutional Balancing in American Presidential and House Elections," argues that polls and interest groups can provide information that allows voters to coordinate their actions.

196. The most obvious example involves appointments to the federal bench, but many other policies are in practice irreversible once instituted because of the difficulty in enacting (or repealing) anything in a divided government.

197. Cantril and Cantril, *Reading Mixed Signals*, at pp. 10–14.

198. Esping-Andersen, *Social Foundations of Postindustrial Economies*, at p. 181, points out that "[t]he extraordinary age-bias in many countries' social transfer systems is difficult to reverse *because the median voter is getting older*") (emphasis added).

199. I thank Mark Graber for this formulation.

CHAPTER 2

1. The arguments that arise in connection with liberal Supreme Court decisions and with a liberal president facing a conservative Congress are obviously precisely parallel.

2. See chapter 5 for additional discussion of the type of analysis sketched here.

3. Perhaps some constellation of interest group pressures might overcome the

NOTES TO CHAPTER 2

ideological elements I discuss here and lead to congressional action overturning a Court decision. But from a justice's point of view, such an event is likely to be random and ought not affect the justice's attempt to secure whatever he or she wants. Of course, the justice also retains the possibility of finding unconstitutional Congress's response to a prior Court decision, as *City of Boerne v. Flores*, 521 US 507 (1997), discussed below, shows.

4. The argument here reconciles the so-called attitudinal and strategic approaches to analyzing Supreme Court decision making. The former approach takes justices as adopting in their opinions the positions they personally prefer; the latter assumes that justices want to maximize the realization of the policies they prefer but take into account the possibility of an adverse congressional reaction to Court decisions and respond strategically by going as far as they can without provoking such a reaction. When government is divided and ideological, a strategic justice can behave just as the attitudinal approach assumes. For a formal model supporting the argument that "the extent [to which] the Court is constrained by politics varies significantly over time," see Mario Bergara, Barak Richman, and Pablo Spiller, "Judicial Politics and the Econometrics of Preferences," available at *http://www.fgys.org/cedi/main—docedi.htm*.

5. Even the Court's support for abortion rights and its enthusiasm about free expression are consistent with a certain kind of libertarianism.

6. The combination of restrictions on national power and protection of liberty of contract is sometimes called "dual federalism." Economic actors were protected against national regulation by the limitations on national power and against state regulation by liberty of contract.

7. *United States v. E. C. Knight Co.*, 156 US 1, 12 (1895).

8. *Carter v. Carter Coal Co.*, 298 US 238, 303 (1936).

9. *A.L.A. Schechter Poultry Corp. v. United States*, 295 US 495, 543 (1935).

10. 317 US 111 (1942).

11. The basic argument was laid out in Herbert Wechsler, "The Political Safeguards of Federalism," in Wechsler, *Principles, Politics, and Fundamental Law* (first published in 1954). It was elaborated in Choper, *Judicial Review and the National Political Process*. Kramer, "Putting the Politics Back into the Political Safeguards of Federalism," offers an updated and sophisticated version of the argument. (My statement in the text is, I believe, a more precise formulation of the argument than generally appears in the literature.)

12. *Garcia v. San Antonio Metropolitan Transit Auth.*, 469 US 528 (1985).

13. *United States v. Lopez*, 514 US 549 (1995).

14. Ibid., at 552.

15. Ibid., at 558–59.

16. Ibid., at 564.

17. Ibid., at 565.

18. Ibid., at 567.

19. Ibid., at 568 (Kennedy, J., concurring)

20. Ibid., at 585–86 (Thomas, J., concurring).

21. Ibid., at 567.

22. 529 US 598 (2000). The provision is 42 U.S.C. § 13981 (1994).

23. Ibid., at 615.

24. Ibid.

25. Ibid.

26. Resnik, "Categorical Federalism," at pp. 644–56, describes the large number of areas in which federal law regulates the family.

27. For academic commentary along these lines, See, e.g., Regan, "How to Think about the Federal Commerce Power," at p. 557 (referring to the Act as a "frolic"); Merritt, "Commerce!" at pp. 693–94, 703–4 (describing "troubling" features of the statute and arguing that the statute could not be justified by a sense of "national urgency"); Friedman, "Legislative Findings and Judicial Signals," at p. 766 (describing Congress's action in enacting the statute as either "careless" or "arrogant").

28. Resnik, "Trial as Error, Jurisdiction as Injury," at p. 1005n. 322 (citing Rehnquist's testimony).

29. Kopel and Reynolds, "Taking Federalism Seriously," at p. 69.

30. *Lopez*, 514 US at 564.

31. Ibid., at 560.

32. Ibid., at 558.

33. 28 U.S.C. § 922(q) as amended.

34. *Morrison*, 529 US at 657. Justice Breyer went on to ask, "How much would be gained" by insisting that Congress employ such a jurisdictional hook? "Complex Commerce Clause rules creating fine distinctions that achieve only random results do little to further the important federalist interest that called them into being" (659).

35. See *Lopez*, 514 US at 568 (Kennedy, J., concurring) ("The history of the judicial struggle to interpret the Commerce Clause during the transition from the economic system the Founders knew to the single, national market still emergent in our own era counsels great restraint before the Court determines that the Clause is insufficient to support an exercise of the national power. That history gives me some pause about today's decision."); *Planned Parenthood of Southeastern Pennsylvania v. Casey*, 505 US 833, 861–62 (1992) (joint opinion of O'Connor, Kennedy, and Souter, JJ.) (approving the overruling of *Lochner*).

36. 501 US 452 (1991).

37. Ibid., at 459.

38. Ibid., at 460.

39. 505 US 144 (1992).

40. Ibid., at 169.

41. Ibid., at 177.

42. Ibid., at 188.

43. 521 US 898 (1997).

44. Ibid., at 905, 922.

45. Ibid., at 938 (Thomas, J., concurring).

46. *Lopez*, 514 US at 583 (Kennedy, J., concurring) (citing *New York v. United States* as a case involving that etiquette).

47. For a development of this argument, see Cox, "Expressivism in Federalism."

48. 528 US 141 (2000).

49. Ibid., at 151.

50. Ibid., at 142.

51. Technically, I suppose, someone could—at enormous expense—create a database of the information from other sources.

52. *Garcia,* 469 US at 580 (Rehnquist, J., dissenting), 589 (O'Connor, J., dissenting).

53. For a discussion of the limits the Constitution places on remedies for state violations of these requirements, see below.

54. See generally Hills, "The Political Economy of Cooperative Federalism."

55. 384 US 641 (1966).

56. *Lassiter v. Northampton County Board of Elections,* 360 US 45 (1959).

57. *South Carolina v. Katzenbach,* 383 US 301 (1966).

58. *Employment Division, Dept. of Human Resources of Oregon v. Smith,* 494 US 872 (1990).

59. *City of Boerne v. Flores,* 521 US 507 (1997).

60. Ibid., at 529.

61. For my discussion of the point, see Tushnet, *Taking the Constitution away from the Courts,* at p. 6.

62. *Massachusetts Board of Retirement v. Murgia,* 427 US 307 (1976).

63. *Kimel v. Florida Bd. of Regents,* 528 US 62 (2000).

64. Ibid., at 89.

65. Ibid.

66. 531 US 356 (2001).

67. Ibid., at 378.

68. Ibid., at 367.

69. Ibid., at 367–68.

70. 531 US 356, 370 (2001).

71. Ibid., at 371n. 7.

72. Ibid., at 370–71.

73. Pub. L. 106–274, 114 Stat. 803 (2000).

74. Post and Siegel, "Equal Protection by Law."

75. A particularly dramatic example is provided by the sit-in cases of the 1960s, where the Court struggled to overturn convictions for protests at private businesses in the face of its own doctrine that the Constitution applied only where state officials engaged in discrimination. Never resolving the state action issue, the Court nonetheless managed to overturn all the convictions in series of decisions, the last of which relied on a provision of the recently enacted Civil Rights Act of 1964. *Hamm v. City of Rock Hill,* 379 US 306 (1964). Another illustration is the interaction between the political branches and the Court in eliminating poll taxes. Congress submitted the Twenty-fourth Amendment, barring the use of poll taxes in elections for federal office, to the states in 1962, and it was ratified in 1964. The Voting Rights Act of 1965 directed the attorney general to challenge the constitutionality of poll taxes for state elections. 42 U.S.C. § 1973 (h) (1994). He did so by participating as an amicus curiae in a pending case, which produced a Court decision invalidating poll taxes for state elections as a violation of the equal protection clause. *Harper v. Virginia State Board of Elections,* 383 US 663 (1966).

76. *Miranda v. Arizona,* 384 US 436, 467 (1966). For a discussion of Con-

gress's response to this invitation, and the Court's reaction, see text accompanying notes 256–57 below. For a broader canvassing of the Court's invitations to Congress on criminal procedure during this period, see Klein, "Identifying and (Re)Formulating Prophylactic Rules, Safe Harbors, and Incidental Rights in Constitutional Criminal Procedure," at pp. 1054–57.

77. In *Garrett*, ex-president Bush submitted a "statement" on behalf of the disabled plaintiffs. Statement of Former President George H. W. Bush as Amicus Curiae in Support of Respondents, *University of Alabama at Birmingham v. Garrett*, No. 99-1240, 1999 U.S. Briefs 1240 (August 11, 2000).

78. Griffin, "Judicial Supremacy and Equal Protection in a Democracy of Rights."

79. *Chisholm v. Georgia*, 2 US (2 Dall.) 419 (1793).

80. The requisite three-quarters of the states ratified the amendment within a year, but the amendment was not officially promulgated until 1797.

81. The best account of the cases and their political and economic setting is Orth, *The Judicial Power of the United States*.

82. *Hans v. Louisiana*, 134 US 1 (1890).

83. *Pennsylvania v. Union Gas Co.*, 491 US 1 (1989).

84. 517 US 44 (1996).

85. Ibid., at 72.

86. 527 US 706 (1999).

87. *Mitchum v. Foster*, 407 US 225, 238 (1972).

88. *Fitzpatrick v. Bitzer*, 427 US 445 (1976).

89. Alden, 527 US at 755.

90. 209 US 123 (1908).

91. Some lower courts have held that *Ex parte Young* suits can be used to enforce the Americans with Disabilities Act even though *Garrett* holds that states are immune from monetary liability under the act. See, e.g., *Gibson v. Arkansas Dept. of Correction*, 265 F3d 718 (8ʰ Cir. 2001).

92. *Pennhurst State School & Hospital v. Halderman*, 465 US 89 (1984).

93. Ibid., at 105.

94. *Idaho v. Coeur d'Alene Tribe of Idaho*, 521 US 261 (1997) (opinion of Kennedy, J., joined by Rehnquist, C.J.).

95. The statute in *Seminole Tribe* authorized injunctions against the state government itself, and the Court held that that provision, though unconstitutional, was intended to make an *Ex parte Young* injunction against the state's governor unavailable.

96. The Court might hold that the remedies provided by the general wage-and-hour law were intended to preclude reliance on *Ex parte Young* suits to enforce that law. Cf. *Luder v. Endicott*, 253 F3d 1020 (7ᵗʰ Cir. 2001) (asserting, in a suit "under the Fair Labor Standards Act," that employees did not fit within the *Ex parte Young* doctrine). Such a holding would not bar Congress from making it clear that the *Ex parte Young* technique was in fact available for enforcement of the wage-and-hour laws.

97. 514 US 779 (1995).

98. Ibid., at 803.

99. *Saenz v. Roe*, 526 US 489 (1999).

100. Rubin, "Puppy Federalism and the Blessings of America," at p. 38.

101. For a discussion, see Caminker, "Judicial Solicitude for State Dignity."

102. *US Term Limits*, 514 US at 838 (Kennedy, J., concurring).

103. 290 US 398 (1934).

104. *United States Trust Co. v. New Jersey*, 431 US 1 (1977).

105. *Allied Structural Steel Co. v. Spannaus*, 438 US 234 (1978).

106. See, e.g., *Energy Reserves Group, Inc. v. Kansas Power and Light Co.*, 459 US 400 (1983); *General Motors Corp. v. Romein*, 503 US 181 (1992).

107. *Lochner v. New York*, 198 US 45 (1905).

108. *West Coast Hotel Co. v. Parrish*, 300 US 379 (1937).

109. *Eastern Enterprises v. Apfel*, 524 US 498 (1998). Four justices joined an opinion finding the act to be an unconstitutional taking of property without compensation. I discuss the takings clause below.

110. *Loretto v. Teleprompter Manhattan CATV Corp.*, 458 US 419 (1982).

111. *Loretto v. Group W. Cable*, 522 NYS2d 543, 545–46 (App. Div. 1987) (discussing proceedings on remand).

112. *Hodel v. Irving*, 481 US 704 (1987); *Babbitt v. Youpee*, 519 US 234 (1997).

113. *Phillips v. Washington Legal Foundation*, 524 US 156 (1998).

114. *Yee v. City of Escondido*, 503 US 519 (1992). Earlier the Court had refused to consider whether a rent-control ordinance barring rent increases over 8 percent a year for tenants who would suffer economic hardship from higher rents was unconstitutional, over a dissent by Justices Scalia and O'Connor. *Pennell v. City of San Jose*, 485 US 1 (1988).

115. *Eastern Enterprises v. Apfel*, 524 US at 528–29.

116. The Court invalidated the program, but Justice Kennedy's vote was predicated on the proposition that the program, understood as imposing a tax, violated the due process clause, not the takings clause.

117. *Nollan v. California Coastal Commission*, 483 US 825 (1987).

118. *Dolan v. City of Tigard*, 512 US 374 (1994).

119. Ibid., at 395–96.

120. *Pennsylvania Coal Co. v. Mahon*, 260 US 393, 415 (1922).

121. *Lucas v. South Carolina Coastal Council*, 505 US 1003, 1029 (1992).

122. *Palazzolo v. Rhode Island*, 533 US 606 (2001).

123. 438 US 104 (1978).

124. Ibid., at 124.

125. Ibid.

126. 533 US at 635–36.

127. It bears noting that the Court has also erected substantial procedural hurdles that increase the litigation costs that those who challenge land-use regulations must bear.

128. *Dolan*, 512 US at 396.

129. Here it may be important to note that the political institutions of the New Deal–Great Society constitutional order placed limits on what governments "wanted" to do during that regime.

130. *J.W. Hampton, Jr., and Co. v. United States*, 276 US 394, 409 (1928).

131. *Panama Refining Co. v. Ryan*, 293 US 388 (1935); *A.L.A. Schechter Poultry Corp. v. United States*, 295 US 495 (1935).

132. Some cases, such as *Immigration and Naturalization Service v. Chadha*, 462 US 919 (1983), which held unconstitutional the legislative veto, dealt with practices that were related to the issue of delegation, but the cases did not invoke the nondelegation doctrine.

133. *Industrial Union Dept., AFL-CIO v. American Petroleum Institute*, 448 US 607 (1980).

134. *Clinton v. City of New York*, 524 US 417 (1998).

135. The most substantial critique is Schoenbrod, *Power without Responsibility*.

136. *Whitman v. American Trucking Associations*, 531 US 457 (2001).

137. Justice Thomas did indicate his willingness to reconsider what the proper standard in nondelegation cases should be, suggesting that the "intelligible principle" standard "strayed too far from our Founders' understanding of separation of powers."

138. Kagan, "Presidential Administration," at pp. 2364–70, discusses the ways in which a revitalized nondelegation doctrine might actually support the techniques of presidential administration discussed in chapter 1.

139. Sidak and Spulber, *Deregulatory Takings and the Regulatory Contract*.

140. For a more extensive discussion of the case, see chapter 5 below.

141. Fleming, "Fidelity, Basic Liberties, and the Specter of *Lochner*," at p. 152.

142. For a similar overview, see Tushnet, *Taking the Constitution away from the Courts*, at pp. 129–53.

143. *Green v. County School Board of New Kent County*, 391 US 430, 438 (1968).

144. Ibid., at 442.

145. At least where the government had at one point required segregation.

146. *Milliken v. Bradley*, 418 US 717 (1974).

147. See, e.g., *Freeman v. Pitts*, 503 US 467 (1992) (authorizing the lower courts to release districts from supervision "in incremental stages, before full compliance has been achieved in every area of school operations"); *Jenkins v. Missouri*, 515 US 70 (1995) (limiting the power of lower courts to require programmatic changes when actual integration is not reasonably achievable).

148. See, e.g., *Eisenberg v. Montgomery County Public Schools*, 197 F3d 123 (4th Cir. 1999).

149. Sometimes that presumption could be overcome. See, e.g., *Hunt v. Cromartie*, 532 US 234 (2001).

150. Having drawn that lesson, the Court may have become more comfortable in developing a law of federalism-based limitations on congressional power. Such limitations had become discredited as the basis for "states' rights" resistance to desegregation, but as the desegregation imperative has receded so too has the stigma of states' rights.

151. *Virginia State Board of Pharmacy v. Virginia Citizens Consumer Council, Inc.*, 425 US 748 (1976).

152. Ibid., at 763.

153. *Central Hudson Gas and Electric Corp. v. Public Service Commission*, 447 US 557 (1980).

154. *Lorillard Tobacco Co. v. Reilly*, 533 US 525, 533 (2001). The attorney general had been defeated in his campaign to become the state's governor.

155. Ibid., at 562.

156. Ibid.

157. Ibid. (emphasis added).

158. See, e.g., *Lorillard*, 533 US at 572 (Thomas, J., concurring in part and concurring in the judgment).

159. *Clark v. Community for Creative Non-Violence*, 468 US 288 (1984).

160. For a summary of the cases, see Stone et al., *Constitutional Law*, at pp. 259–63.

161. *International Society for Krishna Consciousness, Inc. v. Lee*, 505 US 672 (1992).

162. The cases followed a complex course, but culminated in *Hudgens v. NLRB*, 424 US 507 (1976).

163. For a recent example, see *City of Ladue v. Gilleo*, 512 US 43 (1994) (unanimously striking down a city's ban on "visual clutter" as applied to a homeowner who displayed a sign opposing the Persian Gulf War on her front lawn).

164. Two important qualifications involve efforts to suppress anti-abortion protests near clinics where abortions are performed and efforts to suppress pure hate speech.

165. *Griffin v. Illinois*, 351 US 12 (1956); *Douglas v. California*, 372 US 353 (1963).

166. 411 US 1 (1973).

167. *Bowers v. Hardwick*, 478 US 186 (1986).

168. Ibid., at 194, 195 (emphasis added).

169. *Romer v. Evans*, 517 US 620 (1996).

170. Ibid., at 633.

171. Ibid., at 636 (Scalia, J., dissenting).

172. Ibid., at 652 (Scalia, J., dissenting).

173. It may have been how the New Deal–Great Society Court behaved, however, particularly in connection with race, where many of the Court's actions followed important cultural transformations, such as those signaled by the desegregation of the armed forces and professional baseball.

174. *Sherbert v. Verner*, 374 US 398 (1963); *Wisconsin v. Yoder*, 406 US 205 (1972).

175. Government decisions can be challenged on the ground that the regulations are not in fact generally applicable or neutral as between religious activities and other activities. For my analysis of the present state of free exercise doctrine, see Tushnet, "The Redundant Free Exercise Clause."

176. The best recent discussion is Jeffries and Ryan, "A Political History of the Establishment Clause."

177. *Lee v. Weisman*, 505 US 577 (1992); *Santa Fe Independent School Dist. v. Doe*, 530 US 290 (2000).

178. *Zelman v. Simmons-Harris*, 536 US —, 122 SG 2460 (2002).

179. *Rosenberger v. Rector and Visitors of University of Virginia*, 515 US 819 (1995).

180. As Jeffries and Ryan note, "At the federal level, none of the various proposals to grant tuition tax-credits or vouchers for private schools have been enacted." Jeffries and Ryan, "A Political History of the Establishment Clause," at p.

350. Programs at the state and local levels are small-scale so far. Ryan and Heise, "The Political Economy of School Choice," offers an analysis of why choice programs, including vouchers, are likely to remain small-scale.

181. Sunstein, "What Judge Bork Should Have Said," at p. 205.

182. That fact accounts for much of the discomfort among liberal constitutional scholars with the Supreme Court's innovative application of equal protection doctrine in *Bush v. Gore*, 531 US 98 (2000). They do not disagree with the innovation, but they are suspicious about innovations when only deployed by the modern Court to terminate an election in favor of a Republican.

183. Lewis, *The Context of Judicial Activism*, at p. 104.

184. Waxman, "Foreword: Does the Solicitor General Matter?" at p. 1120.

185. Some other federal initiatives, such as some wetlands regulations, have as their justification the protection of biodiversity, and the analysis of such initiatives tracks that of the Endangered Species Act.

186. Nagle, "The Commerce Clause Meets the Delhi Sands Flower-Loving Fly."

187. For lower court holdings to this effect, see *Reickenbacker v. Foster*, 274 F3d 974 (5th Cir. 2001); *Thompson v. Colorado*, 278 F3d 1020 (10th Cir. 2001).

188. *City of Mobile v. Bolden*, 446 US 55 (1980).

189. One part of the question is what to do about the possibility that the number of constitutional violations has decreased precisely because of the existence of section 2.

190. *Boy Scouts of America v. Dale*, 530 US 640, 648 (2000).

191. Ibid., at 653.

192. Ibid., at 651.

193. Ibid., at 648.

194. Ibid., at 653. Assertions to that effect appear to be insufficient standing alone; apparently the courts must be satisfied that the association's claim of impairment is at least reasonable in some minimal sense.

195. Ibid., at 648, 653.

196. Ibid., at 648 (emphasis added).

197. For a real-world example, see Renner, "At Bess Eaton" (describing the decision by the owner of a chain of coffee shops to place Christian messages on the stores' coffee cups and doughnut boxes). I use the example of a business owned by a group of people for expository purposes to avoid being distracted by questions that might arise were the business owned by a single person, whose right of association might be thought not to be implicated in regulations limiting the display of religious materials in the business place. I believe that an individual owner does have a right of expressive association but think it better to discuss the coverage of commercial entities before I discuss the coverage of intimate ones.

198. For examples, see Volokh, "What Speech Does 'Hostile Work Environment' Harassment Law Restrict?" at pp. 630–33.

199. 530 US at 655.

200. Epstein, "The Constitutional Perils of Moderation," at pp. 139–40.

201. Ibid., at p. 140.

202. See *Katzenbach v. McClung*, 379 US 294 (1964) (rejecting claim based on the commerce clause that the 1964 Civil Rights Act could not be applied to Ollie's Barbeque).

203. See Ayres, "Alternative Grounds," at p. 72 (citing Maddox's obituary to support the assertion that "Lester Maddox gained national publicity shortly after passage of the 1964 Civil Rights Act when he distributed ax handles to supporters in order to prevent blacks from patronizing his Atlanta restaurant, the Pickrick").

204. Analogous arguments have been made in connection with claims that these expressions are protected by the free speech clause directly. The literature is extensive. See, e.g., Volokh, "Comment, Freedom of Speech and Workplace Harassment"; Epstein, "Can a 'Dumb Ass Woman' Achieve Equality in the Workplace?" I suspect that supplementing the free speech arguments with an argument drawing on the right of expressive association will change no one's position on where the line should be drawn.

205. For discussions of the commercial/noncommercial line, see Farber, "Speaking in the First Person Plural," at pp. 1499–500; Carpenter, "Expressive Association and Anti-Discrimination Law After *Dale*," at p. 1563; Hills, *The Constitutional Rights of Private Governments*. All these authors agree that the line between commercial and noncommercial enterprises does not correspond precisely to the interests protected by the right of expressive association. They conclude, however, that drawing such a line is likely to protect that right more effectively than any other approach, even though it means that some commercial enterprises will be denied what we would in the abstract describe as their right of expressive association.

206. Wechsler, "Toward Neutral Principles of Constitutional Law."

207. The jurisdictional limitation in federal anti-discrimination law, which extends the scope of coverage only to non-intimate settings, seems to confirm my sense that society recognizes a difference between intimate and non-intimate settings. Of course, this jurisdictional limitation is simply statutory, and I am claiming that the Constitution requires some sort of jurisdictional limitation, at least when claims against forced association rest on concerns about expression, whether religious or political.

208. 530 US at 653.

209. *Pennhurst State School & Hospital v. Halderman*, 451 US 1 (1981).

210. *South Dakota v. Dole*, 483 US 203 (1987).

211. See Baker, "Conditional Spending after *Lopez*."

212. *Jim C. v. Arkansas Department of Education*, 235 F3d 1079 (8th Cir. 2000), *cert. denied*, 533 US 949 (2001).

213. Smith, "*Pennhurst, Chevron*, and the Spending Power," at p. 1190, describes how the Court might move from *Pennhurst* to a more robust doctrine limiting conditional spending in the name of federalism by treating *Pennhurst* "as a structural mechanism to ensure congressional accountability" rather than "as a means to ensure notice—and thus fairness—to the states." Smith argues that the accountability model "require[s] an unrealistic standard of congressional recision" and "converts *Pennhurst*'s rule from an interpretive tool to a substantive limitation on Congress's power to regulate through the spending power." Of course, that conversion is precisely what would have to occur if the Court is to pursue a transformative vision of federalism.

214. The Court's primary interventions in the area of conditional spending have been decisions denying private litigants the right to sue to enforce conditions. See, e.g., *Alexander v. Sandoval*, 532 US 275 (2001) (denying a private

right of action to enforce regulations adopted pursuant to Title VI of the 1964 Civil Rights Act, a conditional spending provision). The states' legal obligation to comply with the conditions imposed by Congress is unimpaired by such decisions, although in practice states will be able to evade compliance more easily when they are free from the threat of private enforcement actions.

215. A LEXIS search indicates that the phrase "presumption against pre-emption" first appeared in *Metropolitan Life Ins. Co. v. Massachusetts*, 471 US 724, 741 (1985). It was then used in three cases in 1992, *Cipollone v. Liggett Group, Inc.*, 505 US 504, 522 (1992); *Gade v. National Solid Wastes Management Ass'n*, 505 US 88, 118 (1992) (Souter, J., dissenting); and *Morales v. Trans World Airlines, Inc.*, 504 US 374, 421 (1992) (Stevens, J., dissenting).

216. See Adler, "State Sovereignty and the Anti-Commandeering Cases," at pp. 168–69.

217. For a more extended discussion, incorporating a treatment of an additional, formalist argument for distinguishing between affirmative and negative commandeering, see Tushnet, "Globalization and Federalism in a Post-*Printz* World."

218. See *Printz*, 521 US at 957–58n. 18 (Stevens, J., dissenting) (asserting that the "diffusion of political responsibility" argument "reflects a gross lack of confidence in the electorate").

219. In *Printz* the equivalent discretionary acts involve deployment of police investigative forces. A neighborhood hit by a rash of burglaries is unlikely to be appeased by a sheriff who says, "I would have had more police cars in the area, but too many of my officers were spending their time doing background checks that Congress made us do."

220. But see Hills, "The Political Economy of Cooperative Federalism," at p. 828 (observing that "the complexity inherent in any system of federalism . . . always has the potential to confuse voters and thereby undermine political accountability").

221. For a capsule political history of Burma over the relevant period, see Dhooge, "The Wrong Way to Mandalay," at pp. 390–92.

222. *Crosby v. National Foreign Trade Council*, 530 US 363 (2000).

223. I think it worth noting that the simple "diffusion of political responsibility" argument, unmodified by the requirement that the action be one as to which state officials have discretion, is equally strong with respect to negative and affirmative commandeering.

224. Of course such a company might challenge the discretionary decision after the fact, alleging that the factor that controlled the exercise of discretion was that it did business in Burma and that Congress directed states to remove that factor from their decisional processes. Such a challenge would undoubtedly be much more difficult to mount than was the one in *Crosby*.

225. Cox, "Expressivism in Federalism," at pp. 1341–43, suggests that the message sent by affirmative commandeering might be more clear than the message sent by alternative modes of regulation (in Cox's example, by conditions imposed on federal grants; in the present example, by negative commandeering/ preemption).

226. Hills, "The Political Economy of Cooperative Federalism." Hills pays pri-

mary attention to conditional spending as an alternative to affirmative commandeering, and I adapt his arguments where appropriate for the different context of
conditional or negative commandeering.

227. It seems worth suggesting, however, that Hills's argument, as adapted to
deal with the question of negative commandeering, incorporates so many qualifications that it may well be unhelpful as a defense of the proposition that affirmative commandeering is problematic while negative commandeering is not. Given
the complexity of the argument, a reasonably broad ban on negative commandeering might be defensible on formalist grounds.

228. Hills concedes that an unlimited power of conditional preemption could
completely displace the ban on affirmative preemption and argues that the power
to preempt on condition must therefore be supplemented by a doctrine of unconstitutional conditions. Hills, "The Political Economy of Cooperative Federalism,"
at pp. 921–27. As noted above, the Court itself has not suggested that it is on
the verge of developing such a doctrine.

229. Hills, ibid., at pp. 871–91, argues that the costs incurring in compromise
should be incurred, because the initial program will impose higher costs than are
necessary: Congress could adopt cost-justified programs by purchasing state cooperation at a price equivalent to the benefits produced by state cooperation.

230. See ibid., at pp. 862–63. See also Hills, "Federalism in Constitutional
Context," at p. 184n. 12 (noting the fact that fewer than half the states have
submitted plans to implement the federal Occupational Safety and Health Act).

231. See Hills, "The Political Economy of Cooperative Federalism," at p. 868
(noting that Congress's exercise of the power to preempt on condition "is constrained by [Congress's] limited regulatory capacity").

232. Hills's proposed unconstitutional-conditions doctrine might foreclose
this option. Hills would "prohibit conditional preemption of state or local policies whenever (1) the condition that the nonfederal government must meet
would, if imposed unconditionally, be unconstitutional, and (2) Congress threatened preemption of nonfederal policy merely to gain leverage to extract compliance with the condition" (924). "Merely" appears to do a lot of work here:
Suppose Congress imposed the condition because it was concerned about guns in
the hands of people unqualified to use them and believed that state-performed
background checks would do a good job in screening out the unqualified. Is the
condition imposed "merely to gain leverage"? In addition, it is easy to rewrite the
proposed statute to avoid imposing a condition at all: No gun sales in states that
cannot provide assurances that guns will not be transferred to an unqualified
buyer, coupled with criteria to identify systems that provide adequate assurance
that, as a practical matter, can only be satisfied by systems that are state operated
or closely supervised by the state.

233. Cf. ibid., at p. 899 (distinguishing affirmative commandeering from preemption on the ground that "federal money cannot buy preemption"). Hills offers another distinction, that "preemption is generally less harmful to useful state
and local political activity than commandeering legislation" (900). This is so,
Hills argues, because preemption expresses Congress's judgment that "nonfederal
interest in [the preempted] topics would be counterproductive," whereas the
point of affirmative commandeering "is to use state and local officials to regulate

in some federal field, presumably because such officials are well-suited for such duties." Everything in this argument turns on the characterization of the "fields" preempted and commandeered: It is hardly contradictory to assert both that a nonfederal interest expressed across a wide field would be counterproductive and that state and local officials are well suited to express an interest within some subfield within the larger one.

234. I have a lurking sense that Hills overlooks this dimension of the analysis because he is inclined to accept the proposition that as a general matter regimes of nonregulation are normatively more desirable than regulatory regimes. That normative proposition may be true, but the problems of concern at this point in the argument arise precisely because the people in some jurisdictions, acting through their democratically selected representatives, prefer some sort of regulatory regime, that is, reject the normative proposition. One indication of the difficulty with Hills's argument on this issue is that his argument that the national government can purchase state-level cooperation does not take into account the possibility that the people in one subnational jurisdiction may have different preferences from those in other subnational jurisdictions and from those of the people of the nation in the aggregate See, e.g., ibid., at pp. 872–73. Instead, Hills appears to assume that all the people in the nation have the same set of preferences, which sometimes leads them to prefer action at a subnational level and sometimes leads them to prefer action at the national level. See, e.g., ibid., at p. 873 (arguing that "smaller-scale governments systematically may be better than larger-scale governments at managing nonfiscal costs"). I think it worth noting, therefore, that some subnational governments are likely to be more attractive targets for successful NGO political organizing. (Hills does note that "local and state governments might be more sensitive to the ideological objections of well-organized interest groups" (887), but the comparison he draws is between state and local governments on the one hand and the national government on the other, not among state and local governments.) If so, we should expect to discover variations in preferences among the people of different states. And, of course, the strongest defense of federalism rests on the proposition that such variations are inevitable and desirable.

235. Hills, "Federalism in Constitutional Context," at pp. 191–92.

236. Ibid., at p. 191.

237. Hills, "The Political Economy of Cooperative Federalism," at pp. 884–86, explains that an individual state's ability to refuse to exercise its regulatory power creates a "hold out" or "race to the bottom" problem in which no state will regulate because each will fear that regulation will drive businesses to locate in some other, nonregulating jurisdiction. This justifies the rule that Congress can regulate directly. This argument suggests to me that the best candidate for a state immunity from preemption would be along the lines of a market-participant doctrine: Market participation is not regulation and therefore does not raise the hold-out problem.

238. As Dan T. Coenen puts it, the doctrine allows a state's citizens "to reap where they have sown." Coenen, "Untangling the Market-Participant Exception to the Dormant Commerce Clause," at p. 441.

239. *Lorillard*, 533 US at 598n. 8 (Stevens, J., concurring in part, concurring in the judgment in part, and dissenting in part).

240. *Lopez*, 514 US at 552.

241. *Boerne*, 521 US at 527–28.

242. *Webster v. Reproductive Health Services*, 492 U.S. 490 (1989).

243. 505 US 833 (1992).

244. Ibid., at 855. All quotations are taken from the joint opinion of Justices O'Connor, Kennedy, and Souter.

245. Ibid.

246. Ibid.

247. Ibid.

248. *Casey*, 505 US at 856.

249. Ibid., at 861.

250. Ibid., at 867.

251. Ibid.

252. For my views, see Tushnet, *Taking the Constitution away from the Courts*, at pp. 27–30.

253. *Dickerson v. United States*, 530 US 428 (2000).

254. Ibid., at 443. For a discussion of this aspect of *Dickerson*, see Mezey, "Law as Culture," at pp. 55–57.

255. The Warren Court was willing to overrule prior decisions, but, notably, it did not adopt a cultural theory of stare decisis.

256. The New Deal–Great Society constitutional order showed that a Court with an expansive view would not invalidate laws adopted by a Congress with similarly expansive views.

257. Again, roughly, these would be laws with support ranging from just over 50 percent to just under 60 percent in the Senate and just over 50 percent in the House, and consistent with the president's views. For a discussion of the potential impact of the present Court's doctrine across a wide doctrinal range, see Rubenfeld, "The Anti-Antidiscrimination Agenda."

258. Here "old" means, roughly, enacted prior to 1992 or, perhaps, 1994. Under this criterion, the Americans with Disabilities Act is an old statute, as are the nation's major environmental laws.

259. For example, the Court's section 5 decisions raise questions about the constitutionality of the proposed Innocence Protection Act, which would require states to make DNA testing available to defendants sentenced to death if the DNA evidence "has the scientific potential to produce new . . . evidence material to the claim . . . that the prisoner" did not commit the crime. The circumstances under which denying convicted criminals DNA tests would violate the Constitution are quite limited, and Congress may not be able to come up with evidence of enough constitutional violations to justify invocation of the remedial section 5 power. Yet, the Innocence Protection Act may be a proposal that the justices would regard as the kind of grandstanding at which their decisions were directed.

260. Colker and Brudney, "Dissing Congress."

261. See, e.g., Posner, *Breaking the Deadlock*.

262. In the past I have suggested that the recent Court could best be described as implementing the political program of country-club Republicans. Mark Tushnet, "The Burger Court in Historical Perspective: The Triumph of Country Club Republicanism," in Schwartz, ed., *The Burger Court*, at p. 203. Political

scientist Mark Graber has suggested that the modern Court allows moderate Republicans to vote for "feel-good" legislation while still ensuring that Republicans' federalism principles will be respected. I now think that these characterizations may have been accurate for the Court in transition from the old constitutional order to the new one, but they do not fit the Court in the new constitutional order as well as the one I develop here.

263. *See* Biskupic and Witt, *The Supreme Court at Work*, at p. 74; O'Brien, "The Rehnquist Court's Shrinking Plenary Docket."

264. The standard points include Congress's near elimination of the Court's mandatory jurisdiction in 1988; Justice Byron White's retirement, which deprived the Court of a strong voice for taking cases to resolve conflicts among the circuits; a decrease in the degree to which a more conservative Supreme Court faced lower courts with which it disagreed ideologically; and the now near universal use of the "cert. pool," in which one law clerk prepares a single memorandum describing petitions for review and recommending a disposition, which tends to produce recommendations against granting review because the law clerk who recommends denial will rarely be seen to have made a mistake whereas the justices and other law clerks may discover after granting review that the law clerk who recommended doing so was mistaken. For a summary of the standard accounts for the reduction in the Court's caseload, see O'Brien, "The Rehnquist Court's Shrinking Plenary Docket," at p. 58; Biskupic, "The Shrinking Docket."

265. My focus here is narrow, on the Court's output. The administrative structure supporting the federal courts appears to have grown recently, as detailed in Resnik, "Judicial Independence and Article III," at pp. 662–64.

Chapter 3

1. The chapter is shorter than the others because, after all, it deals with challenges to the book's main argument, and it is not surprising that I have less to say about the challenges than I do about the argument itself.

2. Dallek, *Hail to the Chief*, at p. 99.

3. Keith E. Whittington, "The Political Foundations of Judicial Supremacy," in Barber and George, eds., *Constitutional Politics*, at p. 264.

4. Klinkner and Smith, *Unsteady March*.

5. Ibid., at pp. 3–4.

6. Klinkner and Smith's conditions differ from Ackerman's criteria for identifying constitutional moments, but on a more abstract level they can be understood as providing a specific account of constitutional moments and normal politics.

7. Dahl, *A Preface to Democratic Theory*, at pp. 132–33.

8. I emphasize that the formulation about reversion to a conservative norm is my generalization from Klinkner and Smith's analysis and is not their own.

9. The metaphors vary. I have used *feeding frenzy*; another metaphor, used in connection with the 1981 tax law, is *Christmas-tree legislation*. (I think it not insignificant that the usual example of Christmas-tree legislation comes from two decades ago.)

10. Ackerman, "The New Separation of Powers."

11. This description should be qualified by noting the possibility that a randomly unified conservative (or liberal) government might be replaced not by di-

vided government but by a randomly unified conservative (or liberal) government, which might be able to repeal what its predecessor had enacted.

12. Ackerman, "Off Balance," in Ackerman, ed., *Bush v. Gore.*

13. Ibid.

14. The arguments that follow accept the proposition that "[j]udges are . . . recruited and chosen . . . through a political process . . . emphasizing partisanship and ideology." Peretti, *In Defense of a Political Court*, at p. 85. Peretti provides support, from the political science literature at pp. 85–93.

15. Yalof focuses on the president's choice of a nominee, Silverstein on confirmation. Yalof, *Pursuit of Justices*; Silverstein, *Judicious Choices.*

16. Watson and Stookey, *Shaping America*, at p. 43. See also at p. 97 (describing some of these interest groups).

17. *See* Denning, "Reforming the New Confirmation Process," at pp. 15–17.

18. See Statement of Mark Tushnet, Subcommittee on the Courts, US Senate Committee on the Judiciary, September 4, 2001, available at *http://judiciary. senate.gov/oldsite/te090401so-tushnet.htm.* An e-mail exchange with Keith Whittington helped me clarify this point. Eisgruber, "Politics and Personalities in the Federal Appointments Process," describes and criticizes the role given personal character in nomination battles as of 2000, at pp. 185–88.

19. Yalof describes a process that can create additional difficulties for presidents. The judicial selection process has become increasingly bureaucratized and, importantly, divided between the Department of Justice and the White House staff. Each bureaucracy ordinarily pursues somewhat different interests, with the staff at the Department of Justice somewhat more concerned with ideology and the policy imprint the president hopes to place on the courts and the White House staff somewhat more concerned with the political dimensions of the confirmation process. Yalof, *Pursuit of Justices*, at pp. 12–13, 180–86.

20. Silverstein, *Judicious Choices*, at p. 158.

21. It is generally said, for example, that President George H. W. Bush had to sign a civil rights bill that he had previously vetoed to reduce the impression caused by the Thomas nomination that Bush was opposed to civil rights.

22. Silverstein, *Judicious Choices*, at p. 100.

23. Yalof, *Pursuit of Justices*, at p. 17.

24. Silverstein, *Judicious Choices*, at p. 163.

25. Yalof, *Pursuit of Justices*, at p. 171.

26. Silverstein, *Judicious Choices*, at p. 171.

27. For accounts that detail recent experience, see Kline, "The Topsy-Turvy World of Judicial Confirmations"; Denning, "The 'Blue Slip.'" Kline offers a highly partisan interpretation, but his recounting of the events appears to be accurate.

28. Tinsley E. Yarbrough, "Clinton and the Courts," in Hernnson and Hill, eds., *The Clinton Presidency*, at p. 54.

29. Stidham, Carp, and Sanger, "The Voting Behavior of President Clinton's Judicial Appointees." On criminal justice support, for district judges the rates are: Carter 38%, Reagan 23%, Bush 29%, and Clinton 34%; for court of appeals judges they are: Carter 40%, Reagan 26%, Bush 22%, and Clinton 31%. On civil liberties support, for district judges the rates are: Carter 52%, Reagan 33%, Bush 33%, and Clinton 39%; for court of appeals judges they are: Carter 42%, Reagan 32%, Bush 33%, and Clinton 41%.

30. Silverstein argues, for example, that President George H. W. Bush "reward[ed] . . . the right wing of the party . . . [with] judicial appointments." Silverstein, *Judicious Choices*, at p. 124.

31. Shortly after Bush took office, liberal interest groups focused on the Court began to build the case against confirming any Bush nominee: They argued that the conservative justices who, in their eyes, put Bush in office should not be able effectively to select their own successors. For a presentation of the argument, a year after Bush's inauguration, see Mikva, "Supreme Patience." That strategy probably would not succeed, but it indicates that Democratic interest groups are not likely to treat Supreme Court nominations as political deals in which one constituency can be "bought off" by simple identity politics.

32. See Lewis, "The 2000 Campaign."

33. This may be particularly true when the Court is closely divided and a single appointment might be thought likely to have substantial long-term effects. Under those conditions, of course, the opposition to the nomination is likely to be particularly intense as well.

34. One reason for Ackerman's skepticism about treating the Reagan era as the opening of a period of constitutional transformation is, I believe, his sense that the nation did not face a crisis on the scale of the prior ones.

35. In what follows I focus specifically on presidential leadership because that is what seems most likely to shift us into a newer constitutional order. But, as my examples will indicate, sometimes political leadership can be provided by prominent members of Congress.

36. Tulis, *The Rhetorical Presidency. See* Dallek, *Hail to the Chief,* p. 1 (quoting Bush).

37. Tulis, *The Rhetorical Presidency*, at pp. 106, 108.

38. Ibid., at pp. 128, 129.

39. See generally Jacobs and Shapiro, *Politicians Don't Pander*.

40. Dallek, *Hail to the Chief,* at pp. 44–45.

41. Tulis, *The Rhetorical Presidency*, at p. 136.

42. Crime rates did decrease substantially in the 1990s, and some part of the decline may be attributed to policies associated with the wars on crime and drugs. But it is not clear to me that the declines are seen to have resulted from anticrime policies, and public perception is what matters for the argument made here.

43. Prescient, and not just randomly correct in retrospect.

44. Abraham Lincoln, "Second Annual Message to Congress," in Nicolay and Hay, *Complete Works*, vol. 8, at p. 131.

45. Keith Whittington, "The Political Foundations of Judicial Supremacy," in Barber and George, eds., *Constitutional Politics*, at pp. 265–66.

46. Dionne, "Conservatism Recast."

47. See generally Whittington, *Constitutional Construction*.

CHAPTER 4

1. 297 US 1, 62 (1936).

2. *Home Building and Loan Association v. Blaisdell,* 290 US 398, 448–49 (1934) (Sutherland, J., dissenting).

3. Martin Shapiro, "Fathers and Sons: The Court, the Commentators, and the Search for Values," in Blasi, ed., *The Burger Court*, at p. 220.

4. The qualification is necessary because of Frankfurter's willingness to enforce the Fourth Amendment and the establishment clause rather vigorously. See, e.g., *Johnson v. United States*, 333 US 10 (1948) (a 5–4 decision written by Justice Robert Jackson with Frankfurter in the majority, finding a constitutional violation when an officer searched apartment without a warrant after smelling opium from outside the apartment); *Zorach v. Clauson*, 343 US 306, 320–23 (1952) (Frankfurter, J., dissenting) (arguing that a program allowing students to be released from school to attend church-run classes was unconstitutional), and his ambivalent but generally supportive stance toward the Court's intervention against the American system of apartheid. See, e.g., *Terry v. Adams*, 345 US 461, 470 (1953) (opinion of Frankfurter, J.); Tushnet, *Making Civil Rights Law*, at pp. 192–95 (describing Frankfurter's role in *Brown v. Board of Education*).

5. See, e.g., *Minersville School Dist. v. Gobitis*, 310 US 586 (1940); *Dennis v. United States*, 341 US 494, 517 (1951) (Frankfurter, J., concurring in affirmance of the judgment).

6. *United States v. Carolene Products Co.*, 304 US 144, 152–53n. 4 (1938).

7. See Horwitz, *The Warren Court and the Pursuit of Justice*, at p. 84 (noting the importance of Arthur Goldberg's appointment to the consolidation of the Warren Court).

8. Cases illustrating this consolidation are *Griswold v. Connecticut*, 381 US 479 (1965), which no one on the Court sought to defend in "footnote 4" terms; *Shapiro v. Thompson*, 394 US 618 (1969), which began the short-lived process of transforming statutory social welfare provisions into constitutional entitlements; and *Goldberg v. Kelly*, 397 US 254 (1970), which extended that process. One can reconstruct these decisions along "footnote 4" lines, though doing so entails a reconstruction of that footnote's meaning as well.

9. *Griffin v. Illinois*, 351 US 12 (1956) (finding unconstitutional a requirement that appeals be allowed in criminal cases only when the defendant supplied a transcript at his or her own expense); *Douglas v. California*, 372 US 353 (1963) (finding unconstitutional a denial of appointed counsel to indigent defendants on appeal unless the appellate court found that counsel would be helpful).

10. The doctrine might have been confined to state-provided goods. Two observations about such a limitation seem appropriate. First, New Deal–Great Society jurisprudence placed some pressure on the state action doctrine in cases including *Shelley v. Kraemer*, 334 US 1 (1948) (finding state action in judicial decisions enforcing racially restrictive property covenants), and *Burton v. Wilmington Parking Auth.*, 365 US 715 (1961) (finding state action where the state benefited from a lease arrangement under which its tenant chose to discriminate on the basis of race). Limiting the equal protection doctrine to state-provided goods might therefore not have limited it much. Second, the government might respond to a finding that it unconstitutionally provided a good to one group but not to another either by expanding the scope of the program to include the previously excluded or by restricting the program to deny the previously included the good as well. Consistent with the proposition that the New Deal–Great Society courts collaborated with the regime's other institutions, the new equal protec-

tion doctrine was actually used to support the already existing trend toward expanding the welfare state's scope.

11. Personal Responsibility and Work Opportunity Reconciliation Act of 199, Pub. L. 104-193, 11 Stat. 2015 (1996). As one analyst put it, "The outcome for the immediate future was that welfare would never again become a federal entitlement: a reversal of the New Deal as it had developed from Roosevelt to Johnson." Dilys M. Hill, "Domestic Policy," in Hernnson and Hill, eds., *The Clinton Presidency*, at p. 117.

12. On this interpretation, the Court's recent invalidations have come after the new regime was put in place. It seems noteworthy as well that the Court's decisions have not precipitated anything like the political reaction that occurred in the New Deal crisis.

13. See, e.g., Wright, "Professor Bickel, the Scholarly Tradition, and the Supreme Court," at p. 777 (describing Bickel as an "academic mandarin").

14. For a suggestion that the Supreme Court can provoke partisan conflict in periods leading up to realigning elections, see John B. Gates, "The Supreme Court and Partisan Change: Contravening, Provoking, and Diffusing Partisan Conflict," in Gillman and Clayton, eds., *The Supreme Court in American Politics*, at pp. 102–4.

15. For a discussion of the three eras of the Warren Court, only the last of which is the programmatic liberal Warren Court, see Powe, *The Warren Court and American Politics*.

16. See Burt, "Alex Bickel's Law School and Ours," at p. 1860 (noting that by the 1950s the "proper goal . . . for governance institutions [was] to foster mutual accommodations among conflicting parties" in the arena of labor-capital struggle).

17. *See Kovacs v. Cooper*, 336 US 77, 90–95 (1949) (Frankfurter, J., concurring) (criticizing the argument that the First Amendment has a preferred position in constitutional adjudication).

18. For a discussion of the way in which the Court-packing struggle during the New Deal shaped understanding of the law-politics distinction, see Friedman, "The History of the Countermajoritarian Difficulty, Part Four: Law's Politics." The next installment of Friedman's work addresses the dilemma, explored in this chapter as well, faced by liberals in the 1950s. Friedman, "The History of The Countermajoritarian Difficulty, Part Five" (unpublished manuscript in the author's possession).

19. For a discussion, see Tushnet, *Making Civil Rights Law*, at pp. 203–4.

20. What follows is a thumbnail sketch of Legal Process theory and its conceptual structure. I ignore many details and, in particular, ignore the sequence in which the elements of Legal Process theory's analysis of constitutional adjudication actually developed. I also ignore the (large) extent to which Legal Process theory was designed to counter claims, emerging from the Soviet Union and its allies, that the legal processes of the United States and its allies were insufficient to secure social justice.

21. To say that courts have a duty that legislatures do not does not imply, however, that legislatures may not develop policy based on principle in the Legal Process sense. The point is that legislatures may do so but they need not, whereas courts must.

22. The Legal Process approach came to be understood as specifying institutional arrangements that would support stability in any society. In invoking the actual conditions of American society, Bickel may have modified the approach in an important way. But cf. Hart and Sacks, *The Legal Process*, at p. 113 ("Are the positions which have been taken thus far in these materials conventional and generally acceptable? Might a representative chairman of the Republic [*sic*] National Committee, for example, be expected to agree with them? A chairman of the Democratic National Committee? . . . A representative member of the Soviet Russian Politburo?").

23. 350 US 891 (1955), after remand, 350 US 985 (1956), discussed in Bickel, *The Least Dangerous Branch*, at p. 174.

24. Fallon, Meltzer, and Shapiro, *Hart and Wechsler's The Federal Courts and the Federal System*, at pp. 653–55, provides a convenient summary of the Naim litigation and its jurisprudential context.

25. Wechsler, *Principle, Politics and Fundamental Law*, at p. 47, originally published as "Toward Neutral Principles of Constitutional Law."

26. Of course, principled application of justiciability doctrines might require that the Court decline to decide some cases where invoking principle would not produce instability.

27. Gunther, "The Subtle Vices of the 'Passive Virtues,'" at p. 3.

28. In addition, Bickel's analysis was in tension with the Legal Process idea that courts lacked the capacity to do a good job in making political judgments.

29. On Warren's appointment, see Powe, *The Warren Court and American Politics*, at p. 24.

30. On Brennan's appointment, see ibid., at pp. 89–90.

31. On Harlan's appointment, see ibid., at pp. 48–49.

32. The best example of this phenomenon is probably Kurland, "Foreword: 'Equal in Origin and Equal in Title to the Legislative and Executive Branches of the Government.'"

33. For a discussion, see Tushnet, *Making Civil Rights Law*, at pp. 192–93, 228–29.

34. Kronman, "Alexander Bickel's Philosophy of Prudence," at p. 1589.

35. Ely pointed out that Legal Process theory imputed characteristics to legislatures that need not always be satisfied. Legislatures would not respond to the interests, preferences, or values of those who were not represented, for example. An incomplete or partial democracy was unlikely to be stable and therefore could not satisfy Legal Process theory's foundational requirement. Ely argued that courts could promote stability by invoking the Constitution to guarantee that legislatures fairly represented all in the society. Ely, *Democracy and Distrust*.

36. Vetter, "Postwar Legal Scholarship on Judicial Decision Making," at p. 420.

37. Ely's critique of *Roe v. Wade* exemplifies the difficulty. Ely, "The Wages of Crying Wolf." For Ely, *Roe* was simply not constitutional law as he understood it, for two related reasons: It was unprincipled in the Legal Process sense, and it identified no problem of democratic representation that justified judicial intervention.

38. Burt, "Alex Bickel's Law School and Ours," at pp. 1864, 1859.

39. At least if, as was true during the New Deal–Great Society constitutional regime, the regime principles point to choosing judges who combine political judgment with a commitment to principle.

40. *Michael H. v. Gerald D.*, 491 US 110, 127–28n. 6 (1989) (opinion of Scalia, J.).

41. *Washington v. Glucksberg*, 521 US 702, 722 (1998) ("the development of this Court's substantive-due-process jurisprudence . . . has been a process whereby the outlines of the 'liberty' specially protected by the Fourteenth Amendment—never fully clarified, to be sure, and perhaps not capable of being fully clarified—have at least been carefully refined by concrete examples involving fundamental rights found to be deeply rooted in our legal tradition. This approach tends to rein in the subjective elements that are necessarily present in due-process judicial review.").

42. Perhaps Justice Scalia's background as an academic has made him sensitive to the concerns of academics for justification. My concern in this chapter is with theorizing about the Supreme Court's role, not with its actual performance. Bickel and other academics worried about justifying the decisions made by the New Deal–Great Society Supreme Court; the justices of that Court rarely did.

43. *County of Sacramento v. Lewis*, 523 US 833, 848n. 8 (1998) ("in a due process challenge to executive action, the threshold question is whether the behavior of the governmental officer is so egregious, so outrageous, that it may fairly be said to shock the contemporary conscience. That judgment may be informed by a history of liberty protection, but it necessarily reflects an understanding of traditional executive behavior, of contemporary practice, and of the standards of blame generally applied to them.").

44. See *County of Sacramento v. Lewis*, 523 US at 860 (Scalia, J., dissenting) ("Today's opinion gives the lie to those cynics who claim that changes in this Court's jurisprudence are attributable to changes in the Court's membership. It proves that the changes are attributable to nothing but the passage of time (not much time, at that), plus application of the ancient maxim, 'That was then, this is now.' Just last Term, in *Washington v. Glucksberg*, the Court specifically rejected the method of substantive-due-process analysis employed by . . . the Court today.") (citation and paragraphing omitted).

45. 505 US 833 (1992).

46. Ibid., at 848–50.

47. Ibid., at 849.

48. Ibid.

49. *Casey*, 505 US at 874.

50. Ibid., at 982 (Scalia, J., dissenting).

51. Ibid., at 983 (Scalia, J., dissenting).

52. Ibid., at 853 (opinion of O'Connor, Kennedy, and Souter, JJ.) ("the *reservations any of us may have* in reaffirming the central holding of *Roe* are outweighed by the explication of individual liberty we have given combined with the force of stare decisis") (emphasis added); 869 ("A decision to overrule *Roe*'s essential holding under the existing circumstances *would address error, if error there was*, at the cost of both profound and unnecessary damage to the Court's legitimacy, and to the Nation's commitment to the rule of law.") (emphasis added).

53. Ibid., at 865, 866.

54. Ibid., at 865.

55. Ibid., at 867.

56. Ibid.

57. The reasoned judgment they defend is that *Roe* offered a defensible, though not necessarily correct, account of the interests at stake. They then erect a reasoned defense of stare decisis, a doctrine that matters only when the initial decision might be erroneous.

58. *Glucksberg*, 521 US at 721.

59. See, e.g., McConnell, "The Right to Die and the Jurisprudence of Tradition," at p. 683 ("In the absence of any reliable basis for resolving moral and philosophical disagreements of this sort [other than whether a position accords with our own opinion!], courts should look to *experience* and to *stable consensus* as an objective basis for decision making. If a practice is adopted by many different communities, and maintained for a considerable period of time, this provides strong evidence that the practice contributes to the common good and accords with the spirit and mores of the people.") (emphasis added); Duncan, "'They Call Me "Eight Eyes,"'" at p. 248 ("Under *Glucksberg*, persons challenging the dual-gender requirement for marriage will be required to establish that an objective historical inquiry based upon a 'careful description' of the asserted liberty interest supports their claim. *In other words*, they will be required to establish that our society has rejected *its traditional concept of marriage as a relationship between one man and one woman* and has formed a new national consensus in support of the equal validity of homosexual marriage.") (emphasis added).

60. *See* Sunstein, *One Case at a Time*, at p. ix ("A majority of five justices merely said that there is no general right to suicide, assisted or otherwise, and it left open the possibility that under special circumstances, people might have a right to physician assisted suicide after all."); xii (a five-justice majority "has rejected the whole approach in Rehnquist's opinion"). Justice O'Connor joined the Court's opinion but wrote a separate concurring opinion indicating her view that "a mentally competent person who is experiencing great suffering [might have] a constitutionally cognizable interest in controlling the circumstances of his or her imminent death." *Washington v. Glucksberg*, 521 US at 736 (O'Connor, J., concurring). Justice Ginsburg concurred in the judgment "substantially for the reasons stated" by Justice O'Connor (789), thereby suggesting her agreement with Justice O'Connor's qualification. Justice Breyer concurred in the judgment and joined Justice O'Connor's opinion "except insofar as [it] joined the Court's opinion" (789n.), and quoted Justice O'Connor's assertion that "a mentally competent person who is experiencing great suffering has a constitutionally cognizable interest in controlling the circumstances of his or her imminent death." Justice Stevens concurred in the judgment and indicated his view that "[a]llowing the individual . . . to make judgments 'about the "quality" of life.' . . . gives proper recognition to the individual's interest in choosing a final chapter that accords with her life story" (746–47) (Stevens, J., concurring in the judgment). Justice Souter recognized a liberty interest that might have a broader scope but believed that the legislature had greater competence to deal with the question "at this time," while not "decid[ing] for all time that respondent's claim should not be

recognized" (789) (Souter, J., concurring in the judgment). McConnell, "The Right to Die and the Jurisprudence of Tradition," at 673–81, argues against drawing strong conclusions about interpretive methods from this analysis of the opinions of the various justices.

61. I do not mean to assert that the Warren Court's decisions were expressed with a lack of seriousness. Yet there clearly is a stylistic difference between the typical opinion by Earl Warren or William O. Douglas and the typical opinion by David Souter or Anthony Kennedy. The word "seriousness" comes as close to capturing that stylistic difference as anything I have been able to come up with.

62. See, e.g., Paulsen and Johnson, "Scalia's Sermonette," at p. 863 ("Scalia is the master of the eminently quotable turn-of-phrase, the arresting quip, the provocatively expressed legal argument"); McAllister, "An Eagle Soaring," at p. 309 (Scalia "articulates his principles with a wit and style that few can match."). These authors admire Justice Scalia's decisions as well as his style, and their judgments about the former may influence their judgments about the latter. But my impression is that even liberals think that Justice Scalia is a good prose stylist.

63. Cf. Price, "Party of Nine" (describing Supreme Court oral arguments as "the best show in America" and labeling individual justices as "Bart Simpson," "Cosmo Kramer," "Ling Woo," "Lisa Simpson," and "Bob Newhart").

64. Or so I interpret Bobbitt, *Constitutional Interpretation*. See Tushnet, "Justification in Constitutional Interpretation."

65. Michelman, *Some Notes on Republicanism and Judicial Review* (alluding to Fried, "The Artificial Reason of the Law").

66. Bickel, *The Least Dangerous Branch*, at p. 23.

67. The term is usually attributed to Baker, "Hun Lacks Seriosity," but Baker had used it earlier in "Taking the Cure." The first use disclosed in a search of the NEXIS database was Gilbert, "Look What's Happening in Chicago."

68. Eskridge and Frickey, "The Supreme Court, 1993 Term—Foreword: Law as Equilibrium."

69. Ibid., at p. 28 (describing a "renaissance" in legal process theory).

70. Ibid.

71. Eskridge and Frickey, "The Supreme Court, 1993 Term—Foreword: Law as Equilibrium," at p. 29 (describing "each branch" in these terms).

72. Ibid.

73. Ibid.

74. Eskridge and Frickey, "The Supreme Court, 1993 Term—Foreword: Law as Equilibrium," at p. 42 (asserting that their theory is both "necessary" and "sufficient"), 29 (offering understanding and explanation as the grounds for theory choice).

75. Epstein, Knight, and Martin, "The Supreme Court as a *Strategic* National Policymaker," at p. 600.

76. Kritzer, "The Impact of *Bush v. Gore* on Public Perceptions and Knowledge of the Supreme Court."

77. See, e.g., Eskridge and Frickey, "The Supreme Court, 1993 Term—Foreword: Law as Equilibrium," at pp. 37–38 (providing a speculative account of *Planned Parenthood of Southeastern Pennsylvania v. Casey*, concluding that

"[t]hese centrist Justices rationally understood that a position rejected by big majorities in Congress and by the public would not be regarded as legitimate").

78. For a general critique of political scientists' efforts to demonstrate that justices' preferences provide the best explanation for their actions, see Gillman, "What's Law Got to Do with It?"

79. Segal and Cover, "Ideological Values and the Votes of U.S. Supreme Court Justices"; Nagel, "Political Party Affiliation and Judges' Decisions."

80. The location of the political center shifts over time so that a judge who is described as "moderate" when appointed might become "liberal" or "conservative" during the judge's tenure. Although his deepest views did not change, Justice Hugo Black was a New Deal liberal when appointed, a strict constructionist semi-conservative late in his career. More recently, Justice John Paul Stevens was a moderate when appointed, a liberal late in his tenure.

81. Gillman, "What's Law Got to Do With It?" at p. 470n. 7. I should note that Gillman is describing what is obviously a hotly contested division among political scientists, which to an outsider seems as much a war over turf as one over substance.

82. For an indication of the difficulty, see Krehbiel, *Pivotal Politics*, at pp. 15–16 (describing difficulties of testing theories in "multidimensional settings").

83. The title of a widely cited public choice work expresses the problem: Shepsle, "Congress Is a 'They,' Not an 'It'."

84. Eskridge and Frickey, "The Supreme Court, 1993 Term—Foreword: Law as Equilibrium," at p. 70.

85. Ibid., at p. 75.

86. Eskridge and Frickey offer a moderately reformist informal public choice account, thereby gaining some advantage from the prestige of law and economics.

87. Eskridge and Frickey, "The Supreme Court, 1993 Term—Foreword: Law as Equilibrium," at p. 29.

88. Ibid.

89. Eskridge and Frickey, "The Supreme Court, 1993 Term—Foreword: Law as Equilibrium," at p. 35. I think it fair to ask whether in Eskridge and Frickey's conception there could be law in any nontotalitarian state that was not a balance among institutions; if there cannot, it is hard to understand the sense in which they use the word "superior."

90. Ibid., at p. 88.

91. Ibid., at p. 77.

92. For critiques of Legal Process theory arguing that the theory was incompatible with some aspects of the New Deal reformism espoused by leading proponents of Legal Process, which however underestimate the degree to which the Legal Process theorists were reformists, see Horwitz, *The Transformation of American Law, 1870–1960*, at pp. 257–58, 264–68; Peller, "*Neutral Principles in the 1950s.*"

93. Rosen, "The Age of Mixed Results."

94. See Sunstein, *One Case at a Time*, at pp. 267–68n. 5 (whereas Bickel believed that "once assumed, jurisdiction should result in the most principled and

full of opinions," Sunstein's view is that "opinions should be self-consciously narrow and shallow, at least some of the time").

95. See ibid., at pp. 11–14. For example, a deep opinion might rely exclusively on the framers' intent, expressly because judges are licensed to overturn contemporary legislative judgments only in the service of the framers' intentions. Or it might invoke economic analysis, expressly because that is the best way to achieve our society's commitment to efficient allocation of resources. Or it might invoke some systematic moral theory like utilitarianism or some other liberal theory of justice, expressly because the Constitution is a justice-seeking document.

96. Ibid., at p. 13 (referring to "concrete judgments backed by . . . unambitious reasoning on which people can converge from diverse foundations").

97. For Sunstein's definition of narrowness, see ibid., at p. 10.

98. "[A] minimalist path usually—not always, but usually—makes a good deal of sense when the Court is dealing with a constitutional issue of high complexity about which many people feel deeply and on which the nation is divided (on moral or other grounds)." Ibid., at p. 5 (emphasis omitted).

99. "[M]inimalism makes sense first because courts may resolve those issues incorrectly, and second because courts may create serious problems even if their answers are right. Courts thus try to economize on moral disagreement by refusing to take on other people's deeply held moral commitments when it is not necessary for them to do so in order to decide the case." Ibid.

100. It is worth noting that the courts' identification of these goals, and more particularly of what constitutes a truly democratic dialogue, almost certainly rests on some deep judgments in democratic theory. Sunstein, for example, holds a theory in which decisions made by those directly responsible to voters are more consistent with democratic premises than decisions made by those only indirectly responsible to voters. See, e.g., ibid., at pp. 38 ("A court might strike down vague laws precisely because they ensure that executive branch officials, rather than elected representatives, will determine the content of the law"); 41 ("the nondelegation and void-for-vagueness doctrines ensure legislative rather than executive law-making"), 130 (asserting that "[t]he proliferation of [affirmative action] programs . . . has proceeded without sustained attention to the underlying issues of principle and policy," but noting as well that "many such programs have their origins in . . . decisions of politically accountable bodies"). See also Rosen, "The Age of Mixed Results," at p. 49 (arguing that Sunstein's reliance on an idea of deliberative democracy "risks substituting his own visions of good policy for those of the people. And that is precisely what minimalism promised to avoid"). But see Sunstein, *One Case at a Time*, at pp. 271–72n. 9 (noting that "there are many different conceptions of democracy").

101. See Gelman, "The Hedgehog, the Fox, and the Minimalist," at p. 2319 (observing that "the crucial question becomes one of circumstances" and arguing that Sunstein does not provide helpful guidance on identifying the circumstances under which minimalism and maximalism are each appropriate).

102. See, e.g., Sunstein, *One Case at a Time*, at p. 267n. 5 ("My argument . . . finds its foundations in the aspiration to deliberative democracy, with an insistence that the principal vehicle is the legislature, not the judiciary; the judiciary is to play a catalytic and supplementary role"); 162 ("The original understanding

was that deliberation about the Constitution's meaning would be part of the function of the President and legislators as well"). Peters, "Assessing the New Judicial Minimalism," argues, with the aim of undermining any claimed democratic superiority of legislatures to courts, that courts are at least as representative as legislatures. If Sunstein's arguments raise questions about the justifications for judicial review, Peters's arguments raise questions, oddly enough, about the justifications for legislative decision making.

103. For example, Sunstein urges minimalism when "things will be quite different in the near future." Sunstein, *One Case at a Time*, at p. 48. When one of the things that might change is "relevant . . . values," it is unclear what is gained by invalidating a statute in such a situation; the invalidated statute would become a derelict anyway.

104. Ibid., at p. 5 ("certain forms of minimalism can be democracy-promoting, not only in the sense that they leave issues open for democratic deliberation, but also and more fundamentally in the sense that they promote reason-giving and ensure that certain important decisions are made by democratically accountable actors"). Minimalist decisions upholding statutes, that is, finding that they do not violate the Constitution, may have a similar effect, if legislatures understand the courts to be saying that they might invalidate the statute if it is unchanged when a slightly different case is presented to them.

105. A slightly more detailed version of the argument that follows can be found in Tushnet, "How to Deny a Constitutional Right." See also Rosen, "The Age of Mixed Results," at p. 44 ("Whether a decision is characterized as narrow or shallow, or deep or broad, seems entirely in the eye of the beholder.").

106. Sunstein addresses this problem under the heading of stare decisis. Sunstein, *One Case at a Time*, at pp. 19–23. I believe the better label would be ratio decidendi. The most acute analysis of the problem is Deutsch, "Precedent and Adjudication." See also Primus, "Canon, Anti-Canon, and Judicial Dissent," at pp. 263 ("Holdings . . . are retrospectively constructed"); 283 (noting "the degree to which the meaning of a judicial opinion is determined by its later construction").

107. Sunstein, *One Case at a Time*, at p. 21. A good example is provided by Justice Scalia's observation about some seemingly maximalist statements about the First Amendment's structure: "Such statements must be taken in context, however, and are [not] . . . literally true." *R.A.V. v. St. Paul*, 505 US 377, 383 (1992).

108. Sunstein, *One Case at a Time*, at p. 22.

109. Ibid.

110. I have tried to rely almost exclusively on Sunstein's classification of these examples to avoid the critique that I have placed the example at the wrong location on the continua between minimalism and maximalism in their various dimensions.

111. Sunstein, *One Case at a Time*, at pp. 131–57. See especially p. 64 (*Romer* "may also be an act of statesmanship.").

112. *Romer v. Evans*, 517 US 620, 623 (1996) (citing *Plessy v. Ferguson*, 163 US 537 [1896], in the opening sentence).

113. *Romer*, 517 US at 634.

114. For a suggestion along these lines, written before the Court decided *Romer* but referring to the litigation at an earlier stage, see Nagel, "Name-Calling and the Clear Error Rule."

115. Sunstein, *One Case at a Time*, at p. 26.

116. Ibid., at p. 76 (describing the decisions as "good minimalist" ones and asserting that "[t]he Court was right not to decide" more broadly).

117. McConnell, "The Right to Die and the Jurisprudence of Tradition."

118. Sunstein, *One Case at a Time*, at pp. 77, 83.

119. This course was available in the assisted-suicide cases themselves. Cf. ibid., at pp. 99–101 (suggesting but rejecting this course). The Court could have held, as had the Court of Appeals for the Ninth Circuit, that a statute making assistance in suicide impermissible in all circumstances was unconstitutional because it swept into the ban circumstances where the Constitution gave people a right to assistance.

120. Ibid., at p. 37.

121. See, e.g., Congregation for the Doctrine of the Faith, "Declaration on Procured Abortion," no. 14 (November 18, 1974) ("[I]n certain cases, . . . by denying abortion one endangers important values . . . which may sometimes even seem to have priority. . . . [I]t may be the importance attributed in different classes of society to considerations of honour or dishonour, of loss of social standing, and so forth. We proclaim only that none of these reasons can ever objectively confer the right to dispose of another's life."); "Abortion and the Right to Live: A Joint Statement of Catholic Archbishops of Great Britain," no. 21 (January 24, 1980, Catholic Truth Society) ("The newly conceived child cannot rightly be made to suffer the penalty of death for a man's violation of the woman."). (I thank Kevin Quinn, S.J., for these references.)

122. See Sunstein, *One Case at a Time*, at p. 82 (noting the existence of "not widely advertised" practices associated with assisted suicide).

123. One might regard the Court's initial decision invalidating the death penalty as such, *Furman v. Georgia*, 408 US 238 (1972), and its aftermath as an illustration of this process. Perhaps *Furman* does not count as wide under Sunstein's definition, although it seems to me that a decision that invalidates all existing capital sentences ought to be called wide. The decision certainly was shallow, with each justice writing a separate opinion and with no obvious holding beyond the bottom line result. Legislatures responded by enacting new death penalty statutes that they correctly believed would satisfy the Court. *Gregg v. Georgia*, 428 US 153 (1976).

124. 60 US (19 How.) 393 (1857).

125. 347 US 483 (1954).

126. 410 US 113 (1973).

127. See Sunstein, *One Case at a Time*, at p. 37, but see p. 17 (chart placing *Roe* outside category of maximalist decisions).

128. Ibid., at pp. 54, 37.

129. Ibid., at p. 158 (noting the "vigorous debates about the impact of *Brown*").

130. Sunstein defends *Brown* as perhaps not truly maximalist because of its reservation of issues of remedy. Ibid., at p. 38. See also Burt, *The Constitution in*

Conflict, at pp. 275–85 (providing a similar account of the relation between *Brown* and the subsequent decision on remedy, *Brown v. Board of Education*, 349 US 294 [1955]).

131. Of course the public's democratic deliberations cannot be immediately effective if they reach a different conclusion from the Court's maximalist one. *See* Sunstein, *One Case at a Time*, at p. 30 (making this point in connection with *Dred Scott* and *Roe*). But obstacles to legislative action mean that such deliberations are rarely immediately effective anyway. The real question is how large the difference is between the time it takes to secure legislation after a minimalist decision and the time it takes to do so after a maximalist one. Here all I can report is my sense that the difference is not as large as the terms *minimal* and *maximal* suggest.

132. Morgentaler v. The Queen, [1988] S.C.R. 30.

133. For a brief discussion of the legislative aftermath, see Morton, *Pro-Choice vs. Pro-Life*.

134. Sunstein, *One Case at a Time*, at p. 56 (emphasis added). See generally Komesar, *Imperfect Alternatives*.

135. Although the story is not yet complete, this may be one way to describe the results of the contemporary Court's affirmative action decisions.

136. Sunstein endorses the virtue of prudence in adjudication. Sunstein, *One Case at a Time*, at p. 161. Cf. ibid., at pp. 254–55 (urging that judges attend more to "fact-filled briefs" describing the effects of alternative legal rules).

137. See Tushnet, "Constitutional Interpretation, Character, and Experience," at pp. 757, 759–60 (describing the justices' backgrounds; the general picture has not changed since 1992).

138. See Tushnet, *Making Civil Rights Law*, at pp. 192–93 (describing Frankfurter's political concerns), 210 (noting Tom Clark's reference to political considerations), 219 (describing Black and Douglas's statements about resistance to *Brown*), 229–30 (quoting Black's statement that *Brown* would be "the end of Southern liberalism for the time being").

139. See, e.g., Black, "The Unfinished Business of the Warren Court," at p. 22.

140. See, e.g., Sunstein, *One Case at a Time*, at p. 57 ("it is worthwhile to attempt a broad and deep solution . . . when judges have considerable confidence in the merits of that solution").

141. See, e.g., *Alden v. Maine*, 527 US 706, 758 (1999) ("In apparent attempt to disparage a conclusion with which it disagrees, the dissent attributes our reasoning to natural law. We seek to discover, however, only what the Framers and those who ratified the Constitution sought to accomplish when they created a federal system."); *College Savings Bank v. Florida Prepaid Postsecondary Ed. Expense Bd.*, 527 US 666, 688 (1999) (asserting that the dissent "reiterates . . . the now-fashionable revisionist accounts of the Eleventh Amendment set forth in other opinions in a degree of repetitive detail that has despoiled our northern woods").

142. 521 US 507 (1997).

143. A similar concern could be raised by Sunstein's suggestion that maximalism is appropriate "for the most compelling cases in which the underlying judg-

ment of (constitutionally relevant) political morality is insistent." Sunstein, *One Case at a Time*, at p. 38. Agreement on what is "insistent" and "compelling" might reflect something other than detached judgment, such as a political consensus among a group with its own interests.

144. Ibid., at p. 38. See also pp. 168–70 (describing the Court's gender discrimination decisions as involving "so many encounters with so many contexts," and as therefore justifying a deep account of gender discrimination's harms). In this aspect, Sunstein's account resembles the process of common-law adjudication. See, e.g., Holmes, *His Book Notices and Uncollected Letters and Papers*, at pp. 63, 90 ("It is the merit of the common law that it decides the case first and determines the principle afterwards."). For a general discussion, see Strauss, "Common Law Constitutional Interpretation."

145. Sunstein, *One Case at a Time*, at p. 118. See also pp. 117–18 (suggesting that the Court's minimalism in affirmative action cases might be "performing a valuable catalytic function").

146. *Gaines ex rel. Missouri v. Canada*, 305 US 337 (1938); *Sipuel v. Oklahoma State Regents*, 332 US 631 (1948); *McLaurin v. Oklahoma State Regents*, 339 US 637 (1950); *Sweatt v. Painter*, 339 US 629 (1950). (*Fisher v. Hurst*, 333 US 147 [1948], was a reappearance of the *Sipuel* case, presenting no new issues.)

147. 515 US 200 (1995). See Stone et al., *Constitutional Law*, at pp. 553–57 (describing the cases). Cf. Sunstein, *One Case at a Time*, at p. 124 (noting that the Court "has decided a large number of cases, but proceeded in a minimalist manner").

148. Burt, "Alex Bickel's Law School and Ours," at p. 1869.

149. 531 US 70 (2000).

150. Sunstein, "The Broad Virtue in a Modest Ruling." Sunstein reiterated his praise for the decision in "Order without Law," in Sunstein and Epstein, eds., *The Vote*.

151. Flaherty, Letter to the Editor.

152. *Bush v. Gore*, 531 US 98, 109 (2000). The decision illustrates as well the fact that minimalism is not an intrinsic characteristic of decisions, as Sunstein recognizes. See "Order without Law." The Court articulated an equal protection doctrine, which remains available for later courts to use more expansively if they choose. The decision's apparent minimalism, that is, is hostage to what courts do with it in the future.

153. Sunstein, "Order without Law."

154. Ibid. (emphasis added).

155. Lund, "The Unbearable Rightness of *Bush v. Gore*," argues that the Court's decision, which vacated the Florida Supreme Court's decision and remanded the case for further action "consistent with" the U.S. Supreme Court's decision, did not in fact foreclose the Florida Supreme Court from taking further action. He suggests that the Florida Supreme Court might have overruled the decisions interpreting Florida law on which the U.S. Supreme Court relied. There is almost no relevant law on the question of what actions on remand are "consistent with" a Supreme Court's decision, but I would be surprised if the Court were to say that overruling decisions on which it had relied was consistent with its decision.

156. For this reason, I find unconvincing Sunstein's specification of the circumstances under which courts should prefer minimalism or maximalism. Because they are not intrinsic characteristics of an opinion, the analysis must focus not on judicial capacity or the nature of the problem posed to the courts but on the reaction of public officials to the courts' decision. Sunstein provides little account of the variables affecting these reactions.

157. See, e.g., Mendelson, "On the Meaning of the First Amendment." Cf. Sunstein, *One Case at a Time*, at p. 53 (referring to narrow decisions that "point[ ] to a range of factors in a particular case").

158. See, e.g., Frantz, "The First Amendment in the Balance."

159. Sunstein, *One Case at a Time*, at p. 48 ("A court that economizes on decision costs for itself may in the process 'export' decision costs to other people, including litigants and judges in subsequent cases who must give content to the law.").

160. 476 US 267 (1986).

161. Carol Steiker, bench memorandum for Thurgood Marshall, no. 87–998, Thurgood Marshall Papers, Library of Congress, box 429, file 4, cited in Tushnet, *Making Constitutional Law*, at p. 137. Sunstein commends the narrowness of Justice Powell's affirmative action opinion in *Regents of the University of California v. Bakke*, 438 US 165 (1978). See Sunstein, *One Case at a Time*, at p. 131.

162. Cf. Sunstein, *One Case at a Time*, at p. 22 (describing "width as a judicial virtue" because "it creates a reliable backdrop for use by citizens and legislators"); Rosen, "The Age of Mixed Results," at p. 46 (noting the power-enhancing aspects of Justice O'Connor's minimalism in cases involving challenges to districting as impermissibly based on race).

163. See Devins, "The Democracy-Forcing Constitution," at p. 1193n. 84 ("where Bickel was criticized for '100% insistence on principle, 20% of the time,' Sunstein seems to ask for 0% principle 100% of the time").

164. We might impute a more strategic view to the Court. I have argued that there are reasons to believe that a new constitutional order has emerged, but those reasons are certainly not conclusive. One might think that the new order is struggling to be born and may not ever fully emerge. In such circumstances it would be imprudent to project today a rule that is to guide the national government in the new constitutional order because that rule might turn out to be incompatible with what in fact takes place. This is one way of understanding Sunstein's arguments for minimalism: When political society is sharply divided over some issue, minimalist positions are strategically desirable for the Court. Resolving the issue definitively would generate severe criticism of the Court by the (large) losing side, and the Court might resolve the issue in a way inconsistent with the way society ends up resolving it. Minimalist decisions allow the Court to endorse a vision of a more limited national government without, however, committing the Court to enforcing strict rules in the event that the new order never consolidates and the old one continues.

165. Some have suggested that Sunstein's analysis should be understood as strategic in another sense. See, e.g., Miller, "Book Says Bolder Isn't Better in Rulings by the Supreme Court" (quoting Professor Michael Klarman: "To a neutral observer, it is suspicious that all of us liberals are making these claims about

limited judicial power at a time when we don't control the power"). According to this view, Sunstein is taken to be a political liberal facing a relatively conservative Court. The best he can hope for in a liberal direction are minimalist decisions like *Romer*. The worst, from his imputed political position, would be maximalist conservative decisions. The presumption in favor of minimalist decisions takes nothing away from what he and his allies can get from the Court anyway and might deprive his opponents of some decisions they might get. This interpretation unattractively attributes disingenuousness to Sunstein and implausibly attributes an inability on the part of conservative justices to see through the purported Machiavellian strategy.

CHAPTER 5

1. For a general analysis, see Thomas, "Constitutional Change and International Government."

2. Strange, "The Defective State," at p. 56. For a different but equally evocative metaphor, see Rhodes, "The Hollowing Out of the State."

3. For other observations along similar lines, see Sassen, *Globalization and Its Discontents*, at p. 92: Globalization involves "the unbundling of sovereignty . . . , the relocation of various components of sovereignty onto supranational, nongovernmental, or private institutions." See also Ruggie, "At Home Abroad, Abroad at Home," at p. 508 (referring to "the denationalisation of control over significant decisions regarding production, exchange, and employment"). For a more complete description, see Dreeg, "Economic Globalization and the Shifting Boundaries of German Federalism," at p. 28 ("[G]lobalization weakens the policy autonomy and capacity of all units of government. Autonomy is weakened because the increased mobility of investment capital narrows the range of policy strategies that governments may use effectively. Capacity is weakened because many conventional economic policy instruments are rendered ineffective in open and competitive markets."). For a balanced introduction to the uses of the term, see Scholte, *Globalization*.

4. For a review of issues on which international influences have domestic effects, see Luard, *The Globalization of Politics* (focusing on environmental regulation, immigration, and social welfare programs). See also Ruggie, "At Home Abroad, Abroad at Home," at p. 508 (referring to the "denationalisation of control over significant decisions regarding production, exchange, and employment; and the growing difficulty experienced by governments in living up to their part of the domestic social compact on which post-war liberalisation . . . hinged"); Gill, "Globalisation, Market Civilisation, and Disciplinary Neoliberalism," at p. 413 ("In effect, new constitutionalism confers privileged rights of citizenship and representation on corporate capital, whilst constraining the democratization process that has involved struggles for representation for hundreds of years. Central, therefore, to new constitutionalism is the imposition of discipline on public institutions, partly to prevent national interference with the property rights and entry and exit options of holders of mobile capital with regard to particular political jurisdictions."); Schneiderman, "Investment Rules and the New Constitutionalism."

5. Sassen, *Globalization and Its Discontents*, at p. 195. See also Cerny, "Globalization and the Changing Logic of Collective Action," at p. 619 (pointing out that "the decay of the cultural underpinnings of the state" will be slower in "more developed states [that] provide infrastructure, education systems, workforce skills, and quality-of-life amenities [usually classed among the immobile factors of capital] to attract mobile, footloose capital of a highly sophisticated kind.").

6. Hiscox, "Supranationalism and Decentralization in the Global Economy."

7. See Whittington, "Dismantling the Modern States?" at p. 516 ("Globalization and post-industrialism have weakened the value of centralization by reducing the autonomy of the national state.").

8. Castells, *The Power of Identity*, at pp. 66–67, 272. See also Rawlings, "The New Model Wales," at p. 469 (arguing that devolution "put[s] in issue the meaning of ideas of 'Britishness,'" and "reinforces the contemporary sense of a more cosmopolitan society, whose people have multiple identities"). Castells continues, "once this decentralization occurs, local and regional governments may seize the initiative on behalf of their populations, and may engage in developmental strategies vis à vis the global system, eventually coming into competition with their own parent states" (272). The Burma Law case discussed in chapter 2 and later in this chapter may be an example of this phenomenon.

9. Koh, "Bringing International Law Home," at p. 642 (describing, inter alia, political and legal "internalization" of international norms).

10. For a general discussion of the integration problem, see Didier Maus, "The Influence of Contemporary International Law on the Exercise of Constituent Power," in Jyränki, ed., *National Constitutions in the Era of Integration*, at p. 45.

11. Precisely because globalization is such a large topic, I focus only on a few cases in which globalization intersects with constitutional law. I do not examine, for example, questions about immigration law and alienage, which arise in new forms because of globalization.

12. For a discussion of the manner in which constitutional doctrine was transformed, stressing that the process took place over a long period and was not directly connected to the New Deal itself, see White, *The Constitution and the New Deal*, at pp. 33–93.

13. Responding in part to Senator Bricker's proposals to amend the Constitution, the consensus came to accept the proposition that this plenary power was limited by the Constitution's individual rights provisions. See *Reid v. Covert*, 354 US 1 (1957). For a discussion of the Bricker proposals, see Tananbaum, *The Bricker Amendment Controversy*.

14. Flaherty, "History Right?" at pp. 2095–96. I do not deal with the possible transformation of executive dominance in foreign affairs, except indirectly in my emphasis on the role of divided government in limiting the possibility of successful assertions of the president's exclusive power to make foreign policy. For a collection of articles speculating on the role of Congress in foreign policy in the new constitutional order, see Symposium, "Congress and Foreign Policy after the Cold War."

15. See Goldsmith, "The New Formalism in United States Foreign Relations

Law," at p. 1409 (asserting that "[t]he Court's traditional rule-like approach to the judicial foreign relations doctrines might have seemed unsatisfactory because any errors of under- or overinclusiveness were thought to be unacceptably costly in the Cold War world").

16. Flaherty, "History Right?" at p. 2096.

17. See Bradley, "A New American Foreign Affairs Law?" at p. 1106 ("The end of the Cold War era also is a likely factor in the shift away from foreign affairs exceptionalism, since there is now a reduced need for the national government to speak with one voice in international relations, and because many of the exceptionalism decisions . . . clearly seem to be a product of the Cold War era."); Spiro, "Foreign Relations Federalism," at pp. 1241–46 (describing the historical cold war context in which foreign affairs doctrine was shaped).

18. Goldsmith, "The New Formalism in United States Foreign Relations Law," at p. 1412.

19. For example, the 2000 Democratic National Platform, available at *http://www.democrats.org*, "demand[s]" that "Congress pass the Convention to Eliminate All Forms of Discrimination Against Women" and asserts that "[w]e will continue to press for human rights, the rule of law, and political freedom." The 2000 Republican platform, available at *http://www.rnc.org*, criticizes the Clinton administration's humanitarian interventions and mentions human rights in connection with Cuba, Chechnya, and Iran.

20. For an overview of these developments and arguments about their effects on the problem of integration, see Ku, "The Delegation of Federal Power to International Organizations."

21. Stephan, "International Governance and American Democracy," at p. 238.

22. For a description of the case at an early stage, see Glaberson, "NAFTA Invoked to Challenge Court Award." As of mid-2001 the arbitration panel had disposed of some preliminary objections the United States raised to its jurisdiction.

23. Arbitration proceedings under NAFTA are not public.

24. For contrasting views on the constitutionality of the NAFTA dispute-resolution mechanism, see Metropoulos, "Constitutional Dimensions of the North American Free Trade Agreement" (arguing that the NAFTA dispute resolution violates article 3), and Senior, "Comment: The Constitutionality of NAFTA's Dispute Resolution Process" (arguing that the dispute resolution process is constitutional). See also Weisburd, "International Courts and American Courts," at pp. 892–900 (discussing article 3 problems that might arise from a treaty authorizing international review of decisions by U.S. courts).

25. A leading study of transnational human rights NGOs is Keck and Sikkink, *Activists beyond Borders*.

26. For a useful skeptical analysis of the role of transnational NGOs in the domestic policy arena, see Anderson, "The Limits of Pragmatism in American Foreign Policy."

27. See, e.g., Peter M. Haas, "Social Constructivism and the Evolution of Multilateral Environmental Governance," in Prakash and Hart, eds., *Globalization and Governance*, at p. 103.

28. Of course they may also have moral interests and almost always press their

policies on public interest grounds. Nonetheless, the element of material interest is so common as to be a structural feature of traditional interest group lobbying.

29. Again, this is not to contend that transnational NGOs do not have or at least are not supported by groups that have material interests (labor unions supporting international human rights claims about working conditions being the obvious example), but only that the place of material interest is substantially smaller than in traditional interest groups.

30. Critics refer, somewhat pejoratively I think, to "foreign affairs exceptionalism." See, e.g., Bradley, "A New American Foreign Affairs Law?" at p. 1104. Peter Spiro pointed out to me that the New Deal–Great Society constitutional order gave primacy to foreign affairs primarily—if not exclusively—with respect to policy concerns rather than constitutional ones.

31. Goldsmith, "The New Formalism in United States Foreign Relations Law," at p. 1399, uses the term "underspecification" to refer to the problems that arise when a norm must be integrated into existing law without clear guidance from the norm itself as to its place in domestic law. Goldsmith continues, "[E]ven if federal law is underspecified [that is, when integration is necessary] . . . , such controversy is no more serious than analogous controversies that arise all the time from underspecification of federal law in domestic cases."

32. *Breard v. Greene*, 523 US 371 (1998). Weisburd, "International Courts and American Courts," at p. 879nn. 7–8, provides citations to the major academic commentaries on the Breard litigation.

33. *Breard*, 523 US at 374.

34. As the government brief put it, "our federal system imposes limits on the federal government's ability to interfere with the criminal justice systems of the States. The 'measures at [the United States'] disposal' under our Constitution may in some cases include only persuasion." Brief for the United States as Amicus Curiae, *Breard v. Greene*, 523 US 371 (1998), at 51. For a critical discussion of the U.S. government's position, see Vagts, "Taking Treaties Less Seriously."

35. *Breard*, 523 US at 378.

36. For the former, see Brief for the United States as Amicus Curiae, *Breard v. Greene*, 523 US 371 (1998), at 10, 12; for the latter, see U.S. Department of State, Pub. No. 10,518, Consular Notification and Access (1998), excerpted in Contemporary Practice of the United States.

37. Germany also sought permission to file a complaint against Arizona in the U.S. Supreme Court, which the Court denied. *Federal Republic of Germany v. United States*, 526 US 111 (1999).

38. The decision is available at *http://www.icj-cij.org/icjwww/idocket/igus/igusframe.htm.*

39. *Soering v. United Kingdom*, 11 EurCt. HR (ser. A), pp. 439, 478, P111 (1989).

40. For a description of the U.S. government's representations, see Djajic, "The Effect of International Court of Justice Decisions on Municipal Courts in the United States," at pp. 79–80.

41. The U.S. Supreme Court has regularly denied review of claims that long-term detention on death row awaiting execution violates the Eighth Amendment's ban on cruel and unusual punishment. For the most recent case, see

Knight v. Florida, 528 US 990 (1999), with separate opinions by Justices Thomas and Breyer.

42. *Printz*, 521 US at 918.

43. Golove, "Treaty-Making and the Nation," at pp. 1149–1210 (describing treaties entered into during the early republic and antebellum periods, as well as contemporaneous political and academic commentary).

44. U.S. Constitution, art. 1, § 8, cl. 10.

45. Golove, "Treaty-Making and the Nation," at pp. 1157–88 (describing the controversy over the Jay Treaty between the United States and Great Britain, which contained a provision allowing British subjects to own real property in the states, thus overriding the common law rule allowing forfeiture of real property owned by aliens). I note that the federal courts followed state common law on real property even during the era of *Swift v. Tyson*. See, e.g., *Jackson v. Chew*, 25 US (12 Wheat.) 153 (1827).

46. Weisburd, "International Courts and American Courts," at p. 900 (discussing *Chirac v. Chirac*, 15 US [2 Wheat.] 259 [1817], and *Hauenstein v. Lynham*, 100 US 483 [1879]).

47. The suggestion that federalism limitations are conceptually inappropriate with respect to foreign affairs rattles around in the literature. Relying on *United States v. Curtiss-Wright Export Corp.*, 299 US 304 (1936), these authors suggest that power over foreign affairs was never lodged in the states, which therefore could not "reserve" any aspect of foreign affairs power from the Constitution's delegations to the national government. See, e.g., Thornberry, "Comment: Federalism vs. Foreign Affairs," at p. 139; Healy, "Note: Is *Missouri v. Holland* Still Good Law?" at pp. 1748–50. The argument could be supplemented by observing that the Court adopted a related view in *U.S. Term Limits v. Thornton*, 514 US 779 (1995). But, as one author observes, "One objection to this position is that it . . . leaves the treaty power virtually unlimited." Healy, "Note: Is *Missouri v. Holland* Still Good Law?" at p. 1750. If accepted, it would terminate the inquiry in which I am engaged here. In addition, adopting the position would be an aggressive assertion of national authority, in an era when the doctrinal trend is in the other direction.

48. See Henkin, *Foreign Affairs and the Constitution*, at pp. 140–41 (describing cases supporting such a limitation).

49. See Bradley, "A New American Foreign Affairs Law?" at pp. 451–52 ("Today, almost any issue can plausibly be labeled 'international.'"). Bradley continues, "[E]ven if there were a workable distinction in theory between international and domestic matters, it seems unlikely that U.S. courts would feel competent to contradict the political branches on this issue. It is far from clear, for example, what standard the courts could use to draw such a line" (453).

50. Goldsmith, "The New Formalism in United States Foreign Relations Law," at p. 1416.

51. The national government clearly has the power to eliminate the juvenile death penalty in federal prosecutions and has done so. 18 U.S.C. § 3591 (a). In the unlikely event that a negotiating partner insisted only that the juvenile death penalty be eliminated in state prosecutions, the federal negotiators might be more willing to concede than if they themselves had to forgo executing juvenile of-

fenders. We might develop a doctrine that treaty provisions must deal even-handedly with the state and national governments, although I am skeptical about the possibility of developing a useful standard for determining when a provision operates in an even-handed way, and more skeptical about the need for a doctrine to guard against what seems to me a quite remote possibility.

52. Mari Matsuda suggested in conversation that one could defend the position that the treaty power had no subject-matter limits even in the absence of explicit trade-offs. The U.S. treaty makers could reasonably take the position that their bargaining position in a range of negotiations is strengthened by a perception among the negotiating partners that the United States is a law-abiding nation that honors international human rights norms. In this argument, even a free-standing treaty banning the death penalty for juvenile offenders would be a permissible exercise of the treaty power because adopting such a treaty would enhance the U.S. position in other negotiations about matters that are unquestionably of international concern.

53. Weisburd, "International Courts and American Courts,"at p. 921.

54. Again, the bi- or multilateral nature of foreign affairs distinguishes these negotiations from policymaking in a purely domestic context, where only Congress and the president decide what policies to pursue. In the treaty context, the U.S. treaty makers initially decide on the nation's preferred policies, but they then must respond to counterproposals by other nations.

55. Bradley, "A New American Foreign Affairs Law?" at p. 456.

56. *United States v. Butler*, 297 US 1 (1936).

57. Of course the procedures for adopting treaties and statutes differ.

58. Professor Golove, while criticizing the view that there are subject-matter limits on the treaty power, agrees that sham treaties cannot be enforced domestically against federalism objections. See Golove, "Treaty-Making and the Nation," at p. 1287 ("the purpose of a treaty cannot be to adopt domestic standards just because the President and Senate believe them to be laudable"). See also Henkin, *Foreign Affairs and the Constitution*, at p. 143 ("A treaty . . . must be a bona fide agreement between states, not a 'mock marriage,' nor a unilateral act by the United States to which a foreign government lends itself as an accommodation.").

59. A somewhat more realistic possibility is a treaty whose domestic implications are strongly favored by the U.S. negotiators even though those implications are otherwise beyond the national government's power. The negotiators might then make larger concessions to the negotiating partners. A doctrine responsive to this concern would have to allow U.S. negotiators to agree to such provisions if they extracted "enough" in exchange and pretty clearly would not be an attractive one for courts to administer.

60. I note another difficulty with the concern for sham treaties. Why would the negotiating partner simply do the U.S. treaty makers a favor? They might see the U.S. offer as an opportunity to extract something in exchange. And if that something is an appropriate subject for international agreement, such as a trade concession, we would again be in the position of having an agreement part of which is within the nation's power and part of which is (by hypothesis) not. As argued in the text above, such mixed agreements would almost certainly survive

constitutional scrutiny. For completeness, I note the possibility of a doctrine condemning treaties as shams where the international component in a mixed agreement was simply a façade for the treaty's true goal. Again, the possibilities that the treaty makers would enter such agreements, and that the courts would be able reliably to identify them, are so small that developing a doctrine along these lines seems inadvisable.

61. "Should" here is both predictive and normative.

62. For example, a law bringing the United States into line with the international consensus that hate speech should be illegal (to the extent that such hate speech laws might violate the First Amendment).

63. See Henkin, *Foreign Affairs and the Constitution*, at pp. 254–66 (describing the liberty-based limitations on the foreign affairs power).

64. *Missouri v. Holland*, 252 US 416, 434 (1920).

65. One formulation is that subject-matter limitations identify internal limits on each enumerated power, limits that are specific to each such power, while individual-rights limitations are external to all the enumerated powers and cut across them all.

66. See, e.g., *State v. Pang*, 132 Wn2d 852, 940 P2d 1293 (1997) (addressing the proper interpretation of the doctrine of speciality while assuming its applicability).

67. 8 U.S.C. § 3192.

68. *United States v. Belmont*, 301 US 324 (1937); *United States v. Pink*, 315 US 203 (1942). Carlos Vázquez suggested this argument to me.

69. That exception to the anti-commandeering principle might not be available, however, because so much of the traditionalist argument relies on assumptions about the scope of the doctrine of specialty, and those assumptions were rarely tested during the older regime.

70. *New York v. United States*, 505 US 144, 1778–79 (1992) (distinguishing *Testa v. Katt*, 330 US 386 [1947]).

71. Vázquez, "*Breard*, *Printz*, and the Treaty Power," at p. 1318 (describing the convention's requirements as commandeering); Healy, "Note: Is *Missouri v. Holland* Still Good Law?" at p. 1746 (same).

72. For a discussion of the difficulty in distinguishing between prohibited affirmative commandeering and negative commandeering, see chapter 2 above. Vázquez, "*Breard*, *Printz*, and the Treaty Power," at pp. 1347–48, 1350, uses *Asakura v. Seattle*, 265 US 332 (1923), which upheld a treaty provision requiring the city to consider license applications from Japanese citizens, to illustrate the proposition that "it is notoriously difficult to draw the line between affirmative and negative obligations."

73. According to the Supreme Court, the anti-commandeering principle would not be implicated if the treaties required only that state courts provide enhanced remedies within a general remedial framework already created by state law. See *New York v. United States*, 505 US 144, 1778–79 (1992) (distinguishing *Testa v. Katt*, 330 US 386 [1947], on the ground that the supremacy clause, directed specifically at state judges, allows them to be "commandeered" to enforce national law).

74. *Printz*, 521 US at 936 (O'Connor, J., concurring) (noting that the Court

"refrains from deciding whether . . . purely ministerial reporting requirements imposed by Congress on state and local authorities pursuant to its Commerce Clause powers are . . . invalid," and referring to a federal law requiring reporting missing children to the Department of Justice).

75. The Court's analysis is expressly formalist, meaning in this context that the Court does not provide functional justifications for large parts of its doctrine. The information-compilation exception might be a formalist exception to a formalist doctrine, in which case there is little to say about it.

76. *Printz*, 521 US at 932–33.

77. See, e.g., Caminker, "State Sovereignty and Subordinacy," at p. 1068–74; Jackson, "Federalism and the Uses and Limits of Law," at pp. 2200–05; Hills, "The Political Economy of Cooperative Federalism," at pp. 824–31.

78. Of course an exception for notification could be an additional formalist exception to a formalist doctrine.

79. See Thornberry, "Comment: Federalism vs. Foreign Affairs," at pp. 134–35 (describing the burdens notification might impose).

80. Ibid., at pp. 126–27. Thornberry notes that of course governors will take the latter course, quoting then-Governor George W. Bush: "In general, I will uphold the laws of the State of Texas, regardless of the nationality of the person involved."

81. I do not mean to claim that the argument is powerful or persuasive in its original context but only that it is no less powerful or persuasive in the present one.

82. The classic discussion is Strauss, "Formal and Functional Approaches to Separation of Powers Questions."

83. Thornberry, "Comment: Federalism vs. Foreign Affairs," at p. 142, suggests that the anti-commandeering principle would be avoided in the Breard context by requiring a determination "at every defendant's initial [judicial] hearing" of whether the defendant is a foreign national and requiring notification of foreign nationals' rights at that time. See also Vázquez, "*Breard, Printz*, and the Treaty Power," at p. 1326n. 30 (making the same suggestion).

84. Weisburd, "International Courts and American Courts," at p. 903. Professor Weisburd's prime example is a convention concluded in 1788 (implementing a treaty made in 1778) requiring a party's "officials competent" to arrest deserters from the other nation's merchant ships. As Professor Weisburd points out, one might mistakenly think that the relevant "officials competent" would be officials of the national government. But there were no such officials in 1788; the Constitution had been completed but the national government was not yet organized. Professor Weisburd acknowledges the possibility that a duty imposed on state officials in 1788 was transferred to federal officials when the national government was organized, but he argues that doing so "would have required the establishment of a substantial federal police force in a good many port cities" (903n. 142), a requirement that he correctly thinks implausible to attribute to the Framers.

85. Deeken, "Note: A New *Miranda* for Foreign Nationals?" at p. 1030, argues that a state's failure to notify foreign nationals of their rights under the Vienna Convention might be said to interfere with the purposes of the conven-

tion. If so, the convention would preempt something, but it is not entirely clear what: the state prosecution? state rules immunizing police officers from monetary liability for unlawful action? Deeken argues that the convention itself does not establish a rule requiring the exclusion of evidence acquired as a result of failure to comply with the convention's notification requirement (1036–38).

86. Vázquez, "*Breard, Printz,* and the Treaty Power."

87. The national government's power to deny state officials authority to arrest or prosecute foreign nationals arises from its power over foreign relations. Other nations might trust the U.S. government but not subnational governments and might insist in negotiations that only the U.S. government prosecute their nationals, even for ordinary crimes. That possibility is sufficient to establish that the U.S. government has the power to preempt the application of state criminal laws to foreign nationals.

88. Vázquez, "*Breard, Printz,* and the Treaty Power," at pp. 1327–28 (suggesting a rewriting of the Brady Act to invoke the power to preempt on condition). See also Carter, "Note, Commandeering under the Treaty Power," at p. 618 (arguing that "finding such proposals to be within Congress's powers would open the door to complete circumvention of states' rights").

89. The example is a bit off-key because barring states from executing juvenile offenders is not precisely a form of affirmative commandeering as would, for example, be a requirement that states that prosecute juvenile offenders confine them in prisons for a federally prescribed number of years.

90. Weisburd, "International Courts and American Courts," at p. 918 (emphasis added). See also *Henkin, Foreign Affairs and the Constitution,* at p. 148 (describing a similar constraint).

91. In their capacity as state voters. Of course in their capacity as national voters, the same people participate in the development of national statutes.

92. See chapter 2 above, discussing preemption.

93. Ruling out a constitutional immunity from preemption is in some tension with the Court's federalism decisions, as I argued in chapter 2.

94. For present purposes it is unimportant to discuss the question of whether Congress can exercise its exclusive power by delegating authority to the states.

95. *Gibbons v. Ogden,* 22 US (9 Wheat.) 1, 227 (1824) (Johnson, J., concurring): "The power of a sovereign state over commerce, therefore, amounts to nothing more than a power to limit and restrain it at pleasure. And since the power to prescribe the limits to its freedom, necessarily implies the power to determine what shall remain unrestrained, it follows, that the power must be exclusive; it can reside but in one potentate; and hence, the grant of this power carries with it the whole subject, leaving nothing for the State to act upon."

96. Ibid., at 209.

97. The power was one to "prescribe the rule by which commerce is to be governed" (ibid., at 196), and commerce was "commercial intercourse . . . in all its branches" (189–90).

98. The idea of preemption in the Constitution remained an important part of constitutional law in the guise of the dormant commerce clause. The dormant commerce clause is invoked when some state regulation interferes with interstate commerce, and yet Congress has not proscribed the interference. (Again, for

present purposes it is unnecessary to discuss the Court's complex set of standards for determining when a state statute unconstitutionally interferes with interstate commerce.) Dormant commerce clause cases are ones in which the mere grant of an unexercised power to Congress displaces state authority to adopt the regulation its legislators think best.

Consistent with its general federalism decisions, the modern Supreme Court has reduced somewhat the reach of dormant commerce clause doctrine. Typically it is said that that doctrine has two branches, one barring states from enacting statutes that discriminate against out-of-state commerce and the other barring states from enacting statutes that place unacceptably high burdens on interstate commerce. The modern Supreme Court has made the first branch a serious limitation on state power by looking quite skeptically on state regulations that draw geographic lines that effectively treat local and interstate commerce differently. Probably the most dramatic recent example, but one of many, is *C and A Carbone, Inc. v. Clarkstown*, 511 US 383 (1994), finding unconstitutional a flow control ordinance that directed that all solid waste generated within the town be deposited at a specified waste transfer station. The formality of using a geographic term in the regulation is crucial here, because the modern Supreme Court appears to be quite reluctant to invalidate statutes that do have a substantial disparate impact on in-state and out-of-state commerce, even without drawing geographic lines. Here the most dramatic example is *Exxon Corp. v. Governor of Maryland*, 437 US 117 (1978), upholding a facially neutral state regulation that adversely affected the large proportion of economic activity—here, integrated gasoline production and retailing—under out-of-state control and the small proportion of that activity under local control. The Court has not invoked the second "excessive burden" branch of dormant commerce clause to invalidate a state regulation in at least a decade. *Kassel v. Consolidated Freightways Corp.*, 450 US 662 (1981), is the most recent case cited in the relevant section of Chemerinsky, *Constitutional Law*, at p. 326. Tribe, *American Constitutional Law*, at pp. 1053, 1070–73, points out that parts of the plurality opinion in *Kassel* and parts of the majority opinion in *Kassel*'s predecessor, *Raymond Motor Transportation v. Rice*, 434 US 429 (1978), suggest that the statutes in those cases were problematic because they contained provisions that the opinions' authors saw as discriminatory. The most recent case cited by Tribe as invalidating a statute on "excessive burden" grounds is *Edgar v. MITE Corp.*, 457 US 624 (1982) (ibid., at p. 1099). On the borderline between discriminatory statutes and nondiscriminatory ones are statutes the Court finds directly to regulate commercial activity in other states. See, e.g., *Healy v. The Beer Institute*, 491 US 324 (1989). Justice O'Connor relied on the "excessive burden" branch of dormant commerce clause doctrine in her opinion concurring in the judgment in *Carbone*. See 511 U.S. at 405–7 (O'Connor, J., concurring in the judgment). (The infrequency with which the "excessive burden" doctrine is invoked to invalidate statutes suggests to me that one should be cautious about describing *Pike v. Bruce Church, Inc.*, 397 US 137 (1970), as a "seminal" case. Tribe, *American Constitutional Law*, at p. 1082. Pike is the governing standard, of course, but the Court rarely employs it to invalidate state regulations.)

99. 389 US 429 (1968). For critiques of *Zschernig*, see Henkin, *Foreign Af-*

fairs and the Constitution, at pp. 163–65; Bilder, "The Role of States and Cities in Foreign Relations," at p. 830; Goldsmith, "Federal Courts, Foreign Affairs, and Federalism."

100. *Zschernig*, 389 US at 435.

101. Justice Harlan concurred in the result.

102. 389 US at 432.

103. Ibid., at 434 (quoting the amicus curiae brief filed by the Department of Justice).

104. Ibid., at 437.

105. Ibid., at 442 (Stewart, J., concurring).

106. As Justice Harlan's concurring opinion pointed out, the Court refrained from relying on the provisions of a treaty that might have been construed to displace the state law (ibid., at 445–51). Notably, the *Crosby* opinion cited *Zschernig* only in describing the ruling of the lower court. *Crosby v. National Foreign Trade Council*, 530 US 363, 371 (2000).

107. 441 US 434, 448 (1979) (quoting *Board of Trustees of Univ. of Ill. v. United States*, 289 US 48, 59 [1933]). See also *Hines v. Davidowitz*, 312 US 52, 68 (1941) (describing "international relations" as "the one aspect of our government that from the first has been most generally conceded imperatively to demand broad national authority").

108. 512 US 298 (1994).

109. Briefs attacking the statute were filed on behalf of the United Kingdom and the member states of the European Communities, as well as by the United States Chamber of Commerce, and the Court quoted a letter from the secretary of state to the governor of California asserting that "[t]he Department of State has received diplomatic notes complaining about state use of the worldwide unitary method of taxation from virtually every developed country in the world" (ibid., at 324n. 22).

110. The solicitor general had argued that "statements of executive branch officials are entitled to substantial evidentiary weight" on the question of whether a state tax system "impairs the federal government's ability to speak with one voice," but the Court found it unnecessary to accept or reject that argument because it found that the executive statements were insufficient to "authorize judicial intervention" "in light of Congress' acquiescence" in California's system (ibid., at 330n. 32).

111. See Spiro, "Foreign Relations Federalism," at p. 1239n. 74 (describing *Barclays Bank* as "a doctrinal watershed"), 1264–65 (asserting that the Breard cases "at least implicitly reject *Zschernig* constraints in the state death penalty context"). It remains possible that there could be constitutionally based preemption, or a presumption of preemption, with respect to some subject matter within but not as comprehensive as the area of foreign affairs. One possibility, consistent with *Crosby*'s outcome, is that states may not treat commerce related to one foreign nation worse than it treats commerce related to another—a requirement that states give "most favored nation" status to all foreign nations. Presumably the scope of such a doctrine would be determined by balancing the national interest in uniformity against whatever interests states might assert in favor of local decision making.

112. Ibid., at pp. 1261–70 (describing "targeted retaliation"). Cf. Dinh, "Reassessing the Law of Preemption," at p. 2106 (suggesting that preemption doctrine can change as "the background against which Congress legislates" changes).

113. But see Denning and McCall, "The Constitutionality of State and Local 'Sanctions' against Foreign Countries," at pp. 330–31 (describing retaliation by the Swiss government against proposed local sanctions; the retaliation would have affected goods produced in states that proposed the sanctions and in states that had not). I should note that Spiro argues only that the possibility of targeted retaliation diminishes the need to invoke a presumption in favor of preemption. Denning and McCall in fact make the stronger argument that the Burma Law was preempted by the Constitution itself and so are unconcerned with claims about positions farther along the spectrum of possibilities for preemption doctrine.

114. Cf. Dinh, "Reassessing the Law of Preemption," at p. 2087 ("Contrary to the prevailing wisdom and the unexplored assumptions of Supreme Court dicta, the constitutional structure of federalism does not admit to a general presumption against federal preemption of state law."), 2092 ("as a matter of constitutional structure, there should be no general systematic presumption against or in favor of preemption"), 2097 (preemption analysis is "garden-variety statutory interpretation").

115. 529 US 861 (2000).

116. Ibid., at 870–71.

117. Ibid., at 898 (Stevens, J., dissenting).

118. Ibid., at 871.

119. Ibid., at 872.

120. In the form of the special burden the defendant should have been required to carry, according to the dissent.

121. The offsetting effect of the two statutory provisions in *Geier* captures the basic intuition in a statutory context.

122. 529 US 89 (2000).

123. The Court acknowledged that what was said in the single voice might be influenced by participation by state authorities in developing national policy (ibid., at 117) ("States, as well as environmental groups and local port authorities, will participate in the process.").

124. Ibid., at 108.

125. Ibid.

126. *Rice v. Santa Fe Elevator Corp.*, 331 US 218, 230 (1947), quoted and distinguished in *Locke*, 530 US at 108. The most prominent recent formulation is that there is a "presumption against the pre-emption of state police power regulations," *Cipollone v. Liggett Group, Inc.*, 505 US 504, 518 (1992).

127. *Crosby*, 530 US at 374n. 8. This conclusion was "based on [the Court's] analysis below." But that analysis did not refer to a presumption against preemption or discuss what it was about the national and state laws that overcame whatever presumption there might have been, because the Court expressly utilized only normal principles of statutory interpretation to decide the preemption question.

128. *Locke*, 530 US at 108 (quoting *Rice*).

129. Ibid., at 99.

130. 426 US 833 (1976).

131. Not surprisingly, there is likely to be an interaction between the characterization of the area involved and the characterization of the history of state and national regulation of that area.

132. As Peter Spiro observes, "*Crosby* is . . . a time-bider, a ruling that allows for future flexibility, either in reaffirming the differential federalism rules that apply to foreign relations or in charting a path towards the differential's elimination." Spiro, "Contextual Determinism and Foreign Relations Federalism," at p. 368. Early academic commentary of *Crosby* reflects a division between traditionalists in foreign affairs matters, who see *Crosby* as reflecting, albeit in a muted form, the notion of national primacy, and revisionists, who treat *Crosby* as neutral on the question of national primacy. For an example of the former, see Vázquez, "W(h)ither *Zschernig*?"; for examples of the latter, see Goldsmith, "Statutory Foreign Affairs Preemption"; Yoo, "Foreign Affairs Federalism and the Separation of Powers."

133. I have added the final clause to this sentence to leave open the possibility that a state might have some constitutionally based immunity from preemption, but not one that extends to the Burma Law. (One possibility, for example, might be that Congress could not require that Massachusetts abstain from a primary boycott of goods made in Burma. Under such a rule Massachusetts could refuse to buy goods made in Burma even if that interfered with congressional policy, but it could not refuse to deal with businesses that themselves did business in Burma.)

134. *Crosby*, 530 US at 373n. 7 (quoting *Wisconsin Dept. of Industry v. Gould, Inc.*, 475 US 282, 287 [1986]). The Court also noted that Massachusetts had "concede[d], as it must," that Congress had the power to preempt the Burma Law (ibid.), and challenged only the assertion that Congress had in fact exercised that power.

135. See *Gould*, 475 US at 289 (asserting that "the 'market participant' doctrine reflects the particular concerns underlying the Commerce Clause, not any general notion regarding the necessary extent of state power in areas where Congress has acted").

136. See, e.g., *Geier*, 530 US at 887 (Stevens, J., dissenting) ("'This is a case about federalism,'" quoting *Coleman v. Thompson*, 501 US 722, 726 [1991]).

137. One might think that relatively recently articulated "presumption against preemption" was related to the Court's concern about the reach of national regulatory power. The justices themselves, however, seem not to think so. Justice Stevens, a persistent dissenter in the federalism cases, is the Court's foremost proponent of the "presumption against regulation." Justice Thomas, the most vigorous proponent of restrictions on national power (see, e.g., *United States v. Lopez*, 514 US 549, 584–85 [1995] [Thomas, J., concurring] [suggesting the appropriateness of rethinking the Court's overall doctrine dealing with congressional power]), did join Justice Stevens's dissent in *Geier*, but his federalism colleagues Chief Justice Rehnquist and Justices O'Connor and Kennedy joined the majority opinion, which was written by Justice Breyer, one of the leading critics of the Court's federalism decisions. See, e.g., *Lopez*, 514 US at 615 (Breyer, J., dissenting). It is tempting to develop a merely political account of the Court's

cases: It is a conservative Court, restricting national power with respect to legislation supported by liberals and restricting state power when states adopt anti-business regulatory programs. The line-ups make such an account implausible.

138. A recent discussion and defense of the practice of making federalism and more specific reservations is Bradley and Goldsmith, "Treaties, Human Rights, and Conditional Consent." On a technical rather than a political level, the federalism understandings might not preclude Congress from enacting constitutionally questionable legislation. They may not be judicially enforceable. More important, they typically state that the national government will implement the treaty to which the declaration is attached only in areas of traditional national authority. That would not bar the government from defending treaty-based legislation on the ground that it did not go beyond the scope of traditional national authority. Nonetheless, a Senate insistent enough on federalism to require that a federalism understanding be attached to a treaty is unlikely to approve treaty-based legislation raising federalism concerns.

139. 138 Cong. Rec. S4781-01 (daily ed., April 2, 1992), available at *http://www1.umn.edu/humanrts/usdocs/civilres.html.*

140. For example, the Carter administration submitted five international human rights agreements to the Senate: the International Covenant on Civil and Political Rights (submitted 1978, ratified 1992); the International Covenant on Economic, Social, and Cultural Rights (submitted 1978); the Convention for the Elimination of All Forms of Racial Discrimination or CERD (submitted 1978, ratified 1994); the American Convention on Human Rights (submitted 1978); and the Convention on the Elimination of All Forms of Discrimination against Women or CEDAW (submitted 1980). The Reagan administration submitted two: the Genocide Convention and the Convention against Torture and Other Cruel, Inhuman or Degrading Treatment, or Punishment. The Bush administration submitted two: the Torture Convention submitted initially by the Reagan administration, and the Covenant on Civil and Political Rights submitted initially by the Carter administration. The Clinton administration also submitted two: CERD (ratified in 1994); and CEDAW.

141. The same dynamic occurs in connection with ordinary legislation, where the requirement of support in both houses of Congress replaces the requirement of two-thirds support in the Senate.

142. For example, another common reservation expressly disclaims any duty to enact legislation required by international treaties but not by the Constitution itself. The version in CERD is:

> That the Constitution and laws of the United States establish extensive protections against discrimination, reaching significant areas of non-governmental activity. Individual privacy and freedom from governmental interference in private conduct, however, are also recognized as among the fundamental values which shape our free and democratic society. The United States understands that the identification of the rights protected under the Convention by reference in article 1 to fields of "public life" reflects a similar distinction between spheres of public conduct that are customarily the subject of governmental regulation, and spheres of private conduct that

are not. To the extent, however, that the Convention calls for a broader regulation of private conduct, the United States does not accept any obligation under this Convention to enact legislation or take other measures under paragraph (1) of article 2, subparagraphs (1) (c) and (d) of article 2, article 3 and article 5 with respect to private conduct except as mandated by the Constitution and laws of the United States.

143. Treaty proponents may be able to move some treaties forward by gaining agreement from some states to accept the treaty's requirements and agreement from the negotiating partners that application of the treaty's requirements everywhere in the United States is unnecessary. (I am grateful to John Jackson for pointing out this possibility to me.)

144. Gerald Neuman suggested that the International Covenant on Civil and Political Rights might be a source of congressional authority to enact the Religious Freedom Restoration Act. Neuman, "The Global Dimension of RFRA." Congress's response to the Supreme Court's invalidation of that statute relied on the commerce and spending powers. Religious Land Use and Institutionalized Persons Act, Pub. L. No. 106-274, 114 Stat. 803 (2000).

145. Again, coming to the matter as an outsider, I was struck by the existence of interpretive ambiguity with respect to the doctrine of speciality in *Soering* with respect to both its application to state-level prosecutions and representations about the application of the death penalty. If interpretive ambiguity exists there, unambiguous provisions raising serious federalism questions must be exceedingly rare.

146. Carlos Vázquez has pointed out that many existing treaties have aspirational provisions that, though not enforceable without supporting legislation, might be invoked to justify legislation not otherwise within an enumerated power. Vázquez, "*Breard, Printz,* and the Treaty Power," at p. 1339n. 75. He also points out that the treaty that provided the basis for statute upheld in *Missouri v. Holland,* 252 US 416 (1920), provided that the United States would propose appropriate legislation, not that it would enact such legislation. He suggests that *Missouri v. Holland* might be limited by denying Congress the power to enact statutes based on such precatory provisions. I wonder, however, whether this makes too much of the difference between an obligation assumed by the national government to propose legislation and an obligation to enact it; why would a treaty partner accept the former without believing that it entailed the latter?

Conclusion

1. Stewart, "Evaluating the New Deal," at p. 240.

2. Coleman, "Clinton and the Party System in Historical Perspective." See also Feigenbaum, Henig, and Hamnett, *Shrinking the State,* at p. 118 (noting that conservative support of privatization was accompanied by "reassur[ances to] the public that their attack on the size and structure of the governmental apparatus did not necessarily entail the wholesale rejection of the broad goals that had come to be associated with liberalism and the welfare state").

3. Feigenbaum, Henig, and Hamnett, *Shrinking the State*, at p. 146.

4. Cerny, "Paradoxes of the Competition State," at p. 266.

5. See Feigenbaum, Henig, and Hamnett, *Shrinking the State*, at pp. 138–39 (describing how privatizing initiatives of the Reagan and first Bush administrations produced a backlash that limited the extent to which further initiatives could be undertaken).

6. See, e.g., Pildes and Sunstein, "Reinventing the Regulatory State."

7. For an overview, see Giddens, *The Third Way*.

8. The projects I discuss can be understood either as a subset of the administration's Reinventing Government initiative or as related to that initiative. Thompson and Riccucci, "Reinventing Government," at pp. 235–37, enumerates the reinvention initiative's principles in terms that place the programs I discuss outside that initiative: "internal deregulation of government agencies," "mak[ing] the administrative agents of government more mission-driven or bottom-line oriented," "decentralization and the empowerment of frontline workers," and "competition and customer service."

9. For a description of several of these programs, see Spence, "The Shadow of the Rational Polluter," at pp. 954–58.

10. For a description of Project XL, see Dorf and Sabel, "The Constitution of Democratic Experimentalism," at pp. 382–87.

11. The program is described in a report to the Clinton administration's National Performance Review, "The New OSHA: Reinventing Worker Safety and Health" (May 1995), and at *http://www.osha-slc.gov/html/Reinventing/index.html*.

12. Sabel, Fung, and Karkkainen, "Beyond Backyard Environmentalism."

13. A convenient summary of democratic experimentalism (with the label "empowered deliberative democracy") is provided in Fung and Wright, "Deepening Democracy."

14. Dorf and Sabel, "The Constitution of Democratic Experimentalism," at p. 287.

15. Ibid., at pp. 287–88.

16. Ibid., at 434.

17. Sabel, "How Experimentalism Can Be Democratic and Constitutional."

18. See, e.g., Dorf and Sabel, "The Constitution of Democratic Experimentalism," at p. 326 (describing reforms in the provision of social services, and observing that "[t]hese reforms are still too new to permit any overall assessment of their effectiveness, or even to say which methods of composition and collaboration encourage effective monitoring and dissemination of best practices").

19. One, for example, involved community participation in planning over pollution discharges at a plant that closed for economic reasons unrelated to pollution, before the anti-pollution plan was put into effect. For a description, see Reich, "Public Administration and Public Deliberation," at pp. 1632–35.

20. For a discussion of these problems, see Young, "Activist Challenges to Deliberative Democracy." As Young points out, many of these problems can be overcome by careful design. See also Dorf and Sabel, "The Constitution of Democratic Experimentalism," at pp. 405–8 (making a similar point). One would need to know, however, the political conditions under which careful design pre-

vails over careless design. The proponents of experimentalist approaches have done little to explore those conditions.

21. *See* Fung and Wright, "Deepening Democracy," at pp. 33–34.

22. Drug courts, for example, might be successful as ways of dealing with people addicted to illegal drugs, but they cannot consider whether the current range of laws making drug use illegal is desirable. See Dorf and Sabel, "Drug Treatment Courts and Emergent Experimentalist Government," at pp. 869–73 (discussing decriminalizing and explaining why drug courts may be a better solution to the problems associated with addiction than decriminalization).

23. Dorf and Sabel, "The Constitution of Democratic Experimentalism," at p. 434 (using Goals 2000 legislation as illustrating how national laws can advance "the goals of federalism understood as experimentalist collaboration between the states and the federal government").

24. See ibid., at pp. 435–38 (criticizing the welfare reform statute on these lines).

25. For a description, see Ross and Nisbett, *The Person and the Situation*, at pp. 210–12.

26. Another, more generous to democratic experimentalism, is that people change their behavior when they know they are being observed and evaluated to meet the observers' expectations.

27. See Fung and Wright, "Deepening Democracy," at p. 37 (referring to the possibility of routinization of participatory processes).

28. See ibid., at pp. 34–36 (describing these and related risks as "forum shopping" and rent seeking).

29. *Chamber of Commerce v. Department of Labor*, 174 F3d 206 (D.C. Cir. 1999).

30. Steinzor, "Reinventing Environmental Regulation," at pp. 131, 138–39.

31. See, e.g., Spence, "The Shadow of the Rational Polluter," at pp. 975–77.

32. Sabel, Fung, and Karkkainen, "Beyond Backyard Environmentalism," at p. 6.

33. Quoted in Spence, "The Shadow of the Rational Polluter," at p. 958n. 184, where it is also observed that the statement "has been reproduced in a number of places."

34. See Dorf and Sabel, "The Constitution of Democratic Experimentalism," at p. 359 (describing the legal action that blocked the adoption of a rule requiring passive restraints in passenger cars, on grounds that I would characterize as involving premature closure).

35. Notably, Dorf and Sabel expressly invoke *Miranda v. Arizona* and its idea of legislative-judicial collaboration in support of democratic experimentalism (ibid., at pp. 403, 459).

36. Steven E. Schier, "American Politics After Clinton," in Scheir, ed., *The Postmodern Presidency*, at p. 260.

37. As the shift in party control of the Senate in 2001 shows, under the right conditions small numbers can have large effects in other institutions as well. But those conditions are unusual, whereas small numbers are a permanent characteristic of the Supreme Court as an institution.

Abramowitz, Alan I. "It's Monica, Stupid: Voting Behavior in the 1998 Midterm Election." 26 *Legislative Studies Quarterly* 211 (2001).

Ackerman, Bruce, ed. *Bush v. Gore: The Question of Legitimacy.* (New Haven: Yale University Press, 2002.

———. "Discovering the Constitution." 93 *Yale Law Journal* 1013 (1984).

———. "A Generation of Betrayal?" 65 *Fordham Law Review* 1519 (1997).

———. "The New Separation of Powers." 113 *Harvard Law Review* 633 (2000).

———. "Revolution on a Human Scale." 108 *Yale Law Journal* 2279 (1999).

———. *We the People: Foundations.* Cambridge, MA: Harvard University Press, 1991.

———. *We the People: Transformations.* Cambridge, MA: Harvard University Press, 1998.

Adler, Matthew D. "State Sovereignty and the Anti-Commandeering Cases." 574 *Annals* 158 (2001).

Aldrich, John H. "Political Parties in a Critical Era." 27 *American Politics Quarterly* 9 (1999).

Aldrich, John H., and David W. Rohde. "The Republican Revolution and the House Appropriations Committee." 62 *Journal of Politics* 1 (2000).

———. "The Transition to Republican Rule in the House: Implications for Theories of Congressional Politics." 112 *Political Science Quarterly* 541 (1997–98).

Amenta, Edwin. *Bold Relief: Institutional Politics and the Origins of Modern Social Policy.* Princeton: Princeton University Press, 1998.

Anderson, Kenneth. "The Limits of Pragmatism in American Foreign Policy: Unsolicited Advice to the Bush Administration on Relations with International Nongovernmental Organizations." 2 *Chicago Journal of International Law* 371 (2001).

Ansolabehere, Stephen, and James M. Snyder, Jr. "Soft Money, Hard Money, Strong Parties." 100 *Columbia Law Review* 598 (2000).

Ansolabehere, Stephen, and Shanto Iyengar. *Going Negative: How Attack Ads Shrink and Polarize the Electorate.* New York: Free Press, 1995.

Ayres, Ian. "Alternative Grounds: Epstein's Discrimination Analysis in Other Market Settings." 31 *San Diego Law Review* 67 (1994).

Baker, Lynn A. "Conditional Spending after *Lopez.*" 95 *Columbia Law Review* 1911 (1995).

Baker, Russell. "Hun Lacks Seriosity." *New York Times,* February 4, 1997, p. A23.

———. "Taking the Cure." *New York Times,* November 7, 1995, p. A23.

Balkin, Jack M. "*Bush v. Gore* and the Boundary between Law and Politics." 110 *Yale Law Journal* 1407 (2001).

———. "How Mass Media Simulate Political Transparency." 3 *Cultural Values* 393 (1999).

Balkin, Jack M., and Sanford Levinson. "Understanding the Constitutional Revolution." 87 *Virginia Law Review* 1045 (2001).

Barber, Sotirios, and Robert P. George, eds. *Constitutional Politics: Essays on Constitution Making, Maintenance, and Change.* Princeton: Princeton University Press, 2001.

Berke, Richard L. "Following Baby-Size Issues into Voters' Hearts." *New York Times,* March 21, 1999, p. E1.

Berkman, Harvey. "After the Hype, Tort Reform Moves Slowly." *National Law Journal,* June 14, 1999, p. A1.

BeVier, Lillian R. "The Communications Assistance for Law Enforcement Act of 1994: A Surprising Sequel to the Break Up of AT & T." 51 *Stanford Law Review* 1049 (1999).

Bickel, Alexander M. *The Least Dangerous Branch: The Supreme Court at the Bar of Politics.* Indianapolis: Bobbs-Merrill, 1962.

Bilder, Richard. "The Role of States and Cities in Foreign Relations." 83 *American Journal of International Law* 821 (1989).

Binder, Sarah A. "The Dynamics of Legislative Gridlock, 1947–96." 93 *American Political Science Review* 519 (1999).

Binder, Sarah A., and Steven S. Smith. *Politics or Principle?: Filibustering in the United States Senate.* Washington: Brookings Institution, 1997.

Biskupic, Joan. "The Shrinking Docket; Attorneys Try to Make an Issue Out of the Dramatic Decline in High Court Rulings." *Washington Post,* March 18, 1996.

Biskupic, Joan, and Elder Witt. *The Supreme Court at Work.* 2d ed. Washington, DC: Congressional Quarterly, 1997.

Black, Charles. "The Unfinished Business of the Warren Court." 46 *Washington Law Review* 3 (1970).

Blasi, Vince, ed. *The Burger Court: The Counter-Revolution That Wasn't.* New Haven: Yale University Press, 1983.

Bobbitt, Philip. *Constitutional Interpretation.* Oxford: Basil Blackwell, 1991.

———. *The Shield of Achilles: The Long War and the Market State.* New York: Knopf, 2002.

Boeckelman, Keith. "The American States in the Postindustrial Economy." 27 *State & Local Government Review* 182 (1995).

Born, Richard. "Policy-Balancing Models and the Split-Ticket Voter, 1972–1996." 28 *American Politics Quarterly* 131 (2000).

Bositis, David A., ed. *Redistricting and Minority Representation: Learning from the Past, Preparing for the Future.* Washington, DC: Joint Center for Political and Economic Studies, 1998.

Bradley, Curtis A. "A New American Foreign Affairs Law?" 70 *University of Colorado* Law Review 1089 (1999).

Bradley, Curtis A., and Jack L. Goldsmith. "Treaties, Human Rights, and Conditional Consent." 149 *University of Pennsylvania Law Review* 399 (2000).

Brady, David W., John F. Cogan, and Morris P. Fiorina, eds. *Continuity and Change in House Elections.* Stanford: Stanford University Press, 2000.

Briffault, Richard. "The Political Parties and Campaign Finance Reform." 100 *Columbia Law Review* 620 (2000).

Burden, Barry C., and David C. Kimball. "A New Approach to the Study of Ticket Splitting." 92 *American Political Science Review* 533 (1998).

Burnham, Walter Dean. *Critical Elections and the Mainsprings of American Politics.* New York: Norton, 1970.

Burt, Robert A. "Alex Bickel's Law School and Ours." 104 *Yale Law Journal* 1853 (1995).

———. *The Constitution in Conflict.* Cambridge, MA: Harvard University Press, 1992.

Calmes, Jackie. "House Divided: Why Congress Hews to the Party Lines on Impeachment." *Wall Street Journal,* December 16, 1998, p. A1.

Cameron, Charles M. *Veto Bargaining: Presidents and the Politics of Negative Power.* New York: Cambridge University Press, 2000.

Caminker, Evan H. "Judicial Solicitude for State Dignity." 574 *Annals* 81 (2001).

———. "State Sovereignty and Subordinacy: May Congress Commandeer State Officers to Implement Federal Law?" 95 *Columbia Law Review* 1001 (1995).

Cantril, Albert H., and Susan Davis Cantril. *Reading Mixed Signals: Ambivalence in American Public Opinion about Government.* Baltimore: Johns Hopkins University Press, 1999.

Carey, John M., Richard G. Niemi, and Lynda W. Powell. *Term Limits in the State Legislatures.* Ann Arbor: University of Michigan Press, 2000.

Carpenter, Dale. "Expressive Association and Anti-Discrimination Law after *Dale*: A Tripartite Approach." 85 *Minnesota Law Review* 1515 (2001).

Carter, Janet R. "Note: Commandeering under the Treaty Power." 76 *New York University Law Review* 598 (2001).

Castells, Manuel. *The Power of Identity.* Malden, MA: Blackwell, 1997.

Catholic Truth Society. "Abortion and the Right to Live: A Joint Statement of Catholic Archbishops of Great Britain." No. 21, January 24, 1980.

Cerny, Philip G. "Globalization and the Changing Logic of Collective Action." 49 *International Organization* 595 (1995).

———. "Paradoxes of the Competition State: The Dynamics of Political Globalization." 32 *Government & Opposition* 251 (1997).

Chemerinsky, Erwin. *Constitutional Law: Principles and Policies.* New York: Aspen Law & Business, 1997.

Choper, Jesse. *Judicial Review and the National Political Process.* Chicago: University of Chicago Press, 1980.

Clarke, Susan E., and Gary L. Gaile. *The Work of Cities.* Minneapolis: University of Minnesota Press, 1998.

Clinton, William J. "State of the Union 1996." 62 *Vital Speeches Of The Day* 258 (Feb. 15, 1996).

Coenen, Dan T. "Untangling the Market-Participant Exception to the Dormant Commerce Clause." 88 *Michigan Law Review* 395 (1989).

Cohen, Richard E. "A Congress Divided." *National Journal,* February 5, 2000.

Coleman, John J. "Clinton and the Party System in Historical Perspective." Paper presented at the 2000 Annual Meeting of the American Political Science Association, August 30–September 3, 2000.

Colker, Ruth, and James J. Brudney. "Dissing Congress." 100 *Michigan Law Review* 80 (2001).

Congregation for the Doctrine of the Faith. "Declaration on Procured Abortion." No. 14, November 18, 1974.

Contemporary Practice of the United States. 92 *American Journal of International Law* 243 (1998).

Cook, Timothy B. *Governing the News: The News Media as a Political Institution.* Chicago: University of Chicago Press, 1998.

Covington, Cary R., and Andrew Bargan. "The Effect of Divided Government on the Ideological Content of Bills Enacted by the House of Representatives." Paper presented at the Annual Meeting of the American Political Science Association, August 30–September 2, 2001.

Cox, Adam. "Expressivism in Federalism: A New Defense of the Anti-Commandeering Rule?" 33 *Loyola Los Angeles Law Review* 1309 (2000).

Cox, Gary, and Mathew D. McCubbins. "Toward a Theory of Legislative Rules Changes: Assessing Schickler and Rich's Evidence." 41 *American Journal of Politics* 1376 (1997).

Dahl, Robert A. *A Preface to Democratic Theory.* Chicago: University of Chicago Press, 1956.

Dallek, Robert. *Hail to the Chief: The Making and Unmaking of American Presidents.* New York: Hyperion, 1996.

Deeken, James A. "Note: A New *Miranda* for Foreign Nationals? The Impact of Federalism on International Treaties That Place Affirmative Obligations on State Governments in the Wake of *Printz v. United States.*" 31 *Vanderbilt Journal of Transnational Law* 997 (1998).

Denning, Brannon P. "The 'Blue Slip': Enforcing the Norms of the Judicial Confirmation Process." 10 *William & Mary Bill of Rights Journal* 75 (2001).

———. "Reforming the New Confirmation Process: Replacing 'Despise and Dissent' with 'Advice and Consent.'" 53 *Administrative Law Review* 1 (2001).

Denning, Brannon P., and Jack H. McCall, Jr. "The Constitutionality of State and Local 'Sanctions' against Foreign Countries: Affairs of State, States' Affairs, or a Sorry State of Affairs?" 26 *Hastings Constitutional Law Quarterly* 307 (1999).

Deutsch, Jan G. "Precedent and Adjudication." 83 *Yale Law Journal* 1553 (1974).

Devins, Neil. "The Democracy-Forcing Constitution." 97 *Michigan Law Review* 1171 (1999).

Dewar, Helen, and Juliet Eilperin, "GOP Fears Agenda Drift as 2000 Elections Near." *Washington Post*, May 24, 1999, p. A3.

Dhooge, Lucien J. "The Wrong Way to Mandalay: The Massachusetts Selective Purchasing Act and the Constitution." 37 *American Business Law Journal* 387 (2000).

Dinh, Viet. "Reassessing the Law of Preemption." 88 *Georgetown Law Journal* 2085 (2000).

Dionne, E. J., Jr. "Conservatism Recast," *Washington Post*, January 27, 2002, p. B1.

Djajic, Sanja. "The Effect of International Court of Justice Decisions on Municipal Courts in the United States: *Breard v. Greene*." 23 *Hastings International & Comparative Law Review* 27 (1999).

Dorf, Michael C., and Charles E. Sabel. "The Constitution of Democratic Experimentalism." 98 *Columbia Law Review* 267 (1998).

———. "Drug Treatment Courts and Emergent Experimentalist Government." 53 *Vanderbilt Law Review* 831 (2000).

Doron, Gideon, and Michael Harris. *Term Limits*. Lanham, MD: Lexington Books, 2000.

Dreeg, Richard. "Economic Globalization and the Shifting Boundaries of German Federalism." 26 *Publius* 27 (1996).

Duncan, Richard F. " 'They Call Me "Eight Eyes': *Hardwick*'s Respectability, *Romer*'s Narrowness, and Same-Sex Marriage." 32 *Creighton Law Review* 241 (1998).

Eisgruber, Christopher L. "Politics and Personalities in the Federal Appointments Process." 10 *William & Mary Bill of Rights Journal* 176 (2001).

Ely, John Hart. *Democracy and Distrust*. Cambridge, MA: Harvard University Press, 1980.

———. "The Wages of Crying Wolf: A Comment on *Roe v. Wade*." 82 *Yale Law Journal* 920 (1973).

Epstein, David, and Sharyn O'Halloran. *Delegating Powers: A Transaction Cost Politics Approach to Policy Making under Separate Powers*. New York: Cambridge University Press, 1999.

———. "The Nondelegation Doctrine and the Separation of Powers: A Political Science Approach." 20 *Cardozo Law Review* 947 (1999).

Epstein, Deborah. "Can a 'Dumb Ass Woman' Achieve Equality in the Workplace?: Running the Gauntlet of Hostile Environment Harassing Speech." 84 *Georgetown Law Journal* 399 (1996).

Epstein, Lee, Jack Knight, and Andrew D. Martin. "The Supreme Court as a *Strategic* National Policymaker." 50 *Emory Law Journal* 583 (2001).

Epstein, Richard A. "The Constitutional Perils of Moderation: The Case of the Boy Scouts." 74 *Southern California Law Review* 119 (2000).

Eskridge, William N., Jr., and Philip P. Frickey. "The Supreme Court, 1993 Term—Foreword: Law as Equilibrium." 108 *Harvard Law Review* 26 (1994).

Esping-Andersen, Gosta. *Social Foundations of Postindustrial Economies*. Oxford: Oxford University Press, 1999.

Evans, Sean F. "The House That Governs Least, Governs Best: Obstruction in the U.S. House of Representatives." Paper presented at the 1999 Annual Meeting of the American Political Science Association, September 2–5, 1999.

Fallon, Richard H., Daniel Meltzer, and David Shapiro. *Hart and Wechsler's The Federal Courts and the Federal System*. 4th ed. Westbury, NY: Foundation Press, 1996.

Farber, Daniel A. "Speaking in the First Person Plural: Expressive Associations and the First Amendment." 85 *Minnesota Law Review* 1483 (2001).

Farrar-Myers, Victoria A. "Controlling the Floor: The Republicans' Use of House Rules with High Visibility Issues." Paper presented at the 1999 Annual Meeting of the American Political Science Association, September 2–5, 1999.

Feigenbaum, Harvey, Jeffrey Henig, and Chris Hamnett. *Shrinking the State: The*

Political Underpinnings of Privatization. New York: Cambridge University Press, 1999.

Fiorina, Morris. *Divided Government.* 2d ed. Boston: Allyn and Bacon, 1996.

Fisk, Catherine, and Erwin Chemerinsky. "The Filibuster." 49 *Stanford Law Review* 181 (1997).

Fitts, Michael A. "The Legalization of the Presidency: A Twenty-Five Year Watergate Retrospective." 43 *St. Louis University Law Journal* 725 (1999).

Flaherty, Martin S. "History Right? Historical Scholarship, Original Understanding, and Treaties as 'Supreme Law of the Land.'" 99 *Columbia Law Review* 2095 (1999).

———. Letter to the Editor. *New York Times,* December 7, 2000, p. A38.

Fleming, James E. "Fidelity, Basic Liberties, and the Specter of *Lochner.*" 41 *William & Mary Law Review* 147 (1999).

Formisano, Ronald P. "The 'Party Period' Revisited." 86 *Journal of American History* 93 (1999).

Fox, Richard L., and Robert W. Van Sickel. *Tabloid Justice: Criminal Justice in an Age of Media Frenzy.* Boulder, CO: Lynn Rienner, 2001.

Frantz, Laurent B. "The First Amendment in the Balance." 71 *Yale Law Journal* 1424 (1962).

Fried, Charles. "The Artificial Reason of the Law, or: What Lawyers Know." 60 *Texas Law Review* 35 (1981).

Friedman, Barry. "The History of the Countermajoritarian Difficulty, Part Five: The Birth of an Academic Obsession." 2000. (Unpublished manuscript in the author's possession.)

———. "The History of the Countermajoritarian Difficulty, Part Four: Law's Politics." 148 *University of Pennsylvania Law Review* 971 (2000).

———. "Legislative Findings and Judicial Signals: A Positive Political Reading of *United States v. Lopez.*" 46 *Case Western Reserve Law Review* 757 (1996).

Fung, Archon, and Erik Olin Wright. "Deepening Democracy: Innovations in Empowered Participatory Governance." 29 *Politics & Society* 5 (2001).

Gant, Michael M., and William Lyons. "Democratic Theory, Nonvoting, and Public Policy: The 1972–1988 Presidential Elections." 21 *American Politics Quarterly* 185 (1993).

Garrett, Elizabeth. "A Fiscal Constitution with Supermajority Voting Rules." 40 *William & Mary Law Review* 471 (1999).

Geer, John G., ed. *Politicians and Party Politics.* Baltimore: Johns Hopkins University Press, 1998.

Gelman, Sheldon. "The Hedgehog, the Fox, and the Minimalist." 89 *Georgetown Law Journal* 2297 (2001).

Giddens, Anthony. *The Third Way: The Renewal of Social Democracy.* Cambridge: Polity Press, 1998.

Gilbert, Bil. "Look What's Happening in Chicago." *Sports Illustrated,* January 9, 1984, p. 54.

Gill, Stephen. "Globalisation, Market Civilisation, and Disciplinary Neoliberalism." 24 *Millennium* 399 (1995).

Gillman, Howard. "What's Law Got to Do with It? Judicial Behavioralists Test the 'Legal Model' of Judicial Decision Making." 26 *Law & Social Inquiry* 465 (2001).

Gillman, Howard, and Cornell Clayton, eds. *The Supreme Court in American Politics: New Institutionalist Interpretations.* Lawrence: University Press of Kansas, 1999.

Gimpel, James G. *Legislating the Revolution: The Contract with America in Its First 100 Days.* Boston: Allyn and Bacon, 1996.

Gimpel, James G., and Jason E. Schuknecht. "Interstate Migration and Electoral Politics." 63 *Journal of Politics* 207 (2001).

Ginsberg, Benjamin, and Martin Shefter. *Politics by Other Means: The Declining Importance of Elections in America.* New York: Basic Books, 1990.

Ginsberg, Benjamin, Walter R. Mebane, Jr., and Martin Shefter. "The Presidency, Social Forces, and Interest Groups: Why Presidents Can No Longer Govern." In *The Presidency and the Political System,* ed. Michael Nelson. 5th ed. Washington, DC: CQ Press, 1998.

Ginsburg, Tom. "Economic Analysis and the Design of Constitutional Courts." 3 *Theoretical Inquiries in Law* (Online Edition), no. 1, article 3 (2002), *http://www.bepress.com/til/default/vol3/Iss1/art3.*

Glaberson, William. "NAFTA Invoked to Challenge Court Award." *New York Times,* January 28, 1999, p. C6.

———. "State Courts Sweeping away Laws Curbing Suits for Injury." *New York Times,* July 18, 1999, p. A1.

Goldsmith, Jack L. "Federal Courts, Foreign Affairs, and Federalism." 83 *Virginia Law Review* 1617 (1997).

———. "The New Formalism in United States Foreign Relations Law." 70 *University of Colorado Law Review* 1395 (1999).

———. "Statutory Foreign Affairs Preemption." 2000 *Supreme Court Review* 175 (2001).

Golove, David M. "Treaty-Making and the Nation: The Historical Foundations of the Nationalist Conception of the Treaty Power." 98 *Michigan Law Review* 1075 (2000).

Green, John C., and Daniel M. Shea, eds. *The States of the Parties: The Changing Role of Contemporary American Parties,* 3d ed. Lanham, MD: Rowman and Littlefield, 1999.

Griffin, Stephen. "Judicial Supremacy and Equal Protection in a Democracy of Rights." 5 *University of Pennsylvania Journal of Constitutional Law* 281 (2002).

Grofman, Bernard, ed. *Race and Redistricting in the 1990s.* New York: Agathon Press, 1998.

Grofman, Bernard, William Koetzle, Michael P. McDonald, and Thomas L. Brunell. "A New Look at Split-Ticket Outcomes for House and President: The Comparative Midpoints Model." 62 *Journal of Politics* 34 (2000).

Gunther, Gerald. "The Subtle Vices of the 'Passive Virtues': A Comment on Principle and Expediency in Judicial Review." 64 *Columbia Law Review* 1 (1964).

Hacker, Jacob. *The Road to Nowhere: The Genesis of President Clinton's Plan for Health Security.* Princeton: Princeton University Press, 1997.

Hall, John A., and Charles Lindholm. *Is America Breaking Apart?* Princeton: Princeton University Press, 1999.

Halpern, Stephen C., and Charles M. Lamb. "The Supreme Court and New Constitutional Eras." 64 *Brooklyn Law Review* 1183 (1998).

Hansen, F. Andrew. "Is There a Politically Optimal Level of Judicial Independence?" Stanford Law School, John M. Olin Program in Law and Economics, Working Paper 218, May 2001.

Hart, Henry M. Jr., and Albert M. Sacks. *The Legal Process: Basic Problems in the Making and Application of Law.* Westbury, NY: Foundation Press, 1994.

Healy, Thomas. "Note: Is *Missouri v. Holland* Still Good Law? Federalism and the Treaty Power." 98 *Columbia Law Review* 1726 (1998).

Henkin, Louis. *Foreign Affairs and the Constitution.* Mineola, NY: Foundation Press, 1972.

Hernnson, Paul S., and Dilys M. Hill, eds. *The Clinton Presidency: The First Term, 1992–96.* New York: St. Martin's Press, 1999.

Hetherington, Marc J. "Resurgent Mass Partisanship: The Role of Elite Polarization." 95 *American Political Science Review* 619 (2001).

Hills, Roderick M., Jr., *"The Constitutional Rights of Private Governments."* University of Michigan Law School, Public Law Research Paper No. 003.

———. "Federalism in Constitutional Context." 22 *Harvard Journal of Law & Public Policy* 181 (1998).

———. "The Political Economy of Cooperative Federalism: Why State Autonomy Makes Sense and 'Dual Sovereignty' Doesn't." 96 *Michigan Law Review* 813 (1998).

Hiscox, Michael J. "Supranationalism and Decentralization in the Global Economy." Paper presented at the Annual Meeting of the American Political Science Association, Washington, DC, September 2000.

Holmes, Oliver Wendell. *His Book Notices and Uncollected Letters and Papers.* Ed. Harry Shriver New York: Central Book Co., 1936.

Horwitz, Morton J. *The Transformation of American Law, 1870–1960: The Crisis of Legal Orthodoxy.* New York: Oxford University Press, 1992.

———. *The Warren Court and the Pursuit of Justice.* New York: Hill and Wang, 1998.

Hurwitz, Mark S., Roger J. Moiles, and David W. Rohde. "Distributive and Partisan Issues in Agriculture Policy in the 104th House." 95 *American Political Science Review* 911 (2001).

Ingberman, Daniel, and John Villani. "An Institutional Theory of Divided Government and Party Polarization." 37 *American Journal of Politics* 429 (1993).

Jackson, Vicki C. "Federalism and the Uses and Limits of Law: *Printz* and Principle?" 111 *Harvard Law Review* 2180 (1998).

Jacobs, Lawrence R., and Robert Y. Shapiro. *Politicians Don't Pander: Political Manipulation and the Loss of Democratic Responsiveness.* Chicago: University of Chicago Press, 2000.

Jacobson, Gary C. "The Electoral Basis of Partisan Polarization in Congress." Paper presented at the 2000 Annual Meeting of the American Political Science Association, August 31–September 3, 2000.

———. *The Electoral Origins of Divided Government: Competition in U.S. House Elections, 1946–1988.* Boulder, CO: Westview Press, 1990.

Jeffries, John C., Jr. and James E. Ryan. "A Political History of the Establishment Clause." 100 *Michigan Law Review* 279 (2001).

Jones, Charles O. *The Presidency in a Separated System.* Washington, DC: Brookings Institution, 1994.

Joyce, Philip G., and Daniel R. Mullins. "The Changing Fiscal Structure of the State and Local Public Sector: The Impact of Tax and Expenditure Limitations." 51 *Public Administration Review* 240 (1991).

Jyränki, Antero, ed. *National Constitutions in the Era of Integration*. Boston: Kluwer Law International, 1999.

Kagan, Elena. "Presidential Administration." 114 *Harvard Law Review* 2245 (2001).

Keck, Margaret E., and Kathryn Sikkink. *Activists beyond Borders: Advocacy Networks in International Politics*. Ithaca: Cornell University Press, 1998.

Keefe, William J. *Parties, Politics, and Public Policy in America*. Washington, DC: CQ Press, 1998.

Keller, Morton P., and R. Shep Melnick, eds. *Taking Stock: American Government in the Twentieth Century*. New York: Cambridge University Press, 1999.

Kennedy, David M. "Bill Clinton in the Eye of History." *New York Times*, November 2, 2000, p. A 31.

Klein, Susan R. "Identifying and (Re)Formulating Prophylactic Rules, Safe Harbors, and Incidental Rights in Constitutional Criminal Procedure." 99 *Michigan Law Review* 1030 (2001).

Kline, Stephan O. "The Topsy-Turvy World of Judicial Confirmations in the Era of Hatch and Lott." 103 *Dickinson Law Review* 247 (1999).

Klinkner, Philip A., with Rogers M. Smith. *The Unsteady March: The Rise and Decline of Racial Equality in America*. Chicago: University of Chicago Press, 1999.

Koh, Harold Hong-ju. "Bringing International Law Home." 35 *Houston Law Review* 623 (1998).

Komesar, Neil K. *Imperfect Alternatives: Choosing Institutions in Law, Economics, and Public Policy*. Chicago: University of Chicago Press, 1994.

Kopel, David B., and Glenn Harlan Reynolds. "Taking Federalism Seriously: *Lopez* and the Partial-Birth Abortion Ban Act." 30 *Connecticut Law Review* 59 (1997).

Kornbluh, Mark Lawrence. *Why America Stopped Voting: The Decline of Participatory Democracy and the Emergence of Modern American Politics*. New York: New York University Press, 2000.

Kramer, Larry. "Putting the Politics Back into the Political Safeguards of Federalism." 100 *Columbia Law Review* 215 (2000).

Krasner, Stephen. "Structural Causes and Regime Consequences: Regimes as Intervening Variables." 36 *International Organization* 185 (1982).

Krehbiel, Keith. "Institutional and Partisan Sources of Gridlock: A Theory of Divided and Unified Government." 8 *Journal of Theoretical Politics* 7 (1996).

———. *Pivotal Politics: A Theory of U.S. Lawmaking*. Chicago: University of Chicago Press, 1998.

Kritzer, Herbert M. "The Impact of *Bush v. Gore* on Public Perceptions and Knowledge of the Supreme Court." 85 *Judicature* 32 (2001).

Kronman, Anthony. "Alexander Bickel's Philosophy of Prudence." 94 *Yale Law Journal* 1567 (1985).

Ku, Julian G. "The Delegation of Federal Power to International Organizations: New Problems with Old Solutions." 85 *Minnesota Law Review* 71 (2000).

Kurland, Philip B. "Foreword: 'Equal in Origin and Equal in Title to the Legislative and Executive Branches of the Government.'" 78 *Harvard Law Review* 143 (1964).

Kurtz, Howard. "Americans Wait for the Punch Line on Impeachment." *Washington Post*, January 26, 1999, p. A1.

Landy, Marc, and Sidney M. Milkis. *Presidential Greatness*. Lawrence: University Press of Kansas, 2000.

Layman, Geoffrey C., Thomas M. Carsey, and Barry S. Rundquist. "The Causes and Effects of Preferences for Party Government: A New Test of Policy Balancing." Paper presented at the 2001 Annual Meeting of the American Political Science Association, August 30–September 3, 2001.

Lewis, Frederick P. *The Context of Judicial Activism: The Endurance of the Warren Court Legacy in a Conservative Age*. Lanham, MD: Rowman and Littlefield, 1999.

Lewis, Neil A. "The 2000 Campaign: The Judiciary: The Candidates Differ Sharply on Judges They Would Appoint to Top Courts." *New York Times*, October 8, 2000, p. A28.

Lincoln, Abraham. "Second Annual Message to Congress." In *Collected Works of Abraham Lincoln*. Ed. Roy Basler. Vol. 5. New Brunswick, NJ: Rutgers University Press.

Lipset, Seymour Martin. *American Exceptionalism: A Double-Edged Sword*. New York: W. W. Norton, 1996.

Luard, Evan. *The Globalization of Politics: The Changed Focus of Political Action in the Modern World*. New York: New York University Press, 1990.

Lucas, DeWayne. "Voters, Parties, and Representatives: Why the House of Representatives Is So Partisan in the 1990s." Paper presented at the 2000 Annual Meeting of the Southern Political Science Association, November 8–11, 2000.

Lund, Nelson. "The Unbearable Rightness of *Bush v. Gore*." 23 *Cardozo Law Review* 1219 (2001).

Mayhew, David. *Divided We Govern: Party Control, Lawmaking, and Investigations, 1946–1990*, New Haven: Yale University Press, 1991.

Mazzoleni, Gianpietro, and Winfried Schulz. "'Mediazation' of Politics: A Challenge for Democracy?" 16 *Political Communication* 247 (1999).

McAllister, Stephen R. "An Eagle Soaring: The Jurisprudence of Justice Antonin Scalia." 19 *Campbell Law Review* 223 (1997).

McConnell, Michael. "The Right to Die and the Jurisprudence of Tradition." 1997 *Utah Law Review* 665 (1997).

Mebane, Walter R., Jr. "Coordination, Moderation, and Institutional Balancing in American Presidential and House Elections." 94 *American Political Science Review* 37 (2000).

Meffert, Michael F., Helmut Norpoth, and Anirudh V. S. Ruhl. "Realignment and Macropartisanship." 95 *American Political Science Review* 953 (2001).

Mendelson, Wallace. "On the Meaning of the First Amendment: Absolutes in the Balance." 50 *Southern California Law Review* 821 (1962).

Menefee-Libey, David. *The Triumph of Campaign-Centered Politics*. New York: Chatham House, 2000.

Merritt, Deborah Jones. "Commerce!" 94 *Michigan Law Review* 674 (1995).

Metropoulos, Demetrios G. "Constitutional Dimensions of the North American Free Trade Agreement." 27 *Cornell International Law Journal* 141 (1994).

Mezey, Naomi. "Law as Culture." 13 *Yale Journal of Law & Humanities* 35 (2001).

Michelman, Frank. "Some Notes on Republicanism and Judicial Review." (March 25, 1999).

Mikva, Abner J. "Supreme Patience." *Washington Post*, January 25, 2002, p. A25.

Milkis, Sidney M. *Political Parties and Constitutional Government: Rethinking American Democracy.* Baltimore: Johns Hopkins University Press, 1999.

———. *The President and the Parties: The Transformation of the American Party System since the New Deal.* New York: Oxford University Press, 1993.

Miller, D. W. "Book Says Bolder Isn't Better in Rulings by the Supreme Court." *Chronicle of Higher Education*, March 5, 1999, p. A19.

Morris, Dick. *Behind the Oval Office: Winning the Presidency in the Nineties.* New York: Random House, 1997.

Morris, Irwin L. "Conventional Politics in Exceptional Times: House Votes, Money, and the Clinton Impeachment." Paper presented at the 2000 Annual Meeting of the American Political Science Association, August 31–September 5, 2000.

Morton, F. L. *Pro-Choice vs. Pro-Life: Abortion and the Courts in Canada.* Norman: University of Oklahoma Press, 1992.

Nagel, Robert F. "Name-Calling and the Clear Error Rule." 88 *Northwestern University Law Review* 193 (1993).

Nagel, Stuart S. "Political Party Affiliation and Judges' Decisions." 55 *American Political Science Review* 843 (1961).

Nagle, John Copeland. "The Commerce Clause Meets the Delhi Sands Flower-Loving Fly." 97 *Michigan Law Review* 174 (1998).

Neuman, Gerald L. "The Global Dimension of RFRA." 14 *Constitutional Commentary* 33 (1997).

Nicolay, John G., and John Hay. *Complete Works of Abraham Lincoln.* Harrogate, TN: Lincoln Memorial University, 1894.

O'Brien, David M. "The Rehnquist Court's Shrinking Plenary Docket." *Judicature* 81 (September–October 1997): 58.

Olson, Mancur. *The Rise and Decline of Nations: Economic Growth, Stagflation, and Social Rigidities.* New Haven: Yale University Press, 1982.

Orren, Karen, and Stephen Skowronek. "Regimes and Regime Building in American Government: A Review of Literature on the 1940s." 113 *Political Science Quarterly* 689 (1998–99).

Orth, John V. *The Judicial Power of the United States: The Eleventh Amendment in American History.* New York: Oxford University Press, 1987.

Pagano, Michael A. "State-Local Relations in the 1990s." 509 *Annals* 94 (1990).

Patterson, James T. *The New Deal and the States: Federalism in Transition.* Princeton: Princeton University Press, 1969.

Paulsen, Michael Stokes, and Steffen N. Johnson. "Scalia's Sermonette." 72 *Notre Dame Law Review* 863 (1997).

Peller, Gary. "*Neutral Principles* in the 1950s," 21 *University of Michigan Journal of Law Reform* 561 (1988).

Peretti, Terri Jennings. *In Defense of a Political Court*. Princeton: Princeton University Press, 1999.

Peters, Christopher J. "Assessing the New Judicial Minimalism." 100 *Columbia Law Review* 1454 (2000).

Pildes, Richard H. "The Politics of Race (Book Review)." 108 *Harvard Law Review* 1384 (1995).

Pildes, Richard H., and Cass R. Sunstein. "Reinventing the Regulatory State." 62 *University of Chicago Law Review* 1 (1995).

Piven, Frances Fox, and Richard Cloward. *Why Americans Don't Vote*. New York: Pantheon Books, 1988.

Pomper, Gerald M. "The 2000 Presidential Election: Why Gore Lost." 116 *Political Science Quarterly* 201 (2001).

Posner, Richard A. *An Affair of State: The Investigation, Impeachment, and Trial of President Clinton*. Cambridge, MA: Harvard University Press, 1999.

————. *Breaking the Deadlock*. Cambridge, MA: Harvard University Press, 2001.

Post, Robert C., and Reva B. Siegel. "Equal Protection by Law: Federal Antidiscrimination Legislation after *Morrison* and *Kimel*." 110 *Yale Law Journal* 441 (2000).

Powe, Lucas A. *The Warren Court and American Politics*. Cambridge, MA: Harvard University Press, 2000.

Prakash, Aseem, and Jeffrey A. Hart, eds. *Globalization and Governance*. New York: Routledge, 1999.

Price, David Andrew. "Party of Nine." *Wall Street Journal*, July 2, 1999, p. W13.

Primus, Richard. "Canon, Anti-Canon, and Judicial Dissent." 48 *Duke Law Journal* 243 (1998).

Rader, Eric W., Charles D. Elder, and Richard C. Elling. "Motivations and Behaviors of the 'New Breed' of Term Limited Legislators." Paper prepared for presentation at the Annual Meeting of the American Political Science Association, August 31–September 3, 2000.

Rawlings, Richard. "The New Model Wales." 25 *Journal of Law & Society* 461 (1998).

Reed, Douglas S. "A New Constitutional Regime: The Juridico-Entertainment Complex." Paper prepared for presentation at the annual meeting of the Law & Society Association, Chicago, May 27, 1999.

Regan, Donald H. "How to Think about the Federal Commerce Power and Incidentally Rewrite *United States v. Lopez*." 94 *Michigan Law Review* 554 (1995).

Reich, Robert B. "Public Administration and Public Deliberation: An Interpretative Essay." 94 *Yale Law Journal* 1617 (1985).

Renner, Gerald. "At Bess Eaton: Coffee, Doughnuts, and the Lord." *Hartford Courant*, August 7, 1993, p. A1.

Resnik, Judith. "Categorical Federalism: Jurisdiction, Gender, and the Globe." 111 *Yale Law Journal* 619 (2001).

————. "Judicial Independence and Article III: Too Little and Too Much." 72 *Southern California Law Review* 657 (1999).

————. "Trial as Error, Jurisdiction as Injury: Transforming the Meaning of Article III." 113 *Harvard Law Review* 924 (2000).

Rhodes, R.A.W. "The Hollowing Out of the State: The Changing Nature of the Public Service in Britain." 65 *Political Quarterly* 138 (1994).

Ribuffo, Leo. "From Carter to Clinton: The Latest Crisis of American Liberalism." 35 *American Studies International* 4 (1997).

Rich, Frank. "All the Presidents Stink." *New York Times Magazine*, Augist 15, 1999, p. 42.

Ripley, Randall, and Grace Franklin. *Congress, the Bureaucracy, and Public Policy.* 4th ed. Pacific Grove, CA: Brooks/Cole Publishing, 1987.

Rohde, David W. "The Gingrich Speakership in Context: Majority Leadership in the House in the Late Twentieth Century." *Extensions: A Journal of the Carl Albert Congressional Research and Studies Center* (fall 2000): 7.

———. *Parties and Leaders in the Post-Reform House.* Chicago: University of Chicago Press, 1991.

Roosevelt, Franklin D. "Annual Message to Congress, January 11, 1944." 10 *Vital Speeches of the Day* 194.

Rosen, Jeffrey. "The Age of Mixed Results," review of *One Case at a Time,* by Cass Sunstein. *The New Republic,* June 28, 1999, p. 43.

Ross, Lee, and Richard Nisbett. *The Person and the Situation.* Philadelphia: Temple University Press, 1991.

Rothenberg, Lawrence S., and Mitchell S. Sanders. "Lame-duck Politics: Impending Departure and the Votes on Impeachment." 53 *Political Research Quarterly* 523 (2000).

Rubenfeld, Jed. "The Anti-Antidiscrimination Agenda." 111 *Yale Law Journal* 1141 (2002).

Rubin, Edward L. "Puppy Federalism and the Blessings of America." 574 *Annals* 37 (2001).

Ruggie, John Gerard. "At Home Abroad, Abroad at Home: International Liberalisation and Domestic Stability in the New World Economy." 25 *Millennium* 507 (1995).

Ryan, James E., and Michael Heise. "The Political Economy of School Choice." 111 *Yale Law Journal* 2043 (2002).

Sabel, Charles. "How Experimentalism Can Be Democratic and Constitutional." Paper presented at the Conference on Democratic Experimentalism, Georgetown University Law Center, November 13, 2001.

Sabel, Charles, Archon Fung, and Bradley Karkkainen. "Beyond Backyard Environmentalism." *Boston Review* 24, no. 5 (October–November 1999): 5.

Salant, Jonathan D. "Number of Congressional Candidates, Funds Spent Down in '98." *The Bulletin's Frontrunner,* April 29, 1999. Available in LEXIS-NEXIS, New Group File, Beyond Two Years.

Sassen, Saskia. *Globalization and Its Discontents.* New York: New Press, 1998.

Schickler, Eric. "Institutional Change in the House of Representatives, 1867–1998: A Test of Partisan and Ideological Power Balances." 94 *American Political Science Review* 269 (2000).

Schier, Steven E., ed. *The Postmodern Presidency: Bill Clinton's Legacy in U.S. Politics.* Pittsburgh: University of Pittsburgh Press, 2000.

Schmitter, Phillipe C. *How to Democratize the European Union . . . and Why Bother?* Lanham, MD: Rowman and Littlefield, 2000.

Schneiderman, David. "Investment Rules and the New Constitutionalism." 25 *Law & Social Inquiry* 757 (2000).

Schoenbrod, David. *Power without Responsibility*. New Haven: Yale University Press, 1993.

Scholte, Jan Aarte. *Globalization: A Critical Introduction*. New York: St. Martin's Press, 2000.

Schwartz, Bernard, ed. *The Burger Court: Counter-Revolution or Confirmation?* New York: Oxford University Press, 1998.

Segal, Jeffrey A., and Albert D. Cover. "Ideological Values and the Votes of U.S. Supreme Court Justices." 83 *American Political Science Review* 557 (1989).

Segura, Gary M., and Stephen P. Nicholson. "Sequential Choices and Partisan Transitions in U.S. Senate Delegations: 1972–1988." 57 *Journal of Politics* 86 (1995).

Senior, Justin. "Comment: The Constitutionality of NAFTA's Dispute Resolution Process." 9 *Florida Journal of International Law* 209 (1994).

Shea, Daniel M. "The Passing of Realignment and the Advent of the 'Base-Less' Party System." 27 *American Politics Quarterly* 33 (1999).

Shepsle, Kenneth A. "Congress Is a 'They,' Not an 'It': Legislative Intent as an Oxymoron." 12 *International Review of Law & Economics* 239 (1992).

Shull, Steven A., ed. *Presidential Policymaking: An End-of-Century Assessment*. Armonk, NY: M. E. Sharpe, 1999.

Sidak, J. Gregory, and Daniel F. Spulber. *Deregulatory Takings and the Regulatory Contract: The Competitive Transformation of Network Industries in the United States*. New York: Cambridge University Press, 1997.

Sigelman, Lee, Paul J. Wahlbeck, and Emmett H. Buell, Jr. "Vote Choice and the Preference for Divided Government: Lessons of 1992." 41 *American Journal of Political Science* 879 (1997).

Silbey, Joel. *The Partisan Imperative*. New York: Oxford University Press, 1985.

Silverstein, Mark. *Judicious Choices: The New Politics of Supreme Court Confirmations*. New York: W. W. Norton, 1994.

Sinclair, Barbara. "Bipartisan Governing: Possible, Yes; Likely, No." 34 *PS: Political Science & Politics* 81 (2001).

——. "Do Parties Matter?" Center for the Study of Democracy, UC Irvine, Research Papers (1998).

——. *Legislators, Leaders, and Lawmaking: The U.S. House of Representatives in the Postreform Era*. Baltimore: Johns Hopkins University Press, 1995.

——. "Structure, Preferences and Outcomes: Explaining When Bills Do—and Don't—Become Law." Paper presented at the Annual Meeting of the American Political Science Association, August 30–September 2, 2001.

——. *The Transformation of the U.S. Senate*. Baltimore: Johns Hopkins University Press, 1989.

——. *Unorthodox Lawmaking: New Legislative Processes in the U.S. Congress*. Washington, DC: CQ Press, 1997.

Skocpol, Theda. *Boomerang: Health Care Reform and the Turn against Government*. New York: W. W. Norton, 1997.

Skocpol, Theda, and Morris P. Fiorina, eds. *Civic Engagement in American Democracy*. Washington, DC: Brookings Institution, 1999.

Skowronek, Stephen. *The Politics Presidents Make: Leadership from John Adams to George Bush.* Cambridge, MA: Harvard University Press, 1993.

Slotnick, Elliot E., and Jennifer A. Segal. *Television News and the Supreme Court: All the News That's Fit to Air?* New York: Cambridge University Press, 1998.

Smith, Peter J. "*Pennhurst, Chevron,* and the Spending Power." 110 *Yale Law Journal* 1187 (2001).

Sokolow, Alvin D. "The Changing Property Tax and State-Local Relations." 28 *Publius* 165 (1998).

Sparrow, Bartholomew. *Uncertain Guardians: The News Media as a Political Institution.* Baltimore: Johns Hopkins University Press, 1999.

Spence, David B. "The Shadow of the Rational Polluter: Rethinking the Role of Rational Actor Models in Environmental Law." 89 *California Law Review* 917 (2001).

Spiro, Peter J. "Contextual Determinism and Foreign Relations Federalism." 2 *Chicago Journal of International Law* 363 (2001).

———. "Foreign Relations Federalism." 70 *University of Colorado Law Review* 1223 (1999).

Spitzer, Robert J. "Clinton's Impeachment Will Have Few Consequences for the Presidency." 33 *PS: Political Science & Politics* 541 (1999).

Stark, Kirk J. "The Right to Vote on Taxes." 96 *Northwestern University Law Review* 191 (2001).

Steinzor, Rena I. "Reinventing Environmental Regulation: The Dangerous Journey from Command to Self-Control." 22 *Harvard Environmental Law Review* 103 (1998).

Stephan, Paul B. "International Governance and American Democracy." 1 *Chicago Journal of International Law* 237 (2000).

Stewart, Richard B. "Evaluating the New Deal." 22 *Harvard Journal of Law & Public Policy* 239 (1998).

Stidham, Ronald, Robert A. Carp, and Donald R. Sanger. "The Voting Behavior of President Clinton's Judicial Appointees." 80 *Judicature* (July–August 1996), 16.

Stone, Geoffrey, L. Michael Seidman, Cass R. Sunstein, and Mark V. Tushnet. *Constitutional Law.* (4th ed. New York: Aspen Law & Business, 2001.

Strange, Susan. "The Defective State." 124 *Daedalus* 55 (1995).

Strauss, David A. "Common Law Constitutional Interpretation." 63 *University of Chicago Law Review* 877 (1996).

Strauss, Peter. "Formal and Functional Approaches to Separation of Powers Questions: A Foolish Inconsistency?" 72 *Cornell Law Review* 488 (1972).

Summers, John H. "What Happened to Sex Scandals?: Politics and Peccadilloes, Jefferson to Kennedy." 67 *Journal of American History* 825 (2000).

Sundquist, James L. Dynamics of the Party System. Rev. ed. Washington, DC: Brookings Institution, 1983.

Sunstein, Cass R. "The Broad Virtue in a Modest Ruling." *New York Times,* December 5, 2000, p. A29.

———. "Impeaching the President." 147 *University of Pennsylvania Law Review* 79 (1998).

———. *One Case at a Time: Judicial Minimalism on the Supreme Court.* Cambridge, MA: Harvard University Press, 1999.

―――. "What Judge Bork Should Have Said." 23 *Connecticut Law Review* 205 (1991).

Sunstein, Cass R., and Richard Epstein eds. *The Vote: Bush, Gore, and the Supreme Court*. Chicago: University of Chicago Press, 2001.

Symposium. "Congress and Foreign Policy after the Cold War." *Extensions: A Journal of the Carl Albert Congressional Research and Studies Center. Spring 2001*.

Tananbaum, Duane. *The Bricker Amendment Controversy: A Test of Eisenhower's Political Leadership*. Ithaca: Cornell University Press, 1988.

Thomas, Chantal. "Constitutional Change and International Government." 52 *Hastings Law Journal* 1 (2000).

Thompson, Frank J., and Norma M. Riccucci. "Reinventing Government." *1998 Annual Review of Political Science* 231 (1998).

Thornberry, Chad. "Comment: Federalism vs. Foreign Affairs: How the United States Can Administer Article 36 of the Vienna Convention on Consular Relations within the States." 31 *McGeorge Law Review* 107 (1999).

Thorson, Gregory R., Nicholas J. Maxwell, and Tasina Nitzschke. "Strategic Decision Making and the Invoking of Cloture in the United States Senate." Paper presented at the 2001 Annual Meeting of the American Political Science Association, August 30–September 2, 2001.

Tilove, Jonathan. "The New Map of American Politics." *The American Prospect* 11 (May–June 1999): 34.

Trebilcock, Michael J., Ron Daniels, and Malcolm Thorburn, "Government by Voucher." 80 *Boston University Law Review* 205 (2000).

Tribe, Laurence. *American Constitutional Law*. 3d ed. New York: Foundation Press, 2000.

Tulis, Jeffrey K. *The Rhetorical Presidency*. Princeton: Princeton University Press, 1987.

Tushnet, Mark. "Constitutional Interpretation, Character, and Experience." 72 *Boston University Law Review* 747 (1992).

―――. "Globalization and Federalism in a Post-*Printz* World." 36 *Tulsa Law Journal* 11 (2000).

―――. "How to Deny a Constitutional Right: Reflections on the Assisted-Suicide Cases." 1 *Green Bag* 2d ser., 55 (1997).

―――. "Justification in Constitutional Interpretation: A Comment on Constitutional Interpretation." 72 *Texas Law Review* 1707 (1994).

―――. *Making Civil Rights Law: Thurgood Marshall and the Supreme Court, 1936–1961*. New York: Oxford University Press, 1994.

―――. *Making Constitutional Law: Thurgood Marshall and the Supreme Court, 1961–1991*. New York: Oxford University Press, 1997.

―――. "The Redundant Free Exercise Clause." 33 *Loyola University Chicago Law Journal* 71 (2001).

―――. *Taking the Constitution away from the Courts*. Princeton: Princeton University Press, 1999.

Tushnet, Mark, and Larry Yackle, "Symbolic Statutes and Real Laws: The Pathologies of the Antiterrorism and Effective Death Penalty Act and the Prison Litigation Reform Act." 47 *Duke Law Journal* 1 (1997).

Vagts, Detlev F. "Taking Treaties Less Seriously." 92 *American Journal of International Law* 458 (1998).

Vázquez, Carlos Manuel. "*Breard, Printz*, and the Treaty Power." 70 *University of Colorado Law Review* 1317 (1999).

———. "W(h)ither *Zschernig*?" 46 *Villanova Law Review* 1259 (2001).

Vetter, Jan. "Postwar Legal Scholarship on Judicial Decision Making." 33 *Journal of Legal Education* 412 (1983).

Volokh, Eugene. "Comment, Freedom of Speech and Workplace Harassment." 39 *UCLA Law Review* 1791 (1992).

———. "What Speech Does 'Hostile Work Environment' Harassment Law Restrict?" 85 *Georgetown Law Journal* 627 (1997).

Watson, George, and John A. Stookey. *Shaping America: The Politics of Supreme Court Appointments.* New York: Longman, 1995.

Wattenberg, Martin P. *The Rise of Candidate-Centered Politics: Presidential Elections of the 1980s.* Cambridge, MA: Harvard University Press, 1991.

Waxman, Seth P. "Foreword: Does the Solicitor General Matter?" 53 *Stanford Law Review* 1115 (2001).

Wayne, Leslie. "Congress Uses Leadership PACs to Wield Power." *New York Times*, March 13, 1997, p. B10.

Weaver, R. Kent, and Bert A. Rockman, eds. *Do Institutions Matter? Government Capabilities in the United States and Abroad.* Washington, DC: Brookings Institution, 1993.

Wechsler, Herbert. *Principle, Politics and Fundamental Law.* Cambridge, MA: Harvard University Press, 1961.

———. "Toward Neutral Principles of Constitutional Law." 73 *Harvard Law Review* 1 (1959).

Weir, Margaret, ed. *The Social Divide: Political Parties and the Future of Activist Government.* Washington, DC: Brookings Institution, 1998.

Weisburd, A. Mark. "International Courts and American Courts." 21 *Michigan Journal of International Law* 877 (2000).

White, G. Edward. *The Constitution and the New Deal.* Cambridge, MA: Harvard University Press, 2000.

Whittington, Keith E. *Constitutional Construction: Divided Powers and Constitutional Meaning.* Cambridge, MA: Harvard University Press, 1999.

———. "Dismantling the Modern State? The Changing Structural Foundations of Federalism." 25 *Hastings Constitutional Law Quarterly* 483 (1998).

Woodward, Bob. *The Agenda: Inside the Clinton White House.* New York: Simon and Schuster, 1994.

Wright, J. Skelly. "Professor Bickel, the Scholarly Tradition, and the Supreme Court." 84 *Harvard Law Review* 769 (1971).

Yalof, David Alistair. *Pursuit of Justices: Presidential Politics and the Selection of Supreme Court Nominees.* Chicago: University of Chicago Press, 1999.

Yoo, John C. "Foreign Affairs Federalism and the Separation of Powers." 46 *Villanova Law Review* 1341 (2001).

Young, Iris Marion. "Activist Challenges to Deliberative Democracy." 29 *Political Theory* 670 (2001).

TABLE OF CASES

INDEX